JOHN DEERE MODEL B

Restoration Guide

Robert N. Pripps

First published in 1995 by Motorbooks International Publishers & Wholesalers, 729 Prospect Avenue, PO Box 1, Osceola, WI 54020-0001 USA

Library of Congress Cataloging-in-Publication Data
Pripps, Robert N.
John Deere Model B Restoration Guide /
Robert N. Pripps.
p. cm. — (Motorbooks International authentic restoration guides)
Includes index.
ISBN 0-87938-974-5
1. John Deere tractors—Conservation and restoration.
I.Title. II. Series.
TL233.5.P762 1995
629.225—dc20 94-39847

On the front cover: A sharply restored unstyled John Deere Model B soaks up the autumn sunshine. *Randy Leffingwell*

On the back cover: Top: A John Deere Model BI Industrial pulls a Caterpillar No. 4 patrol grader. The photo was taken in 1936. *John Deere Archives* Bottom: A John Deere Model B pulls a six-foot John Deere disk on John Deere's experimental farm near Coal Valley, Illinois in 1947. *John Deere Archives*

Printed and bound in United States of America

Contents

Acknowledgments

This is a book about antique tractor restoration. No one knows all the details, least of all the author. This book would not have been possible without the help of people with lifetimes of John Deere experience . The sad fact is, however, that one doesn't know what one doesn't know. Therefore, omissions and errors in the book are mostly because the author didn't know what questions to ask. The august panel of experts, listed below, were extremely helpful and unselfish of their time in providing help and guidance.

Dr. Leslie J. Stegh, Archivist, and Head of the Deere Library and Records Retention Department. Les has been in charge of Deere's record center and Deere's collection of historical equipment since 1977. Besides the full-time job at Deere, Les teaches a class at Augustana College on archive management. He received his Ph.D. degree in U.S. History from Kent State University in 1975. His M.S. degree is from Ohio State, and is also in U.S. History. His B.S. degree is from Kent State, and is in Education. Dr. Stegh has given speeches and written extensively on the subject of archives and institutional records, and also has written and reviewed publications on the subject of historic automobiles and machinery.

Bruce Johnson, Two-cylinder Club Designated Area Expert and President of his local Two-cylinder chapter. Bruce grew up on a farm in Northern Illinois. He is a graduate of Kishwaukee Collage where he received an Associate Degree in Agriculture Mechanics. After graduation, Bruce worked for a John Deere dealer as a mechanic and as service manager. He is presently Maintenance Manager at a major manufacturing company.

Bruce restored his first tractor, an unstyled John Deere B, in 1977. The tractor was given to him by his father, Ralph Johnson, who is, by the way, a prominent International Harvester collector and restorer. Since that first unstyled Model B, Bruce Johnson has built a collection of ten different unstyled Model B tractors. He has restored many other tractors and has had at least one example of his handiwork at every Two-cylinder Club Expo.

Bruce has recently been asked to teach a night class on tractor overhaul by his alma mater, Kishwaukee Collage.

Gerry Ter Hark, Patrick Flanigan, Jerry Montefelt, Bunky Meese, Jon Ter Hark, Jim Wise, and others of the Northwest Illinois Two-cylinder club, Freeport, Illinois. These John Deere experts dismantled Flanigan's 1949 John Deere Model B row-crop and did a complete restoration for the edification of club members and this author. Many of the photos were provided by this team. They also reviewed the manuscript and made suggestions for corrections and improvements.

Jeff McManus is a Two-Cylinder Club Technical Council Advisor, and member of the Board of Directors of the local chapter. Jeff has done restorations of historic tractors for Deere & Company He grew up on a farm and was involved in machinery repair, as he says, since he was old enough to pick up a hammer. Jeff bought his first John Deere, a Model G, at age 13. His hobby became a part-time tractor restoration business and Jeff has done twenty-nine John Deere restorations. His work has been displayed at several John Deere Expos and he has fifteen John Deeres of his own.

J. R. Hobbs has written two books about John Deere tractors and is regular contributor to *Green* magazine. His work has also appeared in *Two-Cylinder* and *Tractor Digest*. J.R. was born and raised on a farm in western Iowa and farmed with John Deere tractors until 1988, when he got into the antique tractor and parts business.

Preface

Restoring antique John Deere tractors has become a very popular hobby. It usually doesn't cost much more to do it right. With the help of some noted experts (see acknowledgments), I have tried to put together a book that will help the restorer figure what is correct for his or her tractor.

This is not a "how to" book. For that kind of help, see my *How To Restore Your Farm Tractor* book, also published by Motorbooks International. This is a "what to" book. It was my objective to put together a technical resource drawn from factory archives, photographs and manuals, and from other experienced restorers.

For comments, corrections, or suggestions, please communicate with the author through the publisher. Subsequent printings will be corrected.

Robert N. Pripps
1995

The author, aboard his 1948 late styled Model B, pulls a clutch of logs out of the woods to be cut into firewood.

Introduction

The John Deere Model B is the most collectible tractor in the world.

"Whoa," you say, "how can that be; they're as common as fleas on a dog."

Well, let's analyze the statement. First, it's a *John Deere*. That makes it more collectible than any other brand of tractor. The reasons why this is so are unknown, but it's true. Basically, I think it's because more people like green and yellow, and because more people like the distinctive exhaust note of the two-cylinder engine.

This 1951 photo shows a Model B with the Quik-Tatch two-row cultivator. The curved plate attached to the pedestal allowed the operator to drive in to attach the cultivator. The plate centered the cultivator to the tractor. The tractor is equipped with wheel weights, clam shell fenders, and lights.

Next, let's look at the Model B in relation to other John Deere tractors. I'll have to admit that the Model R is my personal favorite. Owning and restoring a big bruiser like that, however, puts you into the big leagues of tractor collecting, and I only have a sandlot pocketbook. For small-time players like me, the Model B is as large as we can go. The Models H and L seem like toys, and don't have the authority of the Model B in their exhaust note. The Models M, 40, and their successors always seem to be a little too expensive and their higher-revving engines don't have the charm of the Model B's grunty "tut-tut-tut."

The Model A and the Model G are nice, but with nearly a ton more weight, the problem of trailering is compounded. My 1948 Model B trailers nicely behind a full-size van or a half-

An early styled John Deere Model B pulls a No. 5 combine. The tractor has early tread-pattern Firestone tires, no attach points on the pedestal, and a flat-spoke steering wheel.

ton pickup. Our Jeep Grand Cherokee (with a trailering package) handles it well.

Finally, there are enough rare and expensive variations of the John Deere Model B to excite the most callused collector. As you will see in the following pages, there are interesting sub-models and variations. Also, since the Model B was built over such a long time (seventeen years), the challenge of authenticity and accuracy comes in (one should never put plastic tire valve caps on a pre-war tractor). That's where—I hope—this book will be helpful.

This book is meant to be a technical resource, presenting facts about the John Deere B that will help you do an accurate restoration of your tractor. It has been prepared with the help of the experts listed in the acknowledgments, and with factory records, manuals and photographs. Every effort has been made to strive for accuracy; only time will tell, however, how well we succeeded. If you have comments, corrections, or suggestions, please correspond with the author through the publisher.

Chapter 1

General Overview

The Model B was born in the depths of the Great Depression. Introduced for the 1935 model year, the design of the Model B had begun shortly after such features as the hydraulic power lift, adjustable wheel tread, and one-piece rear axle housing had been proven in experimental Model A tractors. The Model B was approximately two-thirds of the size and weight of the Model A, which was introduced earlier in 1934.

The Model B filled a niche not only because of its smaller size, but also because it cost less and required less fuel than larger tractors.

The John Deere Models A and B were both products of the fertile minds of a Deere engineering team headed by Theo Brown. When Brown and the team began work on the new tractors in 1931–32, the general purpose, or row-crop, tractor had come into its own. The tricycle configuration was the preferred arrangement for general purpose tractors, although wide-front variations were also in limited demand. Except for certain specialized applications, the new General Purpose (GP) tractors—as the A and B were called—vastly outsold standard tread tractors.

A rare four-bolt Model B is shown on display at Deere & Company headquarters in Moline, Illinois. The four-bolt front pedestal was discontinued in favor of an eight-bolt design after serial number 3,042. In fact, the absence of "John Deere" on the radiator tank top probably indicates that this is a rebuilt HX experimental model. The rod-spoke steering wheel is not correct, however. Note the early 1935 hood decal, with the curved-top "G" and the leaping deer.

The A was introduced first simply because of the limitations of manpower and facilities. Therefore, it was almost a year after the debut of the A that the B reached the dealers. The Model B was originally available with pneumatic tires (the A was not). The Model B also had a four-speed transmission, a power take-off (PTO), and a belt pulley. The B engine, a smaller version of the A's, had enough power for one sixteen-inch plow, or two twelves (the A was capable of pulling two fourteens).

The John Deere Model B began life as the "HX" experimental pre-production tractor in September 1933. While the HX was very similar to the production B, several differences are

Four Groups of Model B Production

Description	YearsProduced	Serial Numbers
General Purpose unstyled	1935–38	1,000–59,999
General Purpose styled	1939–47*	60,000–200,999
General Purpose late styled	1947*–52	201,000–up
Standard Tread/ Orchard	1935–47	325,000–up

**Both styled and unstyled models were produced in 1947; the change was made mid-year.*

The John Deere Model B was built in four basic variations over its seventeen-year life span. These break down into two basic types: styled and unstyled. Those built in model year 1938 and before are unstyled. Those built after that time have the styled sheet metal, grille, and other features instigated by famous industrial designer Henry Dreyfuss.

A Model B picture from 1934 John Deere ad literature. The steering wheel is from an HX (experimental) model. The radiator tank without "John Deere" is also indicative of the HX version. Note the four-bolt front end. *John Deere Archives*

A 1935 Model B makes its way pulling a mounted two-way plow. Plow depth is controlled by the roller ahead of the share. *John Deere Archives*

Model	Description
BN	Narrow single front wheel
BW	Wide-front configuration with adjustable width axle
BNH	High clearance; single front wheel
BWH	High clearance; adjustable axle; wide-front
BR	Regular, or standard tread configuration; sometimes called a "Wheatland" tractor
BO	Orchard configuration
BI	Industrial configuration

The basic model designation, Model B, indicates the General Purpose, or Row-Crop, version with the two-wheel tricycle configuration. The variations of the basic model are listed below.

Right, an ad from *The Furrow,* August-September 1935 issue. The ad shows Model A, B, and AO tractors. *John Deere Archives*

Consider Equipment, Too,

WHEN YOU BUY YOUR NEW TRACTOR

• *All over the South—farmers are acclaiming the new John Deere Hydraulic Power Lift Tractor Equipment* •

JOHN DEERE MODEL B GP

Equipment counts BIG in your selection of a tractor. When you choose a John Deere Model B Adjustable-Tread Tractor, you get the most economical row-crop tractor of its size and, in addition, you have available a *complete line* of power lift equipment especially designed for your tractor. Some of the Model B equipment is shown below.

One-Row Bedder

Model B Tractor owners find John Deere B-20 Series Pow- Lift Middlebreaker just the ng for making beds (blind ing). A two-row planting at- hment can be furnished for outfit. Simple. Strong. ms a compact unit with the ctor.

2-Row Planter

Whether you plant your crop beds or in the furrows, this ible John Deere Two-Row nter will do a fast, accurate for you. GPB-202 for use h the Model B Tractor. GPA- for use with the Model A ctor. Has John Deere Natural op Seed Plates for corn and er crops; Saw-Tooth Type el Picker Wheel for Cotton. cial planter available for veg- ble growers.

2-Row Cultivator

n the John Deere line, you will d just the two-row cultivator fit your conditions, with a big iety of rig equipment. Model owners find it easy to cultivate to 30 acres in a 10-hour day, h easier steering, better view the work and greater comfort the operator than ever be- e. A special 2- and 4-row tivator is available for vege- le growers.

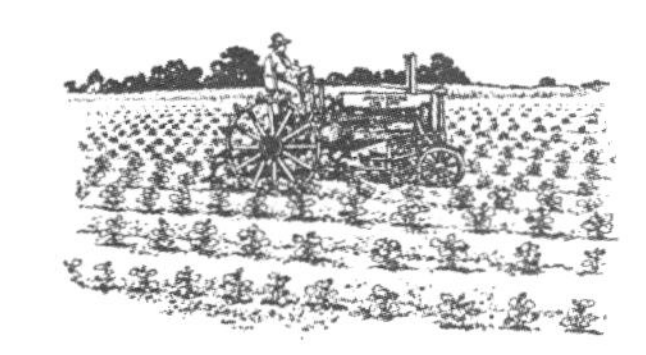

The Model B

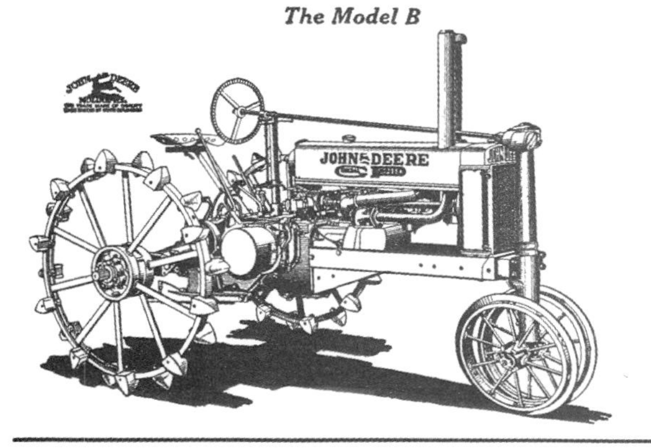

JOHN DEERE MODEL A 

For growers who want a larger-size General Purpose, there is the John Deere Model A Adjustable-Tread, shown below with Southern wheel equipment. This tractor, too, has a complete line of power lift equipment for bedding, planting and cultivating. Handles the load ordinarily pulled by 6 mules. This tractor and the Model B have four forward speeds with a high of 5-1/4 M.P.H.

The Model A

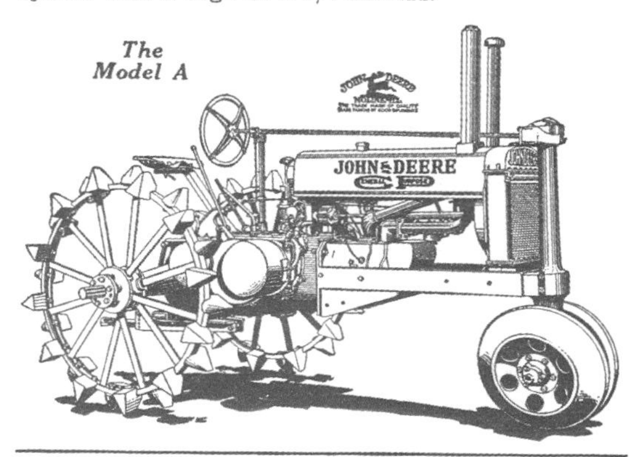

JOHN DEERE "AO" ORCHARD TRACTOR

Specially designed for orchardists is this John Deere Orchard Tractor. Seat and platform are low down. Wide, orchard-type fenders prevent damage to trees. Steers easily. Independent differential brakes make possible extremely short turns. Handles the load that ordinarily requires 6 mules. Four speeds forward adapt the tractor to a wide variety of uses. Special citrus fenders can be furnished as shown.

ASK YOUR JOHN DEERE DEALER WHERE YOU CAN SEE A JOHN DEERE AT WORK . . . *Write to John Deere Plow Co., Atlanta, Georgia, for Literature on Any Model . . .*

readily apparent. Most, if not all, HX tractors did not have "John Deere" cast into either the top radiator tank or rear axle housing. Most pictures of HX tractors also show that they were equipped with the triangle-hub French and Hecht steering wheel also used on the 1934 Model A tractors. The existing records are unclear as to how many HX tractors were built; however, it is known that several were rebuilt to production specifications and sold. Deere & Company owns one, serial number B-1,803, which was rebuilt from experimental tractor HX-60. Others may still exist, and would be a valuable find.

A 1935 Model B works up a test plot at the John Deere Moline Experimental Farm. The implement is a B-30 bedder. It is curious that the tires are on backwards; more tread width was obtained by reversing the wheels, most likely. *John Deere Archives*

Below, the flywheel side of Bruce Johnson's 1937 "long-hood" Model BW.

Above, This cross-sectional cut-away view of the early styled Model B clearly indicates how the heavy components of the tractor were mounted fairly low, contributing to stability despite a high appearance. *John Deere Archives*

A head-on view of a 1938 John Deere Model B with a four-row cultivator and integral fertilizer attachment. The factory setting shows over the white backdrop. *John Deere Archives*

An overhead studio picture of a 1938 John Deere Model B with a four-row cultivator. The cultivator has an integral fertilizer attachment. *John Deere Archives*

An unstyled Model B in pretty much original condition. Even the rear tires are pre-World War II.

LOOK to the YEARS AHEAD
1938
JOHN DEERE
GIVES YOU
Extra Years of Low-Cost Service
THE extra years of service you get from a John Deere two-cylinder tractor . . . its ability to stand up year after year under heavy-duty work . . . spreads your investment over a longer period of time. You make a substantial cash saving because you buy more years of steady, dependable power.
Exclusive two-cylinder engine design gives you simplified construction that reduces your operating costs. There are hundreds fewer moving parts; heavier, more rugged parts that wear longer and require less attention. You also get complete accessibility—the big reason why 82% of John Deere owners do fully 75% of their own service work, as disclosed by a recent survey.
The John Deere two-cylinder engine, mounted horizontally, connects directly with a straight-line, spur-gear transmission. The absence of power-consuming bevel gears means more power on the drawbar. The belt pulley, being mounted directly on the crankshaft, delivers full engine power to the belt-operated machine.
To all of these savings add the unmatched economy of John Deere two-cylinder power with its 13-year record of efficiency in burning the low-cost fuels, and you have the reason why an ever-increasing number of farmers are turning to John Deere for more power, for a longer time, at lower cost.
In 12 models, there is a John Deere that exactly fits your farm needs. Ask your near-by dealer for a field demonstration—and be sure to mail the coupon for big, free book and folders.
Fruit growers like low-built, short turning John Deere Orchard Tractors. Two power sizes.
Steady, dependable, low cost drawbar and belt power are yours with a John Deere Standard Tread Tractor. Three power sizes.
JOHN DEERE, Dep't. B-3, Moline, Illinois
Send me big, new FREE book "Better Farming for 1938," also folders on Tractors checked.
General Purpose Tractors
Orchard Tractors
Model "D" 3-4-Plow Tractor
Model "AR" (medium) and "BR" (light) Standard Tread Tractors
Name
Town
State
RFD
JOHN DEERE 2-CYLINDER TRACTORS

John Deere touted their two-cylinder design in period advertisement. You can tell the tractor in the ad is a Model B due to the distinctive brake cover. Also note the obviously retouched exhaust stack. *John Deere Archive*

By the time this photograph was taken (July 1939), the Model B and its variants were set and production settled to routine. This Model B is cultivating cotton near Mesquite, Texas. *John Deere Archives*

JOHN DEERE
JOHN DEERE

The beautiful rolling hill country near Lebanon, New York, circa 1938. Mr. L. R. Dale plows with his Model B and a John Deere 101 two-way plow. *John Deere Archives*

A May 1937 studio picture of John Deere Model B with a spring-tooth integral cultivator. The tractor seems to be well used. *John Deere Archives*

This studio art shows the late styled Model B. Notice the hood decal is not centered, but is located forward of center, the location that was used on 1950–52 styled Model Bs. Styled Model Bs from 1939–49 centered this decal on the side of the hood. *John Deere Archives*

A very early photo of a styled Model B, taken in May 1938. The tractor has a flat-spoke steering wheel and no medallion decal. Also, the cultivator attachment nuts are missing. *John Deere Archives*

June 1936 on the Donalek farm near Cedar Rapids, Iowa; an early styled Model B cultivates corn. The tires appear to be Goodyear. *John Deere Archives*

Left, an early styled Model B pulls a beet-lifter implement in a field near Fort Collins, Colorado, in November 1939. Notice the two instruments, one above the other. *John Deere Archives*

Right, a 1938 photo shows a Model B operating a PTO-driven corn binder. The caption did not indicate where the photo was taken, but judging from the height of the corn, it must have been a good year. *John Deere Archives*

Besides showing typical configurations and applications of antique tractors, old photos, such as this one taken in 1939, show how users of the period dressed. This picture purportedly shows one neighbor asking the other how he likes his new John Deere B. *John Deere Archives*

A 1939 model John Deere B pulls a John Deere potato planter. Notice the cast steel (weighted) rear wheels. The picture was taken at the Rockefeller farm in Phelps, New York. *John Deere Archives*

JOHN DEERE
JOHN DEERE

JOHN DEERE

A nice restoration job by David Polacek of Polacek Implement of Phillips, Wisconsin. The tractor, a 1944 (early styled) model, is owned by Dwight Frick.

Studio art from 1950 shows a Model B with a John Deere No. 100 one-row corn picker. *John Deere Archives*

This late styled Model B has clam shell fenders and wheel weights. *John Deere Archives*

Left, late styled Model Bs have the stylish pressed steel frame and the 190ci engine. That engine was the final, and largest, engine used in the Model B.

Left, Paul Long, shown on the seat of his John Deere Model B, was so pleased with the performance of his John Deere Pick-Up Press on his 200-acre farm in Ohio that he wrote the company in 1941. "I purchased a 16 x 18 Small Pick-up Press from J.H. Snyder at Edison, Ohio. Two twelve-year-old boys and myself have been operating this press, and we have had this machine in all conditions of hay and straw. Where the hay was extremely heavy, we baled out of the swath, and it takes it up just as good as a hay loader. I am more than pleased with my hay press and would highly recommend this machine to anyone interested," he wrote. *John Deere Archives*

Left, Mr. Zed Hardin of Orion, Illinois, plows with a No. 44 plow and his new Model B in May of 1947. The tractor is a gasoline-only version, as were most of the late styled Bs. *John Deere Archives*

Model BN

Production of the Model B had barely begun when the first of many variations of the basic B design, the BN, was introduced. Equipped with a single front wheel, the BN was first advertised as the B Garden Tractor, intended for the vegetable farmer who needed tractor power. These tractors used four bolts to attach the steering pedestal to the frame, as did all Model B tractors through serial number B-3,042. Beginning in October of 1934, a total of twenty-four of these tractors were built.

Left, a 1939 model John Deere B pulls and powers a No. 11 combine. *John Deere Archives*

Left, an eight-bolt Model BN with a B-614 cultivator in the lettuce fields of the Salinas Valley in California, 1935. The exhaust pipe and air intake seem unusually high. *John Deere Archives*

A 1937 studio photo of a John Deere Model BN. The "Model BN" decal is missing from the seat strut. *John Deere Archives*

Right, studio art photo of the Model BN. The BN used the same AB3677R pedestal as the BW. *John Deere Archives*

Right, studio view of the new Model BN taken in 1938. These tractors had longer axles than normal. *John Deere Archives*

Another studio view of the new Model BN taken in 1938. *John Deere Archives*

Rear studio view of the new BN taken in 1938. The wheels of this one are set at their widest limit. *John Deere Archives*

A late styled Model BN with a No. 88 tool holder. *John Deere Archives*

Model BW

At serial number B-3,043, a new cast iron frame (more properly called a front end support) replaced the welded steel frame. Also at this time, the steering pedestal was modified with an eight-bolt mounting to the frame. Shortly after these changes had been made, at serial number B-3,116, the Model BW made its appearance in the line. The BW was intended for farmers who needed greater stability (for traversing hillsides and the like) or raised crops with narrow row spacings and needed the front and rear wheels to run in the same track.

A 1937 factory sketch of a John Deere Model BW. *John Deere Archives*

Another studio view of the Model BW in 1938. *John Deere Archives*

This studio view of the Model BW tractor was taken in 1938 at the time of their introduction. *John Deere Archives*

This 1937 photo shows a John Deere Model BN running an irrigation pump near Grants Pass, Oregon. Note the tool bar, the dandy umbrella, and that the rear tires are reversed. *John Deere Archives*

An early styled 1939 Model BWH in a studio-retouched photo. *John Deere Archives*

Studio art from 1950 shows a normal two-piece pedestal arrangement for the Model BW. *John Deere Archives*

Studio art work from 1947 showing a late styled Model BW. The front pedestal seems to be unusual and is not covered in the parts book.

Model BR and BO

Farmers who needed a smaller four-wheel standard-type tractor had clamored for a standard tread version of the B, and in the fall of 1935, John Deere responded with two new models, the BR and the BO. The new models shared the same basic design, with the BO modified for orchard and grove work. Some of the orchard modifications included shielding for the air intake and fuel caps, a side-discharge muffler, and differential brakes for increased maneuverability. Ful-coverage (also known as citrus) fenders could be added, as well. The BR and BO shared many parts with the general purpose Model Bs, but were assigned their own serial numbers, which began with serial number 325,000.

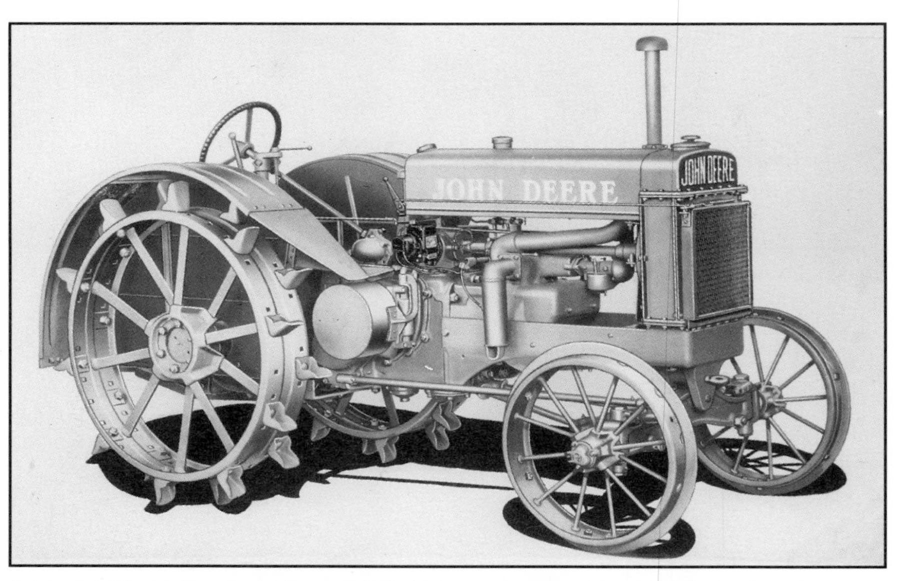

A Model BR studio photo from 1939. When compared to the BO studio photo, the tractors appear to be basically the same except for the steering worm housing and the magneto. *John Deere Archives*

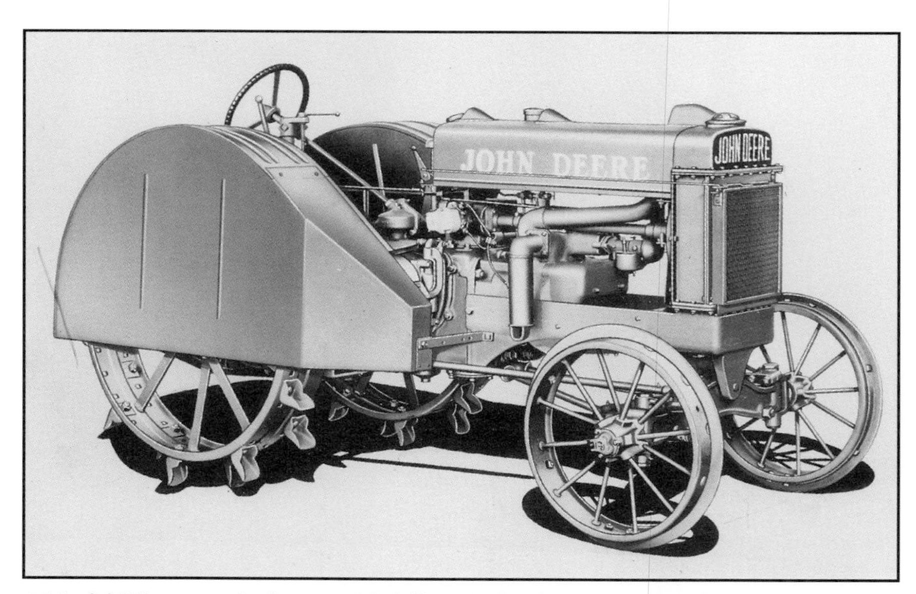

A Model BO tractor is shown with full-cover fenders in this 1939 studio photo. *John Deere Archives*

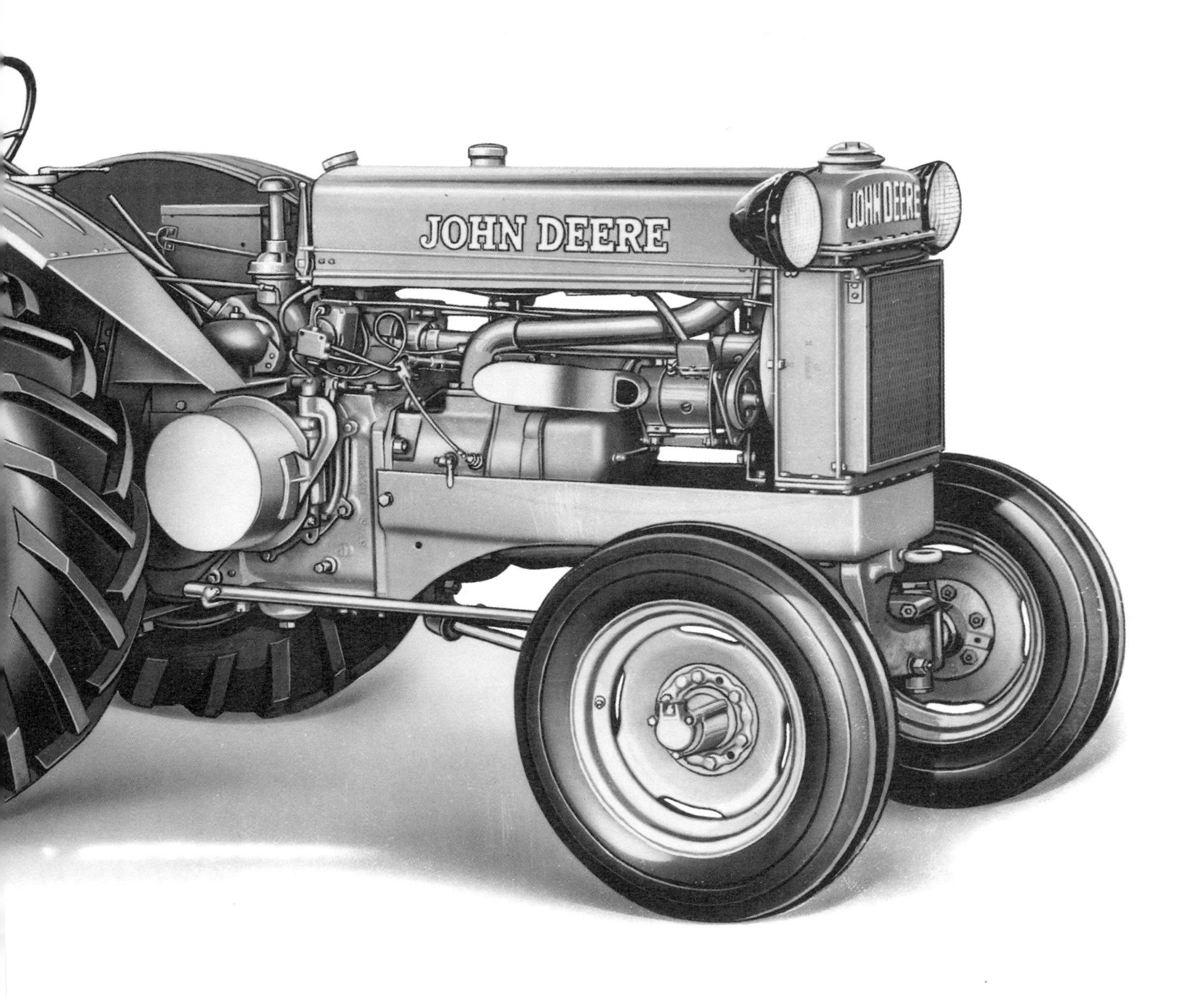

This 1945 studio photo of a John Deere Model BR shows the changes since the previous 1939 photo. Note the addition of the electrical system. *John Deere Archives*

A Model BR on rubber is doing a good job with a John Deere No. 222 disk tiller. The low, aft position of the seat allowed the driver to work controls on the implement. *John Deere Archives*

Right, a Model BO pulls a lawn roller on the Arsenal Golf Course, Rock Island, Illinois. The photo was taken in April of 1936. Notice the hood logo is much different from the type used on row-crop tractors. *John Deere Archives*

The Model BR is shown here for comparison with the venerable John Deere Model D. The standard treads, or "Regulars," as they were known, were especially suited for heavy plowing. *John Deere Archives*

Left, Buena Park, California, orange grove gets tilled by a John Deere Model BO tractor with a John Deere CC disk harrow. The photo was taken in December 1935. *John Deere Archives*

Note the tire tread pattern on this standard-tread Model B. *John Deere Archives*

Model BI

In the spring of 1936, another new member of the B family, the BI, was announced. This new model was intended for industrial customers. It had a different front end support drilled for mounting industrial equipment and sported a 5 1/4in shorter wheelbase for increased maneuverability. The standard Model BI was painted industrial yellow, though a few were painted in custom colors to fulfill special orders.

A 1936 Model BI, with a pusher block installed, appears to be on duty at a trade show in front of a Caterpillar booth. The sign on the radiator of the Diesel RD4 Caterpillar says the price is $2,450; the price of a house in 1936. A Caterpillar D4, today, goes for about $85,000; still the price of a small house in the Mid-west. *John Deere Archives*

This 1937 photo shows a Model BI pulling a John Deere street flusher in its hometown of Waterloo, Iowa. *John Deere Archives*

This 1937 photo shows a Model BI with a Parsons "Landscoop." The scoop is hydraulically operated. *John Deere Archives*

A 1936 Model BI pulls a Caterpillar No. 4 patrol grader. Note the mounting pads on the Model BI front frame that are not included on BR and BO models. *John Deere Archives*

Golf course mowing with a Model BI and a five-gang ground-driven mower, circa 1936. *John Deere Archives*

On the golf links: this Model BI is pulling a John Deere-Van Brunt seeder-spreader. The photo is from 1936. This view clearly shows how the front axle is set back 5.25in on the BI, making the wheelbase shorter. this was done so as not to interfere with front-mounted implements and to provide a shorter turning radius. *John Deere Archives*

A Model BI tractor with street flusher. A 1931 Model A Ford is coming from behind. *John Deere Archives*

Model BNH

By the summer of 1937, another need for a specialized version of the B was recognized. Many specialty crop growers liked the BN but needed a tractor with more vertical clearance. On August 25, 1937, decision number 7250 was published, establishing the specifications of the "BNH" tractor. The new model had two additional inches of crop clearance, accomplished by adopting a 6.50x16in front wheel and 7.50x40in rear wheels. Tread width was increased to a maximum of 104in by providing offset drive wheels and increasing the width of the rear axle housing 5 3/4in. Rear axles were increased 1/8in in diameter to prevent the axle from bending under the increased load when the wheels were at maximum tread position. The process went quickly as the first BNH was shipped on October 1, 1937.

Bruce Johnson's rare BNH. Bruce is a member of the Two-cylinder Clubs Worldwide Technical Council, and is a specialist in unstyled Model Bs.

This BWH is operating with a B-286 cultivator and an AB677 rear toolbar. The photo is from 1938. Note the uneven spacing of the wheels. The photo was taken near Buena Park. *John Deere Archives*

Model BWH

On October 1, 1937, the same day that the first BNH was shipped, decision number 7251 was published, establishing the specifications of the "BWH" tractor, built for much the same purpose as the BNH, but with an adjustable axle for greater stability. Rear wheel and axle equipment was much the same as the BNH. The front axle knees were lengthened 3in to provide additional clearance at the front end.

Shortly after the addition of the BWH, the last member of the B family, an adaptation of the BWH, was authorized for production. This new tractor was a BWH with a special narrow rear axle housing that enabled the rear wheels to set in as close as 42 1/2in, necessitating fenders for operator protection. This special tractor was called the "BWH-40" and since these tractors were serial numbered with the BWH tractors, it is not known how many were produced. Reliable estimates are between six and twenty built, making them one of the rarer variants of the B.

For the 1939 sales season, a new series of Model B tractors appeared sporting a larger engine, more horsepower, and Henry Dreyfuss styling. All of the models received the new engine, although the BR, BO, and BI did not receive the styling treatment.

The new engine was given a 1/4in increase in both bore and stroke, bumping displacement to 175ci. Compression was also increased, making compression relief cocks necessary. Electric starting and lighting became an available option on all models. This series of Model Bs remained unchanged through the 1940 model year.

This BO Lindeman crawler is just about as perfect as you can get. It is owned and was restored by Bruce Johnson of Lily Lake, Illinois. Bruce is one of the experts that advised the author in the preparation of this book. This photo was taken at John Deere's home in Grand Detour, Illinois.

Don Tesker of Salkville, Wisconsin, owns this BO Lindeman crawler. Note the unusual track cleats. Lindeman Brothers of Yakima, Washington, built around 1,800 of these machines. They are randomly disbursed among the standard tread serial numbers. Most were BO models, but there were twenty-five or thirty BRs and one BI.

Deere-Lindeman Crawler

Also in 1939, the Lindeman Power Equipment Company of Yakima, Washington, began limited production of the Deere-Lindeman crawler, using the BO chassis shipped directly to Lindeman, less wheels and steering equipment. A few experimental models had been built prior to this date, but beginning in 1939, the BO crawler became a welcome addition to the line.

Model BW-40

The popularity of the B prompted Deere to experiment with variations of the BN and BW tractors. The first of these to appear were a group of six narrow-tread BW tractors built in the summer and early fall of 1936. These tractors were built with special narrow front and rear axle housings that enabled the rear tread to be set as closely as 40in. To accommodate the narrow wheel spacing, the narrower "BR" crankshaft and belt pulley were adopted, along with a modified first reduction cover. Fenders were standard equipment on these tractors, and they were necessary to shield the operator from the wheels when set into the narrowest spacing. Some of these tractors are known to exist today and are referred to by collectors as the "BW-40," though the factory seems to have referred to them as the "special narrow 'BW.'" Except for the possibility of a surviving "HX" experimental tractor, a BW-40 is the rarest Model B.

Long-Frame Models

In late June 1937, at serial number B-42,200, all General Purpose Model B tractors were given a new front end support that lengthened the wheelbase 5in. This change was mainly so that Model A and B tractors could use the same front-mounted implements. These tractors are referred to as "long-frame" tractors, as the hood, exhaust pipe, and associated components were lengthened to fit the new frame.

Final Revisions

The year 1941 saw another redesign of the Model B line. Engine displacement remained the same, but horsepower was once again increased by adding a little more compression, a larger carburetor, and better breathing. The big news for 1941 was the adoption of rubber tires as standard equipment and a new six-speed transmission for tractors so equipped. Tractors sold with steel wheels continued to use the four-speed transmission but could be converted to six-speed trannies when steel-wheeled tractors were fitted with tires. Aside from minor changes, this series of tractors would continue into early 1947. Also in 1941, the Model BI was discontinued due to lack of demand.

During World War II, advances in technology made gasoline less expensive than distillate. Many tractor companies jumped on the gasoline wagon, but Deere & Company continued to promote the economies afforded by using distillate fuel. Either way, the handwriting was on the wall, and gasoline was the fuel of the future. Accordingly, during 1945 development had begun on gas-burning engines for the Model A and B tractors.

In February 1947, two major changes were made in the Model B line. The BR and BO tractors were discontinued and the final series of Model B General Purpose tractors were introduced. The new engine's bore was opened up to 4 11/16in, but the big news was the availability of factory-built gasoline engines. All-Fuel engines continued to be produced, but the gasoline engines far outsold them.

Other features of the new tractors included a new foam-cushioned seat with the battery mounted underneath. Electric starting and lighting became standard equipment on all models. A new pressed steel front end support was adopted, which made implements easier to attach and was stylish as well. Optional equipment included Roll-O-Matic (see chapter Four) and Powr-Trol (see chapter Six).

The high-clearance Model BNH and BWH were canceled and replaced by a taller tire and wheel option for the BN and BW tractors. A new shift quadrant enabled all six speeds and reverse to be shifted with one lever. Powerful and attractive, these late styled Model Bs sold well. In March 1952, limited availability of copper, due to the Korean War, made steel radiator cores a necessity. To compensate for the reduced cooling capacity, a water pump was incorporated at serial number 306,600 and continued to the end of production. On June 2, 1952, the last Model B rolled off the assembly line, ending seventeen years of Model B production.

General Purpose Row-Crop Version

Years Produced:	1935–52
Total Built	(unstyled): 57,179
Total Built	(styled): 249,203
Total Built	(all GP): 306,382
Price	(1935): $800
Price	(1952): $1,900

			Horsepower	
Serial Numbers	**Bore and Stroke**	**Fuel**	**Drawbar**	**PTO/Belt**
1,000–59,999	4.25x5.25in	All-Fuel*	11.8*	16.0*
60,000–310,775	4.5x5.5in	All-Fuel*	14.0*	18.5*
199,745–310,775**	4.69x5.5in	All-Fuel*	21.1*	23.5*
199,745–310,775**	4.69x5.5in	gasoline	24.6	27.6

**Tested with distillate.* ***Both All-Fuel and gas models were produced for serial numbers 199,745–310,775.*

Serial Numbers	**Engine Displacement**
1,000–59,999	149ci
60,000–200,999	175ci
201,000–310,772	190ci

Serial Numbers	**Engine Rated RPM**
to 200,999	1150
201,000–up	1250

Rear Wheels	**Steel**	**Tire Size**
Unstyled	48x5.25in	9x36in
Styled	10x38in	
Standard Front Wheels		
Styled and Unstyled	22x3.25in	5.5x16in

	Unstyled	**1938–47**	**1947–52**
Length (in.)	120.5	125.5	132.3
Height to Radiator (in.)	56.0	57.0	59.6
Weight (lbs)	2,760	2,880	4,000

Transmission Speeds	
Forward (early)	4
(after serial number 96,000)	6
Reverse	1

Model BR Specifications

Years Produced: 1935–47
(Generally applies to the BO and BI models as well)
Total Built 12,404 (inc. Lindeman)
Price (1947) $2,000

Serial Numbers	Horsepower Bore and Stroke	Fuel	Drawbar	PTO/Belt
325,000–328,999	4.25x5.25in	All-Fuel	9.3	14.3
329,000–337,514	4.5x5.5in	All-Fuel	13.8	17.5

Serial Numbers	Engine Displacement
to 328,999	149ci
329,000–337,514	175ci

Engine Rated RPM	1150
Tires, Standard	
Rear	9.00x28in
	11.25x24in
	11.25x26in
Front	5.50x16in
Length	117.7in
Height to Radiator	50.5in
Weight	3,375 lbs
Transmission Speeds	
Forward	4
Reverse	1

Serial Number Plate

A Model B's serial number is stamped on a brass plate through the 1935 model year, and on an aluminum plate thereafter (except for some steel plates used during World War II). The plate is riveted to the main case belt pulley on styled models and above the flywheel and under the magneto or distributor on unstyled models. The plate is embossed with the words "Model B Tractor, Serial No. B xxxxxx (stamped number), Patents Applied For."

Model B Serial Numbers Versus Year Model

This list is provided as a means of determining a tractor's year model. The model year for the B generally started in August or September of the preceding calendar year, but not always. The number listed is the first serial number of that model year. It should be noted that where a major change occurred, serial numbers were skipped so that the new version could begin with an even number for ready recognition.

Model B Serial Number Chart

Year	B-GP	BI, BO, BR, & BO Lindeman*
1935	1,000	
1936	12,012	325,000
1937	27,389	326,655
1938	46,175	328,111
1939	60,000	329,000
1940	81,600	330,633
1941	96,000	332,039
1942	126,345	332,427
1943	143,420	332,780
1944	152,862	333,156
1945	173,179	334,219
1946	183,673	335,641
1947	199,744	336,746
1948	209,295	
1949	237,346	
1950	258,205	
1951	276,557	
1952	299,175	

**Lindemans are interspersed with other models.*

Special Serial Number Data

The twenty-four Model B Garden tractors had the following serial numbers and build-dates:

Model B Garden Tractor Serial Numbers

Serial Number	Date
1,043–1,048	10/17/34
1,049–1,050	10/30/34
1,080–1,082	10/30/34
1,790–1,799	12/21/34
1,801–1,802	02/15/35

The six BW-40s had the following serial numbers and build dates:

Model BW-40 Serial Numbers

Serial Number	Date
25,150	07/23/36
25,173	07/27/36
26,271	09/04/36
26,965	09/30/36
27,097	10/05/36
27,268	10/09/36

Serial Numbers For Each Generation

Unstyled John Deere B General Purpose tractors used the 149ci engine and four-speed transmission and can be divided into two categories as follows:

Unstyled Model Bs
Short-frame
First built 10-02-34, serial number 1,000
Last built 06-24-37, serial number 42,133
Total production: 41,133

Long-frame
First built 06-24-37, serial number 42,200
Last built 06-14-38, serial number 58,246
Total production: 16,046

Total unstyled production: 57,179

Styled Model Bs
175ci engine
First built 06-16-38, serial number 60,000
Last built 08-29-40, serial number 95,184
Total production: 35,184

Six-speed transmission
First built 09-04-40, serial number 96,000
Last built 05-12-47, serial number 200,247
Total production: 104,247

190ci engine
First built 02-04-47, serial number 201,000
Last built 06-02-52, serial number 310,772
Total production: 109,772

Total styled production: 249,203

Total Model B General Purpose production: 306,282

Unstyled Model B Standard Tread

149ci engine
First built 09-24-35, serial number 325,000
Last built 06-24-38, serial number 328,890
Total production: 3,890

175ci engine
First built 06-14-38, serial number 329,000
Last built 01-28-47, serial number 337,514
Total production: 8,514

Total Model B Standard Tread production: 12,404*

**Of the 12,404 standard tread tractors, 175 were BIs, 3,170 were BOs, 1,884 were BO Lindeman crawlers, and 7,175 were BRs.*

Total Model B Production
(Standard Tread and General Purpose): 318,786

Tractor Build Records

Unlike other tractor makers, John Deere kept a record of the configuration of each tractor built, at least during the time of the Model B. For each tractor serial number, the records list the model configuration (BO, BN, etc.), build date, and shipping destination. In some cases, the record includes codes that indicate how the tractor was equipped.

Tractor build records exist for nearly all John Deere models built from 1914–84 and reside in the John Deere archives. These records can be accessed by writing the archives.

To access the build record for your tractor, send the serial number and model of the tractor along with your name and address to:

Archives
Deere & Company
John Deere Road
Moline, IL 61265

The Two-Cylinder Club can also get build records for your tractor and have some models available on a computer database, although the Model B records were not completely on disk at the time of this printing.

Two-Cylinder Club
Box 219
Grundy Center, IA 50638

The equipment codes that define what was standard on each tractor are somewhat cryptic, and not all codes are understood. Equipment codes known at the time of printing are as follows:

ab4:	48in skeleton drive wheels with cast lugs
ab370:	5.00x15 rubber front tires
ab374:	9.00x36 rubber rear tires
ab3760:	standard cast wheel code, for use with rubber
F and/or G:	Firestone or Goodyear, front and rear
ab1432R:	low-speed transmission
ab1298R:	high-speed transmission

Right, this is an example of what you get when you order a tractor build record. Note the "ab4" code on several of the records. This code is thought to refer to 48in skeleton wheels with cast lugs. See the "Tractor Build Record" section of this chapter for more code information and how to get the build record for your John Deere tractor. *John Deere Archives*

M1227-T-1M-10-29

TRACTOR RECORD

Tractor No.	Warehouse Date	Magneto No.	Equipment, Special Features and Changes in Construction	Date Shipped		SHIPPED TO
B 1000	OCT 2 '34	6383	w/ AB374 Rear R.T.W.	OCT 5 '34	DALLAS	T-8095
1001	OCT 2 '34	6381		[illegible] '34	DALLAS	T-8094
1002	OCT 31 '34		Engy 10/3/34 RB#1 11/14/34 [illegible]	NOV 16 '34	MOLINE	Milwaukee, Wisc.
1003	[illegible] 2 '34	6387		OCT [illegible] '34	SYRACUSE	T-12937
1004	OCT 2 '34	6386		OCT [illegible] '34	SYRACUSE	T-12938
C.M. E1465 1957 1005	NOV 22 1938 / OCT 31 '34	RB#48 11/17/38 Engy 11/9/34	Cm C407 11/31/36 [illegible] October 31, 1935 INVENTORY TAG #[illegible] JUN. 30, 1938 INVENTORY TAG #9375	12/2/38		Reliable Imp. Co., Mattoon, [illegible]
1006	OCT 31 '34			OCT 30 '34	COLUMBUS	T-2832 Moline
1007	OCT 31 '34		Tag #4290 October 31, 1934 INVENTORY	NOV 6 '34	MOLINE	Eldora, Iowa
1008	OCT 11 '34	6388		OCT 11 '34	MOLINE	Mason City, Iowa
1009	OCT 31 '34		Tag #4488 October 31, 1934 INVENTORY	NOV 2 '34	MINNEAPOLIS	Fairmont, Minn.
1010	OCT 31 '34	B-138	Tag #3873 October 31, 1934 INVENTORY w/ AB4	NOV 6 '34	DALLAS	San Antonio, Texas
1011	OCT 31 '34		Tag #4489 October 31, 1934 INVENTORY	NOV 3 '34	ST. LOUIS	Memphis, Tenn.
1012	OCT 31 '34	B-146	Tag #4485 October 31, 1934 INVENTORY w/ AB4	NOV 6 '34	DALLAS	San Antonio, Texas
1013	OCT 31 '34		w/ AB4	OCT 31 '34	DALLAS	T-8247
1014	OCT 31 '34		Tag #4493 October 31, 1934 INVENTORY	NOV 6 '34	MOLINE	La Salle, Illinois
1015	OCT 31 '34			OCT 30 '34	KANSAS CITY	Phoenix, Arizona
1016	OCT 31 '34		w/ AB4	OCT 31 '34	DALLAS	T-8247
1017	OCT 31 '34	RB#167 10/23/34	Tag #4495 October 31, 1934 INVENTORY	NOV 6 '34	MINNEAPOLIS	T-19631
1018	OCT 31 '34	B-142	Tag #4496 October 31, 1934 INVENTORY w/ AB4	NOV 6 '34	DALLAS	San Antonio, Texas
1019	OCT 20 '34			OCT 19 '34	KANSAS CITY	T-41450
1020	OCT 31 '34			OCT 30 '34	LANSING	T-4141
1021	OCT 31 '34		Tag #4497 October 31, 1934 INVENTORY	NOV 6 '34	MINNEAPOLIS	T-19631
1022	OCT 18 '34	6950		OCT 18 '34	DALLAS	T-8216
1023	OCT 18 '34	6956		OCT 1[illegible] '34	KANSAS CITY	Phoenix, Arizona
1024	OCT 31 '34			OCT 30 '34	KANSAS CITY	Phoenix, Arizona
1025	OCT 31 '34	RB#167 10/23/34	Tag #3937 October 31, 1934 INVENTORY	NOV 3 '34	ST. LOUIS	Little Rock, Ark.
1026	OCT 31 '34		w/ AB4	OCT 31 '34	DALLAS	T-8247
1027	OCT 18 '34	6943		OCT 18 '34	DALLAS	T-8216
1028	OCT 18 '34	6951		OCT 18 '34	DALLAS	T-8216
1029	OCT 31 '34	B-139	Tag #3869 October 31, 1934 INVENTORY w/ AB4	NOV 6 '34	DALLAS	San Antonio, Texas
1030	OCT 20 '34			OCT 19 '34	KANSAS CITY	T-41420
1031	OCT 18 '34	6938		OCT [illegible] '34	KANSAS CITY	Phoenix, Arizona
1032	OCT 18 '34	6944	w/ ab374 & ab370 R.T.W.	OCT 18 '34	DALLAS	T-8214
1033	OCT 27 '34			OCT 26 '34	MOLINE	Hampton, Iowa
1034	OCT 27 '34			OCT 22 '34	MOLINE	Union, Iowa
1035	OCT 31 '34		Tag #4494 October 31, 1934 INVENTORY	[illegible] '34	MINNEAPOLIS	T-19631
1036	OCT 18 '34	6853		OCT 19 '34	DALLAS	T-8215
1037	OCT 31 '34	B-144	Tag #3874 October 31, 1934 INVENTORY w/ AB4	NOV 6 '34	DALLAS	San Antonio, Texas
1038	OCT 18 '34	6964		OCT 18 '34	DALLAS	T-8216
1039	OCT 31 '34	Engy 10/20/34	Engy [illegible] RB#28 [illegible] October 31, 1935 INVENTORY TAG #31330	MAR 31 1936	MOLINE	Waterloo, Iowa
1040	OCT 31 '34	B-140	Tag #3872 October 31, 1934 INVENTORY w/ AB4	NOV [illegible]	[illegible]	San Antonio, Texas

Chapter 2

Engine

The John Deere Model B is powered by a horizontal, parallel (side-by-side), two-cylinder engine. The side-by-side pistons operate on a 180º crankshaft, meaning that when one piston is at the top of the stroke the other is at the bottom. The engine fires at 0º and 180º and then rotates 540º before firing again (like a double-barrel shotgun; you fire each barrel, reload, and fire again). This accounts for John Deere two-cylinder engine's unusual pop-pop, space, pop-pop sound.

The engine is mounted with the crankshaft crosswise to the centerline of the tractor. This is known as transverse mounting. Advantages are that the belt pulley is mounted directly to the crankshaft. Bevel gears are not required for the belt pulley or input to the differential.

The John Deere Model B uses an overhead valve, or valve-in-head, engine with two valves per cylinder. The Model B used three different engine displacements: 149, 175, and 190ci. The bore and stroke were increased for 1939, when the B row-crops were styled, and again in 1947 when the pressed-steel frame replaced the angle-iron type. The Model BI was discontinued in 1941, so it got only the first displacement increase. BR and BO models were discontinued in 1947, so they did not receive the final engine increase to 190ci. The 175ci engine was the only one that had decompression taps to ease starting.

A detail of the left side of the B engine. This is an early styled version without electrics.

An interesting characteristic of the Model B, and other John Deeres with transverse engines, was the method of hand starting. Instead of turning a crank, the operator simply rolled the flywheel through a compression stroke, while standing on the ground alongside the tractor.

Engine Summary Table

Model	Year	Serial Numbers	Remarks
B-GP, BN, BW	1935–37	1,000–42,199	unstyled, short frame, 149ci engine
B-GP, BN, BW	1937–38	42,200–59,999	long frame, unstyled
BNH, BWH	1937–38	46,175–59,999	
B-GP, BN, BW, BNH, BWH	1939–40	60,000- 95,999	styled, four-speed, 175ci engine
B-GP, BN, BW, BNH, BWH	1941–47	96,000-200,999	styled, six-speed
B-GP, BN, BW	1947–52	201,000-310,775	late styled, 190ci engine, pressed steel frame,
BR, BO	1935–38	325,000-328,999	149ci engine
BR, BO	1938–47	329,000-337,514	175ci engine
BI	1936–41	325,617-332,157	serial numbers interspersed with BR and BO
BO Lindeman serial	1939–47	329,000-337,506	Lindeman Crawler (1,844 made), numbers interspersed with BO-BN

A Model B's pistons get a thorough cleaning in the wash tank.

This position allowed the operator to actuate any controls, such as the choke or throttle, without having dual controls. This method was touted as being safer than the hand crank, which it likely was, but electric starting was a welcome addition when it appeared in 1939.

Why Two Cylinders?

In the early days of internal combustion engines, one-cylinder engines were the rule. Engineers soon realized that several small cylinders burned fuel more efficiently than one large cylinder. Most manufacturers opted for four-cylinder engines, which were smooth and simple enough to retain reasonable manufacturing costs. Deere, however, elected to stay with two-cylinder engines. Why they did this is not entirely clear, although engineering costs and the success of the Waterloo Boy and the Model D were certainly factors. Whatever the reason, they touted the simplicity of their two-cylinder machines, and brand loyalty later became quite strong, to the point of being fanatical.

For two-cylinder four-cycle engines, a horizontally opposed arrangement is ideal for balance and even power strokes. This type does not package well, however, because of its width. Also, long passages from the carburetor can be a problem, especially with kerosene fuel. Conversely, the side-by-side two-cylinder engine is ideal for kerosene fuel, since the exhaust heat is close by to easily warm the intake tubes and carburetor.

Early engine makers tried three types of two-cylinder side-by-side engines. The first was a two-cycle. The pistons ran in opposite directions on separate crank throws and the engine fired every 180º. This provided smooth, balanced power strokes, but early engineers could not make two-cycle engines work properly. The problems with two-cycle engines were sorted out in more modern times, and the engine has been put to good use in motorcycles, outboard motors, lawn implements, and snowmobiles, to name just a few applications.

Around the turn of the twentieth century, several manufacturers tried the side-by-side two-cylinder four-cycle arrangement with only one crank throw. Henry Ford's first engine and the engine of the gigantic International Harvester Titan were built that way. The pistons operated in unison, providing a power stroke every 360º of rotation. The advantages were even firing and short fuel-air passages. The big disadvantage is excessive vibration that cannot be offset by rotating counterweights.

Finally, consider the two-cylinder four-cycle engine with the pistons on separate throws; that is, the John Deere type (others, such as Rumely and Hart-Parr also used this approach). The advantage of short fuel-air passages can be capitalized upon, and the pistons balance each other. The disadvantage is the uneven firing at 180º and 540º. This disadvantage is readily overcome with a heavy flywheel, which smoothes out the power pulses. John Deere advertising of the day cited the example of the foot treadle-operated grindstone to show how the fly-

The head has been removed.

The crankshaft can be seen after removal of the block, pistons, and rods.

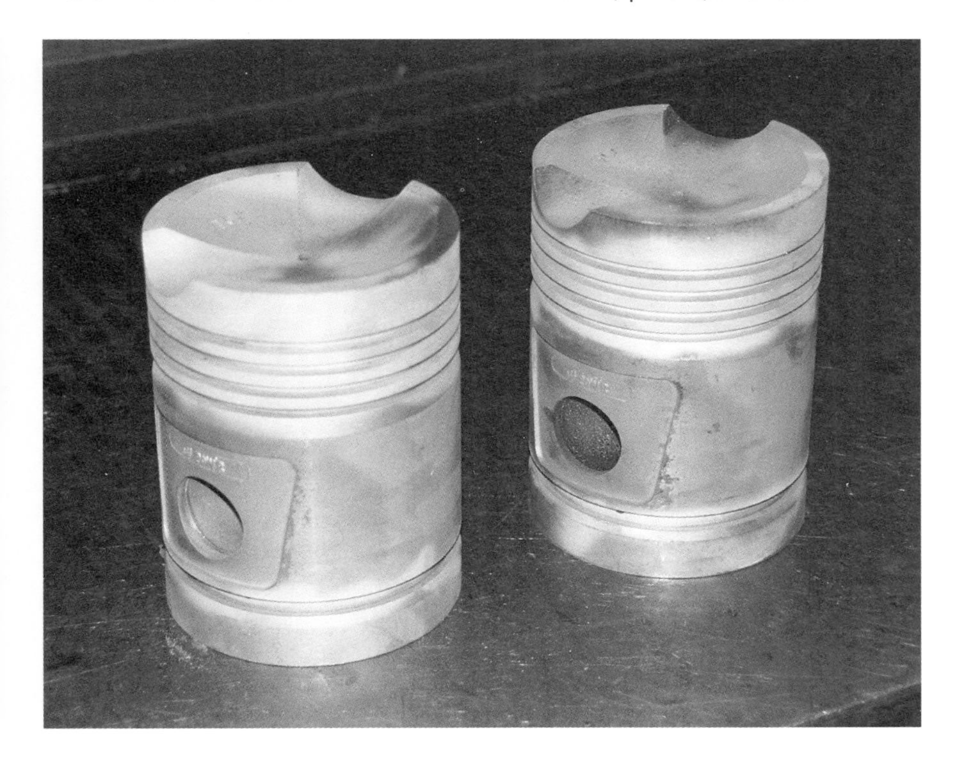

A set of Model B pistons ready for installation.

wheel effect smoothed out the power strokes.

As previously mentioned, John Deere's use of the side-by-side two-cylinder four-cycle engine stems back to their purchase of the Waterloo Boy tractor outfit back in 1918. Waterloo Boy had adopted that configuration as early as 1912, after first experimenting with horizontally opposed and two-cycle engines. Deere touted the advantages of simplicity and fewer parts, as well as the ability of the engine to operate successfully on low-cost distillate fuels. Other brands, such as the Farmall four-

A Model B head, on the bench as valve springs and clips are installed.

cylinder and the Oliver six-cylinder machines, performed adequately on low-cost fuel, although not as well as the simple John Deere two-cylinder.

In the 1930s, gasoline quality stabilized when octane ratings were standardized at seventy. Despite costing about twice as much as distillate-based fuels, gasoline gradually replaced distillates. The advantages of gasoline more than offset the cost; gasoline was more convenient, more fuel efficient, and produced more power. Engines burning distillate used about twenty percent more fuel and produced ten percent less power on distillate. Also, it was more convenient to use gasoline; engines had to be started on gas, so why not just stay with it?

Another view of the Model B head, this time as valve seats are cut.

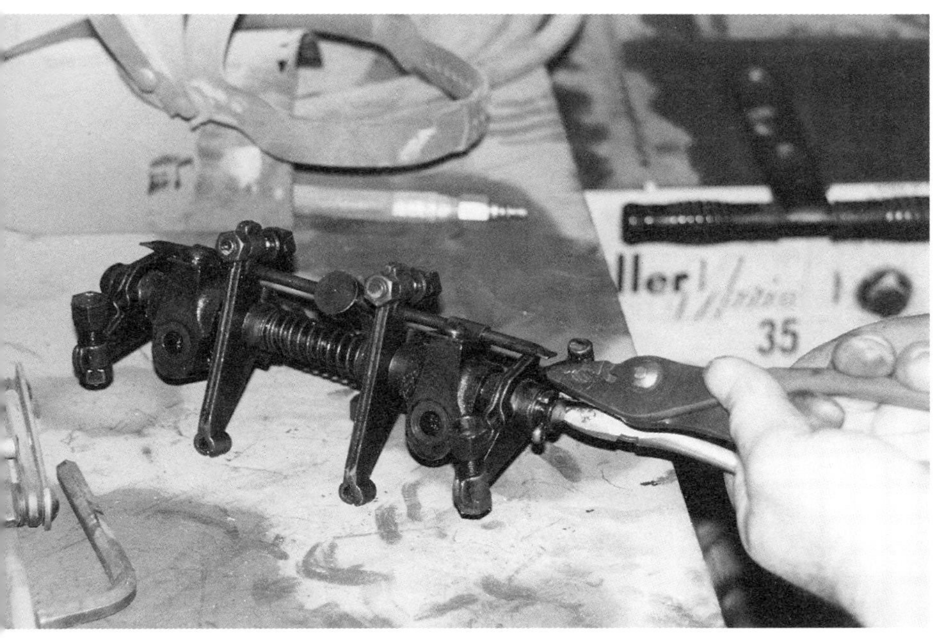

The rocker arms of a John Deere Model B.

Block

The two-cylinder engine block is a one-piece casting which bolts onto the crankcase.

To remove the block from the tractor it is first necessary to remove the upper coolant pipe, head, connecting rods, and pistons. On most Model Bs, it will also be easier to remove the fan shaft and governor. There are oil tubes on some models that must be removed. On tractors with pressed steel frames, it will be necessary to remove the spark plugs to take the block from the tractor.

Cylinder sleeves were not used in the Model B engine, so if re-boring is necessary, it should be done to accommodate the available .045in oversized pistons. The cylinders can also be bored out to receive sleeves, which bring the bore back to standard.

Head

The head assembly includes the valves, tappets, tappet cover, and pushrods. Exhaust and intake manifolds are connected to the head, as is the lower coolant pipe.

The Model B uses removable pushrod sleeves. These need to be inspected when the head is removed, as seal failure and/or corrosion will result in coolant leakage.

With the demise of distillate-based fuel, the two-cylinders' superior use of distillate fuel was no longer a significant advantage. The engine made a good gasoline engine; indeed it made a good diesel. But Deere recognized that they were doing it the hard way with the two-cylinder, and that the new multi-cylinder high-speed diesels were the wave of the future. Even so, John Deere used the traditional two-cylinder engine until 1960, when the New Generation appeared.

6 **TRACTORS—MODELS "B" AND "BR"-"BO" (NOT STYLED)**

ENGINE

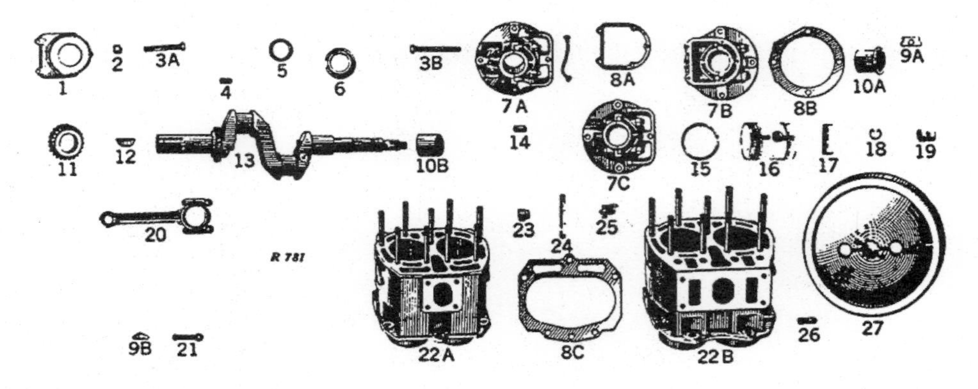

Key	Part No.		B	BR-BO	Description
1	B	131 R	B1000–(——)	325000–	Cover, L.H. Main Bearing
2	B	119 R	B1000–(——)	325000–	Nut, Main Bearing Bolt
3A	B	126 R	B1000–(——)	325000–	Bolt, L.H. Main Bearing
3B	B	118 R	B1000–(——)	325000–	Bolt, R.H. Main Bearing
4	D	1080 R	B1000–(——)	325000–	Screw, Flywheel Locating
5	B	130 R	B1000–(——)	325000–	Washer, Cork, Flywheel Spacer
6	AB	4463 R	B1000–(——)	325000–	Spacer, Flywheel, with B130R Cork Washer (Sub. for AB251R and AB4109R)
7A	AB	511 R	B1000–10168	....	Housing, B597R, Main Bearing, with Cap, R.H., and Oil Line Assembly
7B	AB	3126 R	B1000–(——)	325000–	Housing, B124R or B2031R, Main Bearing, with Cap, L.H. (Sub. for AB250R)
7C	AB	3125 R	B10169–(——)	325000–	Housing, B597R or B2029R, Main Bearing, with Cap, R.H. (Sub. for AB514R)
8A	B	132 R	B1000–(——)	325000–	Gasket, L.H. Main Bearing Cover
8B	B	3026 R	B1000–(——)	325000–	Gasket, L.H. Main Bearing Housing (Sub. for B128R)
8C	B	1332 R	....	329000–	Gasket, Cylinder to Case
	B	356 R	B1000–59999	325000–328999	Gasket, Cylinder to Case
9A	B	120 R	B1000–(——)	325000–	Shim, Main Bearing, Laminated
9B	B	7 R	B1000–(——)	325000–	Shim, Connecting Rod, Laminated
10A	AB	320 R	B1000–(——)	325000–333124	Bearing, L.H. Main (2 Halves, Bronze Backed)
	AB	4273 R	....	333125–	Bearing, L.H. Main (2 Halves, Steel Backed) (Also Parts on B1000–(——) and 325000–333124 Equipped with AB3126R Housing Identified by the Casting No. B2031R) (Sub. for AB3128R)
10B	AB	319 R	B1000–(——)	325000–333124	Bearing, R.H. Main (2 Halves, Bronzed Backed)
	AB	4272 R	....	333125–	Bearing, R.H. Main (2 Halves, Steel Backed) (Also Parts on B1000–(——) and 325000–333124 Equipped with AB3125R Housing Identified by the Casting No. B2029R) (Sub. for AB3127R)
11	B	115 R	B1000–(——)	325000–	Gear, Crankshaft (Sub. for AB4117R)
12	26H	17 R	B1000–(——)	325000–	Key in Crankshaft Gear
13	AB	246 R	B1000–59999	....	Crankshaft, B114R, with Gear (See Page 3 for Special Replacement Assemblies)
	AB	592 R	....	325000–328999	Crankshaft, B767R, with Gear (See Page 3 for Special Replacement Assemblies)
	AB	1561 R	....	329000–	Crankshaft, B1340R, with Gear (See Page 3 for Special Replacement Assemblies)
14	B	122 R	B1000–(——)	325000–	Pin, Dowel, R.H. Main Bearing
15	AB	1055 R	B1000–59999	325000–328999	Ring, Piston, 4-1/4", .030" Oversize (Set of 8) (No Longer Furnished)
	AB	4750 R	B1000–59999	325000–328999	Ring, Piston, Oil Control (2 Rings) (Sub. for AB1282R)
	AB	4751 R	B1000–59999	325000–328999	Ring, Piston, Oil Control, .045" Oversize (2 Rings) (Sub. for AB1464R)
	AB	4752 R	....	329000–	Ring, Piston, Oil Control (2 Rings) (For Use in Used Cylinders only) (Sub. for AB1465R)
	AB	4753 R	....	329000–	Ring, Piston, Oil Control, .045" Oversize (2 Rings) (For Use in Used Cylinders Only) (Sub. for AB1466R)
	AB	2522 R	B1000–59999	325000–328999	Ring, Piston, 4-1/4" Standard (Set of 6 Compression and 2 Oil Control) (For Use in Used Cylinders Only)
	AB	2523 R	B1000–59999	325000–328999	Ring, Piston, 4-1/4", .045" Oversize (Set of 6 Compression and 2 Oil Control) (For Use in Used Cylinders Only)
	AB	3725 R	....	329000–	Ring, Piston, 4-1/2" Standard (Set of 6 Compression and 2 Oil Control) (For Use in Used Cylinders Only) (Sub. for AB3087R)
	AB	3727 R	....	329000–	Ring, Piston, 4-1/2", .045" Oversize (Set of 6 Compression and 2 Oil Control) (For Use in Used Cylinders Only) (Sub. for AB3088R)
16	AB	3914 R	B1000–59999	325000–328999	Piston, 2-B1154R, .045" Oversize, with Rings, Gastets, etc. (Sub. for AB3279R)
	AB	3916 R	....	329000–	Piston, 2-B1349R, .045" Oversize, with Rings, Gaskets, etc. (Sub. for AB3280R)
	AB	3913 R	B1000–59999	325000–328999	Piston, 2-B1R, with Rings, Pins, Gaskets, etc. (Sub. for AB3336R)
	AB	3915 R	....	329000–	Piston, 2-B1308R, with Rings, Pins, Gaskets, etc. (Sub. for AB3337R)
17	B	2 R	B1000–59999	325000–328999	Pin, Piston (2 used) (Sub. for AB1285R)
	B	917 R	B1000–59999	325000–328999	Pin, Piston, .005" Oversize (Marked with Red) (2 used) (Sub. for AB1286R)
	B	1312 R	....	329000–	Pin, Piston (2 used) (Sub. for AB1479R)
	B	1354 R	....	329000–	Pin, Piston, .005" Oversize (Marked with Red) (2 used) (Sub. for AB1480R)
	B	2234 R	B1000–59999	325000–328999	Pin, Piston, .003" Oversize (Marked with Yellow) (2 used) (Sub. for AB3747R)
	B	2235 R	....	329000–	Pin, Piston, .003" Oversize (Marked with Yellow) (2 used) (Sub. for AB3748R)
18	B	3 R	B1000–(——)	325000–	Snap Ring, Piston Pin (4 used)
19	B	413 R	B1000–(——)	325000–	Bushing, Piston Pin (2 used) (Sub. for AB1299R)
20	AB	355 R	B1000–(——)	325000–	Rod, Connecting, B5R, Complete (Exchange Credit Allowable)
21	AB	356 R	B1000–(——)	325000–	Bolt, Connecting Rod, with Nut and Cotter
22A	AB	476 R	B1000–59999	325000–328999	Block, Cylinder, B354R or B560R, with Studs
22B	AB	1450 R	....	329000–	Block, Cylinder, B1305R, with Studs
23	15H	238 R	B1000–(——)	325000–	Plug, Pipe, L.H. Main Bearing (2 used)
	15H	238 R	B1000–(——)	325000–	Plug, Pipe, Crankcase Oil Drain
24	B	355 R	B1000–(——)	325000–	Stud, Cylinder Head, 9/16" x 5-1/4" (9 used)
	B	1333 R	....	329000–	Stud, Cylinder to Case, 5/8" x 2-1/2" (7 used)
	C	719 R	B1000–59999	325000–328999	Stud, Cylinder to Case, 5/8" x 2-5/8" (6 used)
	A	5292 R	B1000–3043	....	Stud, Front End Support to Cylinder 5/8" x 2" (Sub. for C1031R and C1479R)
25	AB	1898 R	....	329000–	Cock, Relief, Compression
26	D	2009 R	B1000–(——)	325000–	Pin, Flywheel Spacer Driving
27	AB	253 R	B1000–14037	325000–325600	Flywheel, B133R, with Bolts and Driving Pin
	AB	705 R	B14038–(——)	325601—	Flywheel, B660R, with Bolts and Driving Pin
(Parts listed below are illustrated in gasket set groupings.)					
	AB	3874 R	B1000–(——)	325000–328999	Gasket Set, Valve Ring or Cylinder Replacement Assembly
	AB	3875 R	B60000–(——)	329000–	Gasket Set, Valve Ring or Cylinder Replacement Assembly
	AB	3878 R	B1000–(——)	325000–328999	Gasket Set, Crankshaft and Bearing Replacement Assembly
	AB	3879 R	B60000–(——)	329000–	Gasket Set, Crankshaft and Bearing Replacement Assembly

PC-676-(2-60)

Unstyled Model B engine (all BR, BO, and BI). *John Deere Archives*

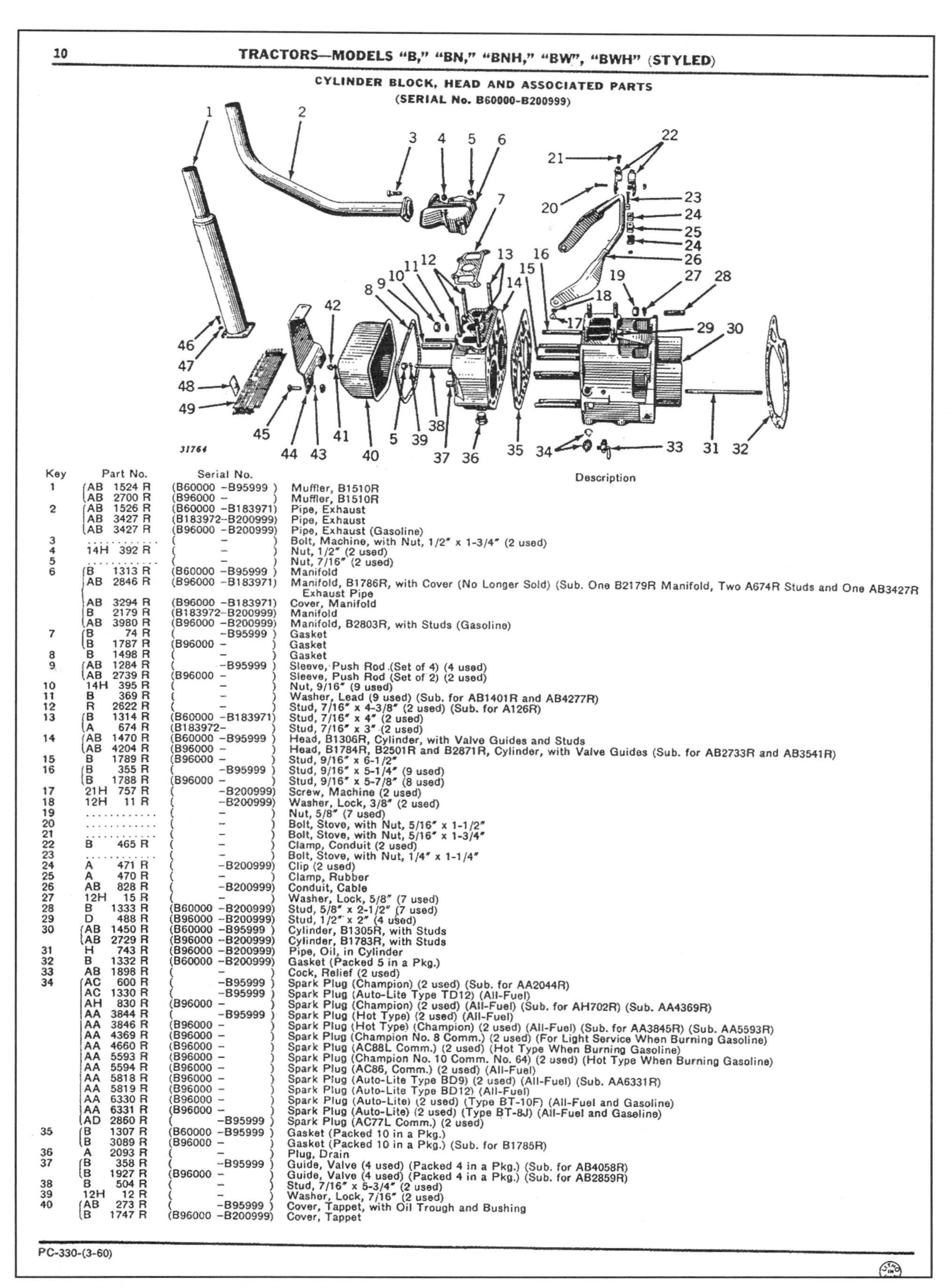

10 TRACTORS—MODELS "B," "BN," "BNH," "BW", "BWH" (STYLED)

CYLINDER BLOCK, HEAD AND ASSOCIATED PARTS
(SERIAL No. B60000-B200999)

Key	Part No.	Serial No.	Description
1	AB 1524 R	(B60000 –B95999)	Muffler, B1510R
	AB 2700 R	(B96000 –)	Muffler, B1510R
2	AB 1526 R	(B60000 –B183971)	Pipe, Exhaust
	AB 3427 R	(B183972–B200999)	Pipe, Exhaust
	AB 3427 R	(B96000 –B200999)	Pipe, Exhaust (Gasoline)
3	....	(–)	Bolt, Machine, with Nut, 1/2" x 1-3/4" (2 used)
4	14H 392 R	(–)	Nut, 1/2" (2 used)
5	....	(–)	Nut, 7/16" (2 used)
6	B 1313 R	(B60000 –B95999)	Manifold
	AB 2846 R	(B96000 –B183971)	Manifold, B1786R, with Cover (No Longer Sold) (Sub. One B2179R Manifold, Two A674R Studs and One AB3427R Exhaust Pipe
	AB 3294 R	(B96000 –B183971)	Cover, Manifold
	B 2179 R	(B183972–B200999)	Manifold
	AB 3980 R	(B96000 –B200999)	Manifold, B2803R, with Studs (Gasoline)
7	B 74 R	(–B95999)	Gasket
	B 1787 R	(B96000 –)	Gasket
8	B 1498 R	(–)	Gasket
9	AB 1284 R	(–B95999)	Sleeve, Push Rod (Set of 4) (4 used)
	AB 2739 R	(B96000 –)	Sleeve, Push Rod (Set of 2) (2 used)
10	14H 395 R	(–)	Nut, 9/16" (9 used)
11	B 369 R	(–)	Washer, Lead (9 used) (Sub. for AB1401R and AB4277R)
12	R 2622 R	(–)	Stud, 7/16" x 4-3/8" (2 used) (Sub. for A126R)
13	B 1314 R	(B60000 –B183971)	Stud, 7/16" x 4" (2 used)
	A 674 R	(B183972–)	Stud, 7/16" x 3" (2 used)
14	AB 1470 R	(B60000 –B95999)	Head, B1306R, Cylinder, with Valve Guides and Studs
	AB 4204 R	(B96000 –)	Head, B1784R, B2501R and B2871R, Cylinder, with Valve Guides (Sub. for AB2733R and AB3541R)
15	B 1789 R	(B96000 –)	Stud, 9/16" x 6-1/2"
16	B 355 R	(–B95999)	Stud, 9/16" x 5-1/4" (9 used)
	B 1788 R	(B96000 –)	Stud, 9/16" x 5-7/8" (8 used)
17	21H 757 R	(–B200999)	Screw, Machine (2 used)
18	12H 11 R	(–B200999)	Washer, Lock, 3/8" (2 used)
19	....	(–)	Nut, 5/8" (7 used)
20	....	(–)	Bolt, Stove, with Nut, 5/16" x 1-1/2"
21	....	(–)	Bolt, Stove, with Nut, 5/16" x 1-3/4"
22	B 465 R	(–)	Clamp, Conduit (2 used)
23	....	(–)	Bolt, Stove, with Nut, 1/4" x 1-1/4"
24	A 471 R	(–B200999)	Clip (2 used)
25	A 470 R	(–)	Clamp, Rubber
26	AB 828 R	(–B200999)	Conduit, Cable
27	12H 15 R	(–)	Washer, Lock, 5/8" (7 used)
28	B 1333 R	(B60000 –B200999)	Stud, 5/8" x 2-1/2" (7 used)
29	D 488 R	(B96000 –B200999)	Stud, 1/2" x 2" (4 used)
30	AB 1450 R	(B60000 –B95999)	Cylinder, B1305R, with Studs
	AB 2729 R	(B96000 –B200999)	Cylinder, B1783R, with Studs
31	H 743 R	(B96000 –B200999)	Pipe, Oil, in Cylinder
32	B 1332 R	(B60000 –B200999)	Gasket (Packed 5 in a Pkg.)
33	AB 1898 R	(–)	Cock, Relief (2 used)
34	AC 600 R	(–B95999)	Spark Plug (Champion) (2 used) (Sub. for AA2044R)
	AC 1330 R	(–B95999)	Spark Plug (Auto-Lite Type TD12) (All-Fuel)
	AH 830 R	(B96000 –)	Spark Plug (Champion) (2 used) (All-Fuel) (Sub. for AH702R) (Sub. AA4369R)
	AA 3844 R	(–B95999)	Spark Plug (Hot Type) (2 used) (All-Fuel)
	AA 3846 R	(B96000 –)	Spark Plug (Hot Type) (Champion) (2 used) (All-Fuel) (Sub. for AA3845R) (Sub. AA5593R)
	AA 4369 R	(B96000 –)	Spark Plug (Champion No. 8 Comm.) (2 used) (For Light Service When Burning Gasoline)
	AA 4660 R	(B96000 –)	Spark Plug (AC88L Comm.) (2 used) (Hot Type When Burning Gasoline)
	AA 5593 R	(B96000 –)	Spark Plug (Champion No. 10 Comm. No. 64) (2 used) (Hot Type When Burning Gasoline)
	AA 5594 R	(B96000 –)	Spark Plug (AC86, Comm.) (2 used) (All-Fuel)
	AA 5818 R	(B96000 –)	Spark Plug (Auto-Lite Type BD9) (2 used) (All-Fuel) (Sub. AA6331R)
	AA 5819 R	(B96000 –)	Spark Plug (Auto-Lite Type BD12) (All-Fuel)
	AA 6330 R	(B96000 –)	Spark Plug (Auto-Lite) (2 used) (Type BT-10F) (All-Fuel and Gasoline)
	AA 6331 R	(B96000 –)	Spark Plug (Auto-Lite) (2 used) (Type BT-8J) (All-Fuel and Gasoline)
	AD 2860 R	(–B95999)	Spark Plug (AC77L Comm.) (2 used)
35	B 1307 R	(B60000 –B95999)	Gasket (Packed 10 in a Pkg.)
	B 3089 R	(B96000 –)	Gasket (Packed 10 in a Pkg.) (Sub. for B1785R)
36	A 2093 R	(–)	Plug, Drain
37	B 358 R	(–B95999)	Guide, Valve (4 used) (Packed 4 in a Pkg.) (Sub. for AB4058R)
	B 1927 R	(B96000 –)	Guide, Valve (4 used) (Packed 4 in a Pkg.) (Sub. for AB2859R)
38	B 504 R	(–)	Stud, 7/16" x 5-3/4" (2 used)
39	12H 12 R	(–)	Washer, Lock, 7/16" (2 used)
40	AB 273 R	(–B95999)	Cover, Tappet, with Oil Trough and Bushing
	B 1747 R	(B96000 –B200999)	Cover, Tappet

PC-330-(3-60)

Early styled Model B cylinder, block, head, and associated parts. *John Deere Archives*

TRACTORS—MODELS "B," "BN," "BNH," "BW," "BWH" (STYLED) 11

CYLINDER BLOCK, HEAD AND ASSOCIATED PARTS—Continued
(Serial No. B60000-B200999)

Key	Part No.	Serial No.	Description
41	A 3439 R	(–)	Washer, Copper (2 used) (Packed 5 in a Pkg.) (Sub. for B214R)
42	14H 664 R	(–)	Nut, 7/16" (2 used)
43	12H 13 R	(–)	Washer, Lock, 1/2" (2 used)
44	B 1917 R	(B60000 –B136661)	Support, Fan Shaft
	B 2014 R	(B136662–B166999)	Support, Fan Shaft (Attaching Hardware Two 19H1131N Cap Screws and Two 12H13R Lock Washers)
	B 2114 R	(B167000–B200999)	Support, Fan Shaft
45	....	(–B136661)	Bolt, Mach., with Nut, 1/2" x 1-1/4" (2 used)
	....	(B167000–)	Bolt, Mach., with Nut, 1/2" x 1-1/4" (2 used)
46	....	(–B95999)	Screw, Cap, 3/8" x 1" (4 used)
	19H 1112 H	(B96000 –)	Screw, Cap, 5/16" x 3/4" (4 used) (Sub. for 19H105R)
47	12H 11 R	(–B95999)	Washer, Lock, 3/8" (4 used)
	12H 10 R	(B96000 –)	Washer, Lock, 5/16" (4 used)
48	B 1673 R	(B60000 –B136661)	Washer, Trash Screen (2 used)
	.	(B167000–B200999)	Washer, Trash Screen (2 used)
49	B 1565 R	(B63800 –B136661)	Screen, Trash
		(B167000–B200999)	Screen, Trash
(Parts listed below are not illustrated)			
	AB 3875 R	(–B95999)	Gasket Set, Valve, Ring and Cylinder Replacement
	AB 3876 R	(B96000 –B200999)	Gasket Set, Valve, Ring and Cylinder Replacement
	AR 21782 R	(B96000 –B200999)	Gasket Set, for Valve Service

Early styled Model B cylinder, block, head, and associated parts (continued). *John Deere Archives*

General Data

Serial Numbers	1,000–59,999	60,000–95,999	96,000–200,999	201,000–up	
Fuel	kerosene	kerosene	kerosene	kerosene	gasoline
Bore (in.)	4.25	4.5	4.5	4.69	4.69
Stroke (in.)	5.25	5.5	5.5	5.5	5.5
Displacement (ci)	149	175	175	190	190
Rated RPM	1,150	1,150	1,150	1,250	1,250
Compression Ratio	4.45	4.71	4.71	4.65	5.87
Cranking Pressure (psi)	70	70	70	70	110
Tappet Gap	.020	.020	.020	.020	.020
Inlet Valve Face Angle	30	30	30	29.75	29.75
Exhaust Valve Face Angle	45	45	45	44.5	44.5
Inlet Valve Seat Angle	30	30	30	30	30
Exhaust Valve Seat Angle	45	45	45	45	45
Spark Plug	Champion No. 8 (for unstyled)				
Spark Plug Gap (in.)	.030	.030	.030	.030	.030
Crankcase Capacity (qts.)	7.5	7.5	7.5	7.0	7.0

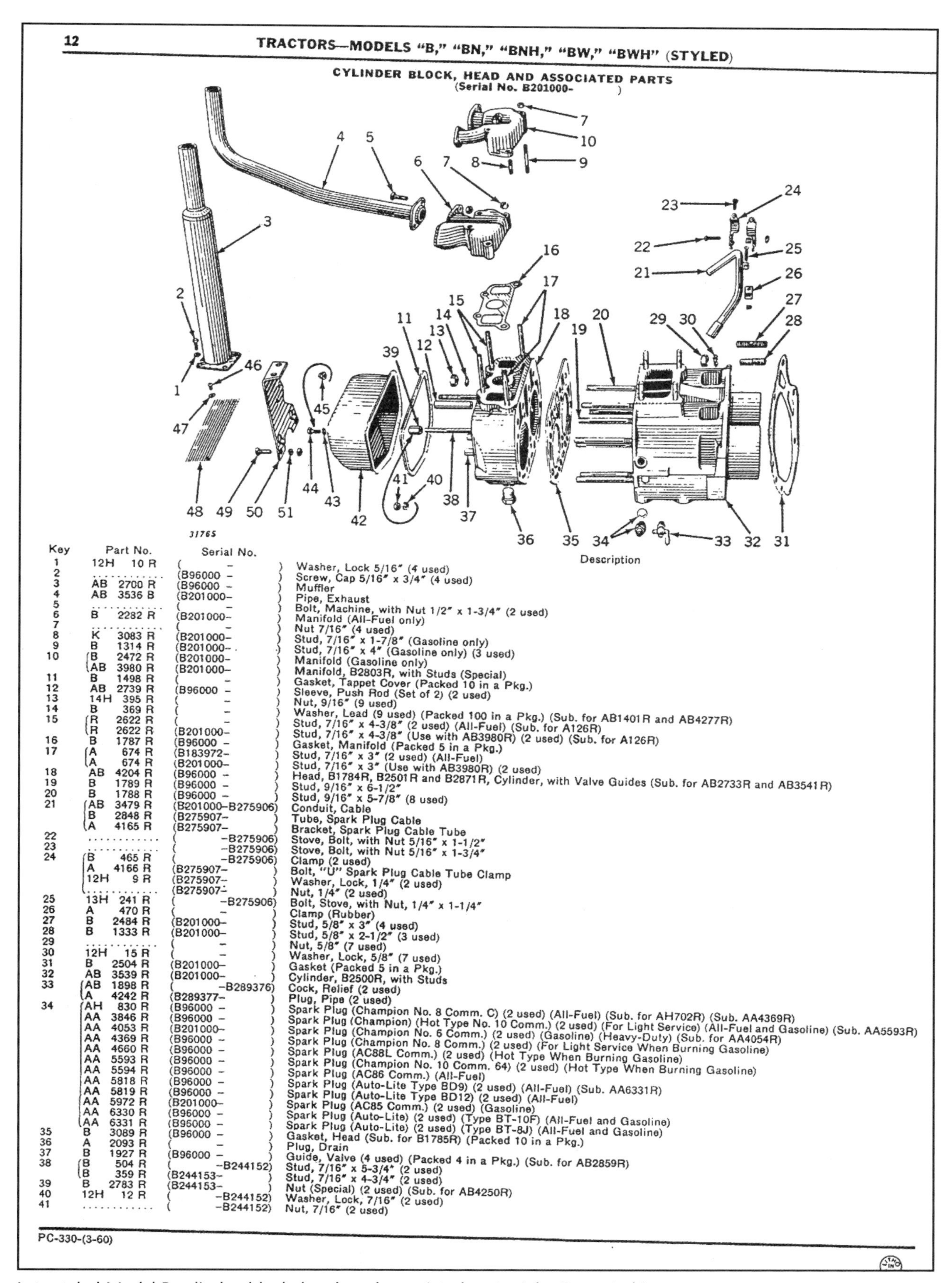

CYLINDER BLOCK, HEAD AND ASSOCIATED PARTS
(Serial No. B201000-)

Key	Part No.	Serial No.	Description
1	12H 10 R	(–)	Washer, Lock 5/16" (4 used)
2	....	(B96000 –)	Screw, Cap 5/16" x 3/4" (4 used)
3	AB 2700 R	(B96000 –)	Muffler
4	AB 3536 B	(B201000–)	Pipe, Exhaust
5	....	(–)	Bolt, Machine, with Nut 1/2" x 1-3/4" (2 used)
6	B 2282 R	(B201000–)	Manifold (All-Fuel only)
7	....	(–)	Nut 7/16" (4 used)
8	K 3083 R	(B201000–)	Stud, 7/16" x 1-7/8" (Gasoline only)
9	B 1314 R	(B201000–)	Stud, 7/16" x 4" (Gasoline only) (3 used)
10	B 2472 R	(B201000–)	Manifold (Gasoline only)
	AB 3980 R	(B201000–)	Manifold, B2803R, with Studs (Special)
11	B 1498 R	(–)	Gasket, Tappet Cover (Packed 10 in a Pkg.)
12	AB 2739 R	(B96000 –)	Sleeve, Push Rod (Set of 2) (2 used)
13	14H 395 R	(–)	Nut, 9/16" (9 used)
14	B 369 R	(–)	Washer, Lead (9 used) (Packed 100 in a Pkg.) (Sub. for AB1401R and AB4277R)
15	R 2622 R	(–)	Stud, 7/16" x 4-3/8" (2 used) (All-Fuel) (Sub. for A126R)
	R 2622 R	(B201000–)	Stud, 7/16" x 4-3/8" (Use with AB3980R) (2 used) (Sub. for A126R)
16	B 1787 R	(B96000 –)	Gasket, Manifold (Packed 5 in a Pkg.)
17	A 674 R	(B183972–)	Stud, 7/16" x 3" (2 used) (All-Fuel)
	A 674 R	(B201000–)	Stud, 7/16" x 3" (Use with AB3980R) (2 used)
18	AB 4204 R	(B96000 –)	Head, B1784R, B2501R and B2871R, Cylinder, with Valve Guides (Sub. for AB2733R and AB3541R)
19	B 1789 R	(B96000 –)	Stud, 9/16" x 6-1/2"
20	B 1788 R	(B96000 –)	Stud, 9/16" x 5-7/8" (8 used)
21	AB 3479 R	(B201000–B275906)	Conduit, Cable
	B 2848 R	(B275907–)	Tube, Spark Plug Cable
	A 4165 R	(B275907–)	Bracket, Spark Plug Cable Tube
22	....	(–B275906)	Stove, Bolt, with Nut 5/16" x 1-1/2"
23	....	(–B275906)	Stove, Bolt, with Nut 5/16" x 1-3/4"
24	B 465 R	(–B275906)	Clamp (2 used)
	A 4166 R	(B275907–)	Bolt, "U" Spark Plug Cable Tube Clamp
	12H 9 R	(B275907–)	Washer, Lock, 1/4" (2 used)
	....	(B275907–)	Nut, 1/4" (2 used)
25	13H 241 R	(–B275906)	Bolt, Stove, with Nut, 1/4" x 1-1/4"
26	A 470 R	(–)	Clamp (Rubber)
27	B 2484 R	(B201000–)	Stud, 5/8" x 3" (4 used)
28	B 1333 R	(B201000–)	Stud, 5/8" x 2-1/2" (3 used)
29	....	(–)	Nut, 5/8" (7 used)
30	12H 15 R	(–)	Washer, Lock, 5/8" (7 used)
31	B 2504 R	(B201000–)	Gasket (Packed 5 in a Pkg.)
32	AB 3539 R	(B201000–)	Cylinder, B2500R, with Studs
33	AB 1898 R	(–B289376)	Cock, Relief (2 used)
	A 4242 R	(B289377–)	Plug, Pipe (2 used)
34	AH 830 R	(B96000 –)	Spark Plug (Champion No. 8 Comm. C) (2 used) (All-Fuel) (Sub. for AH702R) (Sub. AA4369R)
	AA 3846 R	(B96000 –)	Spark Plug (Champion) (Hot Type No. 10 Comm.) (2 used) (For Light Service) (All-Fuel and Gasoline) (Sub. AA5593R)
	AA 4053 R	(B201000–)	Spark Plug (Champion No. 6 Comm.) (2 used) (Gasoline) (Heavy-Duty) (Sub. for AA4054R)
	AA 4369 R	(B96000 –)	Spark Plug (Champion No. 8 Comm.) (2 used) (For Light Service When Burning Gasoline)
	AA 4660 R	(B96000 –)	Spark Plug (AC88L Comm.) (2 used) (Hot Type When Burning Gasoline)
	AA 5593 R	(B96000 –)	Spark Plug (Champion No. 10 Comm. 64) (2 used) (Hot Type When Burning Gasoline)
	AA 5594 R	(B96000 –)	Spark Plug (AC86 Comm.) (All-Fuel)
	AA 5818 R	(B96000 –)	Spark Plug (Auto-Lite Type BD9) (2 used) (All-Fuel) (Sub. AA6331R)
	AA 5819 R	(B96000 –)	Spark Plug (Auto-Lite Type BD12) (2 used) (All-Fuel)
	AA 5972 R	(B201000–)	Spark Plug (AC85 Comm.) (2 used) (Gasoline)
	AA 6330 R	(B96000 –)	Spark Plug (Auto-Lite) (2 used) (Type BT-10F) (All-Fuel and Gasoline)
	AA 6331 R	(B96000 –)	Spark Plug (Auto-Lite) (2 used) (Type BT-8J) (All-Fuel and Gasoline)
35	B 3089 R	(B96000 –)	Gasket, Head (Sub. for B1785R) (Packed 10 in a Pkg.)
36	A 2093 R	(–)	Plug, Drain
37	B 1927 R	(B96000 –)	Guide, Valve (4 used) (Packed 4 in a Pkg.) (Sub. for AB2859R)
38	B 504 R	(–B244152)	Stud, 7/16" x 5-3/4" (2 used)
	B 359 R	(B244153–)	Stud, 7/16" x 4-3/4" (2 used)
39	B 2783 R	(B244153–)	Nut (Special) (2 used) (Sub. for AB4250R)
40	12H 12 R	(–B244152)	Washer, Lock, 7/16" (2 used)
41	....	(–B244152)	Nut, 7/16" (2 used)

PC-330-(3-60)

Late styled Model B cylinder, block, head, and associated parts. *John Deere Archives*

TRACTORS—MODELS "B," "BN," "BNH," "BW," "BWH" (STYLED)

CYLINDER BLOCK, HEAD AND ASSOCIATED PARTS—Continued
(Serial No. B201000-)

Key	Part No.	Serial No.	Description
42	AB 3617 R	(B201000–)	Cover, Tappet, with Bushing
43	A 3439 R	(–B244152)	Washer (2 used) (Packed 5 in a Pkg.) (Sub. for B214R)
	B 425 R	(B244153–)	Washer (2 used) (Packed 5 in a Pkg.)
44	19H 314 R	(B244153–)	Screw, Cap, 7/16" x 1/2" (2 used)
45	14H 664 R	(–B244152)	Nut, Cap, 7/16" (2 used)
46	A 3232 R	(B201000–B223006)	Screw, Machine (2 used) (Sub. for AA4955R)
	A 5748 R	(B223007–)	Stud, Drive (2 used) (Sub. for 25H1151R)
47	24H 143 R	(B201000–B223006)	Washer (2 used)
	24H 846 R	(B223007–)	Washer (2 used)
48	B 2496 R	(B201000–)	Screen, Trash
49	....	(–B306599)	Bolt, Mach., with Nut, 1/2" x 1-1/4" (2 used)
	....	(B306600–)	Bolt, Mach., with Nut, 1/2" x 1" (2 used)
50	B 2656 R	(B201000–B306599)	Support, Fan Shaft
	B 2892 R	(B306600–)	Support, Fan Shaft
51	12H 13 R	(–)	Washer, Lock, 1/2" (2 used)

(Parts listed below are not illustrated.)

Key	Part No.	Serial No.	Description
	24H 4 R	(B306600–)	Washer, Fan Shaft Support (4 used)
	AB 3877 R	(B201000–)	Gasket Set, Valve, Ring and Cylinder Replacement
	AR 21783 R	(B201000–)	Gasket Set for Valve Service

Late styled Model B cylinder, block, head, and associated parts (continued). *John Deere Archives*

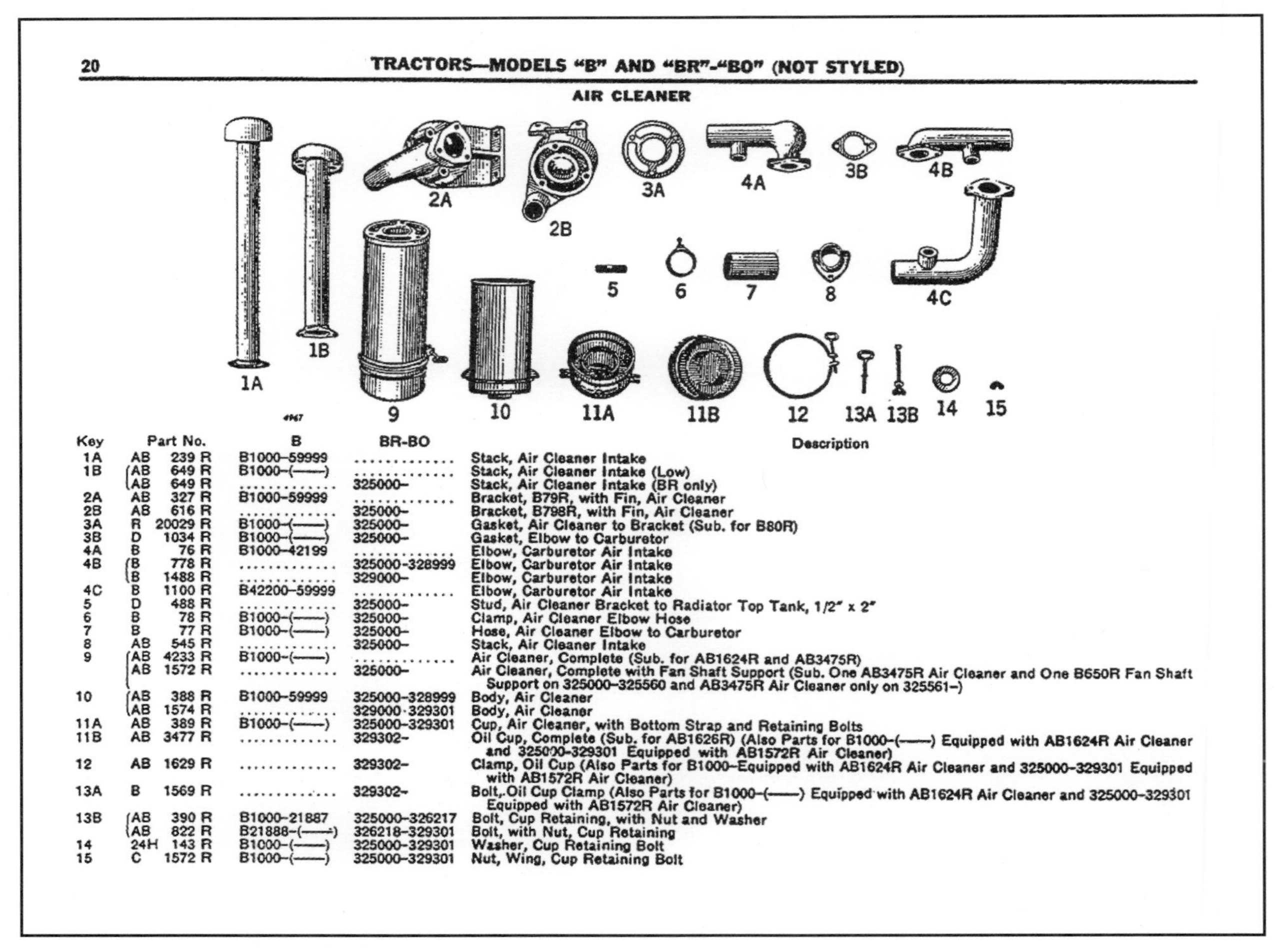

20 TRACTORS—MODELS "B" AND "BR"-"BO" (NOT STYLED)

AIR CLEANER

Key	Part No.	B	BR-BO	Description
1A	AB 239 R	B1000–59999	....	Stack, Air Cleaner Intake
1B	AB 649 R	B1000–(——)	....	Stack, Air Cleaner Intake (Low)
	AB 649 R	....	325000–	Stack, Air Cleaner Intake (BR only)
2A	AB 327 R	B1000–59999	....	Bracket, B79R, with Fin, Air Cleaner
2B	AB 616 R	....	325000–	Bracket, B798R, with Fin, Air Cleaner
3A	R 20029 R	B1000–(——)	325000–	Gasket, Air Cleaner to Bracket (Sub. for B80R)
3B	D 1034 R	B1000–(——)	325000–	Gasket, Elbow to Carburetor
4A	B 76 R	B1000–42199	....	Elbow, Carburetor Air Intake
4B	B 778 R	....	325000–328999	Elbow, Carburetor Air Intake
	B 1488 R	....	329000–	Elbow, Carburetor Air Intake
4C	B 1100 R	B42200–59999	....	Elbow, Carburetor Air Intake
5	D 488 R	....	325000–	Stud, Air Cleaner Bracket to Radiator Top Tank, 1/2" x 2"
6	B 78 R	B1000–(——)	325000–	Clamp, Air Cleaner Elbow Hose
7	B 77 R	B1000–(——)	325000–	Hose, Air Cleaner Elbow to Carburetor
8	AB 545 R	....	325000–	Stack, Air Cleaner Intake
9	AB 4233 R	B1000–(——)	....	Air Cleaner, Complete (Sub. for AB1624R and AB3475R)
	AB 1572 R	....	325000–	Air Cleaner, Complete with Fan Shaft Support (Sub. One AB3475R Air Cleaner and One B650R Fan Shaft Support on 325000–325560 and AB3475R Air Cleaner only on 325561–)
10	AB 388 R	B1000–59999	325000–328999	Body, Air Cleaner
	AB 1574 R	....	329000·329301	Body, Air Cleaner
11A	AB 389 R	B1000–(——)	325000–329301	Cup, Air Cleaner, with Bottom Strap and Retaining Bolts
11B	AB 3477 R	....	329302–	Oil Cup, Complete (Sub. for AB1626R) (Also Parts for B1000–(——) Equipped with AB1624R Air Cleaner and 325000–329301 Equipped with AB1572R Air Cleaner)
12	AB 1629 R	....	329302–	Clamp, Oil Cup (Also Parts for B1000–Equipped with AB1624R Air Cleaner and 325000–329301 Equipped with AB1572R Air Cleaner)
13A	B 1569 R	....	329302–	Bolt, Oil Cup Clamp (Also Parts for B1000–(——) Equipped with AB1624R Air Cleaner and 325000–329301 Equipped with AB1572R Air Cleaner)
13B	AB 390 R	B1000–21887	325000–326217	Bolt, Cup Retaining, with Nut and Washer
	AB 822 R	B21888–(——)	326218–329301	Bolt, with Nut, Cup Retaining
14	24H 143 R	B1000–(——)	325000–329301	Washer, Cup Retaining Bolt
15	C 1572 R	B1000–(——)	325000–329301	Nut, Wing, Cup Retaining Bolt

Unstyled Model B air cleaner. *John Deere Archives*

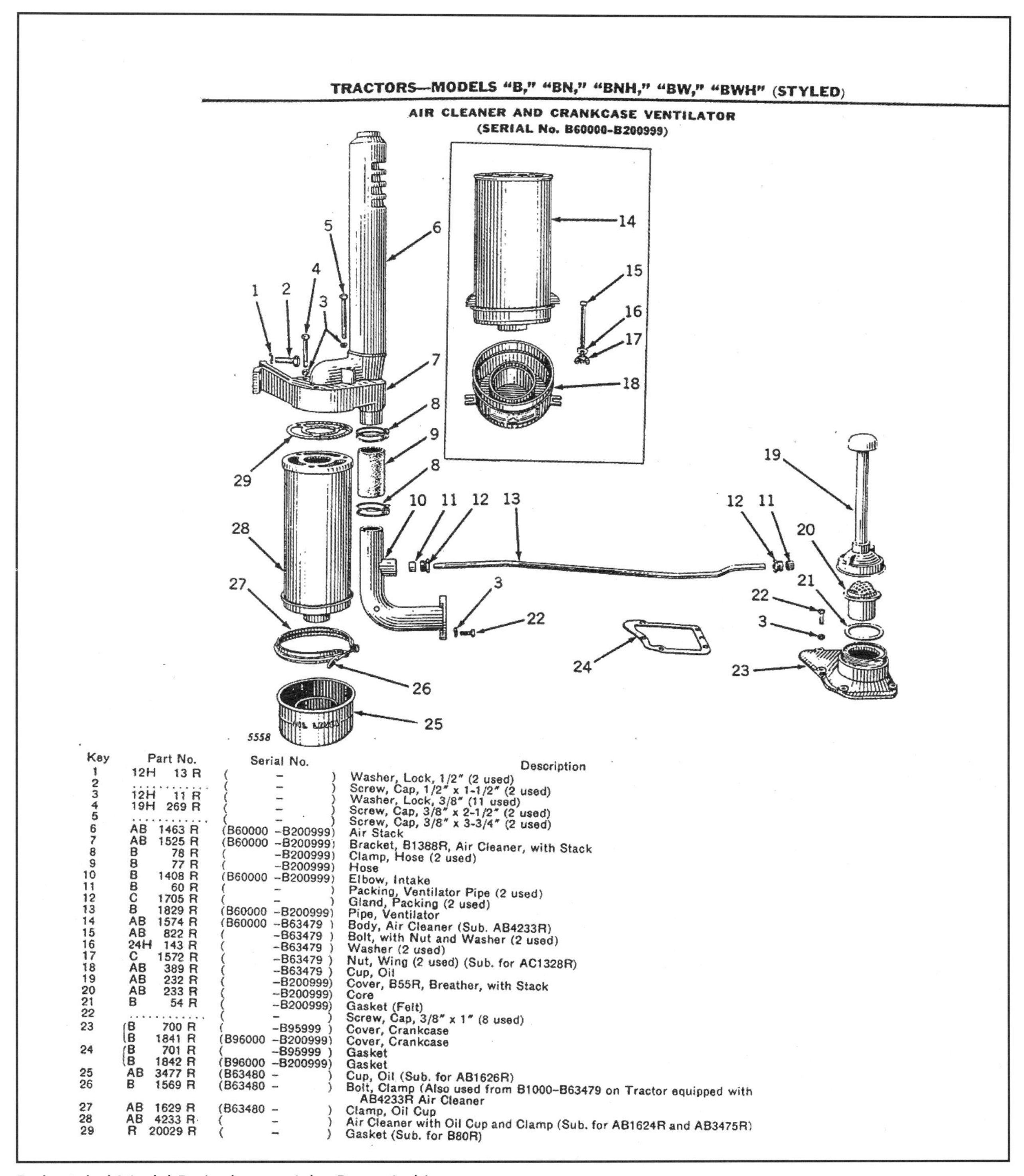

TRACTORS—MODELS "B," "BN," "BNH," "BW," "BWH" (STYLED)

AIR CLEANER AND CRANKCASE VENTILATOR

(SERIAL No. B60000-B200999)

Key	Part No.	Serial No.	Description
1	12H 13 R	(–)	Washer, Lock, 1/2" (2 used)
2	....	(–)	Screw, Cap, 1/2" x 1-1/2" (2 used)
3	12H 11 R	(–)	Washer, Lock, 3/8" (11 used)
4	19H 269 R	(–)	Screw, Cap, 3/8" x 2-1/2" (2 used)
5	....	(–)	Screw, Cap, 3/8" x 3-3/4" (2 used)
6	AB 1463 R	(B60000 –B200999)	Air Stack
7	AB 1525 R	(B60000 –B200999)	Bracket, B1388R, Air Cleaner, with Stack
8	B 78 R	(–B200999)	Clamp, Hose (2 used)
9	B 77 R	(–B200999)	Hose
10	B 1408 R	(B60000 –B200999)	Elbow, Intake
11	B 60 R	(–)	Packing, Ventilator Pipe (2 used)
12	C 1705 R	(–)	Gland, Packing (2 used)
13	B 1829 R	(B60000 –B200999)	Pipe, Ventilator
14	AB 1574 R	(B60000 –B63479)	Body, Air Cleaner (Sub. AB4233R)
15	AB 822 R	(–B63479)	Bolt, with Nut and Washer (2 used)
16	24H 143 R	(–B63479)	Washer (2 used)
17	C 1572 R	(–B63479)	Nut, Wing (2 used) (Sub. for AC1328R)
18	AB 389 R	(–B63479)	Cup, Oil
19	AB 232 R	(–B200999)	Cover, B55R, Breather, with Stack
20	AB 233 R	(–B200999)	Core
21	B 54 R	(–B200999)	Gasket (Felt)
22	....	(–)	Screw, Cap, 3/8" x 1" (8 used)
23	B 700 R	(–B95999)	Cover, Crankcase
	B 1841 R	(B96000 –B200999)	Cover, Crankcase
24	B 701 R	(–B95999)	Gasket
	B 1842 R	(B96000 –B200999)	Gasket
25	AB 3477 R	(B63480 –)	Cup, Oil (Sub. for AB1626R)
26	B 1569 R	(B63480 –)	Bolt, Clamp (Also used from B1000–B63479 on Tractor equipped with AB4233R Air Cleaner
27	AB 1629 R	(B63480 –)	Clamp, Oil Cup
28	AB 4233 R	(–)	Air Cleaner with Oil Cup and Clamp (Sub. for AB1624R and AB3475R)
29	R 20029 R	(–)	Gasket (Sub. for B80R)

Early styled Model B air cleaner. *John Deere Archives*

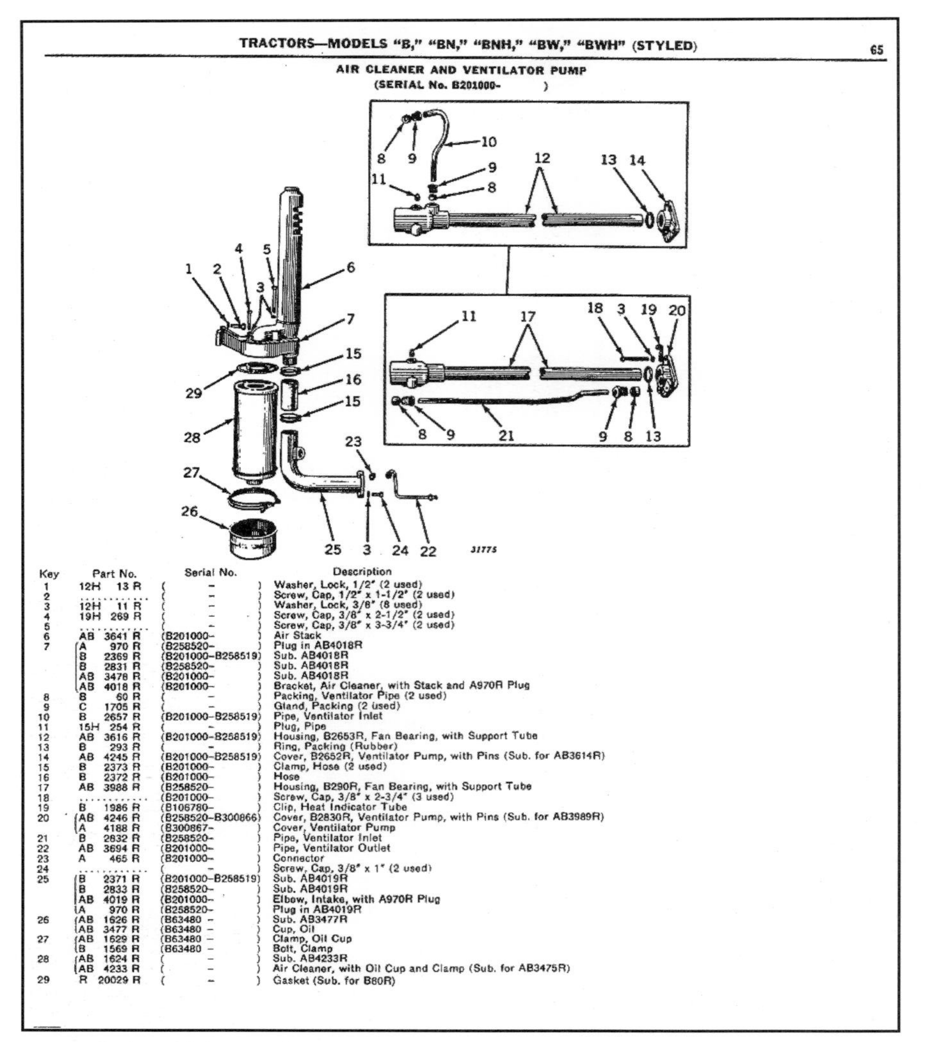

TRACTORS—MODELS "B," "BN," "BNH," "BW," "BWH" (STYLED) 65

AIR CLEANER AND VENTILATOR PUMP
(SERIAL No. B201000-)

31775

Key	Part No.	Serial No.	Description
1	12H 13 R	(–)	Washer, Lock, 1/2" (2 used)
2	....	(–)	Screw, Cap, 1/2" x 1-1/2" (2 used)
3	12H 11 R	(–)	Washer, Lock, 3/8" (8 used)
4	19H 269 R	(–)	Screw, Cap, 3/8" x 2-1/2" (2 used)
5	....	(–)	Screw, Cap, 3/8" x 3-3/4" (2 used)
6	AB 3641 R	(B201000–)	Air Stack
7	A 970 R	(B258520–)	Plug in AB4018R
	B 2369 R	(B201000–B258519)	Sub. AB4018R
	B 2831 R	(B258520–)	Sub. AB4018R
	AB 3478 R	(B201000–)	Sub. AB4018R
	AB 4018 R	(B201000–)	Bracket, Air Cleaner, with Stack and A970R Plug
8	B 60 R	(–)	Packing, Ventilator Pipe (2 used)
9	C 1705 R	(–)	Gland, Packing (2 used)
10	B 2657 R	(B201000–B258519)	Pipe, Ventilator Inlet
11	15H 254 R	(–)	Plug, Pipe
12	AB 3616 R	(B201000–B258519)	Housing, B2653R, Fan Bearing, with Support Tube
13	B 293 R	(–)	Ring, Packing (Rubber)
14	AB 4245 R	(B201000–B258519)	Cover, B2652R, Ventilator Pump, with Pins (Sub. for AB3614R)
15	B 2373 R	(B201000–)	Clamp, Hose (2 used)
16	B 2372 R	(B201000–)	Hose
17	AB 3988 R	(B258520–)	Housing, B290R, Fan Bearing, with Support Tube
18	....	(B201000–)	Screw, Cap, 3/8" x 2-3/4" (3 used)
19	B 1986 R	(B106780–)	Clip, Heat Indicator Tube
20	AB 4246 R	(B258520–B300866)	Cover, B2830R, Ventilator Pump, with Pins (Sub. for AB3989R)
	A 4188 R	(B300867–)	Cover, Ventilator Pump
21	B 2832 R	(B258520–)	Pipe, Ventilator Inlet
22	AB 3694 R	(B201000–)	Pipe, Ventilator Outlet
23	A 465 R	(B201000–)	Connector
24	....	(–)	Screw, Cap, 3/8" x 1" (2 used)
25	B 2371 R	(B201000–B258519)	Sub. AB4019R
	B 2833 R	(B258520–)	Sub. AB4019R
	AB 4019 R	(B201000–)	Elbow, Intake, with A970R Plug
	A 970 R	(B258520–)	Plug in AB4019R
26	AB 1626 R	(B63480 –)	Sub. AB3477R
	AB 3477 R	(B63480 –)	Cup, Oil
27	AB 1629 R	(B63480 –)	Clamp, Oil Cup
	B 1569 R	(B63480 –)	Bolt, Clamp
28	AB 1624 R	(–)	Sub. AB4233R
	AB 4233 R	(–)	Air Cleaner, with Oil Cup and Clamp (Sub. for AB3475R)
29	R 20029 R	(–)	Gasket (Sub. for B80R)

Late styled Model B air cleaner and ventilator pump. *John Deere Archives*

Intake System

Different manifolds are used for kerosene and gasoline engines because of the requirement for more exhaust heat with the kerosene version. Aftermarket gas manifolds were available for unstyled Model Bs.

Model Bs used an oil-bath air cleaner. The body of the filter is filled with a closely crimped wire mesh; the base of the filter is filled with oil. Intake air bubbles through the oil. Dust and dirt get coated with oil, and are either retained in the oil, or pass up into the mesh where they are trapped. When the engine is shut down, most of the dirt and oil caught in the mesh drains down into the dirt cup on the bottom of the filter.

On 1947 models and up, there is a positive crankcase ventilator included in the intake system.

Fuel System and Carburetor

All unstyled Model Bs were configured for kerosene or distillate, as were most of the early styled models.

The fuel system begins with a twelve-gallon tank, the same size for kerosene, All-Fuel, or gasoline. With the kerosene versions, a two-gallon gasoline tank is also provided to hold starting fuel. The first few Model Bs (serial numbers 1,000 to 1,509) had a centered tank opening. The cap's close proximity to the steering shaft made it difficult to fuel up, so the filler opening was offset to the left. This included both the kerosene and gasoline tanks.

Gasoline tank caps should be painted red, while kerosene tank caps should be green. Kerosene tractors have a selec-

Left side, early styled Model B. Note the two fuel caps, and the breather pipe ahead of the steering post.

Model Bs configured for kerosene, or all-fuel, have a gasoline starting tank. The cap for the gasoline tank (rear) should be red. Most collectors now fill the kerosene tank with gasoline. Some, as is the case here, then put the red cap on the front.

tor valve that has a control rod (actuator) on styled models. Unstyled control valves are not accessible from the platform. It should be noted that there are different types of these valves for different serial number tractors. Up to serial number 11,621, part number AD680R valve was used. Unstyled tractors used AB609R after that (see parts breakdown illustrations for details). Also note that tractors with pressed-steel frames (serial number 201,000 and up) have a heat shield under the tank.

A "natural draft" carburetor of the Marvel-Schebler type was

Carburetor of a late styled Model B. The choke rod to the instrument panel is used on models also equipped with electric starters. The coil of fuel line is incorrect.

Nonelectric start Model Bs are not equipped with choke rods.

The valve shown here switches between gasoline and kerosene or distillate. The tractor is an early styled B.

"IN these war times I can't always get just the fuel I'd like to use in my John Deere but I've no fuel problem.

"I can use successfully just about any fuel that's available in my locality—whether it's power fuel, tractor fuel, distillate, or gasoline. I can burn them all.

"I've been using the low-cost fuels ever since I bought my John Deere—because it's designed to burn them and it does burn them at a real saving in cash.

"By burning the less-critical fuels today, I figure I am doing my patriotic duty, for I'm conserving badly-needed gasoline for tanks, planes, and ships and for necessary home use.

"I'm mighty fortunate in owning a John Deere Tractor in times like these."

★ ★ ★

THE owner of a John Deere Tractor is indeed fortunate. He can co-operate in a most effective and patriotic manner in the conservation of gasoline and still SACRIFICE NOTHING OF EFFICIENCY in the operation of his tractor. He doesn't have to make any changes in his tractor, or go to any expense in using lower-priced, more powerful fuels or gasoline. The John Deere was made to operate at utmost effectiveness on distillate, power fuel, tractor fuel, and similar low-cost fuels, but it will operate on practically any fuel that is available.

Yes, the John Deere owner, by using the less-critical fuels, can do his patriotic duty with better performance and greater economy and without detriment to long life and continued, uninterrupted operation.

Talk to your John Deere dealer about tractors and other equipment you need.

★

JOHN DEERE, Moline, Illinois

FOOD FIGHTS for freedom

BUY MORE BONDS ★ GET IN THE SCRA

This war-time (1944) farm magazine ad boasts that the "All-Fuel" John Deere has an advantage over gasoline-only tractors. *John Deere Archives*

used on all Model Bs. Series DLTX-10 were used on all unstyled versions and on styled types up to serial number 95,999. Serial number 96,000–200,999 tractors used the DLTX-34 carburetor. The pressed-steel frame models (serial number 201000 and up) used either the DLTX-67 for gas tractors or the DLTX-73 on the All-Fuel models.

Closing the throttle fully should stop the engine. This is important for magneto-equipped tractors, as there is otherwise no shutoff. Distributor-equipped tractors have an ignition switch. Some replacement magnetos, however, have "kill" buttons.

Only one lever is on the steering post of unstyled and early styled Model Bs. It is the throttle control; pushed forward to open.

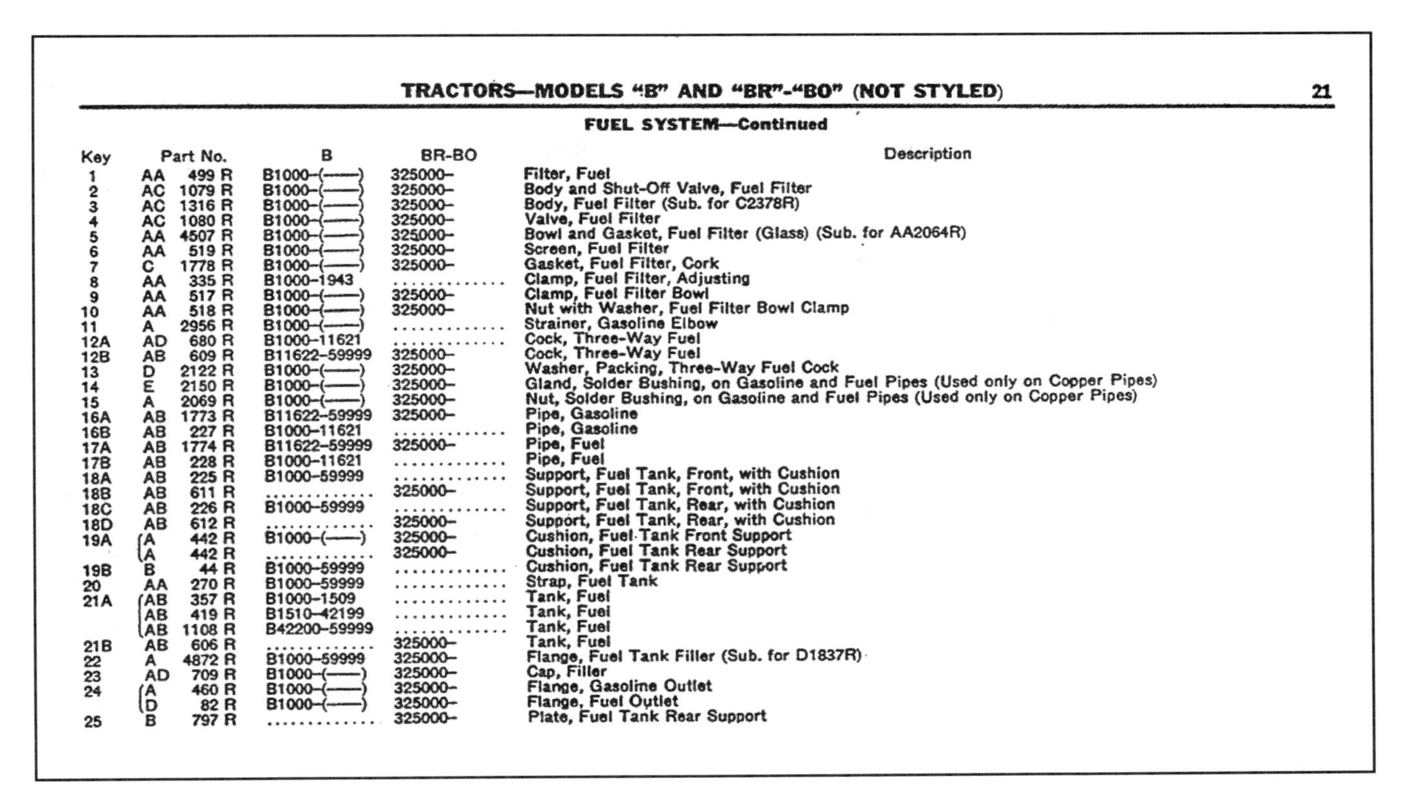

TRACTORS—MODELS "B" AND "BR"-"BO" (NOT STYLED) 21

FUEL SYSTEM—Continued

Key	Part No.	B	BR-BO	Description
1	AA 499 R	B1000-(——)	325000-	Filter, Fuel
2	AC 1079 R	B1000-(——)	325000-	Body and Shut-Off Valve, Fuel Filter
3	AC 1316 R	B1000-(——)	325000-	Body, Fuel Filter (Sub. for C2378R)
4	AC 1080 R	B1000-(——)	325000-	Valve, Fuel Filter
5	AA 4507 R	B1000-(——)	325000-	Bowl and Gasket, Fuel Filter (Glass) (Sub. for AA2064R)
6	AA 519 R	B1000-(——)	325000-	Screen, Fuel Filter
7	C 1778 R	B1000-(——)	325000-	Gasket, Fuel Filter, Cork
8	AA 335 R	B1000-1943	....	Clamp, Fuel Filter, Adjusting
9	AA 517 R	B1000-(——)	325000-	Clamp, Fuel Filter Bowl
10	AA 518 R	B1000-(——)	325000-	Nut with Washer, Fuel Filter Bowl Clamp
11	A 2956 R	B1000-(——)	....	Strainer, Gasoline Elbow
12A	AD 680 R	B1000-11621	....	Cock, Three-Way Fuel
12B	AB 609 R	B11622-59999	325000-	Cock, Three-Way Fuel
13	D 2122 R	B1000-(——)	325000-	Washer, Packing, Three-Way Fuel Cock
14	E 2150 R	B1000-(——)	325000-	Gland, Solder Bushing, on Gasoline and Fuel Pipes (Used only on Copper Pipes)
15	A 2069 R	B1000-(——)	325000-	Nut, Solder Bushing, on Gasoline and Fuel Pipes (Used only on Copper Pipes)
16A	AB 1773 R	B11622-59999	325000-	Pipe, Gasoline
16B	AB 227 R	B1000-11621	....	Pipe, Gasoline
17A	AB 1774 R	B11622-59999	325000-	Pipe, Fuel
17B	AB 228 R	B1000-11621	....	Pipe, Fuel
18A	AB 225 R	B1000-59999	....	Support, Fuel Tank, Front, with Cushion
18B	AB 611 R	....	325000-	Support, Fuel Tank, Front, with Cushion
18C	AB 226 R	B1000-59999	....	Support, Fuel Tank, Rear, with Cushion
18D	AB 612 R	....	325000-	Support, Fuel Tank, Rear, with Cushion
19A	{A 442 R	B1000-(——)	325000-	Cushion, Fuel Tank Front Support
	{A 442 R	....	325000-	Cushion, Fuel Tank Rear Support
19B	B 44 R	B1000-59999	....	Cushion, Fuel Tank Rear Support
20	AA 270 R	B1000-59999	....	Strap, Fuel Tank
21A	{AB 357 R	B1000-1509	....	Tank, Fuel
	{AB 419 R	B1510-42199	....	Tank, Fuel
	{AB 1108 R	B42200-59999	....	Tank, Fuel
21B	AB 606 R	....	325000-	Tank, Fuel
22	A 4872 R	B1000-59999	325000-	Flange, Fuel Tank Filler (Sub. for D1837R)
23	AD 709 R	B1000-(——)	325000-	Cap, Filler
24	{A 460 R	B1000-(——)	325000-	Flange, Gasoline Outlet
	{D 82 R	B1000-(——)	325000-	Flange, Fuel Outlet
25	B 797 R	....	325000-	Plate, Fuel Tank Rear Support

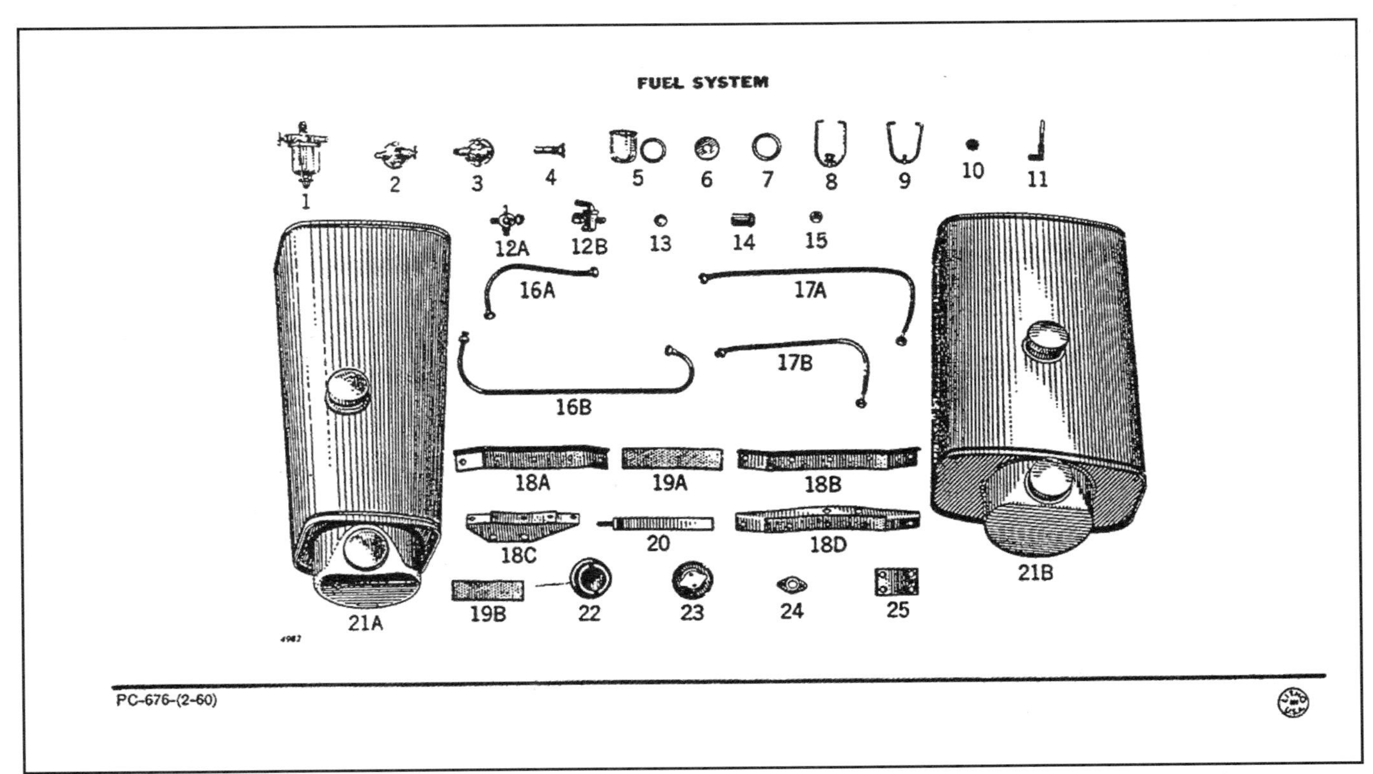

Unstyled Model B, BR, and BO fuel system. *John Deere Archives*

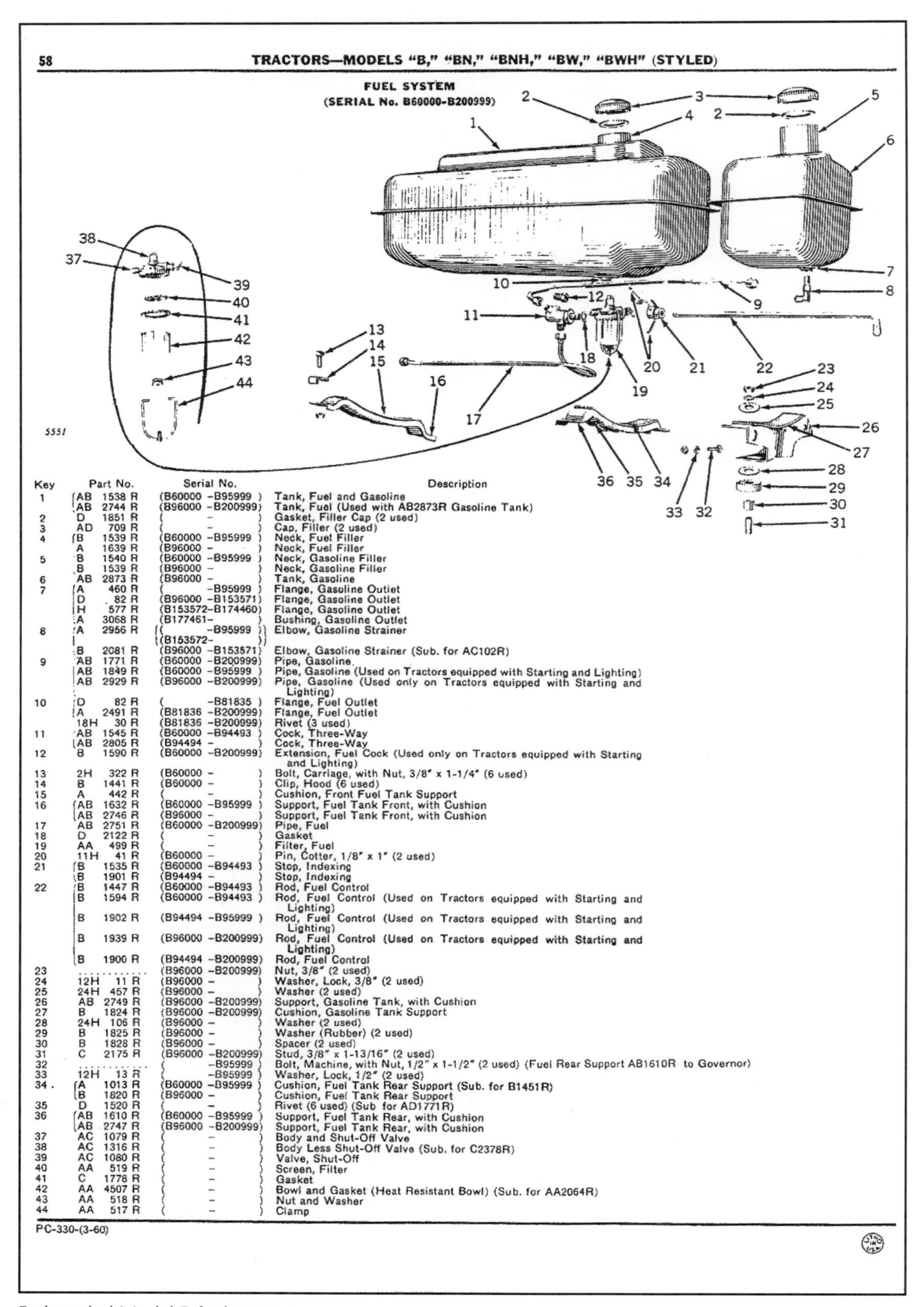

58 TRACTORS—MODELS "B," "BN," "BNH," "BW," "BWH" (STYLED)

FUEL SYSTEM
(SERIAL No. B60000-B200999)

Key	Part No.	Serial No.	Description
1	AB 1538 R	(B60000 –B95999)	Tank, Fuel and Gasoline
	AB 2744 R	(B96000 –B200999)	Tank, Fuel (Used with AB2873R Gasoline Tank)
2	D 1851 R	(–)	Gasket, Filler Cap (2 used)
3	AD 709 R	(–)	Cap, Filler (2 used)
4	B 1539 R	(B60000 –B95999)	Neck, Fuel Filler
	A 1639 R	(B96000 –)	Neck, Fuel Filler
5	B 1540 R	(B60000 –B95999)	Neck, Gasoline Filler
	B 1539 R	(B96000 –)	Neck, Gasoline Filler
6	AB 2873 R	(B96000 –)	Tank, Gasoline
7	A 460 R	(–B95999)	Flange, Gasoline Outlet
	D 82 R	(B96000 –B153571)	Flange, Gasoline Outlet
	H 577 R	(B153572–B174460)	Flange, Gasoline Outlet
	A 3068 R	(B177461–)	Bushing, Gasoline Outlet
8	A 2956 R	(–B95999) (B153572–)	Elbow, Gasoline Strainer
	B 2081 R	(B96000 –B153571)	Elbow, Gasoline Strainer (Sub. for AC102R)
9	AB 1771 R	(B60000 –B200999)	Pipe, Gasoline.
	AB 1849 R	(B60000 –B95999)	Pipe, Gasoline (Used on Tractors equipped with Starting and Lighting)
	AB 2929 R	(B96000 –B200999)	Pipe, Gasoline (Used only on Tractors equipped with Starting and Lighting)
10	D 82 R	(–B81835)	Flange, Fuel Outlet
	A 2491 R	(B81836 –B200999)	Flange, Fuel Outlet
	18H 30 R	(B81836 –B200999)	Rivet (3 used)
11	AB 1545 R	(B60000 –B94493)	Cock, Three-Way
	AB 2805 R	(B94494 –)	Cock, Three-Way
12	B 1590 R	(B60000 –B200999)	Extension, Fuel Cock (Used only on Tractors equipped with Starting and Lighting)
13	2H 322 R	(B60000 –)	Bolt, Carriage, with Nut, 3/8" x 1-1/4" (6 used)
14	B 1441 R	(B60000 –)	Clip, Hood (6 used)
15	A 442 R	(–)	Cushion, Front Fuel Tank Support
16	AB 1632 R	(B60000 –B95999)	Support, Fuel Tank Front, with Cushion
	AB 2746 R	(B96000 –)	Support, Fuel Tank Front, with Cushion
17	AB 2751 R	(B60000 –B200999)	Pipe, Fuel
18	D 2122 R	(–)	Gasket
19	AA 499 R	(–)	Filter, Fuel
20	11H 41 R	(B60000 –)	Pin, Cotter, 1/8" x 1" (2 used)
21	B 1535 R	(B60000 –B94493)	Stop, Indexing
	B 1901 R	(B94494 –)	Stop, Indexing
22	B 1447 R	(B60000 –B94493)	Rod, Fuel Control
	B 1594 R	(B60000 –B94493)	Rod, Fuel Control (Used on Tractors equipped with Starting and Lighting)
	B 1902 R	(B94494 –B95999)	Rod, Fuel Control (Used on Tractors equipped with Starting and Lighting)
	B 1939 R	(B96000 –B200999)	Rod, Fuel Control (Used on Tractors equipped with Starting and Lighting)
	B 1900 R	(B94494 –B200999)	Rod, Fuel Control
23	....	(B96000 –B200999)	Nut, 3/8" (2 used)
24	12H 11 R	(B96000 –)	Washer, Lock, 3/8" (2 used)
25	24H 457 R	(B96000 –)	Washer (2 used)
26	AB 2749 R	(B96000 –B200999)	Support, Gasoline Tank, with Cushion
27	B 1824 R	(B96000 –B200999)	Cushion, Gasoline Tank Support
28	24H 106 R	(B96000 –)	Washer (2 used)
29	B 1825 R	(B96000 –)	Washer (Rubber) (2 used)
30	B 1828 R	(B96000 –)	Spacer (2 used)
31	C 2175 R	(B96000 –B200999)	Stud, 3/8" x 1-13/16" (2 used)
32	....	(–B95999)	Bolt, Machine, with Nut, 1/2" x 1-1/2" (2 used) (Fuel Rear Support AB1610R to Governor)
33	12H 13 R	(–B95999)	Washer, Lock, 1/2" (2 used)
34	A 1013 R	(B60000 –B95999)	Cushion, Fuel Tank Rear Support (Sub. for B1451R)
	B 1820 R	(B96000 –)	Cushion, Fuel Tank Rear Support
35	D 1520 R	(–)	Rivet (6 used) (Sub for AD1771R)
36	AB 1610 R	(B60000 –B95999)	Support, Fuel Tank Rear, with Cushion
	AB 2747 R	(B96000 –B200999)	Support, Fuel Tank Rear, with Cushion
37	AC 1079 R	(–)	Body and Shut-Off Valve
38	AC 1316 R	(–)	Body Less Shut-Off Valve (Sub. for C2378R)
39	AC 1080 R	(–)	Valve, Shut-Off
40	AA 519 R	(–)	Screen, Filter
41	C 1778 R	(–)	Gasket
42	AA 4507 R	(–)	Bowl and Gasket (Heat Resistant Bowl) (Sub. for AA2064R)
43	AA 518 R	(–)	Nut and Washer
44	AA 517 R	(–)	Clamp

PC-330-(3-60)

Early styled Model B fuel system.

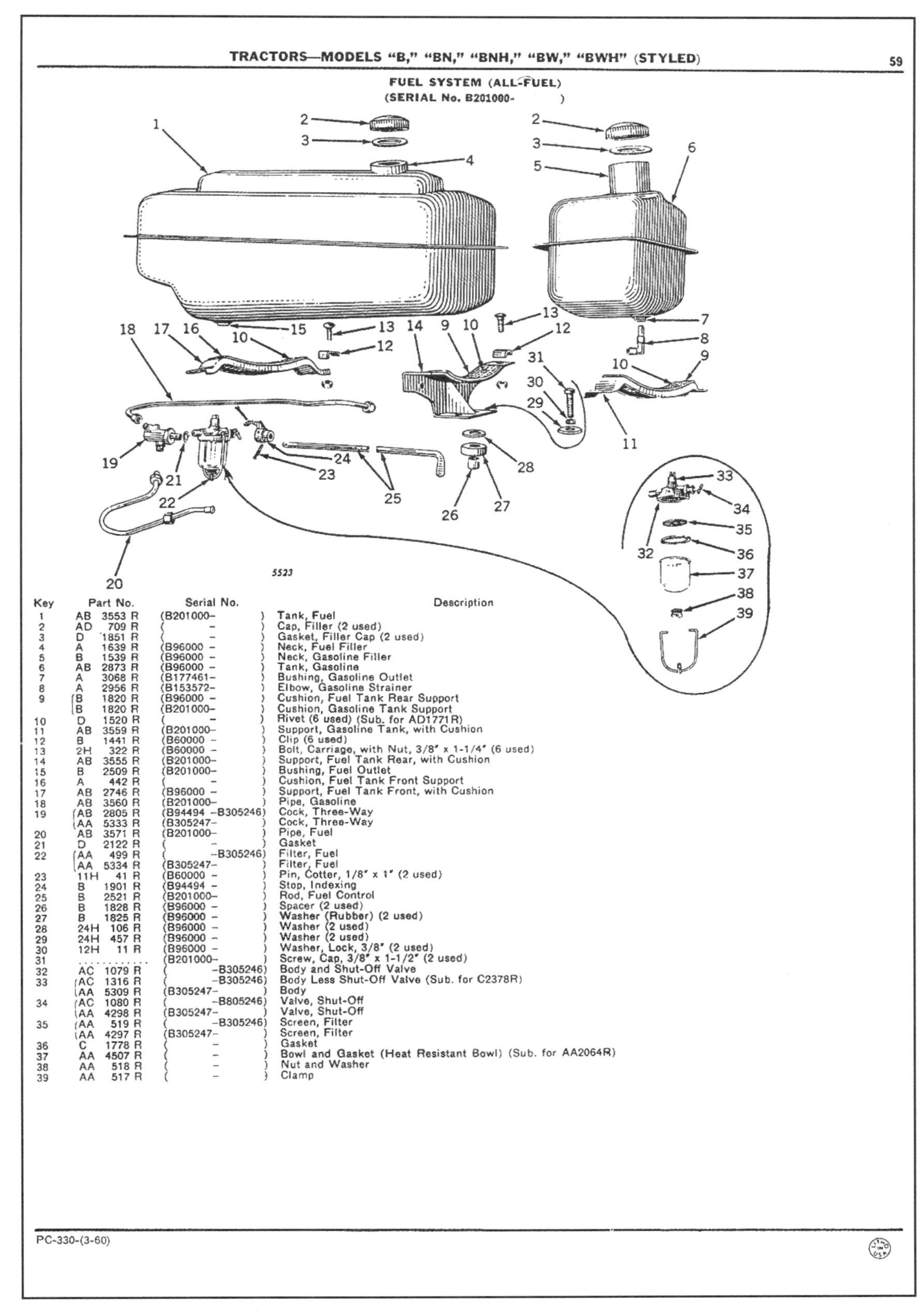

TRACTORS—MODELS "B," "BN," "BNH," "BW," "BWH" (STYLED) 59

FUEL SYSTEM (ALL-FUEL)
(SERIAL No. B201000-)

Key	Part No.	Serial No.	Description
1	AB 3553 R	(B201000–)	Tank, Fuel
2	AD 709 R	(–)	Cap, Filler (2 used)
3	D 1851 R	(–)	Gasket, Filler Cap (2 used)
4	A 1639 R	(B96000 –)	Neck, Fuel Filler
5	B 1539 R	(B96000 –)	Neck, Gasoline Filler
6	AB 2873 R	(B96000 –)	Tank, Gasoline
7	A 3068 R	(B177461–)	Bushing, Gasoline Outlet
8	A 2956 R	(B153572–)	Elbow, Gasoline Strainer
9	B 1820 R	(B96000 –)	Cushion, Fuel Tank Rear Support
	B 1820 R	(B201000–)	Cushion, Gasoline Tank Support
10	D 1520 R	(–)	Rivet (6 used) (Sub. for AD1771R)
11	AB 3559 R	(B201000–)	Support, Gasoline Tank, with Cushion
12	B 1441 R	(B60000 –)	Clip (6 used)
13	2H 322 R	(B60000 –)	Bolt, Carriage, with Nut, 3/8" x 1-1/4" (6 used)
14	AB 3555 R	(B201000–)	Support, Fuel Tank Rear, with Cushion
15	B 2509 R	(B201000–)	Bushing, Fuel Outlet
16	A 442 R	(–)	Cushion, Fuel Tank Front Support
17	AB 2746 R	(B96000 –)	Support, Fuel Tank Front, with Cushion
18	AB 3560 R	(B201000–)	Pipe, Gasoline
19	AB 2805 R	(B94494 –B305246)	Cock, Three-Way
	AA 5333 R	(B305247–)	Cock, Three-Way
20	AB 3571 R	(B201000–)	Pipe, Fuel
21	D 2122 R	(–)	Gasket
22	AA 499 R	(–B305246)	Filter, Fuel
	AA 5334 R	(B305247–)	Filter, Fuel
23	11H 41 R	(B60000 –)	Pin, Cotter, 1/8" x 1" (2 used)
24	B 1901 R	(B94494 –)	Stop, Indexing
25	B 2521 R	(B201000–)	Rod, Fuel Control
26	B 1828 R	(B96000 –)	Spacer (2 used)
27	B 1825 R	(B96000 –)	Washer (Rubber) (2 used)
28	24H 106 R	(B96000 –)	Washer (2 used)
29	24H 457 R	(B96000 –)	Washer (2 used)
30	12H 11 R	(B96000 –)	Washer, Lock, 3/8" (2 used)
31	....	(B201000–)	Screw, Cap, 3/8" x 1-1/2" (2 used)
32	AC 1079 R	(–B305246)	Body and Shut-Off Valve
33	AC 1316 R	(–B305246)	Body Less Shut-Off Valve (Sub. for C2378R)
	AA 5309 R	(B305247–)	Body
34	AC 1080 R	(–B805246)	Valve, Shut-Off
	AA 4298 R	(B305247–)	Valve, Shut-Off
35	AA 519 R	(–B305246)	Screen, Filter
	AA 4297 R	(B305247–)	Screen, Filter
36	C 1778 R	(–)	Gasket
37	AA 4507 R	(–)	Bowl and Gasket (Heat Resistant Bowl) (Sub. for AA2064R)
38	AA 518 R	(–)	Nut and Washer
39	AA 517 R	(–)	Clamp

PC-330-(3-60)

Late styled Model B All-Fuel fuel system.

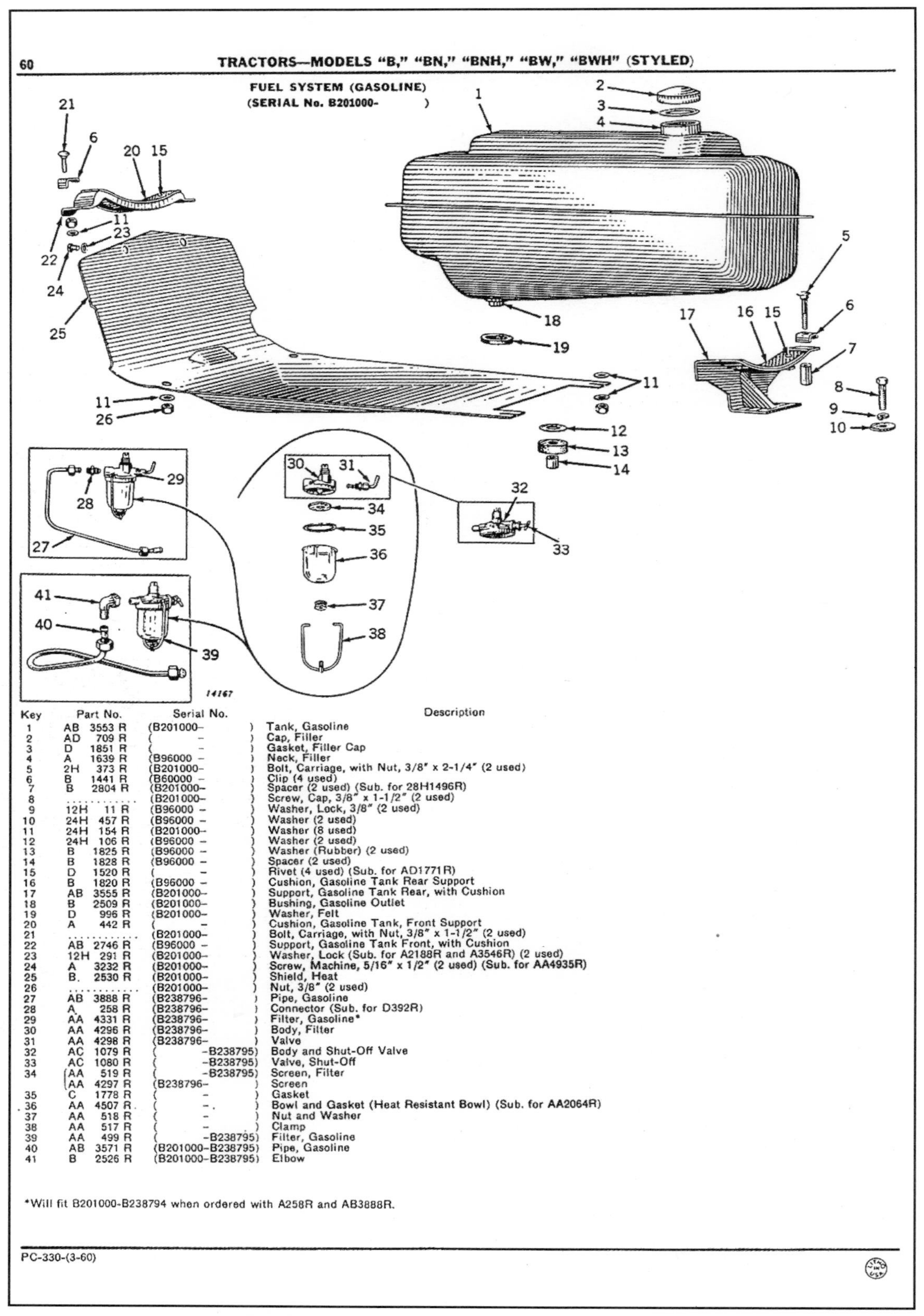

60 TRACTORS—MODELS "B," "BN," "BNH," "BW," "BWH" (STYLED)

FUEL SYSTEM (GASOLINE)
(SERIAL No. B201000-)

Key	Part No.	Serial No.	Description
1	AB 3553 R	(B201000–)	Tank, Gasoline
2	AD 709 R	(–)	Cap, Filler
3	D 1851 R	(–)	Gasket, Filler Cap
4	A 1639 R	(B96000 –)	Neck, Filler
5	2H 373 R	(B201000–)	Bolt, Carriage, with Nut, 3/8" x 2-1/4" (2 used)
6	B 1441 R	(B60000 –)	Clip (4 used)
7	B 2804 R	(B201000–)	Spacer (2 used) (Sub. for 28H1496R)
8	....	(B201000–)	Screw, Cap, 3/8" x 1-1/2" (2 used)
9	12H 11 R	(B96000 –)	Washer, Lock, 3/8" (2 used)
10	24H 457 R	(B96000 –)	Washer (2 used)
11	24H 154 R	(B201000–)	Washer (8 used)
12	24H 106 R	(B96000 –)	Washer (2 used)
13	B 1825 R	(B96000 –)	Washer (Rubber) (2 used)
14	B 1828 R	(B96000 –)	Spacer (2 used)
15	D 1520 R	(–)	Rivet (4 used) (Sub. for AD1771R)
16	B 1820 R	(B96000 –)	Cushion, Gasoline Tank Rear Support
17	AB 3555 R	(B201000–)	Support, Gasoline Tank Rear, with Cushion
18	B 2509 R	(B201000–)	Bushing, Gasoline Outlet
19	D 996 R	(B201000–)	Washer, Felt
20	A 442 R	(–)	Cushion, Gasoline Tank, Front Support
21	....	(B201000–)	Bolt, Carriage, with Nut, 3/8" x 1-1/2" (2 used)
22	AB 2746 R	(B96000 –)	Support, Gasoline Tank Front, with Cushion
23	12H 291 R	(B201000–)	Washer, Lock (Sub. for A2188R and A3546R) (2 used)
24	A 3232 R	(B201000–)	Screw, Machine, 5/16" x 1/2" (2 used) (Sub. for AA4935R)
25	B. 2530 R	(B201000–)	Shield, Heat
26	....	(B201000–)	Nut, 3/8" (2 used)
27	AB 3888 R	(B238796–)	Pipe, Gasoline
28	A 258 R	(B238796–)	Connector (Sub. for D392R)
29	AA 4331 R	(B238796–)	Filter, Gasoline*
30	AA 4296 R	(B238796–)	Body, Filter
31	AA 4298 R	(B238796–)	Valve
32	AC 1079 R	(–B238795)	Body and Shut-Off Valve
33	AC 1080 R	(–B238795)	Valve, Shut-Off
34	AA 519 R	(–B238795)	Screen, Filter
	AA 4297 R	(B238796–)	Screen
35	C 1778 R	(–)	Gasket
36	AA 4507 R	(–)	Bowl and Gasket (Heat Resistant Bowl) (Sub. for AA2064R)
37	AA 518 R	(–)	Nut and Washer
38	AA 517 R	(–)	Clamp
39	AA 499 R	(–B238795)	Filter, Gasoline
40	AB 3571 R	(B201000–B238795)	Pipe, Gasoline
41	B 2526 R	(B201000–B238795)	Elbow

*Will fit B201000-B238794 when ordered with A258R and AB3888R.

PC-330-(3-60)

Late styled Model B gasoline fuel system.

Left side view of a late styled Model B. Note the spark plug wire loom and routing inside the frame.

Ignition System

Battery ignition became standard equipment as of June 1950. Prior to that, magneto ignition was standard. Wico and Fairbanks-Morse magnetos were used throughout production, so check the parts breakdown for the right magneto for a particular serial number.

Most Bs were equipped with Champion No. 8 plugs, although some came from the factory with plugs from other manufacturers (Edison and Autolite are two examples).

Short spark plug wire conduits were used up to serial number 23,576. Longer conduits were used thereafter on unstyled machines. Styled tractors used a different type, and this was again changed at serial number 201,000.

Left side view of an early styled Model B. The plug wires are routed inside the loom, which also protects the plug from damage. Note the starting petcock. These were standard on Model Bs with the 175ci engine.

A detail of the distributor ignition setup on a late styled B. Notice the tractor serial number plate below the plug wires.

A magneto ignition setup on an early styled B. The serial number plate is visible below the magneto. To stop a magneto-equipped Model B, pull the throttle to the fully closed position. Carburetors on these tractors should have an idle cutoff position.

Right, the battery is located in the box beneath the bench-type seat on late styled Model Bs.

Left, the generator and voltage regulator installation on a late styled Model B.

When farmers needed to replace a muffler, they would enlarge the hole in the hood as shown above. While this hole is neater than most (a hammer and chisel were the tools of choice), it will have to be fixed for a correct restoration.

This Model B hood is correct, with the muffler hole intact.

Exhaust and Muffler

The illustrated parts breakdown lists acceptable types of mufflers and exhaust for styled tractors. These can also be used on older tractors if original types are unavailable.

Five different mufflers were used on the Model B. One of these is the "orchard" muffler, which lays alongside the engine on BOs and Lindemans. Underslung exhausts were not available until the Model 50 replaced the B, but a low muffler, part number AB484R (unstyled only), was available when building clearance was insufficient for the standard stack. A shorter-than-standard air intake pipe was also available. The intake and exhaust pipes are mounted side-by-side on unstyled Model Bs. On the styled Bs, the intake is behind and in line with the muffler. The muffler is a bit taller and has a necked-down section on most styled Bs.

Different part number air pipes and exhaust pipes are used on short-frame Model Bs than on the long-frame types (refer to the illustrated parts breakdown).

Governor

There was a change in the governor case late in 1937 for both the standard tread and row-crop Model Bs (serial numbers 40,782 and 327,460). The case was again changed in 1939 with the advent of the styled tractors (serial number 60,000). The final case change was made in 1947 when the pressed-steel frames came out (serial number 201,000). Of course, internal parts changed as well.

The governor is a straightforward fly-weight type, built by John Deere. The magneto or distributor is mounted to, and driven by, the governor.

Note the longer exhaust pipe on this Model B. This photo was taken in 1941, and the tractor has cast rear wheels, which take the place of wheel weights. *John Deere Archives*

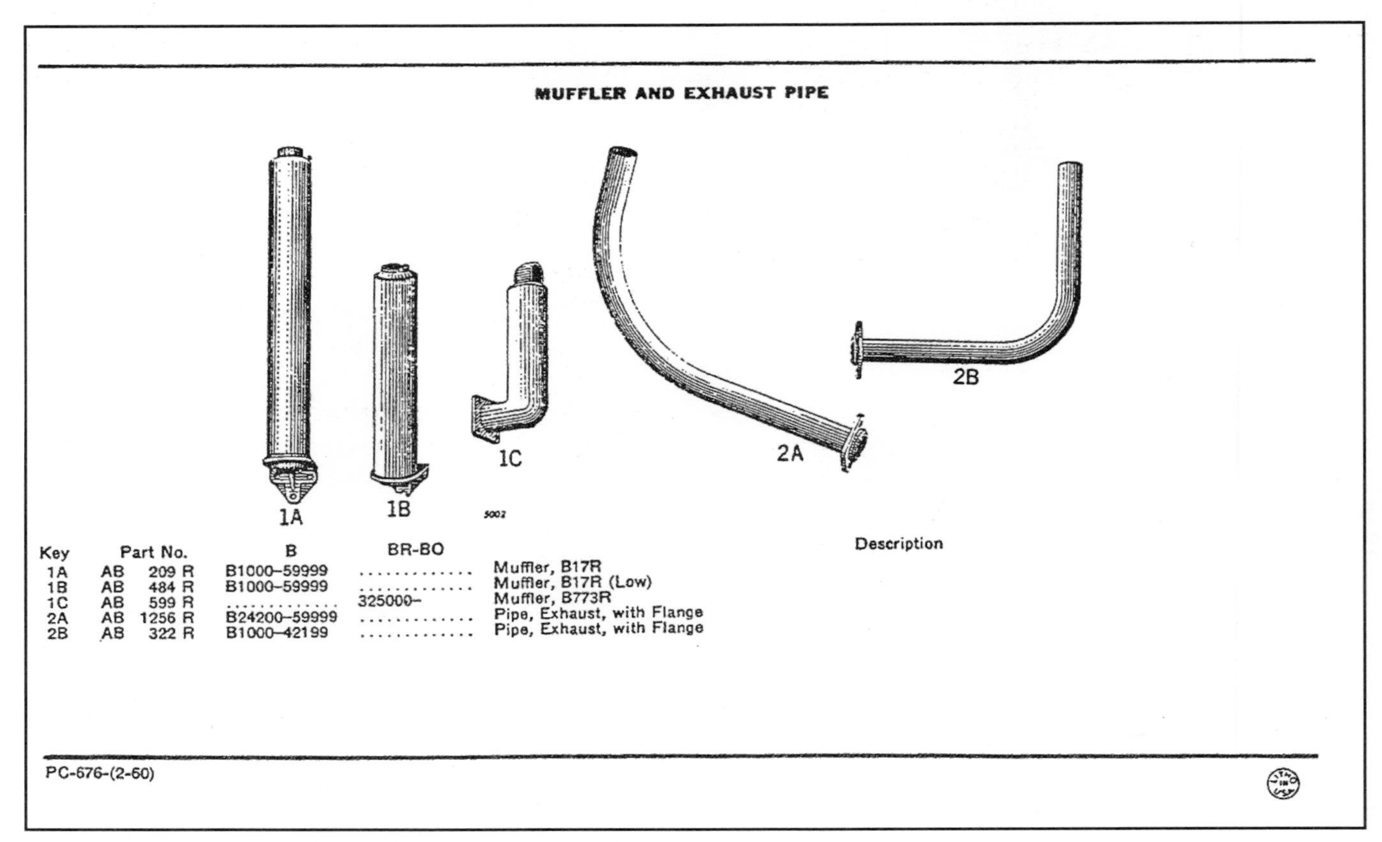

MUFFLER AND EXHAUST PIPE

Key	Part No.	B	BR-BO	Description
1A	AB 209 R	B1000–59999	....	Muffler, B17R
1B	AB 484 R	B1000–59999	....	Muffler, B17R (Low)
1C	AB 599 R	....	325000–	Muffler, B773R
2A	AB 1256 R	B24200–59999	....	Pipe, Exhaust, with Flange
2B	AB 322 R	B1000–42199	....	Pipe, Exhaust, with Flange

PC-676-(2-60)

Muffler and exhaust pipes for Model Bs. *John Deere Archives*

Pines Winter Front Company, Chicago, Illinois, made shutters for the John Deere Model B, as well as for other vehicles. Travis Jorde, the decal expert (see appendix), researched the company and found that this logo was affixed to their products. Jorde now provides this decal to restorers.

Cooling System

A thermosiphon coolant circulation system was employed for almost all John Deere Model B tractors. The system is based on the principle that heated coolant (in the engine block) is lighter than the cooled water in the radiator. The coolant naturally rises into the tank and forces cooler water back into the block. Deere touted the advantage of no water pump, but the requirement for twenty-eight quarts of coolant (late styled) makes the pump look attractive in retrospect. With antifreeze costing a dollar or more per quart, a smaller system would be welcome. In the old days, many tractors were simply stored in the winter with the water drained. By comparison, the 420/430 series tractors had about the same horsepower and, with a water pump system, required only eleven quarts of coolant. The last 4,172 Model Bs used water pumps (serial number 306,600–up). The same radiator was used, but with a bottom tank.

Fan and Shutters

Besides the radiator, water pipes, and coolant (water), the system consisted of a shaft-driven fan and either a curtain or shutters which controlled airflow to the radiator. The curtain was standard until mid-1937, which includes row-crop tractors through serial number 34,951 and standard treads to 327,157. After that, shutters were used. Most unstyled Model Bs were also equipped with radiator guards.

All models used four-bladed fans. The back-side of the blades were painted yellow on unstyled and styled Bs to serial number 95,999. This was done to make the fan more visible and prevent accidental contact with a running fan. Fan bearing housings and shafts were different for the different series. There were no "open fan shaft" Model Bs, as there were with the Model A.

Temperature Gauge

Up to serial number 12,742, no temperature gauge was provided on the John Deere B. A factory retrofit gauge and bracket were made available for those earlier tractors that were built without. Originally, the gauges indicated only "Cold," "Normal," and "Danger," with black, green, and red bands beneath. White-faced instruments were used. Replacement gauges currently available from John Deere have black faces. Correct white face gauges are available from outside suppliers.

WATER PUMP
(SERIAL No. B306600-)

Key	Part No.	Serial No.	Description
1	B 2893 R	(B306600-)	Belt, Drive
2	A 4283 R	(B306600-)	Pulley, Water Pump
3	A 4275 R	(B306600-)	Snap Ring, Bearing Retainer
4	....	(B306600-)	Screw, Cap, 1/2" x 2" (3 used)
	12H 13 R	(B306600-)	Washer, Lock, 1/2" (3 used)
5	AA 5579 R	(B306600-)	Bearing, with Slinger, Washer and Oil Seal
6	AA 5580 R	(B306600-)	Slinger, Washer and Seal
7	AB 4951 R	(B306600-)	Housing, Water Pump (Sub. for B2886R)
8	B 2887 R	(B306600-)	Gasket, Housing (Packed 5 in a Pkg.)
9	B 2897 R	(B306600-)	Impeller, Pump Housing
10	B 2885 R	(B306600-)	Tank, Bottom
11	B 78 R	(B306600-)	Clamp, Hose (4 used)
12	B 2891 R	(B306600-)	Hose, Lower (2 used)
13	B 2890 R	(B306600-)	Pipe, Lower Water
14	B 2889 R	(B306600-)	Pipe, Cylinder Head Water Inlet
15	B 1799 R	(B96000 -)	Gasket (Packed 5 in a Pkg.)
16	K 3083 R	(B96000 -)	Stud, 7/16" x 1-7/8" (2 used)
17	12H 12 R	(B96000 -)	Washer, Lock, 7/16" (2 used)
18	....	(B96000 -)	Nut, 7/16" (2 used)

(Parts listed below are an assembly of parts in this grouping.)

Part No.	Serial No.	Description
AB 4267 R	(B201000–B306599)	**Pump, Water, Complete with Radiator Bottom Tank (ATTACHMENT)**
AB 4262 R	(B306600–)	Water Pump Assembly, Consisting of Seal, Bearing, with Slinger Housing, Pulley, Impeller, Washer, and Snap Ring (Sub. A4283R Pulley and AB4951R Housing)

Water pump for styled Model Bs serial number 306,600 and up. *John Deere Archives*

12 TRACTORS—MODELS "B" AND "BR"-"BO" (NOT STYLED)

PARTS FOR MODEL "B" SERIAL No. B1000-(——) AND MODELS "BR"-"BO" SERIAL No. (325000-334149) EQUIPPED WITH FAN WITH FRICTION DRIVE PARTS

Key	Part No.	B	BR-BO	Description
1	AB 3316 R	B1000-(——)	325000-334149	Fan, Friction Drive
2	B 2122 R	B1000-(——)	325000-334149	Keeper on Fan Shaft
3	D 399 R	B1000-(——)	325000-334149	Washer, Fan Friction (2 used)
4	AB 3314 R	B1000-(——)	325000-334149	Disk, Fan Drive (Set of 2)
5	H 1039 R	B1000-(——)	325000-334149	Spring, Fan Friction
6	B 2124 R	B1000-(——)	325000-334149	Pulley, Generator Drive
7	B 2129 R	B1000-(——)	325000-334149	Spacer, Fan Bearing
8	B 2127 R	B1000-(——)	325000-334149	Packing, Fan Bearing Rear
9	D 1736 R	B1000-(——)	325000-334149	Washer, Fan Bearing Packing
10	B 2121 R	B1000-(——)	325000-334149	Retainer, Fan Bearing Packing

FAN

Key	Part No.	B	BR-BO	Description
1	AB 1630 R	B1000-59999	325000-334149	Fan Blades with Hub, Complete (Sub. AB3301R)
	AB 3301 R	B1000-59999	325000-334149	Fan with Friction Drive Parts (Sub. for AB1630R)
	AB 3316 R	....	334150-	Fan, Friction Drive
2	15H 254 R	B1000-(——)	325000-	Plug, Pipe, in Fan Bearing Housing
3	D 1720 R	B1000-(——)	325000-	Washer, Lock (Half) Fan Shaft
4	AB 1258 R	B422000-59999	....	Shaft, Fan
	B 286 R	B1000-42199	....	Shaft, Fan
	B 724 R	....	325000-334149	Shaft, Fan
	B 2128 R	....	334150-	Shaft, Fan
5A	26H 17 R	B1000-(——)	325000-	Key, Fan Drive Bevel Gear
5B	D 403 R	B1000-(——)	325000-	Key, Fan Drive Bevel Pinion
6	A 369 R	B1000-(——)	325000-	Snap Ring Fan Shaft, Rear End
7	AB 1406 R	B1000-(——)	325000-	Gear and Pinion, Fan Drive Bevel (B279R and B289R)
8A	B 295 R	B1000-(——)	325000-	Spring, Fan Bearing Take-Up
8B	H 1039 R	....	334150-	Spring, Fan Friction
9	AB 296 R	B1000-21230	....	Housing, B290R, Fan Bearing, with Support Tube
	AB 573 R	....	325000-326194	Housing, B290R, Fan Bearing, with Support Tube
	AB 748 R	B21231-42199	....	Housing, B290R, Fan Bearing, with Support Tube
	AB 750 R	....	326195-	Housing, B290R, Fan Bearing, with Support Tube
	AB 1259 R	B42200-59999	....	Housing, B290R, Fan Bearing, with Support Tube
10A	B 298 R	B1000-(——)	325000-	Retainer, Front Fan Bearing Felt Washer
10B	A 286 R	B7744-(——)	325000-334149	Retainer, Front Fan Bearing Packing, Rear
	B 2121 R	....	334150-	Retainer, Fan Bearing Packing
11	B 297 R	B1000-(——)	325000-	Washer, Felt, Front Fan Bearing (Sub. for AB518R)
12	B 292 R	B1000-21230	325000-326194	Clamp, Fan Shaft Tube Packing Rear
13	B 293 R	B1000-(——)	325000-	Packing Ring, Rear of Fan Shaft Tube (Rubber)
14A	24H 239 R	B1000-(——)	325000-334149	Washer, Grease Retainer, Rear, Front Fan Bearing
	D 1736 R	....	334150-	Washer, Fan Bearing Packing
14B	24H 847 R	B1000-(——)	325000-	Washer, Retainer, for Fan Bearing Felt Washer
14C	A 393 R	B7744-(——)	325000-334149	Washer, Packing, Rear of Front Fan Bearing (Cork)
14D	24H 43 R	B1000-(——)	325000-	Washer on Front Fan Bearing to Housing Screws (2 used)
	24H 4 R	B19070-42199	326053-	Washer, Fan Shaft Support (1-1/2" Outside Diameter, 17/32" Inside Diameter)
15A	B 300 R	B1000-3042	....	Support, Fan Shaft, Front
15B	B 650 R	B3043-42199	325000-	Support, Fan Shaft
15C	B 1006 R	B42200-59999	....	Support, Fan Shaft
16	JD 7655 R	B1000-(——)	325000-	Cup, Front and Rear Bearing
17	JD 7656 R	B1000-(——)	325000-	Cone, Front and Rear Bearing
18	JD 7657 R	B1000-(——)	325000-	Balls and Retainer, Front and Rear Bearing
19A	B 287 R	B1000-21230	325000-326194	Housing, Fan Shaft Rear Bearing
19B	B 1141 R	B42200-(——)	....	Housing, Fan Shaft Rear Bearing
	B 870 R	B21231-42199	326195-	Housing, Fan Shaft Rear Bearing
20	A 407 R	B1000-(——)	325000-	Gasket, Rear Fan Bearing Housing (Thick)
	B 571 R	B1000-(——)	325000-	Gasket, Rear Fan Bearing Housing (Thin)
21	B 2122 R	....	334150-	Keeper on Fan Shaft
22	D 399 R	....	334150-	Washer, Fan Friction
23	AB 3314 R	....	334150-	Disk, Fan Drive (Set of 2)
24	B 2124 R	....	334150-	Pulley, Generator Drive
25	B 2127 R	....	334150-	Packing, Fan Bearing Rear
26	B 2129 R	....	....	Spacer, Fan Bearing

(Part listed below is not illustrated.)

Key	Part No.	B	BR-BO	Description
	AA 6240 R	....	334150-	Bearing Kit, Front Fan, Consisting of Packings, Retainers, Washers, and Bearings (Will Fit B1000-B59999 and 325000-334149, if AB3301R Fan Assembly has been Installed)

PC-676-(2-60)

Friction-drive fan for unstyled Model Bs. *John Deere Archives*

Lubrication

The engines of all John Deere Model B tractors have full, positive-pressure oil lubrication systems, which probably accounts for much of their famed reliability. The oil is pressurized to about 15psi by the positive displacement gear pump. The oil is forced through a full-flow filter and through drilled passages to the main bearings, connecting rods, and piston pin bushings). Oil thrown off by the revolving crankshaft bathes the cylinder walls, governor gears, and camshaft. Oil pipes carry lubricant to the governor, tappets, pushrods, and valves. An oil pressure adjustment can be made at the governor housing up to serial number 40,781 (327,459 for standard treads). After that the adjustment is found inside the crankcase.

All unstyled Model Bs used the same basic oil pump, but several types were used on the styled tractors. (See the illustrated breakdown pictures for details).

The oil filter of the Model B was originally a permanent brass mesh type. Replaceable type paper filters are now commonly available. Styled tractors have always used replaceable filter elements.

TRACTORS—MODELS "B," "BN," "BNH," "BW," "BWH" (STYLED) 25

FAN ASSEMBLY AND VENTILATOR PUMP—Continued
(SERIAL No. B201000-)

Key	Part No.	Serial No.	Description
1	D 1720 R	(–)	Lock, Fan Retaining (2 used)
2	B 2122 R	(B171992–B246911)	Keeper
	A 3645 R	(B246912–)	Keeper, Fan
3	AB 3314 R	(B171992–)	Disk, Fan Drive (Carton of 2) (2 used)
4	D 399 R	(B171992–)	Washer, Fan Friction (2 used)
5	A 4059 R	(B258510–)	Cup, Fan Drive (2 used)
6	AB 3315 R	(B171992–)	Fan, with Cups
7	H 1039 R	(B171992–)	Spring, Fan Friction
8	B 2124 R	(B171992–B283673)	Pulley, Generator Drive
	B 2874 R	(B283674–)	Pulley, Generator Drive
9	A 3190 R	(B201000–)	O-Ring (Rubber)
10	B 298 R	(–)	Retainer
11	B 297 R	(–)	Felt (Sub. for AB518R)
12	24H 847 R	(–)	Washer (Sub. for B296R)
13	JD 7656 R	(–)	Cone (2 used)
14	JD 7657 R	(–)	Balls and Retainer (2 used)
15	JD 7655 R	(–)	Cup (2 used)
	JD 7654 R	(–)	Bearing, Complete (2 used) (Composed of JD7655R, JD7656R and JD7657R)
16	B 295 R	(–)	Spring
17	B 2278 R	(B201000–B258519)	Retainer
	B 2121 R	(B258520–)	Retainer
18	B 2127 R	(B171992–)	Packing, Fan Bearing
19	D 1736 R	(B171992–)	Washer, Fan Bearing Packing
20	....	(–)	Screw, Cap, 3/8" x 3/4" (2 used)
21	12H 11 R	(–)	Washer, Lock, 3/8" (5 used)
22	24H 43 R	(–)	Washer (2 used)
23	AB 3988 R	(B258520–)	Housing, B290R, Fan Bearing, with Support Tube
24	15H 254 R	(–)	Plug, Pipe
25	AB 3616 R	(B201000–B258519)	Housing, B2653R, Fan Bearing, with Support Tube
26	AB 3612 R	(B201000–B246911)	Shaft, Fan (Sub, one AB3961R and one A3645R)
	AB 3961 R	(B246912–)	Shaft, Fan
27	D 403 R	(B201000–)	Key
28	D 403 R	(B201000–B300866)	Key
29	....	(B201000–)	Screw, Cap, 3/8" x 2-3/4" (3 used)
30	B 293 R	(–)	Ring, Packing (Rubber)
31	B 1986 R	(B106780–)	Clip, Heat Indicator Tube
32	A 4188 R	(B300867–)	Cover, Ventilator Pump
33	A 4190 R	(B300867–)	Gasket, Ventilator Pump Cover
34	R 820 R	(B300867–)	Roller, Ventilator Pump Rotor (2 used)
35	A 4191 R	(B300867–)	Rotor, Ventilator Pump
36	A 4189 R	(B300867–)	Housing, Fan Shaft Rear Bearing
37	B 2642 R	(B201000–)	Gasket (Thin) (2 used)
	B 2643 R	(B201000–)	Gasket (Thick) (Sub. B2642R)
38	AB 3706 R	(B201000–)	Gear and Pinion, B289R and B2637R
39	A 369 R	(–)	Snap Ring
40	AB 4246 R	(B258520–B300866)	Cover, B2830R, Ventilator Pump, with Pins (Sub. for AB3989R)
41	B 2646 R	(B201000–B300866)	Gasket (Front)
42	B 2644 R	(B201000–B300866)	Body, Pump (Sub. for AB4242R)
43	B 2648 R	(B201000–B300866)	Roller, Pump
44	B 2647 R	(B201000–B300866)	Eccentric, Pump
45	B 2645 R	(B201000–B300866)	Gasket (Rear)
46	AB 4244 R	(B201000–B300866)	Housing, B2640R, Rear Bearing, with Pins (Sub. for AB3613R)
47	B 2649 R	(B201000–B300866)	Spacer
48	B 2641 R	(B201000–B300866)	Pin, Dowel (4 used)
49	B 2730 R	(B201000–B300866)	Vane, Pump (Sub. for B2650R)
50	B 2283 R	(B201000–B222825)	Retainer (Sub. one B2730R and one B2731R)
	B 2731 R	(B222826–B300866)	Retainer
51	B 2651 R	(B201000–B300866)	Spring, Pump Vane (2 used)
52	AB 4245 R	(B201000–B258519)	Cover, B2652R, Ventilator Pump, with Pins (Sub. for AB3614R)
..	AA 5595 R	(B201000–B300866)	Kit, Ventilator Pump Conversion (On B201000–B258519 also furnish one AB4019R, one B2832R and one A970R)

(Parts listed below are assemblies of some of the parts in this grouping.)

Key	Part No.	Serial No.	Description
	AA 6239 R	(B201000–B258519)	Bearing Kit, Front Fan, Consisting of Packings, Retainers, Washers and Bearing
	AA 6240 R	(B258520–B310772)	Bearing Kit, Front Fan, Consisting of Packings, Retainers, Washers and Bearing

Late styled Model B fan and ventilator pump (continued). *John Deere Archives*

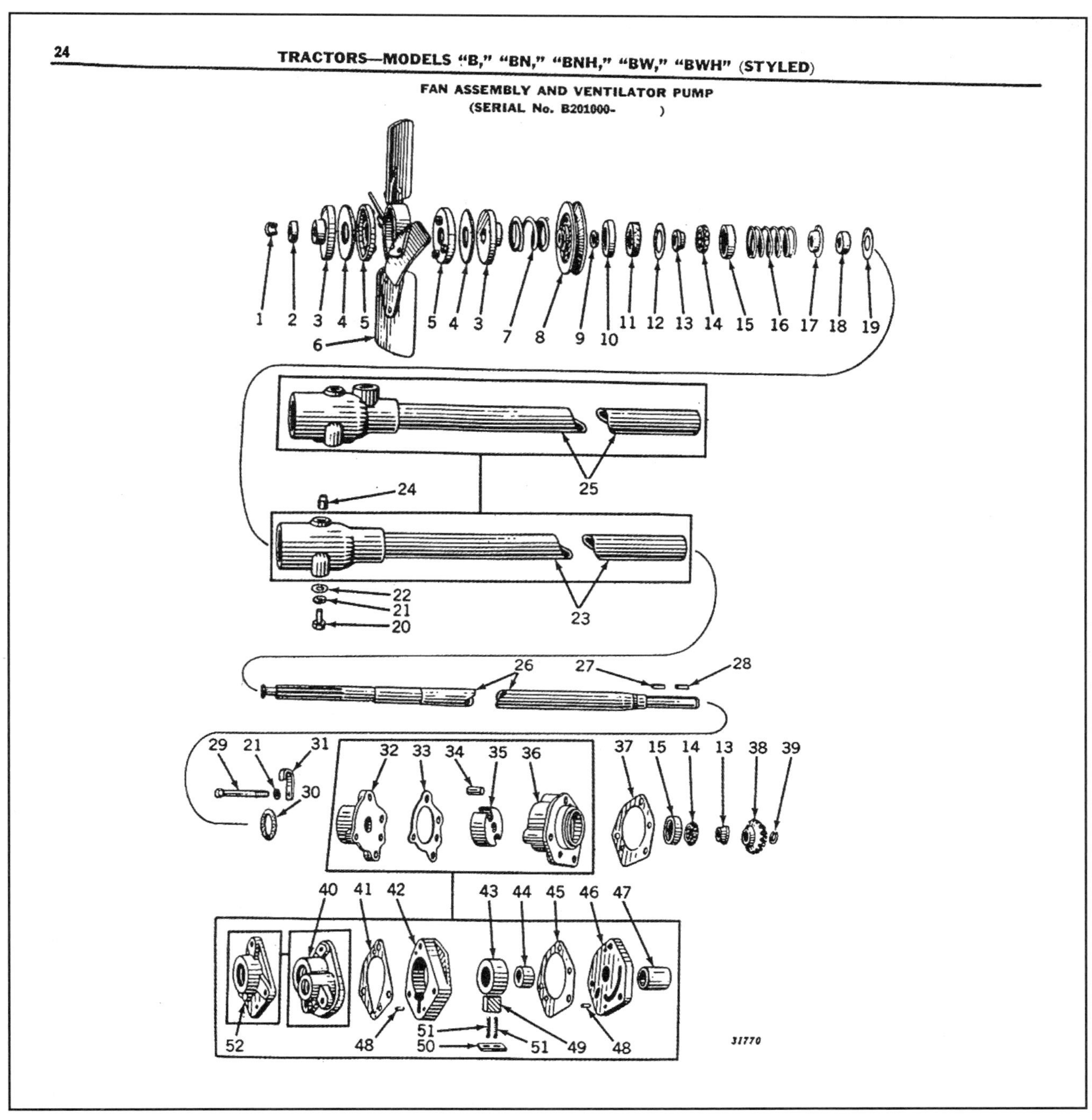

Late styled Model B fan and ventilator pump. *John Deere Archives*

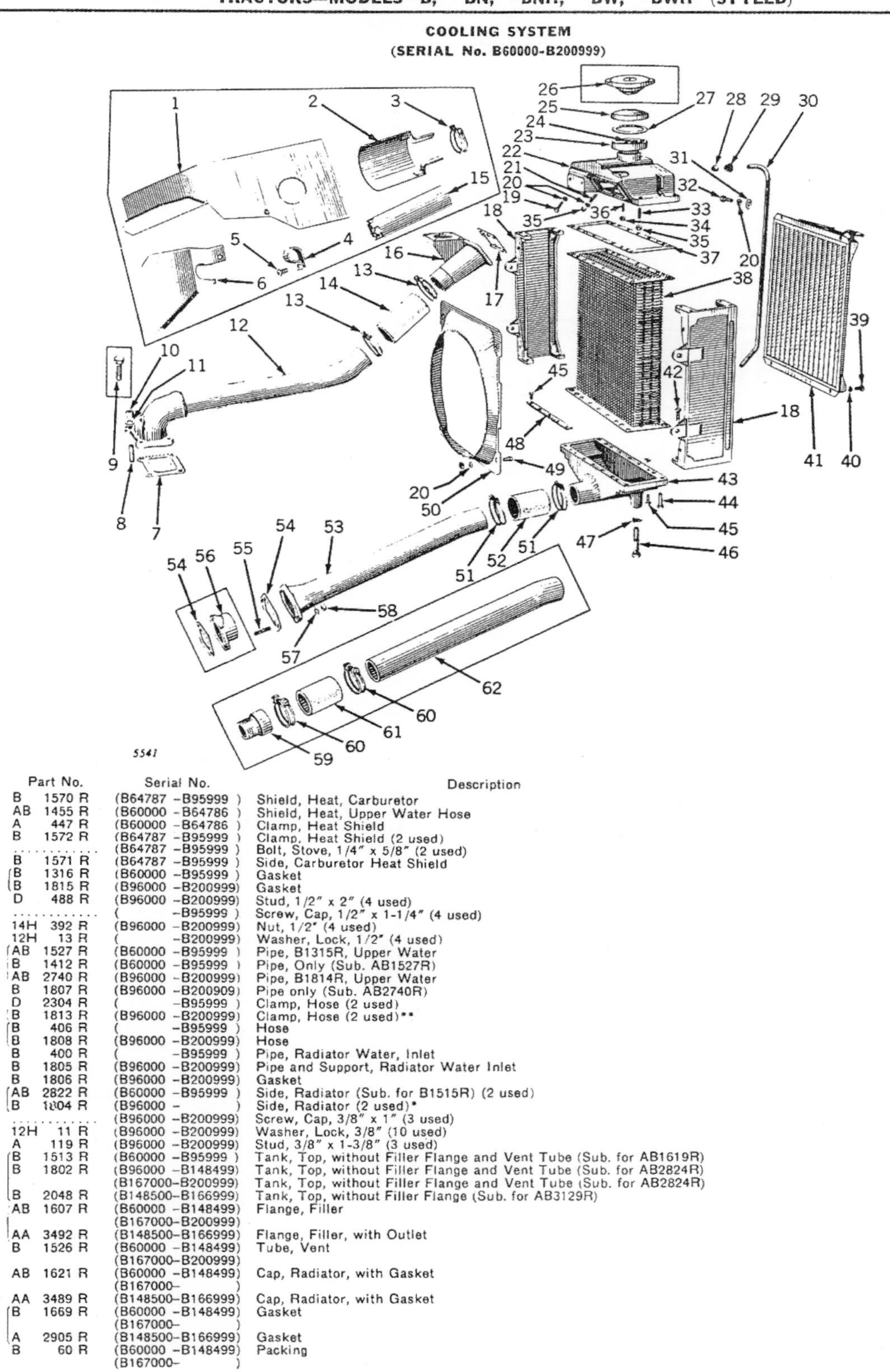

52 TRACTORS—MODELS "B," "BN," "BNH," "BW," "BWH" (STYLED)

COOLING SYSTEM
(SERIAL No. B60000-B200999)

5541

Key	Part No.	Serial No.	Description
1	B 1570 R	(B64787 –B95999)	Shield, Heat, Carburetor
2	AB 1455 R	(B60000 –B64786)	Shield, Heat, Upper Water Hose
3	A 447 R	(B60000 –B64786)	Clamp, Heat Shield
4	B 1572 R	(B64787 –B95999)	Clamp, Heat Shield (2 used)
5	. . . .	(B64787 –B95999)	Bolt, Stove, 1/4" x 5/8" (2 used)
6	B 1571 R	(B64787 –B95999)	Side, Carburetor Heat Shield
7	B 1316 R	(B60000 –B95999)	Gasket
	B 1815 R	(B96000 –B200999)	Gasket
8	D 488 R	(B96000 –B200999)	Stud, 1/2" x 2" (4 used)
9	. . . .	(–B95999)	Screw, Cap, 1/2" x 1-1/4" (4 used)
10	14H 392 R	(B96000 –B200999)	Nut, 1/2" (4 used)
11	12H 13 R	(–B200999)	Washer, Lock, 1/2" (4 used)
12	AB 1527 R	(B60000 –B95999)	Pipe, B1315R, Upper Water
	B 1412 R	(B60000 –B95999)	Pipe, Only (Sub. AB1527R)
	AB 2740 R	(B96000 –B200999)	Pipe, B1814R, Upper Water
	B 1807 R	(B96000 –B200909)	Pipe only (Sub. AB2740R)
13	D 2304 R	(–B95999)	Clamp, Hose (2 used)
	B 1813 R	(B96000 –B200999)	Clamp, Hose (2 used)**
14	B 406 R	(–B95999)	Hose
	B 1808 R	(B96000 –B200999)	Hose
15	B 400 R	(–B95999)	Pipe, Radiator Water, Inlet
16	B 1805 R	(B96000 –B200999)	Pipe and Support, Radiator Water Inlet
17	B 1806 R	(B96000 –B200999)	Gasket
18	AB 2822 R	(B60000 –B95999)	Side, Radiator (Sub. for B1515R) (2 used)
	B 1804 R	(B96000 –)	Side, Radiator (2 used)*
19	. . . .	(B96000 –B200999)	Screw, Cap, 3/8" x 1" (3 used)
20	12H 11 R	(B96000 –B200999)	Washer, Lock, 3/8" (10 used)
21	A 119 R	(B96000 –B200999)	Stud, 3/8" x 1-3/8" (3 used)
22	B 1513 R	(B60000 –B95999)	Tank, Top, without Filler Flange and Vent Tube (Sub. for AB1619R)
	B 1802 R	(B96000 –B148499)	Tank, Top, without Filler Flange and Vent Tube (Sub. for AB2824R)
		(B167000–B200999)	Tank, Top, without Filler Flange and Vent Tube (Sub. for AB2824R)
	B 2048 R	(B148500–B166999)	Tank, Top, without Filler Flange (Sub. for AB3129R)
23	AB 1607 R	(B60000 –B148499)	Flange, Filler
		(B167000–B200999)	
	AA 3492 R	(B148500–B166999)	Flange, Filler, with Outlet
24	B 1526 R	(B60000 –B148499)	Tube, Vent
		(B167000–B200999)	
25	AB 1621 R	(B60000 –B148499)	Cap, Radiator, with Gasket
		(B167000–)	
26	AA 3489 R	(B148500–B166999)	Cap, Radiator, with Gasket
27	B 1669 R	(B60000 –B148499)	Gasket
		(B167000–)	
	A 2905 R	(B148500–B166999)	Gasket
28	B 60 R	(B60000 –B148499)	Packing
		(B167000–)	

Early styled Model B cooling system. *John Deere Archives*

TRACTORS—MODELS "B," "BN," "BNH," "BW," "BWH" (STYLED) 53

COOLING SYSTEM—Continued

(Serial No. B60000-B200999)

Key	Part No.	Serial No.	Description
29	C 1705 R	(B60000 –B148499)	Gland, Packing
		(B167000–)	Gland, Packing
30	AB 1458 R	(B60000 –B63799)	Tube, Radiator Vent Drain, with Trash Screen
	B 3076 R	(B63800 –B148499)	Tube, Radiator Vent Drain° (Sub. for B1527R) (Sub. One A4780R, One B3251R, and One B3252R)
		(B167000–)	Tube, Radiator Vent Drain° (Sub. for B1527R) (Sub. One A4780R, One B3251R, and One B3252R)
	AB 3130 R	(B148500–B166999)	Tube, Radiator Vent Drain, with Clip
31	24H 154 R	(B148500–B166999)	Washer
32	....	(B148500–B166999)	Screw, Cap, 3/8" x 3/4"
33	A 119 R	(B60000 –)	Stud, 3/8" x 1-3/8" (2 used)
34	....	(B60000 –)	Nut, 5/16" (5 used)
35	....	(B60000 –)	Nut, 3/8" (2 used)
	....	(B96000 –B200999)	Nut, 3/8" (3 used)
36	B 1504 R	(B60000 –)	Stud, 5/16" x 15/16" (5 used)
37	B 1507 R	(B60000 –)	Gasket (2 used)
38	AB 3599 R	(B60000 –)	Core, Radiator (Sub. for AB1608R)
39	A 3232 R	(B60000 –)	Screw, Machine, 5/16" x 1/2" (4 used) (Sub. for AA4955R)
40	12H 10 R	(B60000 –)	Washer, Lock, 5/16" (4 used)
41	AB 1622 R	(B60000 –)	Shutter, Radiator
42	7H 328 R	(B60000 –)	Bolt, Machine, 3/8" x 1-1/8" (6 used)
43	AB 2823 R	(B60000 –B95999)	Tank, Bottom, with Lower Water Pipe and Hose (Sub. for B1514R)
	B 1803 R	(B96000 –B13661)	Tank, Bottom**
		(B167000–B200999)	Tank, Bottom**
	B 2023 R	(B136662–B166999)	Tank, Bottom
44	....	(B60000 –)	Screw, Cap, 7/16" x 1-1/2" (8 used)
45	....	(B60000 –)	Bolt, Machine, with Nut, 5/16" x 7/8" (15 used)
46	....	(B60000 –B200999)	Screw, Cap, 5/8" x 3-1/4" (2 used)
47	12H 15 R	(B60000 –B200999)	Washer, Lock, 5/8" (2 used)
48	B 398 R	(–)	Strap, Radiator (4 used)
49	....	(B60000 –)	Bolt, Machine, 3/8" x 3/4" (4 used)
50	AB 4775 R	(B60000 –)	Shroud, Fan (Sub. for B1512R)
51	B 1813 R	(B96000 –)	Clamp, Hose (2 used)**
52	B 1812 R	(B96000 –B200999)	Hose**
53	B 2115 R	(B167000–)	Pipe, Lower Water
54	B 1799 R	(B96000 –)	Gasket
55	K 3083 R	(B96000 –)	Stud, 7/16" x 1-7/8" (2 used)
56	B 1798 R	(B96000 –B166999)	Pipe, Cylinder Head Water Inlet
57	12H 12 R	(B96000 –)	Washer, Lock, 7/16" (2 used)
58	....	(B96000 –)	Nut, 7/16" (2 used)
59	C 251 R	(–B95999)	Pipe, Cylinder Head Inlet
60	D 2304 R	(–)	Clamp, Hose (2 used)
61	B 402 R	(–B95999)	Hose
62	B 1387 R	(B60000 –B95999)	Pipe, Lower Water
	B 1810 R	(B60000 –B95999)	Pipe, Lower Water (Part of AB2823R)**
	B 1811 R	(B96000 –B166999)	Pipe, Lower Water

*Also parts for Tractors B60000–B95999 on which the Radiator Side has been replaced by Part Assembly AB2822R Radiator Side identified by the No. B1804R appearing on the Radiator Side.

**Also parts for Tractors B60000–B95999 on which the Bottom Tank has been replaced by the Part assembly AB2823R Bottom Tank with Lower Water Pipe and Hose, identified by the No. B1803R appearing on the Bottom Tank.

°Also parts for Tractor B60000–B63799 on which AB1458R Radiator Vent Tube and Trash Screen has been installed.

Early styled Model B cooling system (continued). *John Deere Archives*

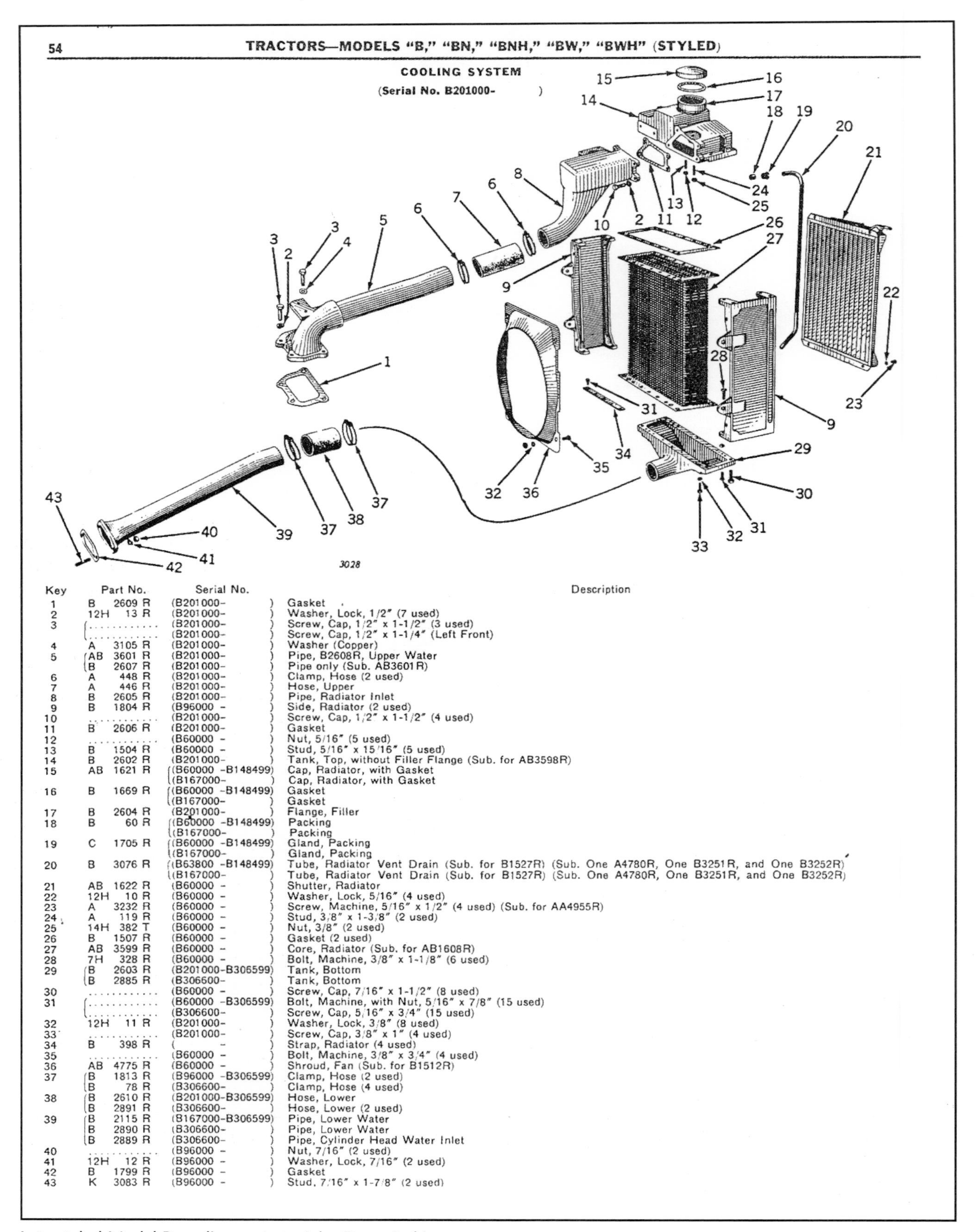

54 TRACTORS—MODELS "B," "BN," "BNH," "BW," "BWH" (STYLED)

COOLING SYSTEM

(Serial No. B201000-)

3028

Key	Part No.	Serial No.	Description
1	B 2609 R	(B201000-)	Gasket
2	12H 13 R	(B201000-)	Washer, Lock, 1/2" (7 used)
3	....	(B201000-)	Screw, Cap, 1/2" x 1-1/2" (3 used)
	....	(B201000-)	Screw, Cap, 1/2" x 1-1/4" (Left Front)
4	A 3105 R	(B201000-)	Washer (Copper)
5	AB 3601 R	(B201000-)	Pipe, B2608R, Upper Water
	B 2607 R	(B201000-)	Pipe only (Sub. AB3601R)
6	A 448 R	(B201000-)	Clamp, Hose (2 used)
7	A 446 R	(B201000-)	Hose, Upper
8	B 2605 R	(B201000-)	Pipe, Radiator Inlet
9	B 1804 R	(B96000 -)	Side, Radiator (2 used)
10	....	(B201000-)	Screw, Cap, 1/2" x 1-1/2" (4 used)
11	B 2606 R	(B201000-)	Gasket
12	....	(B60000 -)	Nut, 5/16" (5 used)
13	B 1504 R	(B60000 -)	Stud, 5/16" x 15/16" (5 used)
14	B 2602 R	(B201000-)	Tank, Top, without Filler Flange (Sub. for AB3598R)
15	AB 1621 R	(B60000 -B148499)	Cap, Radiator, with Gasket
		(B167000-)	Cap, Radiator, with Gasket
16	B 1669 R	(B60000 -B148499)	Gasket
		(B167000-)	Gasket
17	B 2604 R	(B201000-)	Flange, Filler
18	B 60 R	(B60000 -B148499)	Packing
		(B167000-)	Packing
19	C 1705 R	(B60000 -B148499)	Gland, Packing
		(B167000-)	Gland, Packing
20	B 3076 R	(B63800 -B148499)	Tube, Radiator Vent Drain (Sub. for B1527R) (Sub. One A4780R, One B3251R, and One B3252R)
		(B167000-)	Tube, Radiator Vent Drain (Sub. for B1527R) (Sub. One A4780R, One B3251R, and One B3252R)
21	AB 1622 R	(B60000 -)	Shutter, Radiator
22	12H 10 R	(B60000 -)	Washer, Lock, 5/16" (4 used)
23	A 3232 R	(B60000 -)	Screw, Machine, 5/16" x 1/2" (4 used) (Sub. for AA4955R)
24	A 119 R	(B60000 -)	Stud, 3/8" x 1-3/8" (2 used)
25	14H 382 T	(B60000 -)	Nut, 3/8" (2 used)
26	B 1507 R	(B60000 -)	Gasket (2 used)
27	AB 3599 R	(B60000 -)	Core, Radiator (Sub. for AB1608R)
28	7H 328 R	(B60000 -)	Bolt, Machine, 3/8" x 1-1/8" (6 used)
29	B 2603 R	(B201000-B306599)	Tank, Bottom
	B 2885 R	(B306600-)	Tank, Bottom
30	....	(B60000 -)	Screw, Cap, 7/16" x 1-1/2" (8 used)
31	....	(B60000 -B306599)	Bolt, Machine, with Nut, 5/16" x 7/8" (15 used)
	....	(B306600-)	Screw, Cap, 5/16" x 3/4" (15 used)
32	12H 11 R	(B201000-)	Washer, Lock, 3/8" (8 used)
33	....	(B201000-)	Screw, Cap, 3/8" x 1" (4 used)
34	B 398 R	(-)	Strap, Radiator (4 used)
35	....	(B60000 -)	Bolt, Machine, 3/8" x 3/4" (4 used)
36	AB 4775 R	(B60000 -)	Shroud, Fan (Sub. for B1512R)
37	B 1813 R	(B96000 -B306599)	Clamp, Hose (2 used)
	B 78 R	(B306600-)	Clamp, Hose (4 used)
38	B 2610 R	(B201000-B306599)	Hose, Lower
	B 2891 R	(B306600-)	Hose, Lower (2 used)
39	B 2115 R	(B167000-B306599)	Pipe, Lower Water
	B 2890 R	(B306600-)	Pipe, Lower Water
	B 2889 R	(B306600-)	Pipe, Cylinder Head Water Inlet
40	....	(B96000 -)	Nut, 7/16" (2 used)
41	12H 12 R	(B96000 -)	Washer, Lock, 7/16" (2 used)
42	B 1799 R	(B96000 -)	Gasket
43	K 3083 R	(B96000 -)	Stud, 7/16" x 1-7/8" (2 used)

Late styled Model B cooling system. *John Deere Archives*

Chapter 3

Transmission, Final Drive, and PTO

Clutch and Belt Pulley

The clutch transmits power from the engine to the transmission and belt pulley. The clutch is engaged by moving the hand-lever forward through an over-center detent. To release the clutch, the lever is pulled back. When the lever is pulled back with some force, it actuates a brake on the belt pulley. If the transmission is in neutral, the weight of the pulley will spin the transmission gears for quite a while, making it impossible to shift into gear. The pulley brake will quickly stop this rotation. If the transmission is in gear, this brake can also be used for stopping the tractor, but it is best to use the foot brakes.

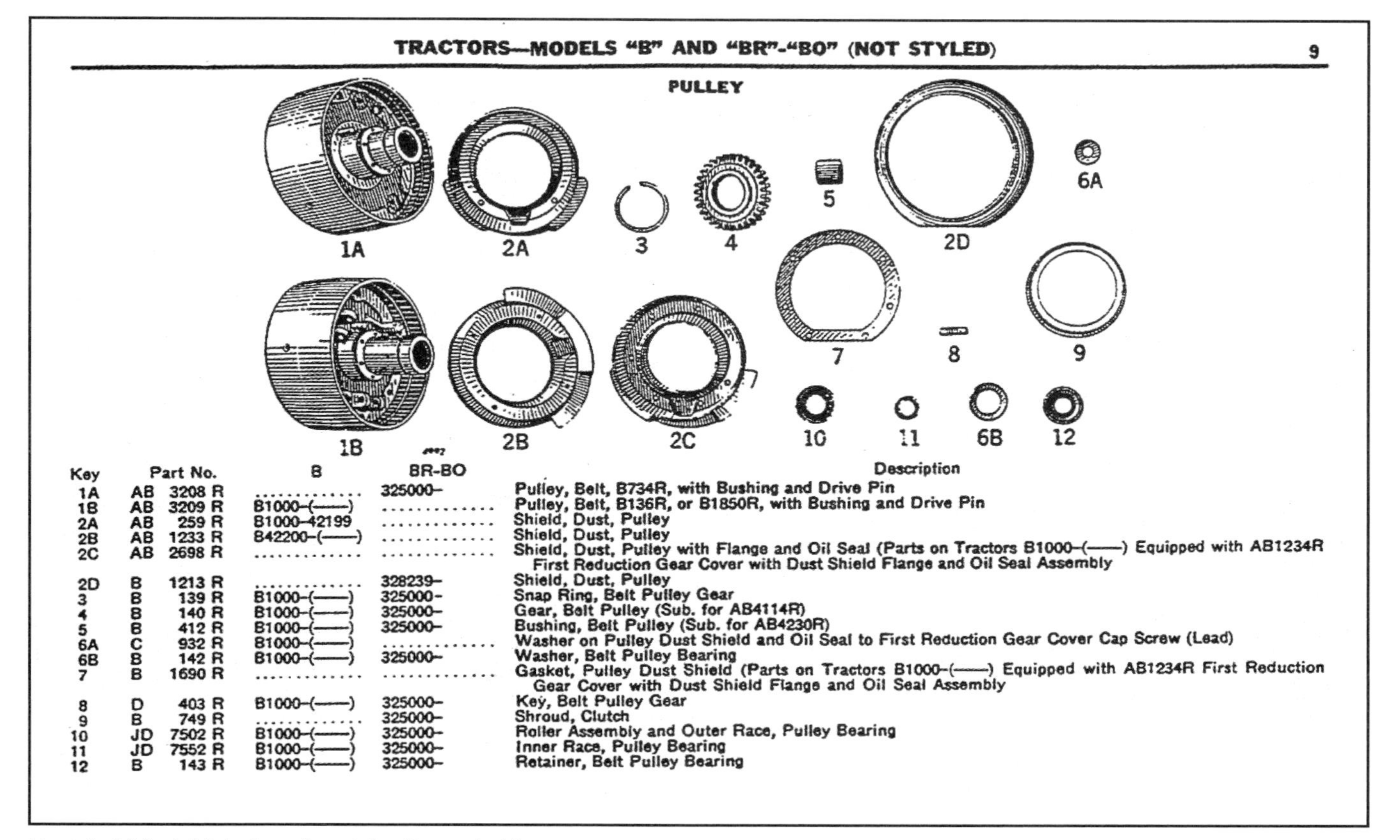

TRACTORS—MODELS "B" AND "BR"-"BO" (NOT STYLED) 9

PULLEY

Key	Part No.	B	BR-BO	Description
1A	AB 3208 R	....	325000–	Pulley, Belt, B734R, with Bushing and Drive Pin
1B	AB 3209 R	B1000–(——)	....	Pulley, Belt, B136R, or B1850R, with Bushing and Drive Pin
2A	AB 259 R	B1000–42199	....	Shield, Dust, Pulley
2B	AB 1233 R	B42200–(——)	....	Shield, Dust, Pulley
2C	AB 2698 R	....	....	Shield, Dust, Pulley with Flange and Oil Seal (Parts on Tractors B1000–(——) Equipped with AB1234R First Reduction Gear Cover with Dust Shield Flange and Oil Seal Assembly
2D	B 1213 R	....	328239–	Shield, Dust, Pulley
3	B 139 R	B1000–(——)	325000–	Snap Ring, Belt Pulley Gear
4	B 140 R	B1000–(——)	325000–	Gear, Belt Pulley (Sub. for AB4114R)
5	B 412 R	B1000–(——)	325000–	Bushing, Belt Pulley (Sub. for AB4230R)
6A	C 932 R	B1000–(——)	....	Washer on Pulley Dust Shield and Oil Seal to First Reduction Gear Cover Cap Screw (Lead)
6B	B 142 R	B1000–(——)	325000–	Washer, Belt Pulley Bearing
7	B 1690 R	....	....	Gasket, Pulley Dust Shield (Parts on Tractors B1000–(——) Equipped with AB1234R First Reduction Gear Cover with Dust Shield Flange and Oil Seal Assembly
8	D 403 R	B1000–(——)	325000–	Key, Belt Pulley Gear
9	B 749 R	....	325000–	Shroud, Clutch
10	JD 7502 R	B1000–(——)	325000–	Roller Assembly and Outer Race, Pulley Bearing
11	JD 7552 R	B1000–(——)	325000–	Inner Race, Pulley Bearing
12	B 143 R	B1000–(——)	325000–	Retainer, Belt Pulley Bearing

Unstyled Model B belt pulley. *John Deere Archives*

This early advertisement for the Model B touts the use of the belt pulley. Until tractor horsepower went over fifty, many farm implements depended on flat belt power (higher horsepower tractors relied more heavily on shaft-driven PTO). This particular tractor seems to be an HX experimental; note the swept-triangle in the center of the steering wheel and that the photo appears to have been retouched to add the "John Deere" type on the rear axle housing. *John Deere Archives*

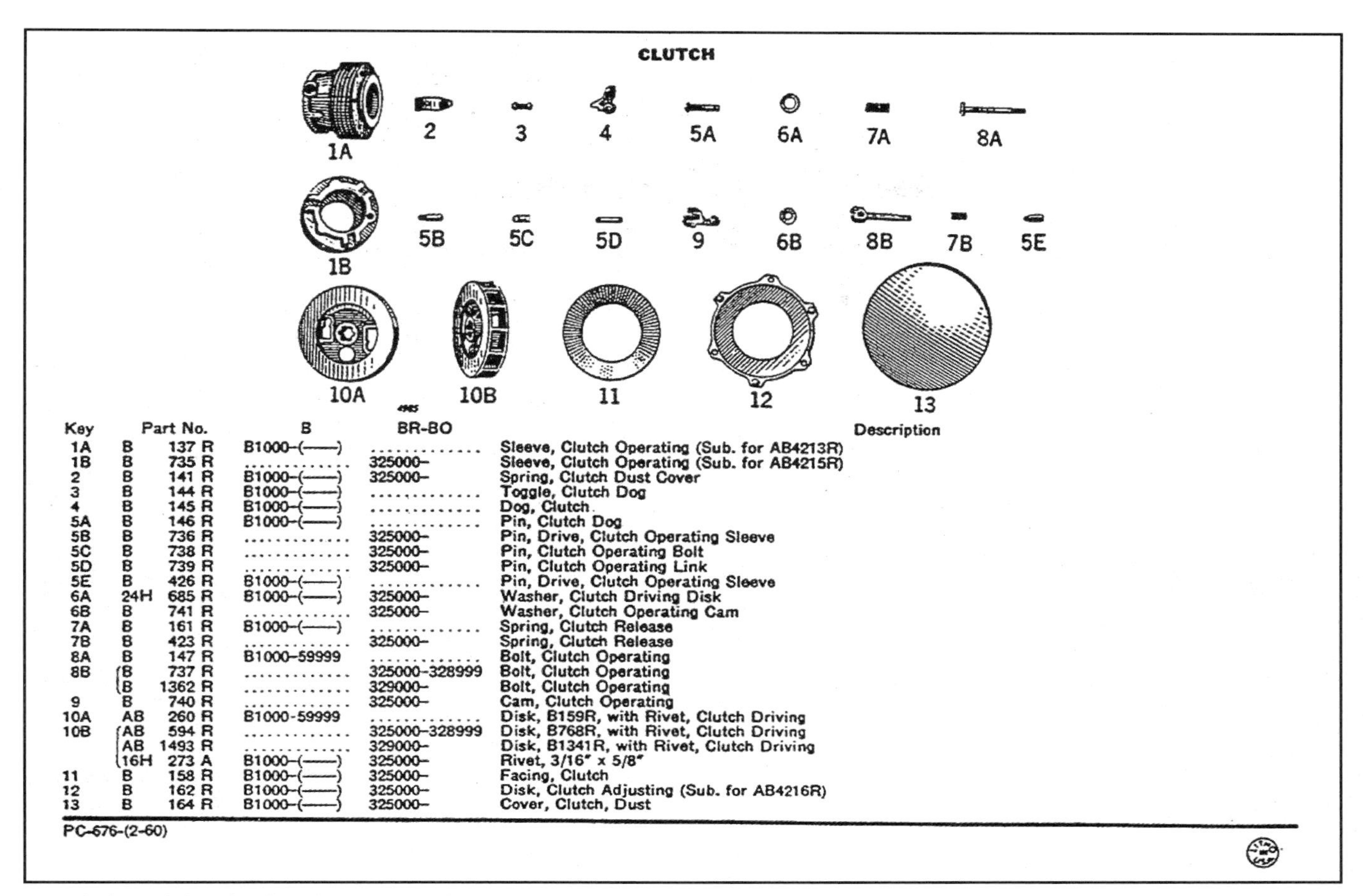
CLUTCH

Key	Part No.		B	BR-BO	Description
1A	B	137 R	B1000-(——)	....	Sleeve, Clutch Operating (Sub. for AB4213R)
1B	B	735 R	....	325000–	Sleeve, Clutch Operating (Sub. for AB4215R)
2	B	141 R	B1000-(——)	325000–	Spring, Clutch Dust Cover
3	B	144 R	B1000-(——)	....	Toggle, Clutch Dog
4	B	145 R	B1000-(——)	....	Dog, Clutch
5A	B	146 R	B1000-(——)	....	Pin, Clutch Dog
5B	B	736 R	....	325000–	Pin, Drive, Clutch Operating Sleeve
5C	B	738 R	....	325000–	Pin, Clutch Operating Bolt
5D	B	739 R	....	325000–	Pin, Clutch Operating Link
5E	B	426 R	B1000-(——)	....	Pin, Drive, Clutch Operating Sleeve
6A	24H	685 R	B1000-(——)	325000–	Washer, Clutch Driving Disk
6B	B	741 R	....	325000–	Washer, Clutch Operating Cam
7A	B	161 R	B1000-(——)	....	Spring, Clutch Release
7B	B	423 R	....	325000–	Spring, Clutch Release
8A	B	147 R	B1000-59999	....	Bolt, Clutch Operating
8B	B	737 R	....	325000-328999	Bolt, Clutch Operating
	B	1362 R	....	329000–	Bolt, Clutch Operating
9	B	740 R	....	325000–	Cam, Clutch Operating
10A	AB	260 R	B1000-59999	....	Disk, B159R, with Rivet, Clutch Driving
10B	AB	594 R	....	325000-328999	Disk, B768R, with Rivet, Clutch Driving
	AB	1493 R	....	329000–	Disk, B1341R, with Rivet, Clutch Driving
	16H	273 A	B1000-(——)	325000–	Rivet, 3/16" x 5/8"
11	B	158 R	B1000-(——)	325000–	Facing, Clutch
12	B	162 R	B1000-(——)	325000–	Disk, Clutch Adjusting (Sub. for AB4216R)
13	B	164 R	B1000-(——)	325000–	Cover, Clutch, Dust

PC-676-(2-60)

Unstyled Model B clutch. *John Deere Archives*

John Deere heavily promoted its hand-operated clutch. For belt work, it is much more convenient, as there is no need to stand on the platform to engage the pulley. Also, when operating the tractor from a standing position, the hand clutch is much quicker to operate than the foot variety. Deere's claim, however, that implement hookup was a one-man job probably would not withstand scrutiny by OSHA today.

Finally, trying to back the tractor into a tight parking spot in a crowded shed can test the vocabulary of the most experienced operator. When twisted around far enough to look directly behind the tractor, it's tough to reach the clutch with either hand. The clutch can be slipped by placing one's foot gently against the lever, but pushing a little too hard and fully engaging the clutch can have disastrous results when maneuvering in a tight spot.

The Model B uses a multiple-disk dry clutch that is contained within the belt pulley. One of the big advantages of John Deere two-cylinder tractors with transverse engines is the ease with which the clutch can be adjusted or repaired. The clutch dust cover, on the end of the belt pulley, is removed like a hub cap. The clutch is adjusted by three castellated nuts. Adjustment is a five-minute job. A complete clutch plate replacement takes only about fifteen minutes.

Removal of the heavy driving disk will probably require the use of a gear puller. When replacing this element, be sure the V mark lines up with the flat spot, or V mark, on the end of the crankshaft spline. Failure to do so will cause excessive vibration, especially at idle. On row-crop tractors, the vibration will cause sympathetic vibration in the steering shaft. Also, when reinstalling the driving disk, be sure the cap screw holding it to the crankshaft is tight.

Clutch and belt pulley variations within the different configurations of the Model B were few. The row-crop types used different components than those of the standard treads (see the parts illustrations for details.)

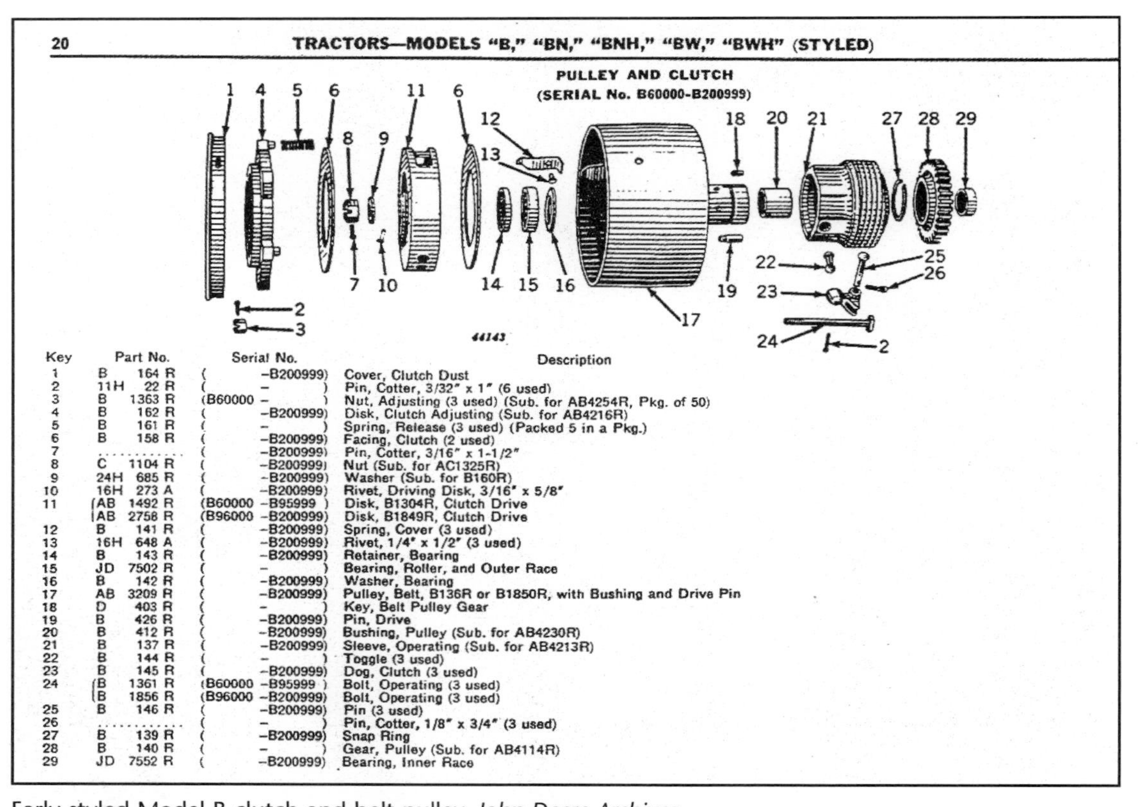

20 TRACTORS—MODELS "B," "BN," "BNH," "BW," "BWH" (STYLED)

PULLEY AND CLUTCH
(SERIAL No. B60000-B200999)

Key	Part No.	Serial No.	Description
1	B 164 R	(-B200999)	Cover, Clutch Dust
2	11H 22 R	(–)	Pin, Cotter, 3/32" x 1" (6 used)
3	B 1363 R	(B60000 –)	Nut, Adjusting (3 used) (Sub. for AB4254R, Pkg. of 50)
4	B 162 R	(-B200999)	Disk, Clutch Adjusting (Sub. for AB4216R)
5	B 161 R	(–)	Spring, Release (3 used) (Packed 5 in a Pkg.)
6	B 158 R	(-B200999)	Facing, Clutch (2 used)
7	....	(-B200999)	Pin, Cotter, 3/16" x 1-1/2"
8	C 1104 R	(-B200999)	Nut (Sub. for AC1325R)
9	24H 685 R	(-B200999)	Washer (Sub. for B160R)
10	16H 273 A	(-B200999)	Rivet, Driving Disk, 3/16" x 5/8"
11	(AB 1492 R	(B60000 -B95999)	Disk, B1304R, Clutch Drive
	(AB 2758 R	(B96000 -B200999)	Disk, B1849R, Clutch Drive
12	B 141 R	(-B200999)	Spring, Cover (3 used)
13	16H 648 A	(-B200999)	Rivet, 1/4" x 1/2" (3 used)
14	B 143 R	(-B200999)	Retainer, Bearing
15	JD 7502 R	(–)	Bearing, Roller, and Outer Race
16	B 142 R	(-B200999)	Washer, Bearing
17	AB 3209 R	(-B200999)	Pulley, Belt, B136R or B1850R, with Bushing and Drive Pin
18	D 403 R	(–)	Key, Belt Pulley Gear
19	B 426 R	(-B200999)	Pin, Drive
20	B 412 R	(-B200999)	Bushing, Pulley (Sub. for AB4230R)
21	B 137 R	(-B200999)	Sleeve, Operating (Sub. for AB4213R)
22	B 144 R	(–)	Toggle (3 used)
23	B 145 R	(-B200999)	Dog, Clutch (3 used)
24	(B 1361 R	(B60000 -B95999)	Bolt, Operating (3 used)
	(B 1856 R	(B96000 -B200999)	Bolt, Operating (3 used)
25	B 146 R	(-B200999)	Pin (3 used)
26	....	(–)	Pin, Cotter, 1/8" x 3/4" (3 used)
27	B 139 R	(-B200999)	Snap Ring
28	B 140 R	(–)	Gear, Pulley (Sub. for AB4114R)
29	JD 7552 R	(-B200999)	Bearing, Inner Race

Early styled Model B clutch and belt pulley. *John Deere Archives*

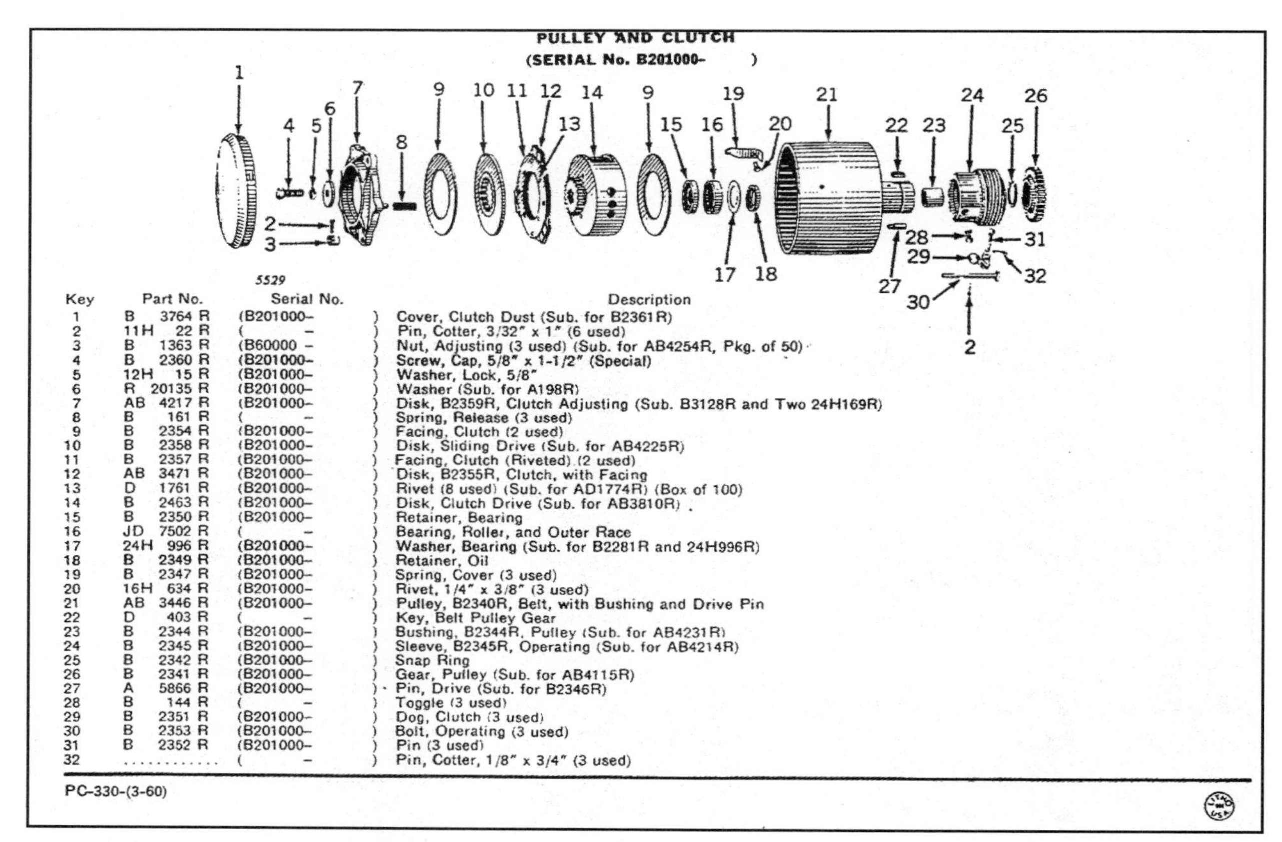

PULLEY AND CLUTCH
(SERIAL No. B201000-)

Key	Part No.	Serial No.	Description
1	B 3764 R	(B201000-)	Cover, Clutch Dust (Sub. for B2361R)
2	11H 22 R	(–)	Pin, Cotter, 3/32" x 1" (6 used)
3	B 1363 R	(B60000 –)	Nut, Adjusting (3 used) (Sub. for AB4254R, Pkg. of 50)
4	B 2360 R	(B201000-)	Screw, Cap, 5/8" x 1-1/2" (Special)
5	12H 15 R	(B201000-)	Washer, Lock, 5/8"
6	R 20135 R	(B201000-)	Washer (Sub. for A198R)
7	AB 4217 R	(B201000-)	Disk, B2359R, Clutch Adjusting (Sub. B3128R and Two 24H169R)
8	B 161 R	(–)	Spring, Release (3 used)
9	B 2354 R	(B201000-)	Facing, Clutch (2 used)
10	B 2358 R	(B201000-)	Disk, Sliding Drive (Sub. for AB4225R)
11	B 2357 R	(B201000-)	Facing, Clutch (Riveted) (2 used)
12	AB 3471 R	(B201000-)	Disk, B2355R, Clutch, with Facing
13	D 1761 R	(B201000-)	Rivet (8 used) (Sub. for AD1774R) (Box of 100)
14	B 2463 R	(B201000-)	Disk, Clutch Drive (Sub. for AB3810R)
15	B 2350 R	(B201000-)	Retainer, Bearing
16	JD 7502 R	(–)	Bearing, Roller, and Outer Race
17	24H 996 R	(B201000-)	Washer, Bearing (Sub. for B2281R and 24H996R)
18	B 2349 R	(B201000-)	Retainer, Oil
19	B 2347 R	(B201000-)	Spring, Cover (3 used)
20	16H 634 R	(B201000-)	Rivet, 1/4" x 3/8" (3 used)
21	AB 3446 R	(B201000-)	Pulley, B2340R, Belt, with Bushing and Drive Pin
22	D 403 R	(–)	Key, Belt Pulley Gear
23	B 2344 R	(B201000-)	Bushing, B2344R, Pulley (Sub. for AB4231R)
24	B 2345 R	(B201000-)	Sleeve, B2345R, Operating (Sub. for AB4214R)
25	B 2342 R	(B201000-)	Snap Ring
26	B 2341 R	(B201000-)	Gear, Pulley (Sub. for AB4115R)
27	A 5866 R	(B201000-)	Pin, Drive (Sub. for B2346R)
28	B 144 R	(–)	Toggle (3 used)
29	B 2351 R	(B201000-)	Dog, Clutch (3 used)
30	B 2353 R	(B201000-)	Bolt, Operating (3 used)
31	B 2352 R	(B201000-)	Pin (3 used)
32	....	(–)	Pin, Cotter, 1/8" x 3/4" (3 used)

PC-330-(3-60)

Late styled Model B clutch and belt pulley. *John Deere Archives*

The six-speed cast shift gate used on the single-lever late styled Model B.

Transmission

Several different transmissions were used over the seventeen years of Model B. All standard tread models used a four-speed transmission. Row-crop tractors through serial number 95,184 (built in 1940) used four-speed transmissions in all cases. Serial number 96,000 (built in 1941) and up were standardly equipped with rubber tires. These rubber-tired tractors used a new six-speed unit that featured three ratios with a separate two-speed auxiliary providing a hi-lo option in each gear. Wartime restrictions on rubber tires resulted in reversion to steel wheels, and some Model Bs were built in 1942 and 1943 with the old four-speed transmission when equipped with these steel wheels. Conversion kits were available to convert these tractors to six-speed transmissions and rubber tires. After serial number 201,000 (1947), the six-speed transmission used a single shift lever with a cast shift gate. Models equipped with the four-speed and the late styled models had just one reverse gear. Early styled Bs with the three-ratio, two-speed box had a high- and low-speed reverse controlled by the two-speed lever.

Components of the standard tread models' transmissions were much the same as those of the row-crops. The shift levers were different, however. All gears were straight-cut spur gears.

There were some differences in transmission covers (see illustrations). Prior to serial number 10,526 (row-crops), a different shift fulcrum was used. Standard tread models were not involved in this change. Early Bs did not have shift positions cast into the covers. No data remains as to when these were added.

High-speed transmissions were available on unstyled Model Bs from serial number 14,783 on row-crops and serial number 325,582 on standard treads. Low-speed transmissions were available from serial number 54,634 on row-crop models and serial number 325,582 on the standard treads. Both are extremely rare, so if you have one, its valuable. Check the part numbers and/or gear-tooth counts as indicated in the parts breakdowns.

This view shows the three-speed shift gate used on early styled Bs. The lever to the right (forward) is the range shifter. The aft bent lever is for the PTO.

Final Drive

Several types of final drive assemblies were used on both the standard tread Model Bs and on the row-crops. Naturally, the row-crop types with wide or narrow stances have different assemblies from the normal types. For the standard tread models, there was a change at serial number 329,000 (1939). Note that axle housings are one piece, which was unique back in the early thirties. Housings for unstyled tractors have the words "John Deere" on the rear of the housing (except for the very narrow ones), while the styled tractors do not.

This view shows the rear axle of a pre-1950, late styled Model B. Model Bs built from 1950 through 1952 had square axle housings.

Above, early styled Model Bs have "John Deere" written on the rear axle. This one is not equipped with a hydraulic lift.

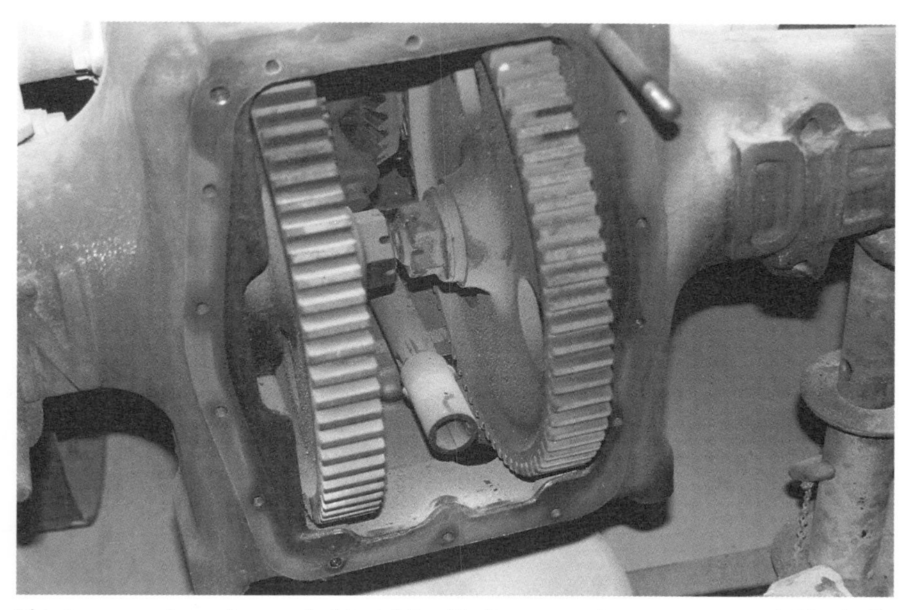

This is a rear view of an early Model B with the rear axle cover removed. The bull gears and the PTO shaft can be seen.

Note that the differential is in the transmission case, rather than in the axle. The differential assemblies are different for styled, unstyled, and standard tread versions, but didn't change during each production run.

Standard tread Model Bs, of course, did not have splined axles for adjusting the wheel tread. Several different types were used on the row-crop tractors. The common axle for unstyled Model Bs has ten spline grooves. Unstyled BWHs and BNHs with 40in rear tires used splines with twelve grooves, as did the early styled Bs. Early styled BNs and BWs used a fifteen-groove spline, which could also be specified for regular Bs in "heavy duty" conditions. Late styled Model Bs all used the fifteengroove spline.

The rear axle of an unstyled Model B equipped with hydraulics. Note that the PTO cover is missing.

TRACTORS—MODELS "B" AND "BR"-"BO" (NOT STYLED) 27

FINAL DRIVE—Continued

Key	Part No.	B	BR-BO	Description
12B	AB 716 R	....	325000-328999	Shaft, Rear Axle, R.H., with Nut
	AB 1331 R	B46175-(——)	....	Shaft, Rear Axle, with Nut (BNH, BWH only)
	AB 1343 R	B46175-(——)	....	Shaft, Rear Axle with Nut, R.H. (Narrow Adjustable Tread) (BWH only)
	AB 1344 R	B46175-(——)	....	Shaft, Rear Axle, with Nut, L.H. (Narrow Adjustable Tread) (BWH only)
	AB 717 R	....	325000-328999	Shaft, Rear Axle, L.H., with Nut
	AB 804 R	....	325000-	Shaft, Rear Axle, R.H. with Nut (For BR Tractors Equipped with Rear Wheel Brakes)
	AB 807 R	....	325000-	Shaft, Rear Axle, L.H., with Nut (For BR Tractors Equipped with Rear Wheel Brakes)
	AB 1593 R	....	329000-	Shaft, Rear Axle, R.H. with Nut
	AB 1594 R	....	329000-	Shaft, Rear Axle, L.H. with Nut
13	B 350 R	B1000-(——)	325000-	Nut, Rear Axle Shaft
14	A 4231 R	B1000-(——)	325000-	Washer, Final Drive Gear Retaining (Sub. for A2764R)
15	AB 4141 R	....	329000-	Gear, Final Drive, with B2118R Spider (Sub. for B1184R, AB2990R and AB3299R) (BNH, BWH only)
	AB 4140 R	B1000-59999	325000-328999	Gear, Final Drive, with B2118R Spider (Sub. for B179R, AB3095R and AB3311R)
	AB 4140 R	....	325000-	Gear, Final Drive, with B2118R Spider (Sub. for B179R and AB3095R) (For BR Tractors Equipped with Rear Wheel Brakes) (Sub. for AB3311R)
16	A 1892 R	B42200-(——)	....	Nut, Special Hex. on A5290R Stud for Quick Implement Attachment (12 used) (Sub. for AA4963R Pkg. of 25)
17	A 5292 R	B42200-(——)	....	Stud, for Quick Implement Attachment to Rear Axle Housing, 5/8" x 2-1/4" (12 used) (Sub. for C1479R)
	D 488 R	B1000-(——)	325000-	Stud, Rear Axle Housing to Main Case, 1/2" x 2" (2 used)
18	C 1220 R	B1000-(——)	325000-	Pin, Dowel, Rear Axle Housing to Transmission Case (2 used)
19	JD 7760	B1000-(——)	325000-	Fitting, Grease, No. 1612
20	AB 2726 R	B42200-59999	....	Housing, B1174R, Rear Axle, with Two B2190R Spacers, Two B2409R Retainers, Two B2412R Retainers and Two B2408R Felt Washers, Studs and Nuts
	AB 3184 R	....	329000-	Housing, B1336R, Rear Axle, with Studs and Nuts
	AB 2688 R	B1000-42199	....	Housing, B345R, Rear Axle with Studs
	AB 2877 R	B46175-(——)	....	Housing, B1178R Rear Axle, with Studs, Nuts, Retainer and Felt Washers (BNH, BWH only)
	AB 2983 R	B46175-(——)	....	Housing, B1222R, Rear Axle (Narrow Adjustable Tread) (BWH only)
	AB 3179 R	....	325000-	Housing, B669R, Rear Axle, with Studs (For BR Tractors Equipped with Rear Wheel Brakes)
	AB 2725 R	....	325000-328999	Housing, B729R, Rear Axle with Studs

Unstyled Model B final drive (continued). *John Deere Archives*

26 TRACTORS—MODELS "B" AND "BR"-"BO" (NOT STYLED)

FINAL DRIVE

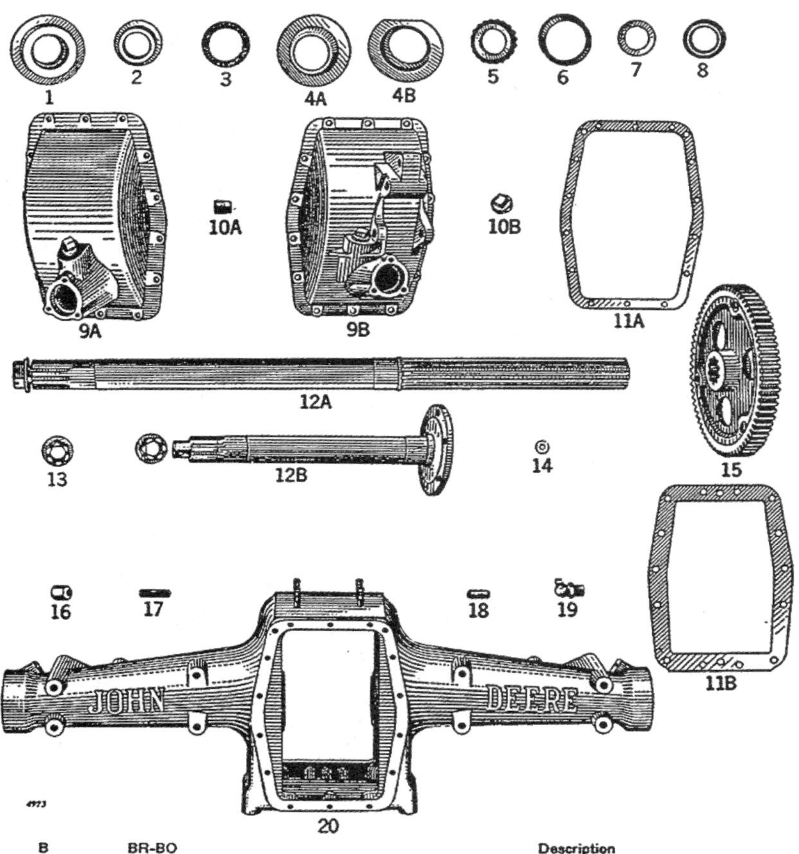

Key	Part No.	B	BR-BO	Description
1	AB 1301 R	B35335–59999	....	Excluder, Dust, Retainer and Bearing Spacer, Rear Axle (BN only)
	B 1182 R	B46175–(——)	....	Excluder, Dust, Rear Axle (BNH, BWH only)
2	B 347 R	B1000–59999	325000–328999	Spacer, Rear Axle Bearing (Sub. for AB4102R)
	B 674 R	....	325000–	Spacer, Rear Axle Bearing (For BR Tractors Equipped with Rear Wheel Brakes) (Sub. for AB4107R)
	B 1180 R	B46175–(——)	....	Spacer, Rear Axle Bearing (BNH, BWH only) (Sub. for AB4103R)
	B 1344 R	....	329000–	Spacer, Rear Axle Bearing (Sub. for AB4106R)
3	AA 666 R	....	325000–	Washer, Felt, Rear Axle Oil Seal (For BR Tractors Equipped with Rear Wheel Brakes)
	B 348 R	B1000–(——)	325000–	Washer, Felt, Rear Axle Oil Seal (Sub. for AB475R)
4A	B 349 R	B1000–59999	....	Retainer, Rear Axle Felt
	B 672 R	....	325000–	Retainer, Rear Axle Felt (For BR Tractors Equipped with Rear Wheel Brakes)
	B 1181 R	B46175–(——)	....	Retainer, Rear Axle Felt (BNH, BWH only)
4B	B 733 R	....	325000–328999	Retainer, Rear Axle Felt
	B 1397 R	....	329000–	Retainer, Rear Axle Felt
5	JD 7242 R	....	325000–	Cone, with Rollers, Rear Axle Bearing, Outer (For BR Tractors Equipped with Rear Wheel Brakes)
	JD 7365 R	....	325000–	Cone, with Rollers, Rear Axle Bearing, Inner (For BR Tractors Equipped with Rear Wheel Brakes)
	JD 7365 R	B1000–59999	325000–328999	Cone, with Rollers, Rear Axle Bearing, Inner
	JD 7366 R	B1000–59999	325000–328999	Cone, with Rollers, Rear Axle Bearing, Outer
	JD 7393 R	....	329000–	Cone, with Rollers, Rear Axle Bearing, Inner (Except B, BN, BW) (B46175–)
	JD 7394 R	....	329000–	Cone, with Rollers, Rear Axle Bearing, Outer (Except B, BN, BW) (B46175–)
6	JD 7272 R	B1000–59999	325000–328999	Cup, Rear Axle Bearing, Inner and Outer
	JD 7272 R	....	325000–	Cup, Rear Axle Bearing, Inner (For BR Tractors Equipped with Rear Wheel Brakes)
	JD 7292 R	....	325000–	Cup, Rear Axle Bearing, Outer (For BR Tractors Equipped with Rear Wheel Brakes)
	JD 7417 R	....	329000–	Cup, Rear Axle Inner and Outer Bearing (BNH, BWH only)
7	B 409 R	B1000–59999	325000–328999	Washer, Rear Axle Oil Seal (Steel)
	B 409 R	....	325000–	Washer, Rear Axle Oil Seal (Steel) (For BR Tractors Equipped with Rear Wheel Brakes)
	B 1183 R	....	329000–	Washer, Rear Axle Oil Seal (BNH, BWH only)
8	B 399 R	....	325000–	Oil Seal, Rear Axle, Inner Bearing (For BR Tractors Equipped with Rear Wheel Brakes) (Sub. for AB718R)
	B 399 R	B1000–59999	325000–328999	Oil Seal, Rear Axle, Inner Bearing (Sub. for AB718R)
	AB 1325 R	B46175–(——)	....	Seal, Oil, Rear Axle Housing, Inner Bearing (BNH, BWH only)
	AB 1326 R	....	329000–	Seal, Oil, Rear Axle, Inner Bearing (Sub. for AB1325R)
9A	AB 2519 R	B1000–(——)	....	Cover, B306R, Rear Axle Housing, with Filler Plug
9B	AB 2520 R	....	325000–	Cover, B769R, Rear Axle Housing, with Filler Plug
10A	15H 239 R	....	330264–	Plug, Pipe, Rear Axle Housing Cover Oil Filler (1")
10B	15H 280 R	....	332092–	Plug, Pipe, Rear Axle Housing Drain
	15H 281 R	B1000–(——)	325000–332091	Plug, Pipe, Rear Axle Housing Drain
	15H 240 R	B1000–(——)	325000–330246	Plug, Pipe, Rear Axle Housing Cover Oil Filler
11A	B 3346 R	B1000–(——)	325000–	Gasket, Rear Axle Cover to Housing (Sub. for B308R)
11B	B 3622 R	B1000–(——)	325000–	Gasket, Rear Axle Housing to Case (Sub. for B351R)
12A	AB 715 R	B11506–59999	....	Shaft, Rear Axle, with Nut
	AB 1278 R	B1000–11505	....	Shaft, Rear Axle, with Nut

PC-676-(2-60)

Unstyled Model B final drive. *John Deere Archives*

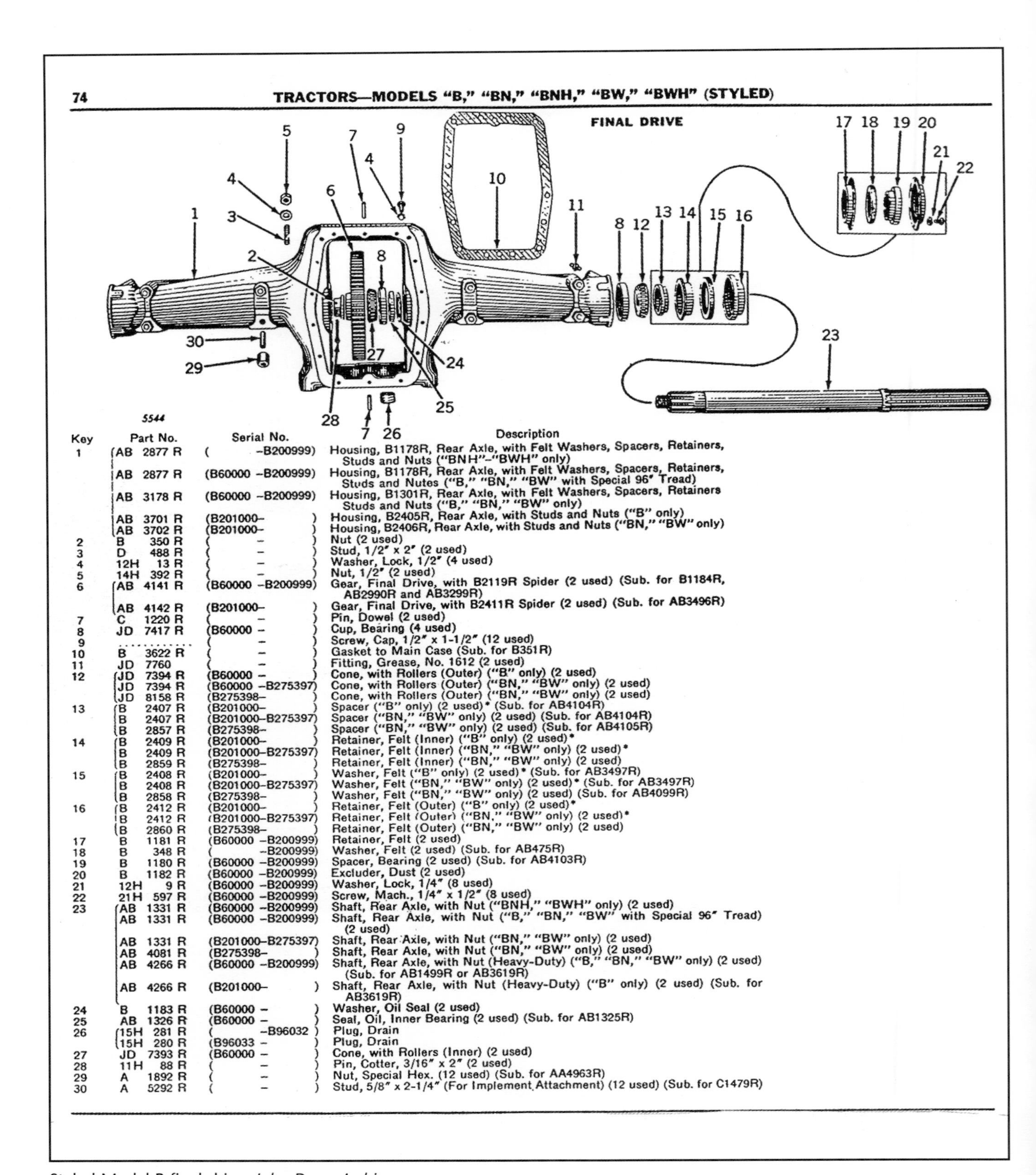

74 TRACTORS—MODELS "B," "BN," "BNH," "BW," "BWH" (STYLED)

FINAL DRIVE

5544

Key	Part No.	Serial No.	Description
1	AB 2877 R	(–B200999)	Housing, B1178R, Rear Axle, with Felt Washers, Spacers, Retainers, Studs and Nuts ("BNH"–"BWH" only)
	AB 2877 R	(B60000 –B200999)	Housing, B1178R, Rear Axle, with Felt Washers, Spacers, Retainers, Studs and Nutes ("B," "BN," "BW" with Special 96" Tread)
	AB 3178 R	(B60000 –B200999)	Housing, B1301R, Rear Axle, with Felt Washers, Spacers, Retainers Studs and Nuts ("B," "BN," "BW" only)
	AB 3701 R	(B201000–)	Housing, B2405R, Rear Axle, with Studs and Nuts ("B" only)
	AB 3702 R	(B201000–)	Housing, B2406R, Rear Axle, with Studs and Nuts ("BN," "BW" only)
2	B 350 R	(–)	Nut (2 used)
3	D 488 R	(–)	Stud, 1/2" x 2" (2 used)
4	12H 13 R	(–)	Washer, Lock, 1/2" (4 used)
5	14H 392 R	(–)	Nut, 1/2" (2 used)
6	AB 4141 R	(B60000 –B200999)	Gear, Final Drive, with B2119R Spider (2 used) (Sub. for B1184R, AB2990R and AB3299R)
	AB 4142 R	(B201000–)	Gear, Final Drive, with B2411R Spider (2 used) (Sub. for AB3496R)
7	C 1220 R	(–)	Pin, Dowel (2 used)
8	JD 7417 R	(B60000 –)	Cup, Bearing (4 used)
9	....	(–)	Screw, Cap, 1/2" x 1-1/2" (12 used)
10	B 3622 R	(–)	Gasket to Main Case (Sub. for B351R)
11	JD 7760	(–)	Fitting, Grease, No. 1612 (2 used)
12	JD 7394 R	(B60000 –)	Cone, with Rollers (Outer) ("B" only) (2 used)
	JD 7394 R	(B60000 –B275397)	Cone, with Rollers (Outer) ("BN," "BW" only) (2 used)
	JD 8158 R	(B275398–)	Cone, with Rollers (Outer) ("BN," "BW" only) (2 used)
13	B 2407 R	(B201000–)	Spacer ("B" only) (2 used)* (Sub. for AB4104R)
	B 2407 R	(B201000–B275397)	Spacer ("BN," "BW" only) (2 used) (Sub. for AB4104R)
	B 2857 R	(B275398–)	Spacer ("BN," "BW" only) (2 used) (Sub. for AB4105R)
14	B 2409 R	(B201000–)	Retainer, Felt (Inner) ("B" only) (2 used)*
	B 2409 R	(B201000–B275397)	Retainer, Felt (Inner) ("BN," "BW" only) (2 used)*
	B 2859 R	(B275398–)	Retainer, Felt (Inner) ("BN," "BW" only) (2 used)
15	B 2408 R	(B201000–)	Washer, Felt ("B" only) (2 used)* (Sub. for AB3497R)
	B 2408 R	(B201000–B275397)	Washer, Felt ("BN," "BW" only) (2 used)* (Sub. for AB3497R)
	B 2858 R	(B275398–)	Washer, Felt ("BN," "BW" only) (2 used) (Sub. for AB4099R)
16	B 2412 R	(B201000–)	Retainer, Felt (Outer) ("B" only) (2 used)*
	B 2412 R	(B201000–B275397)	Retainer, Felt (Outer) ("BN," "BW" only) (2 used)*
	B 2860 R	(B275398–)	Retainer, Felt (Outer) ("BN," "BW" only) (2 used)
17	B 1181 R	(B60000 –B200999)	Retainer, Felt (2 used)
18	B 348 R	(–B200999)	Washer, Felt (2 used) (Sub. for AB475R)
19	B 1180 R	(B60000 –B200999)	Spacer, Bearing (2 used) (Sub. for AB4103R)
20	B 1182 R	(B60000 –B200999)	Excluder, Dust (2 used)
21	12H 9 R	(B60000 –B200999)	Washer, Lock, 1/4" (8 used)
22	21H 597 R	(B60000 –B200999)	Screw, Mach., 1/4" x 1/2" (8 used)
23	AB 1331 R	(B60000 –B200999)	Shaft, Rear Axle, with Nut ("BNH," "BWH" only) (2 used)
	AB 1331 R	(B60000 –B200999)	Shaft, Rear Axle, with Nut ("B," "BN," "BW" with Special 96" Tread) (2 used)
	AB 1331 R	(B201000–B275397)	Shaft, Rear Axle, with Nut ("BN," "BW" only) (2 used)
	AB 4081 R	(B275398–)	Shaft, Rear Axle, with Nut ("BN," "BW" only) (2 used)
	AB 4266 R	(B60000 –B200999)	Shaft, Rear Axle, with Nut (Heavy-Duty) ("B," "BN," "BW" only) (2 used) (Sub. for AB1499R or AB3619R)
	AB 4266 R	(B201000–)	Shaft, Rear Axle, with Nut (Heavy-Duty) ("B" only) (2 used) (Sub. for AB3619R)
24	B 1183 R	(B60000 –)	Washer, Oil Seal (2 used)
25	AB 1326 R	(B60000 –)	Seal, Oil, Inner Bearing (2 used) (Sub. for AB1325R)
26	15H 281 R	(–B96032)	Plug, Drain
	15H 280 R	(B96033 –)	Plug, Drain
27	JD 7393 R	(B60000 –)	Cone, with Rollers (Inner) (2 used)
28	11H 88 R	(–)	Pin, Cotter, 3/16" x 2" (2 used)
29	A 1892 R	(–)	Nut, Special Hex. (12 used) (Sub. for AA4963R)
30	A 5292 R	(–)	Stud, 5/8" x 2-1/4" (For Implement Attachment) (12 used) (Sub. for C1479R)

Styled Model B final drive. *John Deere Archives*

Unstyled Model Bs had brake drum covers as shown, which were not used on the Model As or Gs, or styled Bs after 1940.

Brakes

The Model B row-crop had independent internal expanding brakes. Each brake could be applied independently.

Standard tread Model B brakes fall into two categories. Most BR tractors built before 1938 have a single "service" brake. Independent brakes were available from the start, however, as they were standard equipment on the Model BO (orchard). The standard tread service (single) brakes were of the external contracting type. Independent brakes were internal expanding. Model BI (Industrial) tractors had the single brake, although dual brakes were provided with rubber tires, or could be special ordered. When independent brakes were provided on BI models, there were either individual pedals, or a single lever that operated both brakes, or both the lever and pedals.

Row-crop differential brakes from serial number 1,000 to 96,000 did not change much, if at all. These brakes have a part number B218R cover over the drum. After serial number 96,000 (1941), a different brake was used up to serial number 232,467. To reline or repair this brake, it is necessary to remove the entire brake unit from the tractor. After serial number 232,468 (late 1948), a brake unit was used that was much like that of the Model G. The drum can be removed without removing the brake unit from the tractor.

Speeds in Gears (mph)

Serial Numbers	1st	2nd	3rd	4th	5th	6th	R
1,000–36,814 steel wheels, regular transmission, row-crop	2.2	3.0	4.8	6.3	—	—	3.7
36,815–58,246 steel wheels, regular transmission, row-crop	2.3	3.0	2.9	5.2	—	—	3.8
36,815–58,246 rubber tires, regular transmission, row-crop	2.4	3.1	4.0	5.4	—	—	3.9
14,783–58,246 rubber tires, high-speed transmission (P/N AB1298R), row-crop	2.4	3.1	7.1	9.4	—	—	3.9
54,634–58,246 rubber tires, low-speed transmission (AB1432R), row-crop	1.4	3.4	3.7	6.4	—	—	2.3
54,634–58,246 steel wheels, low-speed transmission (AB1432R), row-crop	1.4	2.3	3.6	6.2	—	—	2.2
325,000–337,514 rubber tires, regular transmission, BR, BO, BI	2.0	3.3	4.3	6.8	—	—	3.5
BO Lindeman Crawlers	1.3	2.0	2.8	4.0	—	2.0	—
60,000–95,184 steel wheels	2.3	3.0	4.0	5.3	—	—	3.8
96,000 and up rubber tires	1.5	2.5	3.5	4.5	5.8	10	2.5

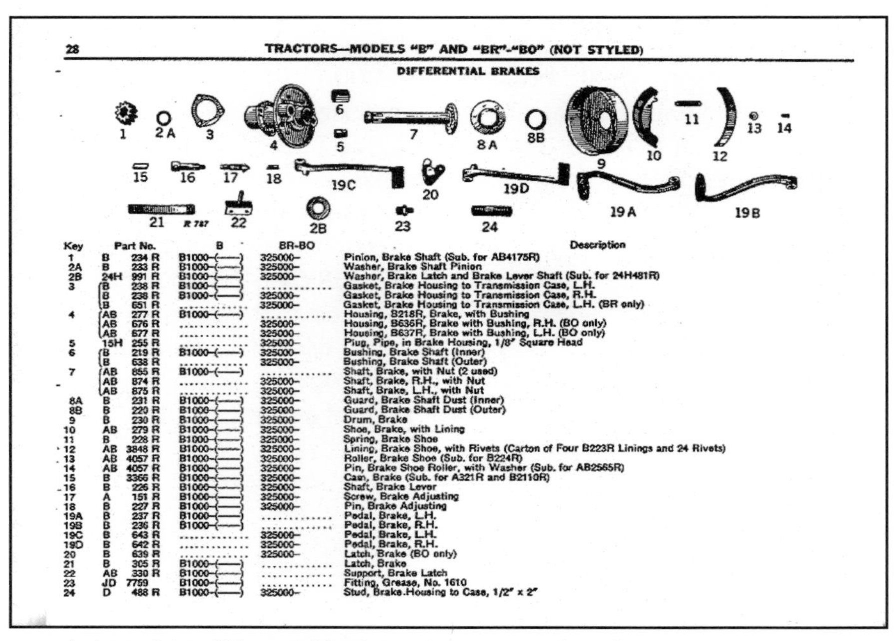

28 TRACTORS—MODELS "B" AND "BR"-"BO" (NOT STYLED)

DIFFERENTIAL BRAKES

Key	Part No.		B	BR-BO	Description
1	B	234 R	B1000–(——)	325000–	Pinion, Brake Shaft (Sub. for AB4175R)
2A	B	233 R	B1000–(——)	325000–	Washer, Brake Shaft Pinion
2B	24H	991 R	B1000–(——)	325000–	Washer, Brake Latch and Brake Lever Shaft (Sub. for 24H481R)
3	B	238 R	B1000–(——)	....	Gasket, Brake Housing to Transmission Case, L.H.
	B	238 R	B1000–(——)	325000–	Gasket, Brake Housing to Transmission Case, R.H.
	B	651 R	....	325000–	Gasket, Brake Housing to Transmission Case, L.H. (BR only)
4	AB	277 R	B1000–(——)	....	Housing, B218R, Brake, with Bushing
	AB	676 R	....	325000–	Housing, B636R, Brake with Bushing, R.H. (BO only)
	AB	677 R	....	325000–	Housing, B637R, Brake with Bushing, L.H. (BO only)
5	15H	255 R	....	325000–	Plug, Pipe, in Brake Housing, 1/8" Square Head
6	B	219 R	B1000–(——)	325000–	Bushing, Brake Shaft (Inner)
	B	638 R	....	325000–	Bushing, Brake Shaft (Outer)
7	AB	855 R	B1000–(——)	....	Shaft, Brake, with Nut (2 used)
	AB	874 R	....	325000–	Shaft, Brake, R.H., with Nut
	AB	875 R	....	325000–	Shaft, Brake, L.H., with Nut
8A	B	231 R	B1000–(——)	325000–	Guard, Brake Shaft Dust (Inner)
8B	B	220 R	B1000–(——)	325000–	Guard, Brake Shaft Dust (Outer)
9	B	230 R	B1000–(——)	325000–	Drum, Brake
10	AB	279 R	B1000–(——)	325000–	Shoe, Brake, with Lining
11	B	228 R	B1000–(——)	325000–	Spring, Brake Shoe
12	AB	3848 R	B1000–(——)	325000–	Lining, Brake Shoe, with Rivets (Carton of Four B223R Linings and 24 Rivets)
13	AB	4057 R	B1000–(——)	325000–	Roller, Brake Shoe (Sub. for B224R)
14	AB	4057 R	B1000–(——)	325000–	Pin, Brake Shoe Roller, with Washer (Sub. for AB2565R)
15	B	3366 R	B1000–(——)	325000–	Cam, Brake (Sub. for A321R and B2110R)
16	B	226 R	B1000–(——)	325000–	Shaft, Brake Lever
17	A	151 R	B1000–(——)	325000–	Screw, Brake Adjusting
18	B	227 R	B1000–(——)	325000–	Pin, Brake Adjusting
19A	B	237 R	B1000–(——)	....	Pedal, Brake, L.H.
19B	B	236 R	B1000–(——)	....	Pedal, Brake, R.H.
19C	B	643 R	....	325000–	Pedal, Brake, L.H.
19D	B	642 R	....	325000–	Pedal, Brake, R.H.
20	B	639 R	....	325000–	Latch, Brake (BO only)
21	B	305 R	B1000–(——)	....	Latch, Brake
22	AB	330 R	B1000–(——)	....	Support, Brake Latch
23	JD	7759	B1000–(——)	....	Fitting, Grease, No. 1610
24	D	488 R	B1000–(——)	325000–	Stud, Brake.Housing to Case, 1/2" x 2"

Unstyled Model B differential brakes. *John Deere Archives*

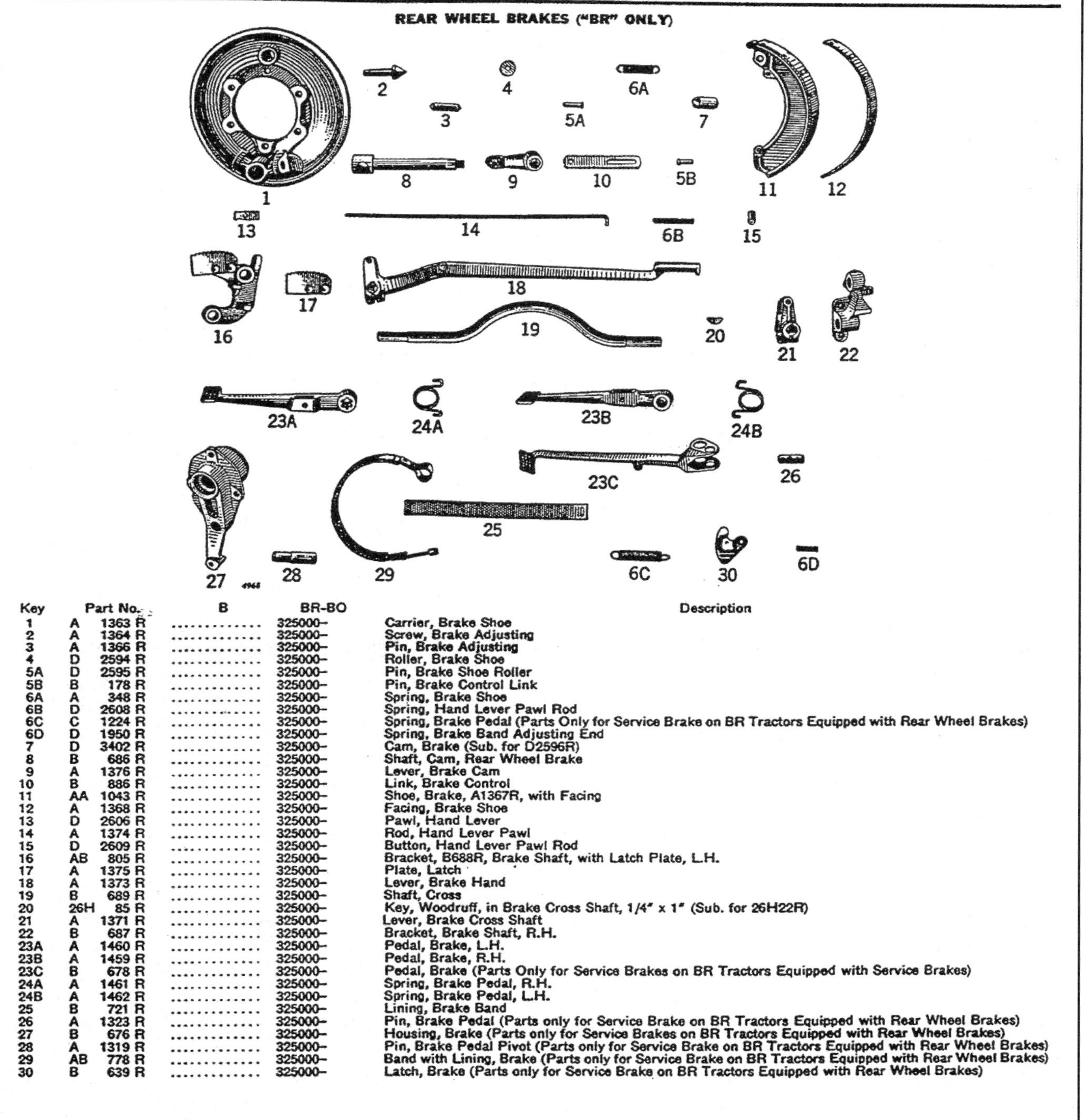

TRACTORS—MODELS "B" AND "BR"-"BO" (NOT STYLED) 29

REAR WHEEL BRAKES ("BR" ONLY)

Key		Part No.	B	BR-BO	Description
1	A	1363 R	....	325000–	Carrier, Brake Shoe
2	A	1364 R	....	325000–	Screw, Brake Adjusting
3	A	1366 R	....	325000–	Pin, Brake Adjusting
4	D	2594 R	....	325000–	Roller, Brake Shoe
5A	D	2595 R	....	325000–	Pin, Brake Shoe Roller
5B	B	178 R	....	325000–	Pin, Brake Control Link
6A	A	348 R	....	325000–	Spring, Brake Shoe
6B	D	2608 R	....	325000–	Spring, Hand Lever Pawl Rod
6C	C	1224 R	....	325000–	Spring, Brake Pedal (Parts Only for Service Brake on BR Tractors Equipped with Rear Wheel Brakes)
6D	D	1950 R	....	325000–	Spring, Brake Band Adjusting End
7	D	3402 R	....	325000–	Cam, Brake (Sub. for D2596R)
8	B	686 R	....	325000–	Shaft, Cam, Rear Wheel Brake
9	A	1376 R	....	325000–	Lever, Brake Cam
10	B	886 R	....	325000–	Link, Brake Control
11	AA	1043 R	....	325000–	Shoe, Brake, A1367R, with Facing
12	A	1368 R	....	325000–	Facing, Brake Shoe
13	D	2606 R	....	325000–	Pawl, Hand Lever
14	A	1374 R	....	325000–	Rod, Hand Lever Pawl
15	D	2609 R	....	325000–	Button, Hand Lever Pawl Rod
16	AB	805 R	....	325000–	Bracket, B688R, Brake Shaft, with Latch Plate, L.H.
17	A	1375 R	....	325000–	Plate, Latch
18	A	1373 R	....	325000–	Lever, Brake Hand
19	B	689 R	....	325000–	Shaft, Cross
20	26H	85 R	....	325000–	Key, Woodruff, in Brake Cross Shaft, 1/4" x 1" (Sub. for 26H22R)
21	A	1371 R	....	325000–	Lever, Brake Cross Shaft
22	B	687 R	....	325000–	Bracket, Brake Shaft, R.H.
23A	A	1460 R	....	325000–	Pedal, Brake, L.H.
23B	A	1459 R	....	325000–	Pedal, Brake, R.H.
23C	B	678 R	....	325000–	Pedal, Brake (Parts Only for Service Brakes on BR Tractors Equipped with Service Brakes)
24A	A	1461 R	....	325000–	Spring, Brake Pedal, R.H.
24B	A	1462 R	....	325000–	Spring, Brake Pedal, L.H.
25	B	721 R	....	325000–	Lining, Brake Band
26	A	1323 R	....	325000–	Pin, Brake Pedal (Parts only for Service Brake on BR Tractors Equipped with Rear Wheel Brakes)
27	B	676 R	....	325000–	Housing, Brake (Parts only for Service Brakes on BR Tractors Equipped with Rear Wheel Brakes)
28	A	1319 R	....	325000–	Pin, Brake Pedal Pivot (Parts only for Service Brake on BR Tractors Equipped with Rear Wheel Brakes)
29	AB	778 R	....	325000–	Band with Lining, Brake (Parts only for Service Brake on BR Tractors Equipped with Rear Wheel Brakes)
30	B	639 R	....	325000–	Latch, Brake (Parts only for Service Brake on BR Tractors Equipped with Rear Wheel Brakes)

Model BR rear brake. *John Deere Archives*

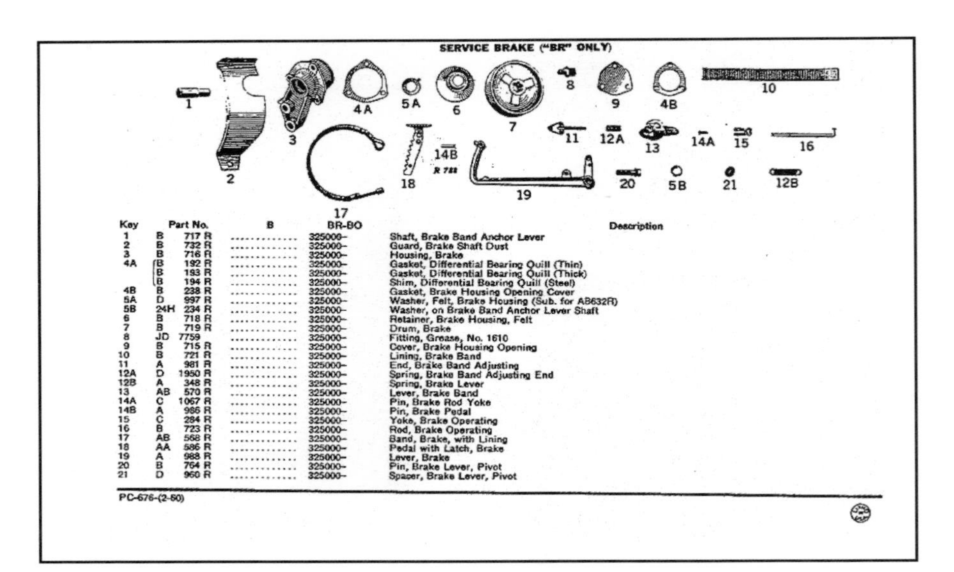

SERVICE BRAKE ("BR" ONLY)

Key	Part No.	B	BR-BO	Description
1	B 717 R	....	325000–	Shaft, Brake Band Anchor Lever
2	B 732 R	....	325000–	Guard, Brake Shaft Dust
3	B 716 R	....	325000–	Housing, Brake
4A	B 192 R	....	325000–	Gasket, Differential Bearing Quill (Thin)
	B 193 R	....	325000–	Gasket, Differential Bearing Quill (Thick)
	B 194 R	....	325000–	Shim, Differential Bearing Quill (Steel)
4B	B 238 R	....	325000–	Gasket, Brake Housing Opening Cover
5A	D 997 R	....	325000–	Washer, Felt, Brake Housing (Sub. for AB632R)
5B	24H 234 R	....	325000–	Washer, on Brake Band Anchor Lever Shaft
6	B 718 R	....	325000–	Retainer, Brake Housing, Felt
7	B 719 R	....	325000–	Drum, Brake
8	JD 7759	....	325000–	Fitting, Grease, No. 1610
9	B 715 R	....	325000–	Cover, Brake Housing Opening
10	B 721 R	....	325000–	Lining, Brake Band
11	A 981 R	....	325000–	End, Brake Band Adjusting
12A	D 1950 R	....	325000–	Spring, Brake Band Adjusting End
12B	A 348 R	....	325000–	Spring, Brake Lever
13	AB 570 R	....	325000–	Lever, Brake Band
14A	C 1067 R	....	325000–	Pin, Brake Rod Yoke
14B	A 986 R	....	325000–	Pin, Brake Pedal
15	C 284 R	....	325000–	Yoke, Brake Operating
16	B 723 R	....	325000–	Rod, Brake Operating
17	AB 568 R	....	325000–	Band, Brake, with Lining
18	AA 586 R	....	325000–	Pedal with Latch, Brake
19	A 988 R	....	325000–	Lever, Brake
20	B 764 R	....	325000–	Pin, Brake Lever, Pivot
21	D 960 R	....	325000–	Spacer, Brake Lever, Pivot

PC-676-(2-60)

Model BR service brake. *John Deere Archives*

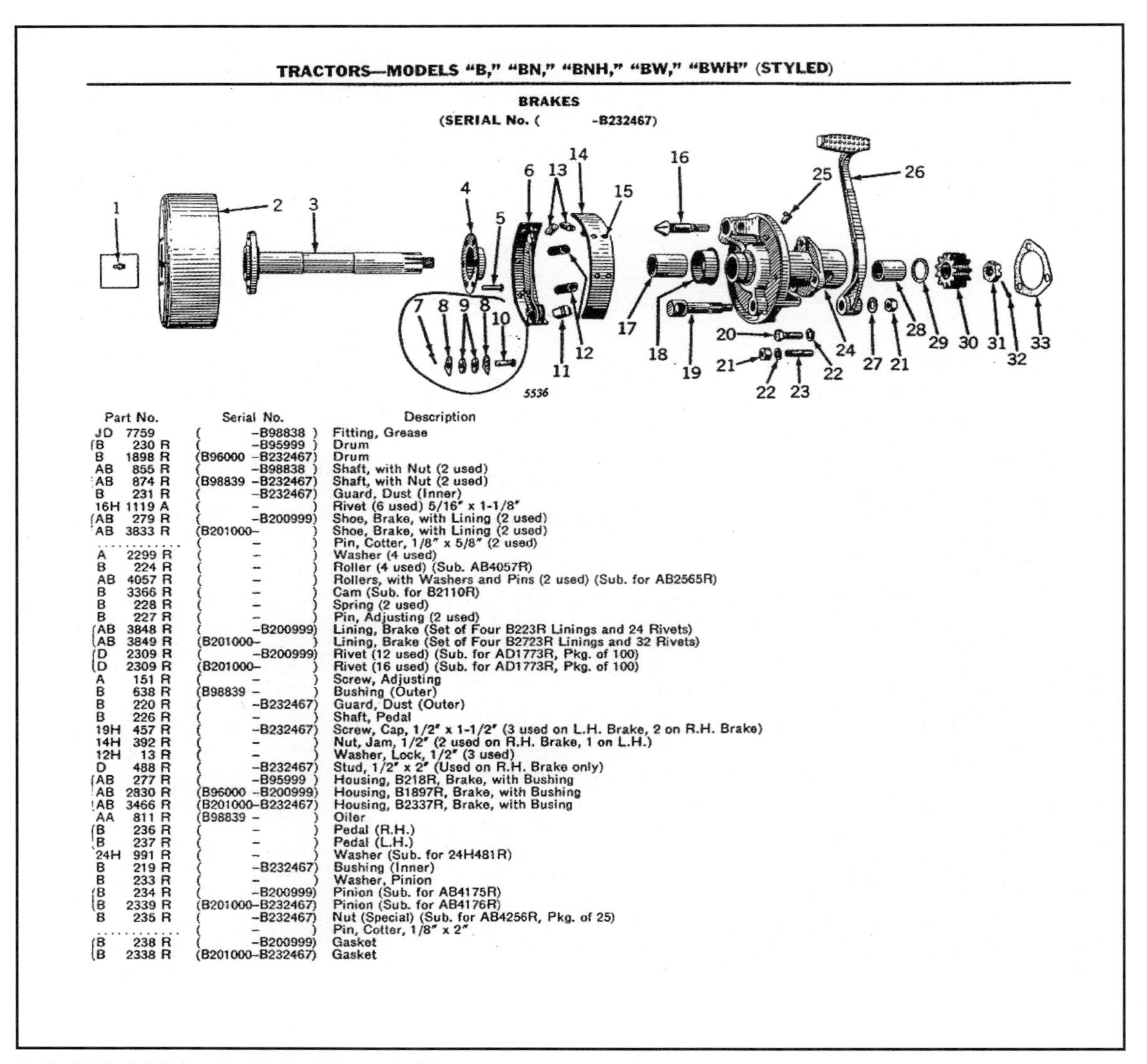

TRACTORS—MODELS "B," "BN," "BNH," "BW," "BWH" (STYLED)

BRAKES

(SERIAL No. (-B232467)

Part No.	Serial No.	Description
JD 7759	(-B98838)	Fitting, Grease
B 230 R	(-B95999)	Drum
B 1898 R	(B96000 -B232467)	Drum
AB 855 R	(-B98838)	Shaft, with Nut (2 used)
AB 874 R	(B98839 -B232467)	Shaft, with Nut (2 used)
B 231 R	(-B232467)	Guard, Dust (Inner)
16H 1119 A	(–)	Rivet (6 used) 5/16" x 1-1/8"
AB 279 R	(-B200999)	Shoe, Brake, with Lining (2 used)
AB 3833 R	(B201000–)	Shoe, Brake, with Lining (2 used)
....	(–)	Pin, Cotter, 1/8" x 5/8" (2 used)
A 2299 R	(–)	Washer (4 used)
B 224 R	(–)	Roller (4 used) (Sub. AB4057R)
AB 4057 R	(–)	Rollers, with Washers and Pins (2 used) (Sub. for AB2565R)
B 3366 R	(–)	Cam (Sub. for B2110R)
B 228 R	(–)	Spring (2 used)
B 227 R	(–)	Pin, Adjusting (2 used)
AB 3848 R	(-B200999)	Lining, Brake (Set of Four B223R Linings and 24 Rivets)
AB 3849 R	(B201000–)	Lining, Brake (Set of Four B2723R Linings and 32 Rivets)
D 2309 R	(-B200999)	Rivet (12 used) (Sub. for AD1773R, Pkg. of 100)
D 2309 R	(B201000–)	Rivet (16 used) (Sub. for AD1773R, Pkg. of 100)
A 151 R	(–)	Screw, Adjusting
B 638 R	(B98839 –)	Bushing (Outer)
B 220 R	(-B232467)	Guard, Dust (Outer)
B 226 R	(–)	Shaft, Pedal
19H 457 R	(-B232467)	Screw, Cap, 1/2" x 1-1/2" (3 used on L.H. Brake, 2 on R.H. Brake)
14H 392 R	(–)	Nut, Jam, 1/2" (2 used on R.H. Brake, 1 on L.H.)
12H 13 R	(–)	Washer, Lock, 1/2" (3 used)
D 488 R	(-B232467)	Stud, 1/2" x 2" (Used on R.H. Brake only)
AB 277 R	(-B95999)	Housing, B218R, Brake, with Bushing
AB 2830 R	(B96000 -B200999)	Housing, B1897R, Brake, with Bushing
AB 3466 R	(B201000-B232467)	Housing, B2337R, Brake, with Busing
AA 811 R	(B98839 –)	Oiler
B 236 R	(–)	Pedal (R.H.)
B 237 R	(–)	Pedal (L.H.)
24H 991 R	(–)	Washer (Sub. for 24H481R)
B 219 R	(-B232467)	Bushing (Inner)
B 233 R	(–)	Washer, Pinion
B 234 R	(-B200999)	Pinion (Sub. for AB4175R)
B 2339 R	(B201000-B232467)	Pinion (Sub. for AB4176R)
B 235 R	(-B232467)	Nut (Special) (Sub. for AB4256R, Pkg. of 25)
....	(–)	Pin, Cotter, 1/8" x 2"
B 238 R	(-B200999)	Gasket
B 2338 R	(B201000-B232467)	Gasket

Styled Model B brakes. John Deere Archives

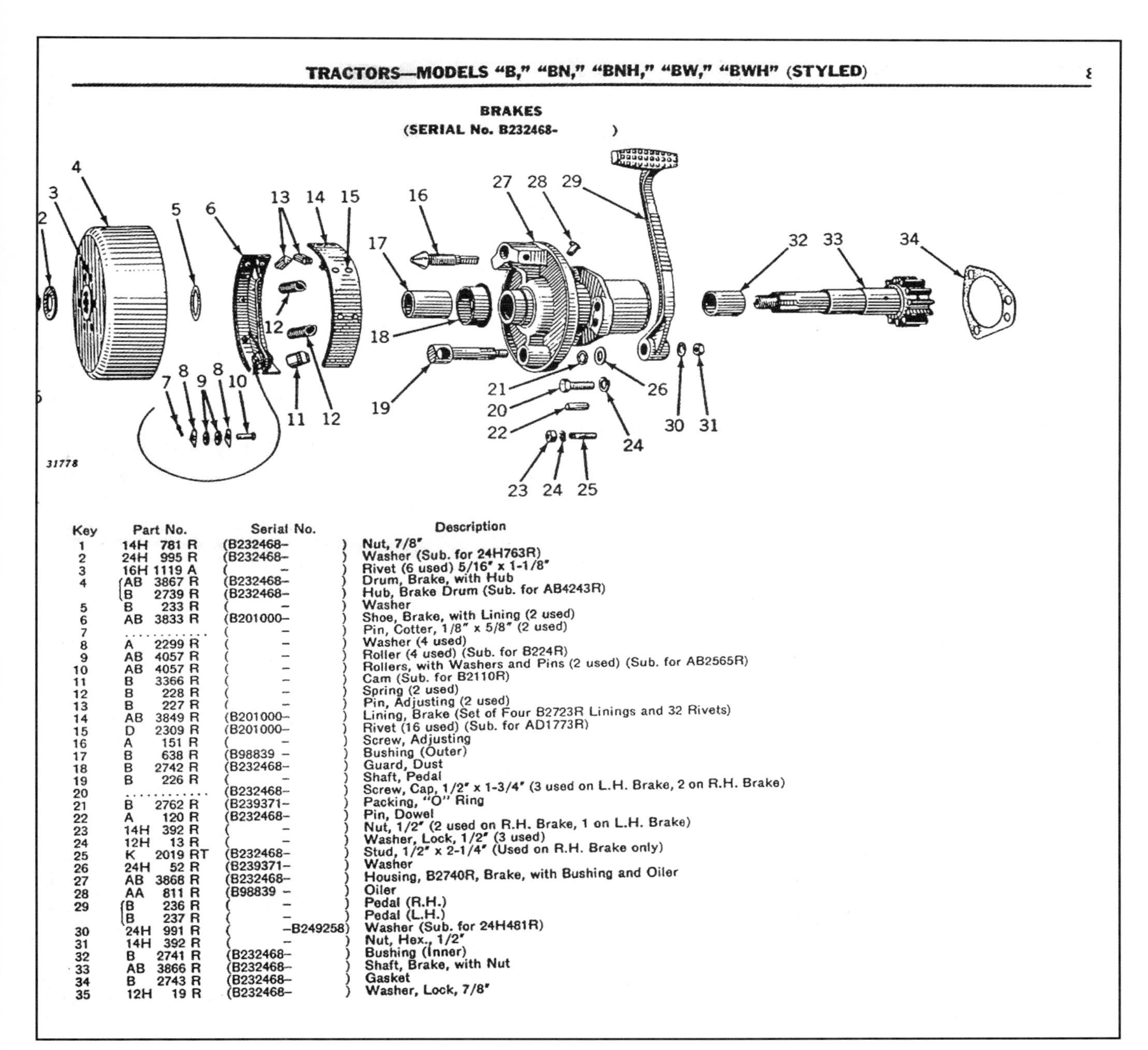

TRACTORS—MODELS "B," "BN," "BNH," "BW," "BWH" (STYLED)

BRAKES
(SERIAL No. B232468-)

Key	Part No.	Serial No.	Description
1	14H 781 R	(B232468-)	Nut, 7/8"
2	24H 995 R	(B232468-)	Washer (Sub. for 24H763R)
3	16H 1119 A	(-)	Rivet (6 used) 5/16" x 1-1/8"
4	AB 3867 R	(B232468-)	Drum, Brake, with Hub
	B 2739 R	(B232468-)	Hub, Brake Drum (Sub. for AB4243R)
5	B 233 R	(-)	Washer
6	AB 3833 R	(B201000-)	Shoe, Brake, with Lining (2 used)
7	....	(-)	Pin, Cotter, 1/8" x 5/8" (2 used)
8	A 2299 R	(-)	Washer (4 used)
9	AB 4057 R	(-)	Roller (4 used) (Sub. for B224R)
10	AB 4057 R	(-)	Rollers, with Washers and Pins (2 used) (Sub. for AB2565R)
11	B 3366 R	(-)	Cam (Sub. for B2110R)
12	B 228 R	(-)	Spring (2 used)
13	B 227 R	(-)	Pin, Adjusting (2 used)
14	AB 3849 R	(B201000-)	Lining, Brake (Set of Four B2723R Linings and 32 Rivets)
15	D 2309 R	(B201000-)	Rivet (16 used) (Sub. for AD1773R)
16	A 151 R	(-)	Screw, Adjusting
17	B 638 R	(B98839 -)	Bushing (Outer)
18	B 2742 R	(B232468-)	Guard, Dust
19	B 226 R	(-)	Shaft, Pedal
20	....	(B232468-)	Screw, Cap, 1/2" x 1-3/4" (3 used on L.H. Brake, 2 on R.H. Brake)
21	B 2762 R	(B239371-)	Packing, "O" Ring
22	A 120 R	(B232468-)	Pin, Dowel
23	14H 392 R	(-)	Nut, 1/2" (2 used on R.H. Brake, 1 on L.H. Brake)
24	12H 13 R	(-)	Washer, Lock, 1/2" (3 used)
25	K 2019 RT	(B232468-)	Stud, 1/2" x 2-1/4" (Used on R.H. Brake only)
26	24H 52 R	(B239371-)	Washer
27	AB 3868 R	(B232468-)	Housing, B2740R, Brake, with Bushing and Oiler
28	AA 811 R	(B98839 -)	Oiler
29	B 236 R	(-)	Pedal (R.H.)
	B 237 R	(-)	Pedal (L.H.)
30	24H 991 R	(-B249258)	Washer (Sub. for 24H481R)
31	14H 392 R	(-)	Nut, Hex., 1/2"
32	B 2741 R	(B232468-)	Bushing (Inner)
33	AB 3866 R	(B232468-)	Shaft, Brake, with Nut
34	B 2743 R	(B232468-)	Gasket
35	12H 19 R	(B232468-)	Washer, Lock, 7/8"

Styled Model B brakes. *John Deere Archives*

Power Take-Off (PTO)

The John Deere Models A and B were the only models to use the one-piece axle housing in 1934. This feature allowed the PTO shaft to protrude from the axle cover almost on the centerline of the tractor. Being on the centerline made the geometry of the implement power shaft virtually the same as that of the hitch, which was also on the centerline. This reduces stress on the universal joints and slip splines.

An open-end tubular PTO guard was used on all Model Bs through serial number 12,011 (1935). This item had the part number A740R. A new A1242R guard was used beginning with serial number 12,012. This guard had a closed, rounded end. The closed-end guard was standard equipment up through serial number 200,999 (1946) on tractors not equipped with the safety shield and flipper cover. The safety shield and flipper cover was "retrofitable" on all standard treads and row-crops that were originally built without them. Therefore, either configuration is now acceptable. However, if you have a 1935 model John Deere B, and can find the open-end guard, so much the better.

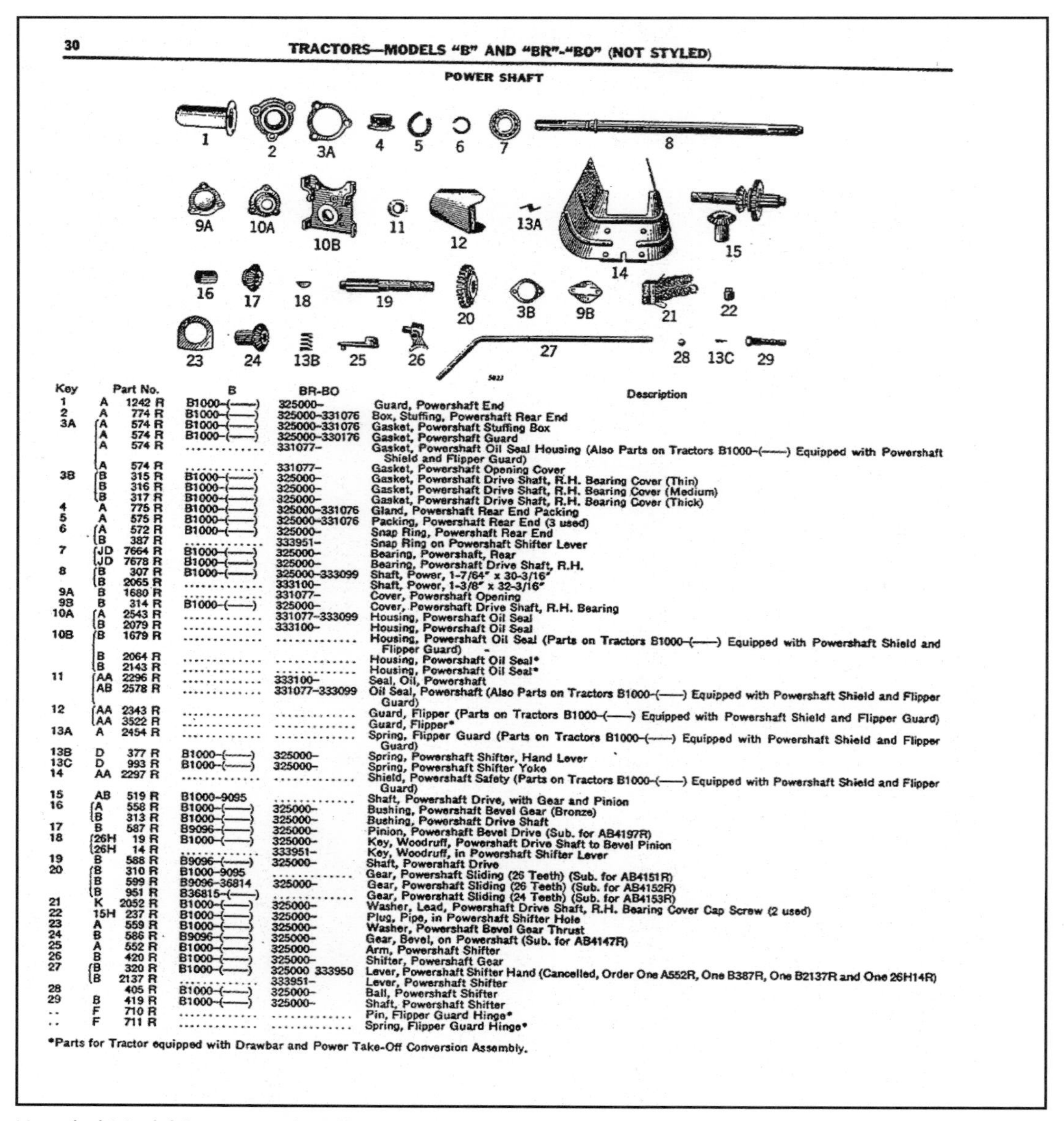

30 TRACTORS—MODELS "B" AND "BR"-"BO" (NOT STYLED)

POWER SHAFT

Key	Part No.	B	BR-BO	Description
1	A 1242 R	B1000-(——)	325000–	Guard, Powershaft End
2	A 774 R	B1000-(——)	325000-331076	Box, Stuffing, Powershaft Rear End
3A	A 574 R	B1000-(——)	325000-331076	Gasket, Powershaft Stuffing Box
	A 574 R	B1000-(——)	325000-330176	Gasket, Powershaft Guard
	A 574 R	....	331077–	Gasket, Powershaft Oil Seal Housing (Also Parts on Tractors B1000-(——) Equipped with Powershaft Shield and Flipper Guard)
	A 574 R	....	331077–	Gasket, Powershaft Opening Cover
3B	B 315 R	B1000-(——)	325000–	Gasket, Powershaft Drive Shaft, R.H. Bearing Cover (Thin)
	B 316 R	B1000-(——)	325000–	Gasket, Powershaft Drive Shaft, R.H. Bearing Cover (Medium)
	B 317 R	B1000-(——)	325000–	Gasket, Powershaft Drive Shaft, R.H. Bearing Cover (Thick)
4	A 775 R	B1000-(——)	325000-331076	Gland, Powershaft Rear End Packing
5	A 575 R	B1000-(——)	325000-331076	Packing, Powershaft Rear End (3 used)
6	A 572 R	B1000-(——)	325000–	Snap Ring, Powershaft Rear End
	B 387 R	....	333951–	Snap Ring on Powershaft Shifter Lever
7	JD 7664 R	B1000-(——)	325000–	Bearing, Powershaft, Rear
	JD 7678 R	B1000-(——)	325000–	Bearing, Powershaft Drive Shaft, R.H.
8	B 307 R	B1000-(——)	325000-333099	Shaft, Power, 1-7/64" x 30-3/16"
	B 2065 R	....	333100–	Shaft, Power, 1-3/8" x 32-3/16"
9A	B 1680 R	....	331077–	Cover, Powershaft Opening
9B	B 314 R	B1000-(——)	325000–	Cover, Powershaft Drive Shaft, R.H. Bearing
10A	A 2543 R	....	331077-333099	Housing, Powershaft Oil Seal
	B 2079 R	....	333100–	Housing, Powershaft Oil Seal
10B	B 1679 R	....	....	Housing, Powershaft Oil Seal (Parts on Tractors B1000-(——) Equipped with Powershaft Shield and Flipper Guard)
	B 2064 R	....	....	Housing, Powershaft Oil Seal*
	B 2143 R	....	....	Housing, Powershaft Oil Seal*
11	AA 2296 R	....	333100–	Seal, Oil, Powershaft
	AB 2578 R	....	331077-333099	Oil Seal, Powershaft (Also Parts on Tractors B1000-(——) Equipped with Powershaft Shield and Flipper Guard)
12	AA 2343 R	....	....	Guard, Flipper (Parts on Tractors B1000-(——) Equipped with Powershaft Shield and Flipper Guard)
	AA 3522 R	....	....	Guard, Flipper*
13A	A 2454 R	....	....	Spring, Flipper Guard (Parts on Tractors B1000-(——) Equipped with Powershaft Shield and Flipper Guard)
13B	D 377 R	B1000-(——)	325000–	Spring, Powershaft Shifter, Hand Lever
13C	D 993 R	B1000-(——)	325000–	Spring, Powershaft Shifter Yoke
14	AA 2297 R	....	....	Shield, Powershaft Safety (Parts on Tractors B1000-(——) Equipped with Powershaft Shield and Flipper Guard)
15	AB 519 R	B1000-9095	....	Shaft, Powershaft Drive, with Gear and Pinion
16	A 558 R	B1000-(——)	325000–	Bushing, Powershaft Bevel Gear (Bronze)
	B 313 R	B1000-(——)	325000–	Bushing, Powershaft Drive Shaft
17	B 587 R	B9096-(——)	325000–	Pinion, Powershaft Bevel Drive (Sub. for AB4197R)
18	26H 19 R	B1000-(——)	325000–	Key, Woodruff, Powershaft Drive Shaft to Bevel Pinion
	26H 14 R	....	333951–	Key, Woodruff, in Powershaft Shifter Lever
19	B 588 R	B9096-(——)	325000–	Shaft, Powershaft Drive
20	B 310 R	B1000-9095	....	Gear, Powershaft Sliding (26 Teeth) (Sub. for AB4151R)
	B 599 R	B9096-36814	325000–	Gear, Powershaft Sliding (26 Teeth) (Sub. for AB4152R)
	B 951 R	B36815-(——)	....	Gear, Powershaft Sliding (24 Teeth) (Sub. for AB4153R)
21	K 2052 R	B1000-(——)	325000–	Washer, Lead, Powershaft Drive Shaft, R.H. Bearing Cover Cap Screw (2 used)
22	15H 237 R	B1000-(——)	325000–	Plug, Pipe, in Powershaft Shifter Hole
23	A 559 R	B1000-(——)	325000–	Washer, Powershaft Bevel Gear Thrust
24	B 586 R	B9096-(——)	325000–	Gear, Bevel, on Powershaft (Sub. for AB4147R)
25	A 552 R	B1000-(——)	325000–	Arm, Powershaft Shifter
26	B 420 R	B1000-(——)	325000–	Shifter, Powershaft Gear
27	B 320 R	B1000-(——)	325000 333950	Lever, Powershaft Shifter Hand (Cancelled, Order One A552R, One B387R, One B2137R and One 26H14R)
	B 2137 R	....	333951–	Lever, Powershaft Shifter
28	405 R	B1000-(——)	325000–	Ball, Powershaft Shifter
29	B 419 R	B1000-(——)	325000–	Shaft, Powershaft Shifter
..	F 710 R	....	....	Pin, Flipper Guard Hinge*
..	F 711 R	....	....	Spring, Flipper Guard Hinge*

*Parts for Tractor equipped with Drawbar and Power Take-Off Conversion Assembly.

Unstyled Model B power take-off. *John Deere Archives*

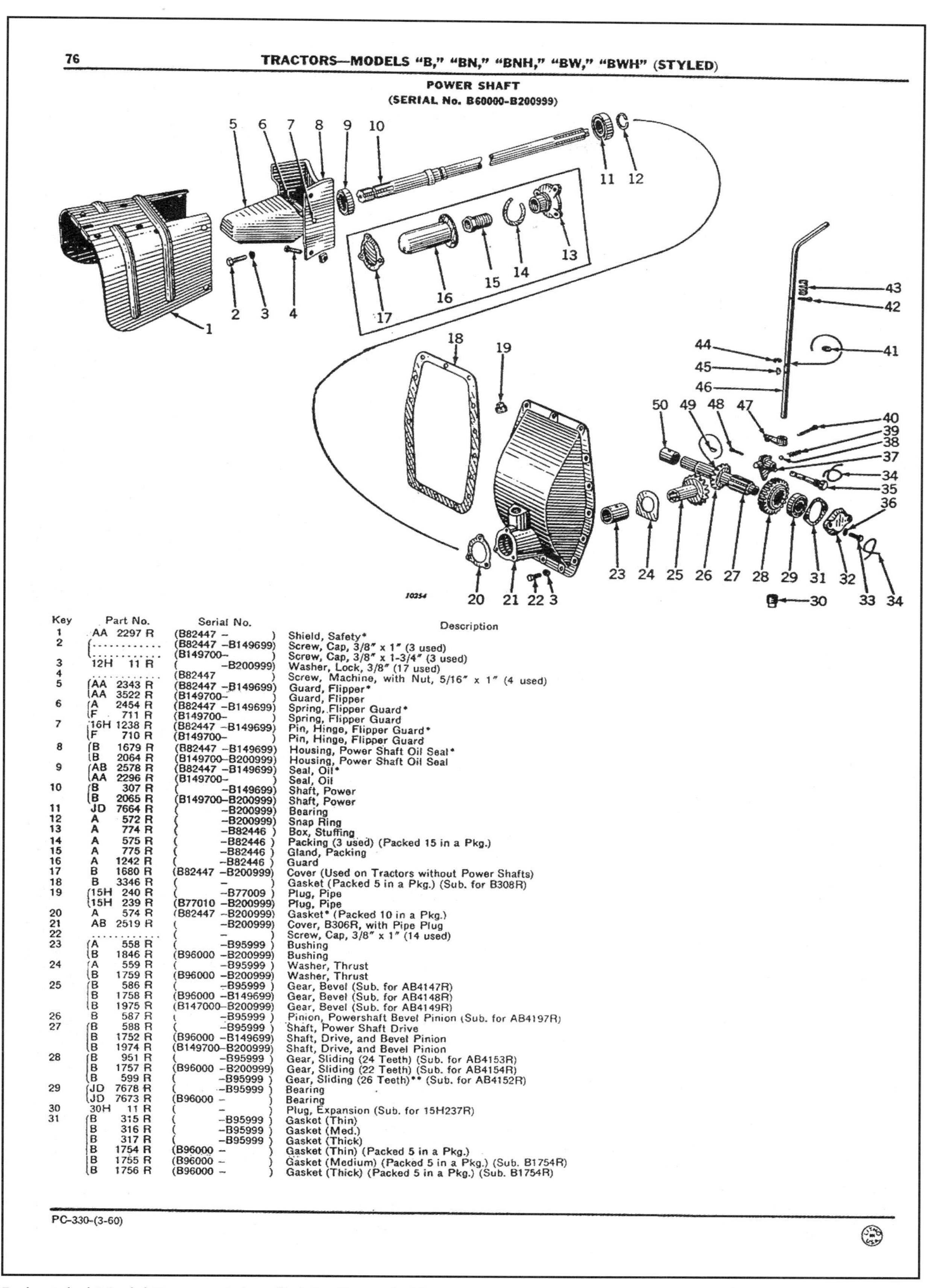

76 TRACTORS—MODELS "B," "BN," "BNH," "BW," "BWH" (STYLED)

POWER SHAFT

(SERIAL No. B60000-B200999)

Key	Part No.	Serial No.	Description
1	AA 2297 R	(B82447 –)	Shield, Safety*
2	....	(B82447 –B149699)	Screw, Cap, 3/8" x 1" (3 used)
	....	(B149700–)	Screw, Cap, 3/8" x 1-3/4" (3 used)
3	12H 11 R	(–B200999)	Washer, Lock, 3/8" (17 used)
4	....	(B82447)	Screw, Machine, with Nut, 5/16" x 1" (4 used)
5	AA 2343 R	(B82447 –B149699)	Guard, Flipper*
	AA 3522 R	(B149700–)	Guard, Flipper
6	A 2454 R	(B82447 –B149699)	Spring, Flipper Guard*
	F 711 R	(B149700–)	Spring, Flipper Guard
7	16H 1238 R	(B82447 –B149699)	Pin, Hinge, Flipper Guard*
	F 710 R	(B149700–)	Pin, Hinge, Flipper Guard
8	B 1679 R	(B82447 –B149699)	Housing, Power Shaft Oil Seal*
	B 2064 R	(B149700–B200999)	Housing, Power Shaft Oil Seal
9	AB 2578 R	(B82447 –B149699)	Seal, Oil*
	AA 2296 R	(B149700–)	Seal, Oil
10	B 307 R	(–B149699)	Shaft, Power
	B 2065 R	(B149700–B200999)	Shaft, Power
11	JD 7664 R	(–B200999)	Bearing
12	A 572 R	(–B200999)	Snap Ring
13	A 774 R	(–B82446)	Box, Stuffing
14	A 575 R	(–B82446)	Packing (3 used) (Packed 15 in a Pkg.)
15	A 775 R	(–B82446)	Gland, Packing
16	A 1242 R	(–B82446)	Guard
17	B 1680 R	(B82447 –B200999)	Cover (Used on Tractors without Power Shafts)
18	B 3346 R	(–)	Gasket (Packed 5 in a Pkg.) (Sub. for B308R)
19	15H 240 R	(–B77009)	Plug, Pipe
	15H 239 R	(B77010 –B200999)	Plug, Pipe
20	A 574 R	(B82447 –B200999)	Gasket* (Packed 10 in a Pkg.)
21	AB 2519 R	(–B200999)	Cover, B306R, with Pipe Plug
22	....	(–)	Screw, Cap, 3/8" x 1" (14 used)
23	A 558 R	(–B95999)	Bushing
	B 1846 R	(B96000 –B200999)	Bushing
24	A 559 R	(–B95999)	Washer, Thrust
	B 1759 R	(B96000 –B200999)	Washer, Thrust
25	B 586 R	(–B95999)	Gear, Bevel (Sub. for AB4147R)
	B 1758 R	(B96000 –B149699)	Gear, Bevel (Sub. for AB4148R)
	B 1975 R	(B147000–B200999)	Gear, Bevel (Sub. for AB4149R)
26	B 587 R	(–B95999)	Pinion, Powershaft Bevel Pinion (Sub. for AB4197R)
27	B 588 R	(–B95999)	Shaft, Power Shaft Drive
	B 1752 R	(B96000 –B149699)	Shaft, Drive, and Bevel Pinion
	B 1974 R	(B149700–B200999)	Shaft, Drive, and Bevel Pinion
28	B 951 R	(–B95999)	Gear, Sliding (24 Teeth) (Sub. for AB4153R)
	B 1757 R	(B96000 –B200999)	Gear, Sliding (22 Teeth) (Sub. for AB4154R)
	B 599 R	(–B95999)	Gear, Sliding (26 Teeth)** (Sub. for AB4152R)
29	JD 7678 R	(–B95999)	Bearing
	JD 7673 R	(B96000 –)	Bearing
30	30H 11 R	(–)	Plug, Expansion (Sub. for 15H237R)
31	B 315 R	(–B95999)	Gasket (Thin)
	B 316 R	(–B95999)	Gasket (Med.)
	B 317 R	(–B95999)	Gasket (Thick)
	B 1754 R	(B96000 –)	Gasket (Thin) (Packed 5 in a Pkg.)
	B 1755 R	(B96000 –)	Gasket (Medium) (Packed 5 in a Pkg.) (Sub. B1754R)
	B 1756 R	(B96000 –)	Gasket (Thick) (Packed 5 in a Pkg.) (Sub. B1754R)

PC-330-(3-60)

Early styled Model B power take-off. *John Deere Archives*

TRACTORS—MODELS "B," "BN," "BNH," "BW," "BWH" (STYLED) 77

POWER SHAFT—Continued
(SERIAL No. B60000-B200999)

Key	Part No.	Serial No.	Description
32	B 314 R	(–B95999)	Cover, Bearing
	B 1753 R	(B96000 –)	Cover, Bearing
33	D 459 R	(–)	Screw, Cap, 3/8" x 1" (Drilled) (2 used)
34	....	(–B200999)	Wire, 16 Gauge x 24" (2 used)
35	B 419 R	(–B95999)	Shaft, Shifter
	B 1761 R	(B96000 –B200999)	Shaft, Shifter
	B 1172 R	(–B95999)	Shaft, Shifter**
36	K 2052 R	(–)	Washer, Lead (2 used) (Packed 50 in a Pkg.) (Sub. for AD1770R)
37	B 420 R	(–B95999)	Shifter, Gear
	B 1760 R	(B96000 –)	Shifter, Gear
	B 1171 R	(–B95999)	Shifter, Gear**
38	405 R	(–)	Ball, Shifter
39	D 993 R	(–)	Spring, Shifter
40	....	(–B168698)	Pin, Cotter, 1/4" x 1-1/2"
41	30H 9 R	(–B200999)	Plug, Welch (Used on Tractors without Power Shaft)
42	11H 80 R	(–)	Pin, Cotter, 3/16" x 1"
43	D 377 R	(–)	Spring
44	B 387 R	(B168699-)	Snap Ring** (Packed 5 in a Pkg.)
45	26H 14 R	(B168699–)	Key, Woodruff**
46	B 320 R	(–B95999)	Lever, Shifter (Sub. one B2137R Lever, one A552R Arm, one B387R Snap Ring and one 26H14R Woodruff Key)
	B 1762 R	(B96000 –B168698)	Lever, Shifter (Sub. one B2136R Lever, one A552 Arm, one B387R Snap Ring and one 26H14R Woodruff Key)
	B 2136 R	(B168699–)	Lever, Shifter°
	B 2137 R	(–B95999)	Lever, Shifter†
47	A 552 R	(–B200999)	Arm, Shifter
48	11H 41 R	(–)	Pin, Cotter, 1/8" x 1"
49	26H 19 R	(–B95999)	Key, Woodruff
50	B 313 R	(–B95999)	Bushing
	B 1844 R	(B96000 –B200999)	Bushing (Sub. for AB3131R)

*Parts from B1000–B82446 equipped with Power Shaft Safety Shield and Flipper Guard.
**Parts from B1000–B95999 when furnished with one B2137R, and one A552R as parts for B320R. Also parts for B96000–B168698 when furnished with one B2136R and one A552R as parts for B1762R.
°Part from B96000–B168698 when furnished with one A552R, one B387R and one 26H14R as parts for B1762R.
†Part from B1000–B95999 when furnished with one A552R, one B387R and one 26H14R as parts for B320R.
°°Used on tractors equipped with high speed gear assemblies.

Late styled Model B power take-off (continued). *John Deere Archives*

TRACTORS—MODELS "B," "BN," "BNH," "BW," "BWH" (STYLED) 79

POWERSHAFT—Continued
(Serial No. B201000-)

Key	Part No.	Serial No.	Description
55	B 2323 R	(B201000–)	Shaft, Shifter
56	B 2322 R	(B201000–)	Shifter, Gear
57	405 R	(–)	Ball, Shifter
58	D 993 R	(–)	Spring, Shifter
59	B 2498 R	(B201000–)	Bushing
60	11H 41 R	(–)	Pin, Cotter, 1/8" x 1"
61	A 552 R	(B201000–)	Arm, Shifter
62	B 2324 R	(B201000–)	Lever, Shifter
63	26H 14 R	(B168699–)	Key, Woodruff
64	B 387 R	(B168699–)	Snap Ring (Packed 5 in a Pkg.)
65	11H 80 R	(–)	Pin, Cotter, 3/16" x 1"
66	D 377 R	(–)	Spring
67	15H 237 R	(–)	Plug, Pipe (Sub. 30H11R)

Late styled Model B power take-off (continued). *John Deere Archives*

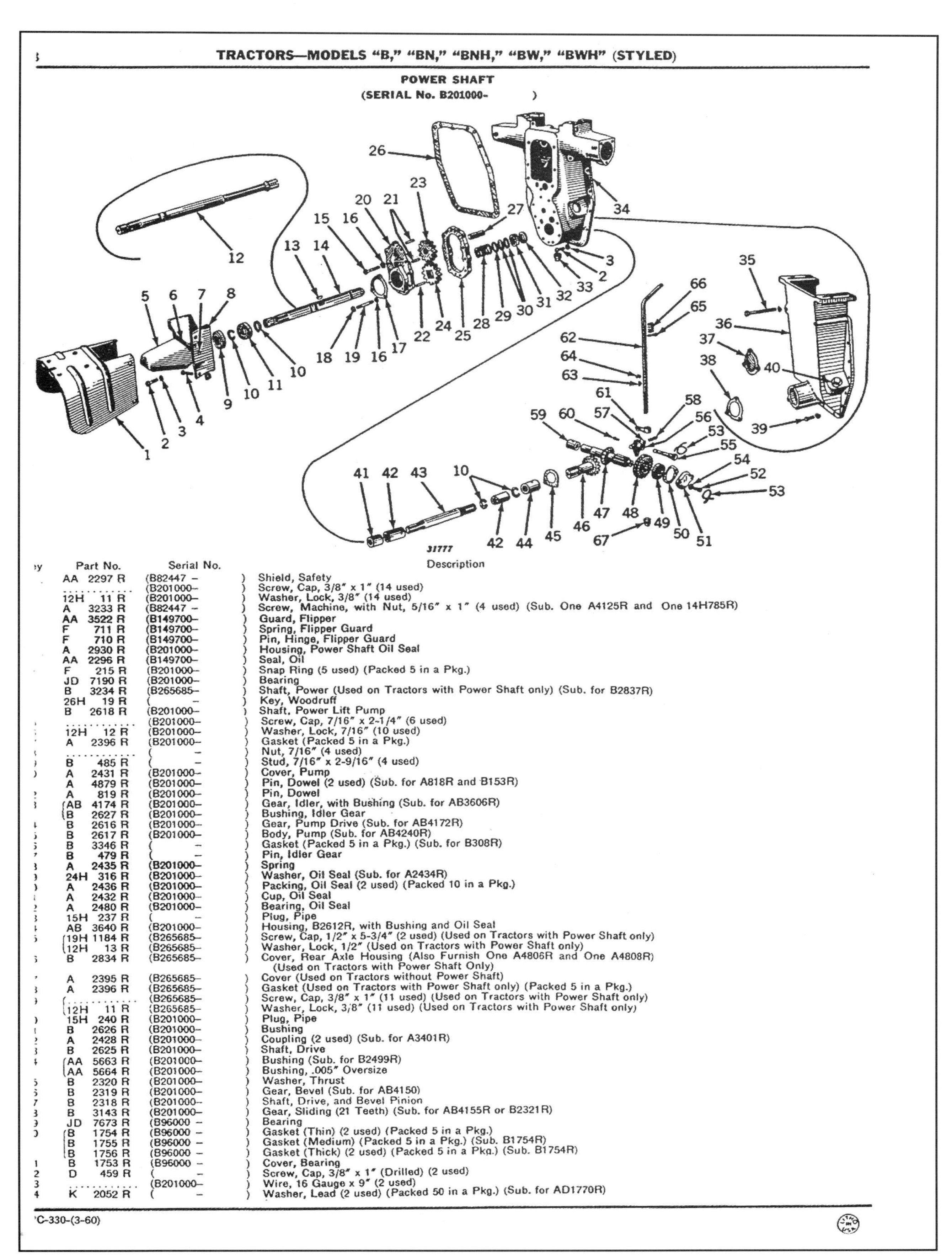

TRACTORS—MODELS "B," "BN," "BNH," "BW," "BWH" (STYLED)

POWER SHAFT

(SERIAL No. B201000-)

Key	Part No.	Serial No.	Description
	AA 2297 R	(B82447 –)	Shield, Safety
	....	(B201000–)	Screw, Cap, 3/8" x 1" (14 used)
	12H 11 R	(B201000–)	Washer, Lock, 3/8" (14 used)
	A 3233 R	(B82447 –)	Screw, Machine, with Nut, 5/16" x 1" (4 used) (Sub. One A4125R and One 14H785R)
	AA 3522 R	(B149700–)	Guard, Flipper
	F 711 R	(B149700–)	Spring, Flipper Guard
	F 710 R	(B149700–)	Pin, Hinge, Flipper Guard
	A 2930 R	(B201000–)	Housing, Power Shaft Oil Seal
	AA 2296 R	(B149700–)	Seal, Oil
	F 215 R	(B201000–)	Snap Ring (5 used) (Packed 5 in a Pkg.)
	JD 7190 R	(B201000–)	Bearing
	B 3234 R	(B265685–)	Shaft, Power (Used on Tractors with Power Shaft only) (Sub. for B2837R)
	26H 19 R	(–)	Key, Woodruff
	B 2618 R	(B201000–)	Shaft, Power Lift Pump
	....	(B201000–)	Screw, Cap, 7/16" x 2-1/4" (6 used)
	12H 12 R	(B201000–)	Washer, Lock, 7/16" (10 used)
	A 2396 R	(B201000–)	Gasket (Packed 5 in a Pkg.)
	....	(–)	Nut, 7/16" (4 used)
	B 485 R	(–)	Stud, 7/16" x 2-9/16" (4 used)
	A 2431 R	(B201000–)	Cover, Pump
	A 4879 R	(B201000–)	Pin, Dowel (2 used) (Sub. for A818R and B153R)
	A 819 R	(B201000–)	Pin, Dowel
	AB 4174 R	(B201000–)	Gear, Idler, with Bushing (Sub. for AB3606R)
	B 2627 R	(B201000–)	Bushing, Idler Gear
	B 2616 R	(B201000–)	Gear, Pump Drive (Sub. for AB4172R)
	B 2617 R	(B201000–)	Body, Pump (Sub. for AB4240R)
	B 3346 R	(–)	Gasket (Packed 5 in a Pkg.) (Sub. for B308R)
	B 479 R	(–)	Pin, Idler Gear
	A 2435 R	(B201000–)	Spring
	24H 316 R	(B201000–)	Washer, Oil Seal (Sub. for A2434R)
	A 2436 R	(B201000–)	Packing, Oil Seal (2 used) (Packed 10 in a Pkg.)
	A 2432 R	(B201000–)	Cup, Oil Seal
	A 2480 R	(B201000–)	Bearing, Oil Seal
	15H 237 R	(–)	Plug, Pipe
	AB 3640 R	(B201000–)	Housing, B2612R, with Bushing and Oil Seal
	19H 1184 R	(B265685–)	Screw, Cap, 1/2" x 5-3/4" (2 used) (Used on Tractors with Power Shaft only)
	12H 13 R	(B265685–)	Washer, Lock, 1/2" (Used on Tractors with Power Shaft only)
	B 2834 R	(B265685–)	Cover, Rear Axle Housing (Also Furnish One A4806R and One A4808R) (Used on Tractors with Power Shaft Only)
	A 2395 R	(B265685–)	Cover (Used on Tractors without Power Shaft)
	A 2396 R	(B265685–)	Gasket (Used on Tractors with Power Shaft only) (Packed 5 in a Pkg.)
	....	(B265685–)	Screw, Cap, 3/8" x 1" (11 used) (Used on Tractors with Power Shaft only)
	12H 11 R	(B265685–)	Washer, Lock, 3/8" (11 used) (Used on Tractors with Power Shaft only)
	15H 240 R	(B201000–)	Plug, Pipe
	B 2626 R	(B201000–)	Bushing
	A 2428 R	(B201000–)	Coupling (2 used) (Sub. for A3401R)
	B 2625 R	(B201000–)	Shaft, Drive
	AA 5663 R	(B201000–)	Bushing (Sub. for B2499R)
	AA 5664 R	(B201000–)	Bushing, .005" Oversize
	B 2320 R	(B201000–)	Washer, Thrust
	B 2319 R	(B201000–)	Gear, Bevel (Sub. for AB4150)
	B 2318 R	(B201000–)	Shaft, Drive, and Bevel Pinion
	B 3143 R	(B201000–)	Gear, Sliding (21 Teeth) (Sub. for AB4155R or B2321R)
	JD 7673 R	(B96000 –)	Bearing
	B 1754 R	(B96000 –)	Gasket (Thin) (2 used) (Packed 5 in a Pkg.)
	B 1755 R	(B96000 –)	Gasket (Medium) (Packed 5 in a Pkg.) (Sub. B1754R)
	B 1756 R	(B96000 –)	Gasket (Thick) (2 used) (Packed 5 in a Pkg.) (Sub. B1754R)
1	B 1753 R	(B96000 –)	Cover, Bearing
2	D 459 R	(–)	Screw, Cap, 3/8" x 1" (Drilled) (2 used)
3	....	(B201000–)	Wire, 16 Gauge x 9" (2 used)
4	K 2052 R	(–)	Washer, Lead (2 used) (Packed 50 in a Pkg.) (Sub. for AD1770R)

'C-330-(3-60)

Late styled Model B power take-off. *John Deere Archives*

Chapter 4

Front System and Steering

General Purpose Model B tractors, from serial number 1,000 to serial number 3,042, used an early style welded-steel frame and four-bolt pedestal. These are known to collectors as four-bolt Bs. After that, a cast frame and an eight-bolt pedestal were used.

As stated in chapter 1, the single front wheel version of the Model B, the BN, was available almost from the beginning of production. John Deere Tractor Company Decision Number 5170 was issued on November 30, 1934, calling for a Model B tractor better suited for beet, lettuce, and other vegetable cultivation. The first 24 of these BNs, with the four-bolt pedestal, are known as Model B Garden Tractors. John Deere production records indicate that around 1,000 unstyled Model BNs, including the Garden Tractors, were built. Steel front wheel size was 22.5in in diameter by 8in wide. The optional tire size was 7.50x10.

It should be noted at this point that it is not possible, without referring to the official build records, to determine the original configuration. It is wise to do some checking before investing in a rare configuration. Ordering a build record from the John Deere archives would be the best way to authenticate a rare model.

Decision Number 5252, issued January 29, 1935, added the adjustable wide front arrangement to the Model B lineup. The main reason for the wide-front, or Model BW, was that only two tracks would be made as the tractor went across the field, lessening the amount of soil compaction. There were other advantages, and other than for cultivation of tall crops, one now wonders why the tricycle arrangement (dual or single front wheel) was so popular. Principal in the other advantages was the ease of plowing, with less attention to steering required by running the right front wheel in the furrow. Also, the increased weight of 233lb at the extreme front added to the stability under heavy pulling loads. The longer wheelbase gave better steering authority and better lateral holding power, although the turning radius was decreased. Conversely, front-mounted implements were cheaper to make and easier to mount on narrow front end models.

The first BW was built February 25, 1935, and was serial number 3,116. The first twenty-five of these (up to serial number 8,974) had front axle adjustments fixed by set screws. After that serial number an improved design with a through-bolt was used. Only about 246 unstyled BWs were built.

Remember, there were both short-frame and long-frame versions of the BN and BW. Most of the limited production was of the short-frame variety, so long-frame unstyled types are even more rare and valuable. There was a part number change for the upper steering shaft bearing for all "General Purpose" Model Bs at the time of the frame-length change. Short-frame models used part number AB214R (casting B36R). Long-frame models used part number AB1253R (casting B1101R).

This photo shows an early Model B, but later than serial number 3,042. Up to serial number 3,042, a pedestal with only four bolts was used. Note the cap and two bolts at the top-front of the pedestal; these do not appear on the Model A.

Model BNH and BWH

August 25, 1937, saw the issuance of Decision Number 7250, calling for a high-clearance version of the Model BN to be known as the BNH. Front ground clearance increased 4.25in by going to a 6.50x16 front tire (with a corresponding yoke change) from the 7.50x10 tire of the BN. The rear tires were mounted to 40in, rather than 36in wheels. Steel wheels were not an option for the Model BNH.

John Deere Model BNH production began with serial number 46,175, built October 1, 1937. Only sixty-six unstyled BNHs were made.

The same day the first BNH was built, Decision Number 7251 came out, describing the Model BWH, another high-clearance version with an adjustable wide front end. Additional height was provided by lengthening the king pin struts (axle knees, as Deere called them). Front axle extension assemblies of seven and thirteen inches were available to provide greater width than the standard BW. With the 7in assembly, tread widths of from 56.625 to 68.625in were possible. With the 13in assembly, tread widths from 68.625 to 80.625in were available.

A variation on the BWH theme was the BWH-40 with the wide-type front axle (as opposed to the tricycle arrangement), but with narrower tread for certain row spacing. Front axle spacing was 42in to 80in(matching that of the rear). Unstyled BW-40 and BWH-40 tractors do not have "John Deere" on the rear axles, as there was insufficient room.

The first BWH was serial number 51,679, and it was built on December 15, 1937. There were only fifty-one unstyled BWHs made. Both BNHs and BWHs used different rear axle housings. The rear axles were also longer and had twelve-groove splines.

Models BNH and BWH continued in the lineup through 1946. After serial number 201,000, when the pressed-steel frame was introduced, high-clearance (H) designations were dropped. It should be noted that none of these were Hi-Crop tractors as were some

Note the acorn nuts (lower) and bolts (upper) for mounting implements. The rounded upper cover (with the John Deere decal) is called the medallion.

of John Deere Model As, which feature a chain drive drop box for the rear axles. Nevertheless, pressed-steel frame BW and BN tractors were available with either 38in or 42in rear wheels. Such BN tractors with 42in rears used a 7.50x16 front tire and corresponding yoke. BW tractors used front spindles that were 2in longer. So even though there were no BNH or BWH designations, there were high-clearance tractors.

Styled John Deere Model BN or BW tractors with pressed-steel frames have special front pedestals that can receive either the single front wheel or wide front ends.

Roll-O-Matic

Roll-O-Matic dual tricycle front end mechanisms were introduced as an option in 1947 at serial number 201,000. The Roll-O-Matic was a system with a pair of gears between the left and right wheels. The wheels were mounted on trailing arm knuckles which were geared together so that when one moved up, the other moved down a like amount. Thus, when one wheel encountered an obstacle, such as a rock, it could move up a maximum of 5in. The opposite wheel would move down a like 5in, maintaining contact with level ground. Because of this differential movement of the wheels, the nose of the tractor only had to go up 2.5in. Actually, the effect was exactly the same as that experienced with a wide front, thereby making the two versions ride equally well.

For row-crop Model Bs, steering wobble or shimmy can be a problem, especially on hard road surfaces. The cause is usually slop between the worm and sector gear in the nose of the tractor. On the older tractors, free play can be adjusted with an eccentric bushing under the sector gear. On later Bs, shim stock can be removed to close up the space. Often, the problem can be lessened by turning the sector gear over. If all these actions fail, it is time for some new parts.

Steering Wheel

Steering wheels for unstyled Bs used flat steel spokes, while styled versions used round steel spokes. Current Deere replacement wheels have covered spokes. These are fine for work tractors, but for correct restoration the original wheel type must be used. See the sources section in the appendix for the addresses of steering wheel restoration services.

An unstyled Model B with the optional adjustable wide front.

A BNH-BWH rear axle housing, which was supposed to create more crop clearance.

The regular Model B rear axle housing.

A BNH yoke. The BNH wheel is 16in high and 6in higher than the standard wheel.

A BN yoke. The 10in wheel is standard with the BN.

A non-Roll-O-Matic front end on a John Deere B.

The operation of the Roll-O-Matic front end is demonstrated above. The front ends of the Model B equipped with Roll-O-Matic sit with their fronts higher than normal, but as you can see, it is necessary to provide clearance. Roll-O-Matic front ends greatly improve the steering and ride in rough going, and add interest to a collectible tractor.

Left, Replacement steering wheels from Deere are functional but not historically correct. This late styled B should have a wheel with exposed rod spokes. Note the two levers on the steering post: The top one is the throttle, the lower one is for controlling the radiator shutters.

Right, this round-spoked steering wheel is correct for styled (both early and late) Model Bs. While this wheel is in good condition, it could be brought to new condition by Minn-Kota, a steering wheel restoration company in Milbank, South Dakota.

Left, this flat-spoked steering wheel is correct for unstyled Model Bs, and was restored by Minn-Kota (see appendix).

38 TRACTORS—MODELS "B" AND "BR"-"BO" (NOT STYLED)

FRONT AXLE

Key	Part No.		B	BR-BO	Description
1A	A	880 R	B1000-(——)	....	Pin, Front Axle Pivot (Front) (BW only)
	A	881 R	B1000-(——)	....	Pin, Front Axle Pivot (Rear) (BW only)
	B	816 R	....	325000-	Pin, Front Axle Pivot
1B	B	817 R	....	325000-	Pin, Front Axle Pivot Pin (Drilled)
1C	B	809 R	....	325000-	Pin, Spindle
1D	F	1743 R	B8974-(——)	....	Pin, Thrust Washer Anchor (BW only) (Sub. for D186R)
2A	B	818 R	....	325000-	Bolt, Taper, Spindle Pin
2B	A	1101 R	B8974-(——)	....	Bolt, Front Axle Lock (BW only)
3	AB	870 R	....	325000-	Knuckle, Front Wheel, with Bushings, Dust Excluders and Studs
4	B	811 R	....	325000-	Axle, Front
5	D	1881 R	....	325000-	Cap, Dust Knuckle
6A	B	810 R	....	325000-	Washer, Spindle Pin
6B	A	561 R	B1000-(——)	....	Washer on Front Axle Pivot Pin (Rear) (BW only)
	D	2629 R	....	325000-	Washer, Radius Rod Pivot
6C	A	890 R	B1000-(——)	....	Washer, Front Wheel Knuckle Thrust (BW only)
7A	A	876 R	B1000-(——)	....	Bushing, Front Axle Pivot Pin (Front) (BW only)
	A	882 R	B1000-(——)	....	Bushing, Front Axle Pin (Rear) (BW only)
	B	815 R	....	325000-	Bushing, Radius Rod Pivot
	B	842 R	....	325000-	Bushing, Front Wheel Knuckle (4 used)
7B	A	877 R	B1000-(——)	....	Bushing, Knuckle Pin (4 used) (BW only) (Sub. for AB5539R)
8	B	814 R	....	325000-	Stud, Radius Rod Pivot, 3/4" x 3-3/4"
	C	1494 R	B51679-(——)	....	Stud, Front Axle Housing, Extension, 5/8" x 2-7/8" (BWH only)
9A	JD	7759	....	325000-	Fitting, Grease, No. 1610, Front Axle and Knuckle (5 used)
	JD	7759	B1000-(——)	....	Fitting, Grease, No. 1610, in Front Axle Pivot Pin (BW only)
	JD	7759	B1000-(——)	....	Fitting, Grease, No. 1610, in Front Axle Knee (BW only)
9B	JD	7760	....	325000-	Fitting, Grease, No. 1612, Radius Rod Pivot
10A	A	886 R	B1000-8973	....	Screw, Lock, Tapered (BW only)
10B	B	550 R	B1000-(——)	....	Screw, Front Axle Lock Plate (BN only)
11	AA	3505 R	B1000-(——)	....	Spindle, Knuckle, with Nuts (BW only)
	AB	3134 R	B51679-(——)	....	Spindle, with Nut (BWH only)
12	AA	1168 R	B1000-(——)	....	Knuckle, with Spindle and Dust Excluders (BW, and BWH only)
	AB	1396 R	B51679-(——)	....	Knuckle, with Spindle, Dust Excluder, Nut and Screw (BWH only)
13	A	887 R	B1000-(——)	....	U-Bolt, Front Axle (BW only)
14	AA	649 R	B1000-8973	....	Housing, A879R, Front Axle, with Pivot Pins (BW only)
	AA	729 R	B8974-(——)	....	Housing, A1100R, Front Axle, with Pivot Pins (BW only)
	AB	1354 R	B41679-(——)	....	Housing, B1207R, Front Axle, with Pivot Pins (BWH only)
15	AB	618 R	....	325000-	Rod, Radius, with Pivot
16A	AB	429 R	B1000-1803	....	Axle, Front, with Bearing Spacer (BN only)
16B	AB	411 R	B1804-(——)	....	Axle, Front, with Bearing Spacer (BN only)
17	B	547 R	B1804-(——)	....	Spacer, Front Axle Bearing (BN only)
18A	B	548 R	B1804-(——)	....	Nut, Front Axle Bearing Adjusting (BN only)
18B	B	551 R	B1000-(——)	....	Nut, Front Axle (BN only)
19	B	549 R	B1000-(——)	....	Plate, Lock Front Axle Nut (BN only)

PC-676-(2-60)

Unstyled Model B front axle. *John Deere Archives*

TRACTORS—MODELS "B" AND "BR"-"BO" (NOT STYLED) 39

FRONT AXLE—Continued

Key	Part No.		B	BR-BO	Description
20	AB	452 R	B1000-(——)	....	Bracket, B574R, Front Axle Pivot, with Bushing (BW only)
21A	AA	730 R	B8974-(——)	....	Knee with Bushing and Pin, Front Axle (BW only)
	AB	1355 R	B51679-(——)	....	Knee with Bushings, Front Axle (BWH only)
21B	AA	650 R	B1000-8973	....	Knee with Bushings, Front Axle (BW only)
(Parts listed below are not illustrated.)					
	AB	1352 R	B51679-(——)	....	Housing Extension, B1210R, Front Axle, Short (BWH only)
	AB	1353 R	B51679-(——)	....	Housing Extension, B1211R, Front Axle, Long (BWH only)

Unstyled Model B front axle (continued). *John Deere Archives*

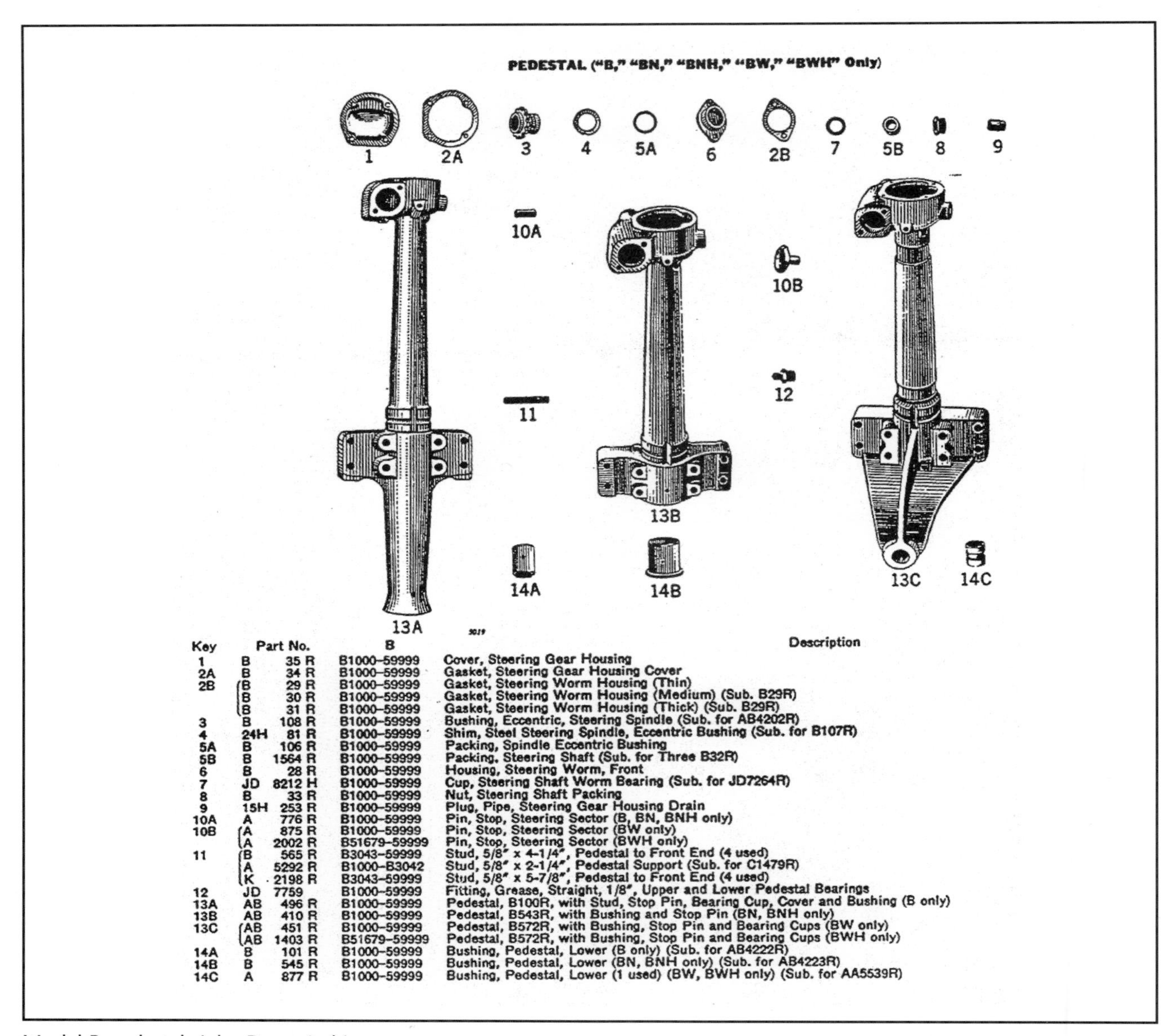

Key	Part No.		B	Description
1	B	35 R	B1000–59999	Cover, Steering Gear Housing
2A	B	34 R	B1000–59999	Gasket, Steering Gear Housing Cover
2B	B	29 R	B1000–59999	Gasket, Steering Worm Housing (Thin)
	B	30 R	B1000–59999	Gasket, Steering Worm Housing (Medium) (Sub. B29R)
	B	31 R	B1000–59999	Gasket, Steering Worm Housing (Thick) (Sub. B29R)
3	B	108 R	B1000–59999	Bushing, Eccentric, Steering Spindle (Sub. for AB4202R)
4	24H	81 R	B1000–59999	Shim, Steel Steering Spindle, Eccentric Bushing (Sub. for B107R)
5A	B	106 R	B1000–59999	Packing, Spindle Eccentric Bushing
5B	B	1564 R	B1000–59999	Packing, Steering Shaft (Sub. for Three B32R)
6	B	28 R	B1000–59999	Housing, Steering Worm, Front
7	JD	8212 H	B1000–59999	Cup, Steering Shaft Worm Bearing (Sub. for JD7264R)
8	B	33 R	B1000–59999	Nut, Steering Shaft Packing
9	15H	253 R	B1000–59999	Plug, Pipe, Steering Gear Housing Drain
10A	A	776 R	B1000–59999	Pin, Stop, Steering Sector (B, BN, BNH only)
10B	A	875 R	B1000–59999	Pin, Stop, Steering Sector (BW only)
	A	2002 R	B51679–59999	Pin, Stop, Steering Sector (BWH only)
11	B	565 R	B3043–59999	Stud, 5/8" x 4-1/4", Pedestal to Front End (4 used)
	A	5292 R	B1000–B3042	Stud, 5/8" x 2-1/4", Pedestal Support (Sub. for C1479R)
	K	2198 R	B3043–59999	Stud, 5/8" x 5-7/8", Pedestal to Front End (4 used)
12	JD	7759	B1000–59999	Fitting, Grease, Straight, 1/8", Upper and Lower Pedestal Bearings
13A	AB	496 R	B1000–59999	Pedestal, B100R, with Stud, Stop Pin, Bearing Cup, Cover and Bushing (B only)
13B	AB	410 R	B1000–59999	Pedestal, B543R, with Bushing and Stop Pin (BN, BNH only)
13C	AB	451 R	B1000–59999	Pedestal, B572R, with Bushing, Stop Pin and Bearing Cups (BW only)
	AB	1403 R	B51679–59999	Pedestal, B572R, with Bushing, Stop Pin and Bearing Cups (BWH only)
14A	B	101 R	B1000–59999	Bushing, Pedestal, Lower (B only) (Sub. for AB4222R)
14B	B	545 R	B1000–59999	Bushing, Pedestal, Lower (BN, BNH only) (Sub. for AB4223R)
14C	A	877 R	B1000–59999	Bushing, Pedestal, Lower (1 used) (BW, BWH only) (Sub. for AA5539R)

Model B pedestal. *John Deere Archives*

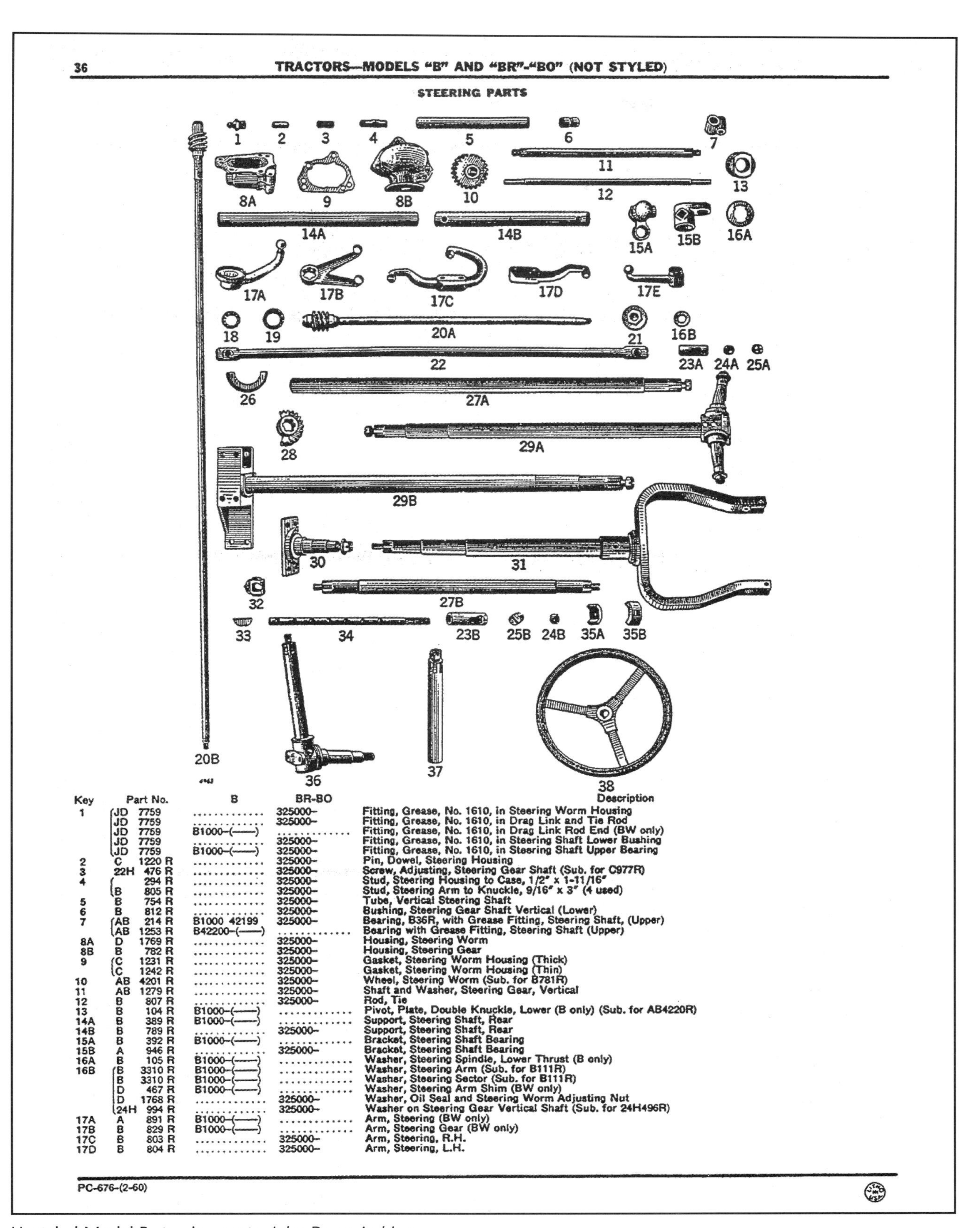

36 TRACTORS—MODELS "B" AND "BR"-"BO" (NOT STYLED)

STEERING PARTS

Key	Part No.	B	BR-BO	Description
1	JD 7759	....	325000–	Fitting, Grease, No. 1610, in Steering Worm Housing
	JD 7759	....	325000–	Fitting, Grease, No. 1610, in Drag Link and Tie Rod
	JD 7759	B1000–(——)	....	Fitting, Grease, No. 1610, in Drag Link Rod End (BW only)
	JD 7759	....	325000–	Fitting, Grease, No. 1610, in Steering Shaft Lower Bushing
	JD 7759	B1000–(——)	325000–	Fitting, Grease, No. 1610, in Steering Shaft Upper Bearing
2	C 1220 R	....	325000–	Pin, Dowel, Steering Housing
3	22H 476 R	....	325000–	Screw, Adjusting, Steering Gear Shaft (Sub. for C977R)
4	294 R	....	325000–	Stud, Steering Housing to Case, 1/2" x 1-11/16"
	B 805 R	....	325000–	Stud, Steering Arm to Knuckle, 9/16" x 3" (4 used)
5	B 754 R	....	325000–	Tube, Vertical Steering Shaft
6	B 812 R	....	325000–	Bushing, Steering Gear Shaft Vertical (Lower)
7	AB 214 R	B1000 42199	325000–	Bearing, B36R, with Grease Fitting, Steering Shaft, (Upper)
	AB 1253 R	B42200–(——)	....	Bearing with Grease Fitting, Steering Shaft (Upper)
8A	D 1769 R	....	325000–	Housing, Steering Worm
8B	B 782 R	....	325000–	Housing, Steering Gear
9	C 1231 R	....	325000–	Gasket, Steering Worm Housing (Thick)
	C 1242 R	....	325000–	Gasket, Steering Worm Housing (Thin)
10	AB 4201 R	....	325000–	Wheel, Steering Worm (Sub. for B781R)
11	AB 1279 R	....	325000–	Shaft and Washer, Steering Gear, Vertical
12	B 807 R	....	325000–	Rod, Tie
13	B 104 R	B1000–(——)	....	Pivot, Plate, Double Knuckle, Lower (B only) (Sub. for AB4220R)
14A	B 389 R	B1000–(——)	....	Support, Steering Shaft, Rear
14B	B 789 R	....	325000–	Support, Steering Shaft, Rear
15A	B 392 R	B1000–(——)	....	Bracket, Steering Shaft Bearing
15B	A 946 R	....	325000–	Bracket, Steering Shaft Bearing
16A	B 105 R	B1000–(——)	....	Washer, Steering Spindle, Lower Thrust (B only)
16B	B 3310 R	B1000–(——)	....	Washer, Steering Arm (Sub. for B111R)
	B 3310 R	B1000–(——)	....	Washer, Steering Sector (Sub. for B111R)
	D 467 R	B1000–(——)	....	Washer, Steering Arm Shim (BW only)
	D 1768 R	....	325000–	Washer, Oil Seal and Steering Worm Adjusting Nut
	24H 994 R	....	325000–	Washer on Steering Gear Vertical Shaft (Sub. for 24H496R)
17A	A 891 R	B1000–(——)	....	Arm, Steering (BW only)
17B	B 829 R	B1000–(——)	....	Arm, Steering Gear (BW only)
17C	B 803 R	....	325000–	Arm, Steering, R.H.
17D	B 804 R	....	325000–	Arm, Steering, L.H.

PC-676–(2-60)

Unstyled Model B steering parts. *John Deere Archives*

TRACTORS—MODELS "B" AND "BR"-"BO" (NOT STYLED) 37

STEERING PARTS—Continued

Key	Part No.	B	BR-BO	Description
17E	B 788 R	....	325000–	Arm, Steering Gear
	AB 4685 R	B51679–(——)	....	Arm, Steering, R.H. (BWH only) (Sub. for B1236R)
	AB 4686 R	B51679–(——)	....	Arm, Steering, L.H. (BWH only) (Sub. for B1204R)
18	JD 7205 R	....	325000–	Roller Assembly, Steering Worm
	JD 7364 R	B1000–59999	....	Cone, with Rollers Steering Shaft Worm
19	JD 7253 R	....	325000–	Cup, Steering Worm Bearing
	JD 8212 R	B1000–59999	....	Cup, Steering Worm Bearing (Sub. for JD7264R)
20A	AA 567 R	....	325000–	Shaft, Steering with Worm
20B	AB 212 R	B1000–42199	....	Shaft, Steering with Worm
	AB 1257 R	B42200–59999	....	Shaft and Worm, Steering
21	D 1766 R	....	325000–	Nut, Adjusting, Steering Worm
22	AB 644 R	....	325000–	Link, Drag
23A	B 808 R	....	325000–	End, Tie Rod
23B	H 982 R	B1000–(——)	....	End, Drag Link Rod (BW only) (Sub. for C1109R)
24A	B 786 R	....	325000–	Bearing, Ball Stud, Drag Link and Tie Rod
24B	C 838 R	B1000–(——)	....	Bearing, Ball Stud (BW only)
25A	B 787 R	....	325000–	Plug, Screw, Drag Link and Tie Rod
25B	C 840 R	B1000–(——)	....	Plug, Screw, Drag Link End (BW only)
26	A 1424 R	B24657–(——)	326452–	Excluder, Dust, Front Wheel (BW, BR and BO only)
	B 888 R	B26055–(——)	....	Excluder, Dust, Front Wheel (B only)
	B 888 R	B1000–(——)	....	Excluder, Dust, Front Wheel (Offset)
27A	AB 3133 R	B1000–(——)	....	Spindle, Steering, with Nut (B only)
27B	AB 1281 R	B1000–59999	....	Spindle, Steering (BW only)
28	B 110 R	B1000–59999	....	Sector, Steering (Sub. for AB4198R)
29A	AB 243 R	B1000–800	....	Knuckle, Double, with Spindle (B only)
	AB 863 R	B8001–(——)	....	Knuckle, Double, with Spindle, Dust Excluder and Hub Caps (B only)
29B	AB 1439 R	B1000–(——)	....	Knuckle Hub with Spindle (Offset)
30	AB 1433 R	B1000–(——)	....	Knuckle with Dust Excluder (Offset)
31	AB 408 R	B1000–(——)	....	Yoke and Spindle, Front Wheel (BN only)
	AB 1320 R	B46175–(——)	....	Yoke, Front Wheel (BNH only)
32	AC 352 R	B1000–(——)	....	Cover, Drag Link, Dust (BW only)
33	26H 17 R	B1000–(——)	325000–	Key, Steering Wheel
34	A 892 R	B1000–(——)	....	Rod, Drag Link (BW only)
	B 1205 R	B51679–(——)	....	Rod, Drag Link, 13-7/8" Long (BWH only)
	B 1206 R	B51679–(——)	....	Rod, Drag Link, L.H., 11" Long (BWH only)
	B 1212 R	B51679–(——)	....	Rod, Drag Link, R.H., 20-1/2" Long (Used with AB1353R) (BWH only)
	B 1221 R	B51679–(——)	....	Rod, Drag Link, L.H., 17-3/8" Long (Used with AB1353R) (BWH only)
	B 1221 R	B51679–(——)	....	Rod, Drag Link, R.H. and L.H., 17-3/8" Long (Used with AB1352R) (BWH only)
35A	A 893 R	B1000–50849	....	Clamp Half, Drag Link (8 used) (BW only)
35B	B 1233 R	B50850–(——)	....	Clamp Half, Drag Link Lower (BW only)
36	AA 1168 R	B1000–(——)	....	Knuckle with Spindle and Dust Excluder (BW only)
	AB 1396 R	B51679–(——)	....	Knuckle with Spindle and Dust Excluder (BWH only)
37	AA 3505 R	B1000–(——)	....	Spindle, Knuckle, with Nut (BW only)
	AB 3134 R	B51679–(——)	....	Spindle, Knuckle, with Nut (BWH only)
38	AA 380 R	B1000–(——)	325000–	Wheel, Steering (Sub. for AB218R)

Unstyled Model B steering parts (continued). *John Deere Archives*

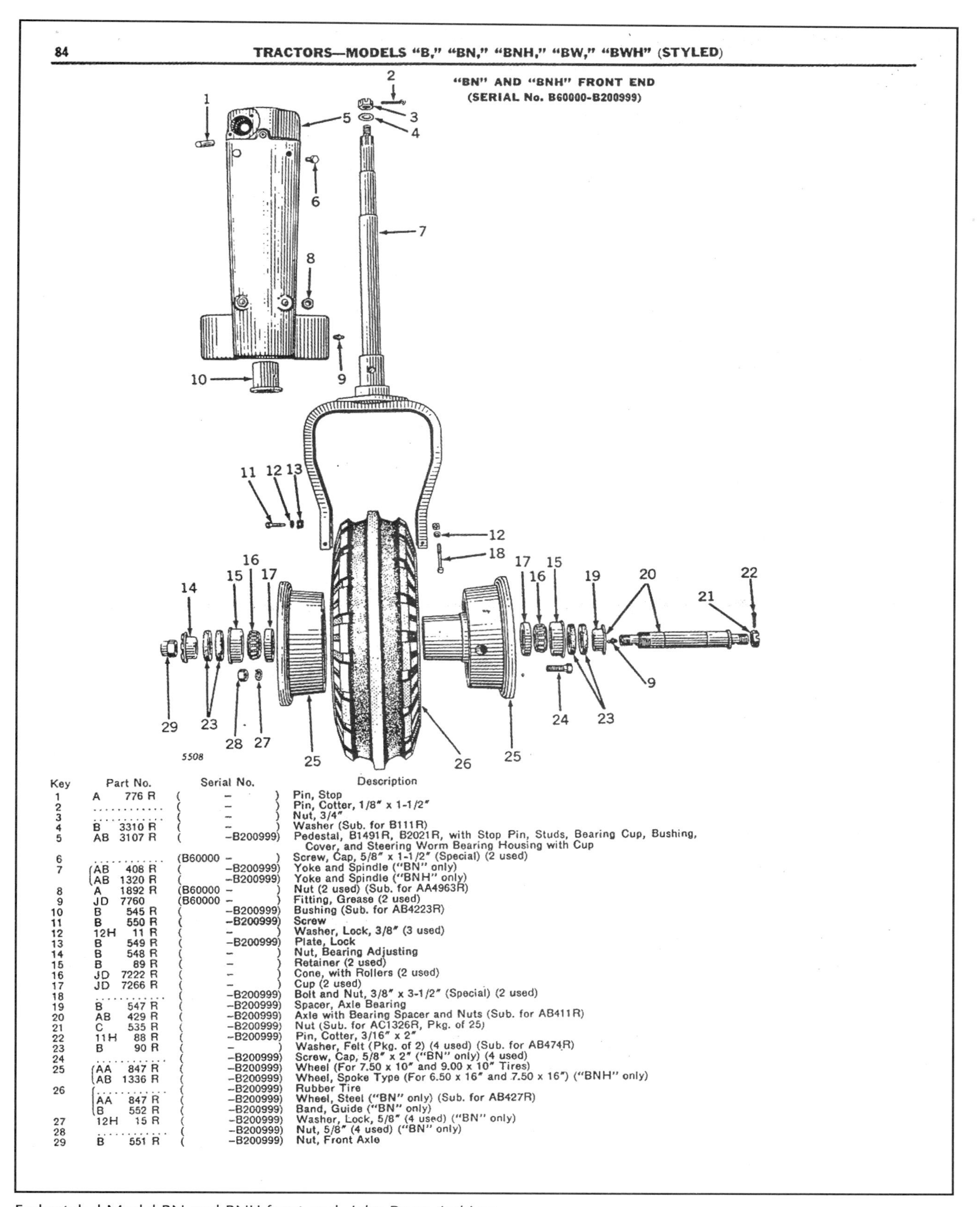

84 TRACTORS—MODELS "B," "BN," "BNH," "BW," "BWH" (STYLED)

"BN" AND "BNH" FRONT END (SERIAL No. B60000-B200999)

Key	Part No.	Serial No.	Description
1	A 776 R	(–)	Pin, Stop
2	....	(–)	Pin, Cotter, 1/8" x 1-1/2"
3	....	(–)	Nut, 3/4"
4	B 3310 R	(–)	Washer (Sub. for B111R)
5	AB 3107 R	(–B200999)	Pedestal, B1491R, B2021R, with Stop Pin, Studs, Bearing Cup, Bushing, Cover, and Steering Worm Bearing Housing with Cup
6	....	(B60000 –)	Screw, Cap, 5/8" x 1-1/2" (Special) (2 used)
7	AB 408 R	(–B200999)	Yoke and Spindle ("BN" only)
	AB 1320 R	(–B200999)	Yoke and Spindle ("BNH" only)
8	A 1892 R	(B60000 –)	Nut (2 used) (Sub. for AA4963R)
9	JD 7760	(B60000 –)	Fitting, Grease (2 used)
10	B 545 R	(–B200999)	Bushing (Sub. for AB4223R)
11	B 550 R	(–B200999)	Screw
12	12H 11 R	(–)	Washer, Lock, 3/8" (3 used)
13	B 549 R	(–B200999)	Plate, Lock
14	B 548 R	(–)	Nut, Bearing Adjusting
15	B 89 R	(–)	Retainer (2 used)
16	JD 7222 R	(–)	Cone, with Rollers (2 used)
17	JD 7266 R	(–)	Cup (2 used)
18	....	(–B200999)	Bolt and Nut, 3/8" x 3-1/2" (Special) (2 used)
19	B 547 R	(–B200999)	Spacer, Axle Bearing
20	AB 429 R	(–B200999)	Axle with Bearing Spacer and Nuts (Sub. for AB411R)
21	C 535 R	(–B200999)	Nut (Sub. for AC1326R, Pkg. of 25)
22	11H 88 R	(–B200999)	Pin, Cotter, 3/16" x 2"
23	B 90 R	(–)	Washer, Felt (Pkg. of 2) (4 used) (Sub. for AB474R)
24	....	(–B200999)	Screw, Cap, 5/8" x 2" ("BN" only) (4 used)
25	AA 847 R	(–B200999)	Wheel (For 7.50 x 10" and 9.00 x 10" Tires)
	AB 1336 R	(–B200999)	Wheel, Spoke Type (For 6.50 x 16" and 7.50 x 16") ("BNH" only)
26	....	(–B200999)	Rubber Tire
	AA 847 R	(–B200999)	Wheel, Steel ("BN" only) (Sub. for AB427R)
	B 552 R	(–B200999)	Band, Guide ("BN" only)
27	12H 15 R	(–B200999)	Washer, Lock, 5/8" (4 used) ("BN" only)
28	....	(–B200999)	Nut, 5/8" (4 used) ("BN" only)
29	B 551 R	(–B200999)	Nut, Front Axle

Early styled Model BN and BNH front end. *John Deere Archives*

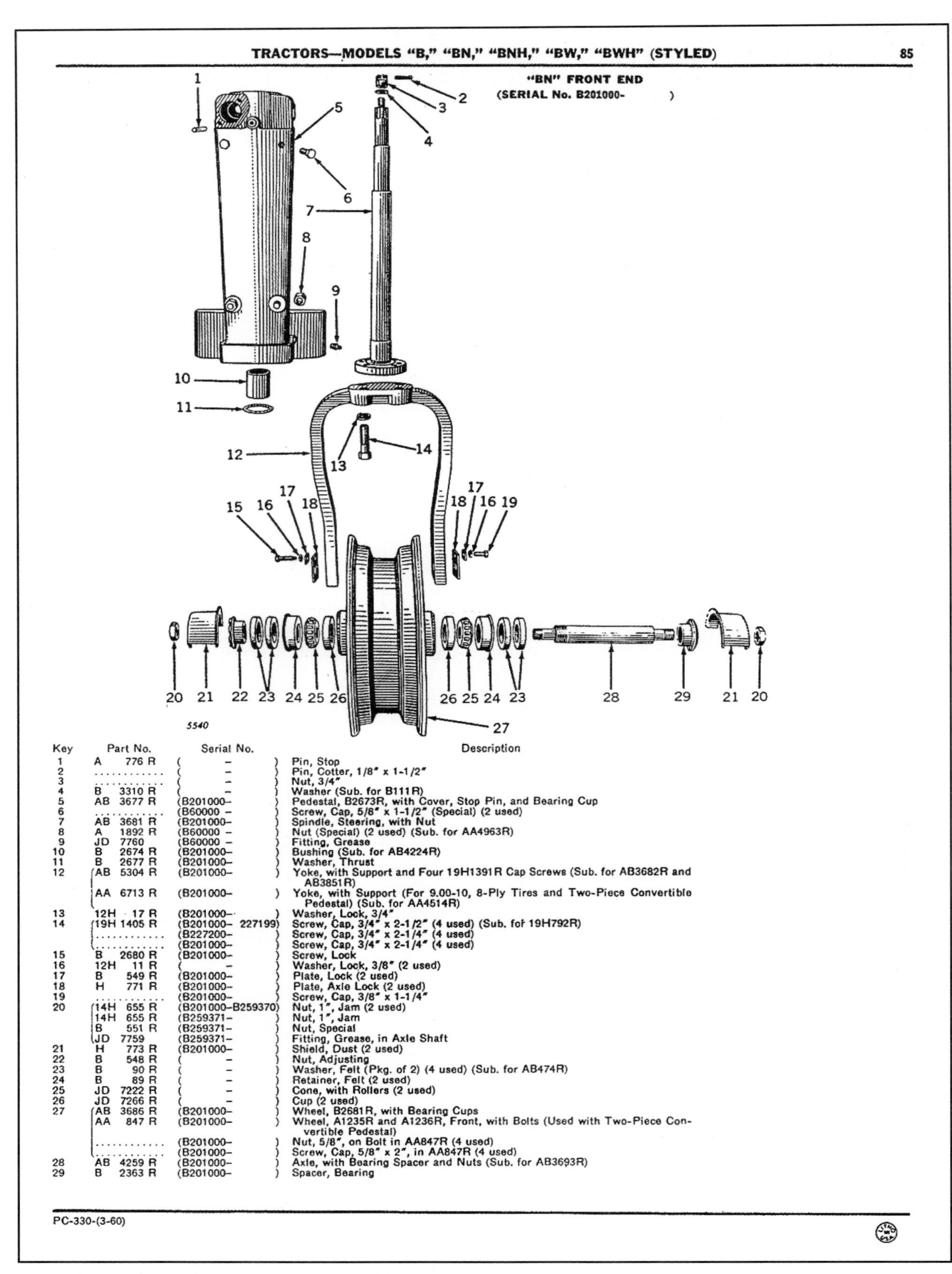

TRACTORS—MODELS "B," "BN," "BNH," "BW," "BWH" (STYLED) 85

"BN" FRONT END
(SERIAL No. B201000-)

Key	Part No.	Serial No.	Description
1	A 776 R	(–)	Pin, Stop
2	....	(–)	Pin, Cotter, 1/8" x 1-1/2"
3	....	(–)	Nut, 3/4"
4	B 3310 R	(–)	Washer (Sub. for B111R)
5	AB 3677 R	(B201000–)	Pedestal, B2673R, with Cover, Stop Pin, and Bearing Cup
6	....	(B60000 –)	Screw, Cap, 5/8" x 1-1/2" (Special) (2 used)
7	AB 3681 R	(B201000–)	Spindle, Steering, with Nut
8	A 1892 R	(B60000 –)	Nut (Special) (2 used) (Sub. for AA4963R)
9	JD 7760	(B60000 –)	Fitting, Grease
10	B 2674 R	(B201000–)	Bushing (Sub. for AB4224R)
11	B 2677 R	(B201000–)	Washer, Thrust
12	AB 5304 R	(B201000–)	Yoke, with Support and Four 19H1391R Cap Screws (Sub. for AB3682R and AB3851R)
	AA 6713 R	(B201000–)	Yoke, with Support (For 9.00-10, 8-Ply Tires and Two-Piece Convertible Pedestal) (Sub. for AA4514R)
13	12H 17 R	(B201000–)	Washer, Lock, 3/4"
14	19H 1405 R	(B201000– 227199)	Screw, Cap, 3/4" x 2-1/2" (4 used) (Sub. for 19H792R)
	....	(B227200–)	Screw, Cap, 3/4" x 2-1/4" (4 used)
	....	(B201000–)	Screw, Cap, 3/4" x 2-1/4" (4 used)
15	B 2680 R	(B201000–)	Screw, Lock
16	12H 11 R	(–)	Washer, Lock, 3/8" (2 used)
17	B 549 R	(B201000–)	Plate, Lock (2 used)
18	H 771 R	(B201000–)	Plate, Axle Lock (2 used)
19	....	(B201000–)	Screw, Cap, 3/8" x 1-1/4"
20	14H 655 R	(B201000–B259370)	Nut, 1", Jam (2 used)
	14H 655 R	(B259371–)	Nut, 1", Jam
	B 551 R	(B259371–)	Nut, Special
	JD 7759	(B259371–)	Fitting, Grease, in Axle Shaft
21	H 773 R	(B201000–)	Shield, Dust (2 used)
22	B 548 R	(–)	Nut, Adjusting
23	B 90 R	(–)	Washer, Felt (Pkg. of 2) (4 used) (Sub. for AB474R)
24	B 89 R	(–)	Retainer, Felt (2 used)
25	JD 7222 R	(–)	Cone, with Rollers (2 used)
26	JD 7266 R	(–)	Cup (2 used)
27	AB 3686 R	(B201000–)	Wheel, B2681R, with Bearing Cups
	AA 847 R	(B201000–)	Wheel, A1235R and A1236R, Front, with Bolts (Used with Two-Piece Convertible Pedestal)
	....	(B201000–)	Nut, 5/8", on Bolt in AA847R (4 used)
	....	(B201000–)	Screw, Cap, 5/8" x 2", in AA847R (4 used)
28	AB 4259 R	(B201000–)	Axle, with Bearing Spacer and Nuts (Sub. for AB3693R)
29	B 2363 R	(B201000–)	Spacer, Bearing

PC-330-(3-60)

Late styled Model BN front end. *John Deere Archives*

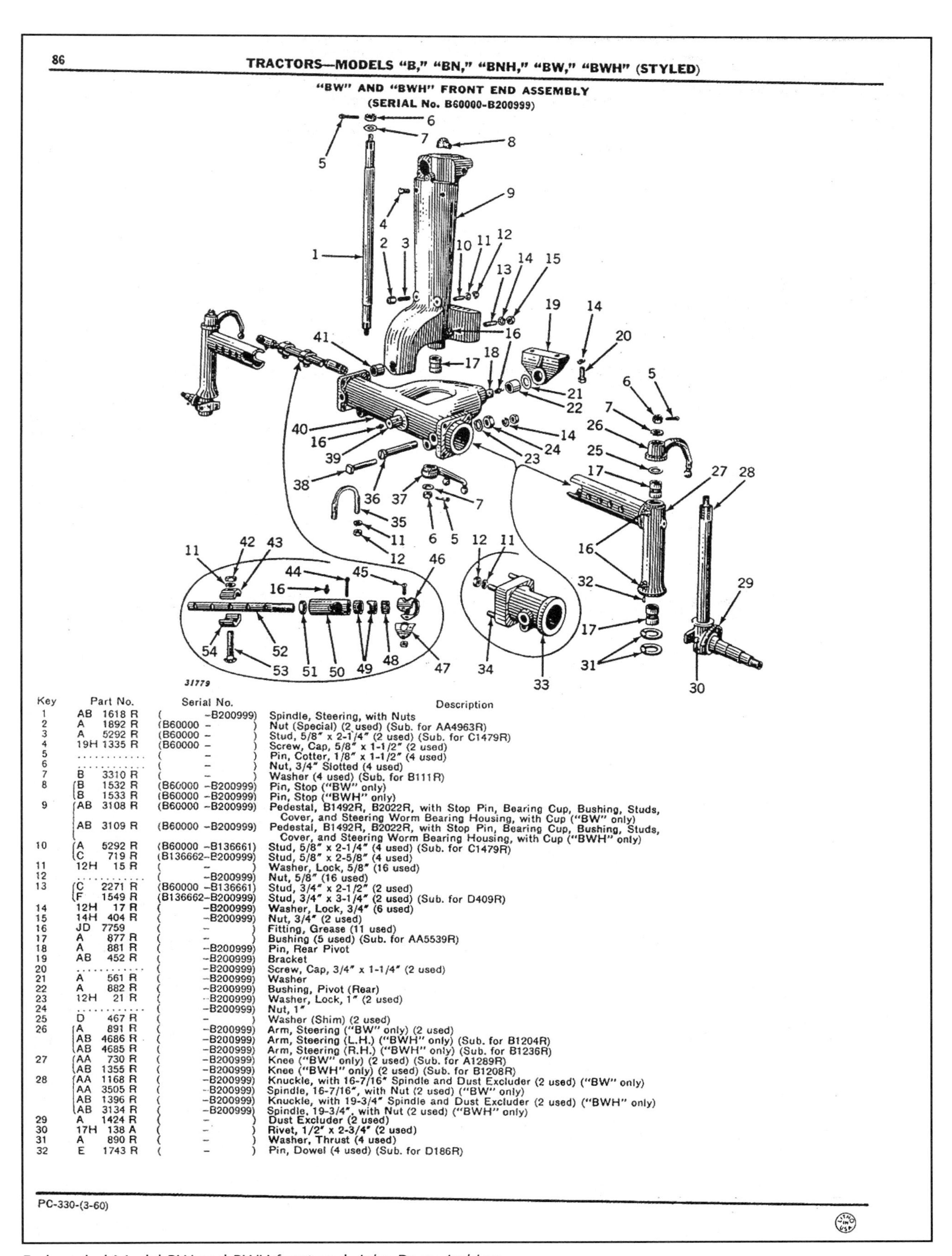

86 TRACTORS—MODELS "B," "BN," "BNH," "BW," "BWH" (STYLED)

"BW" AND "BWH" FRONT END ASSEMBLY
(SERIAL No. B60000-B200999)

Key	Part No.	Serial No.	Description
1	AB 1618 R	(-B200999)	Spindle, Steering, with Nuts
2	A 1892 R	(B60000 -)	Nut (Special) (2 used) (Sub. for AA4963R)
3	A 5292 R	(B60000 -)	Stud, 5/8" x 2-1/4" (2 used) (Sub. for C1479R)
4	19H 1335 R	(B60000 -)	Screw, Cap, 5/8" x 1-1/2" (2 used)
5	....	(-)	Pin, Cotter, 1/8" x 1-1/2" (4 used)
6	....	(-)	Nut, 3/4" Slotted (4 used)
7	B 3310 R	(-)	Washer (4 used) (Sub. for B111R)
8	B 1532 R	(B60000 -B200999)	Pin, Stop ("BW" only)
	B 1533 R	(B60000 -B200999)	Pin, Stop ("BWH" only)
9	AB 3108 R	(B60000 -B200999)	Pedestal, B1492R, B2022R, with Stop Pin, Bearing Cup, Bushing, Studs, Cover, and Steering Worm Bearing Housing, with Cup ("BW" only)
	AB 3109 R	(B60000 -B200999)	Pedestal, B1492R, B2022R, with Stop Pin, Bearing Cup, Bushing, Studs, Cover, and Steering Worm Bearing Housing, with Cup ("BWH" only)
10	A 5292 R	(B60000 -B136661)	Stud, 5/8" x 2-1/4" (4 used) (Sub. for C1479R)
	C 719 R	(B136662-B200999)	Stud, 5/8" x 2-5/8" (4 used)
11	12H 15 R	(-)	Washer, Lock, 5/8" (16 used)
12	....	(-B200999)	Nut, 5/8" (16 used)
13	C 2271 R	(B60000 -B136661)	Stud, 3/4" x 2-1/2" (2 used)
	F 1549 R	(B136662-B200999)	Stud, 3/4" x 3-1/4" (2 used) (Sub. for D409R)
14	12H 17 R	(-B200999)	Washer, Lock, 3/4" (6 used)
15	14H 404 R	(-B200999)	Nut, 3/4" (2 used)
16	JD 7759	(-)	Fitting, Grease (11 used)
17	A 877 R	(-)	Bushing (5 used) (Sub. for AA5539R)
18	A 881 R	(-B200999)	Pin, Rear Pivot
19	AB 452 R	(-B200999)	Bracket
20	....	(-B200999)	Screw, Cap, 3/4" x 1-1/4" (2 used)
21	A 561 R	(-B200999)	Washer
22	A 882 R	(-B200999)	Bushing, Pivot (Rear)
23	12H 21 R	(-B200999)	Washer, Lock, 1" (2 used)
24	....	(-B200999)	Nut, 1"
25	D 467 R	(-)	Washer (Shim) (2 used)
26	A 891 R	(-B200999)	Arm, Steering ("BW" only) (2 used)
	AB 4686 R	(-B200999)	Arm, Steering (L.H.) ("BWH" only) (Sub. for B1204R)
	AB 4685 R	(-B200999)	Arm, Steering (R.H.) ("BWH" only) (Sub. for B1236R)
27	AA 730 R	(-B200999)	Knee ("BW" only) (2 used) (Sub. for A1289R)
	AB 1355 R	(-B200999)	Knee ("BWH" only) (2 used) (Sub. for B1208R)
28	AA 1168 R	(-B200999)	Knuckle, with 16-7/16" Spindle and Dust Excluder (2 used) ("BW" only)
	AA 3505 R	(-B200999)	Spindle, 16-7/16", with Nut (2 used) ("BW" only)
	AB 1396 R	(-B200999)	Knuckle, with 19-3/4" Spindle and Dust Excluder (2 used) ("BWH" only)
	AB 3134 R	(-B200999)	Spindle, 19-3/4", with Nut (2 used) ("BWH" only)
29	A 1424 R	(-)	Dust Excluder (2 used)
30	17H 138 A	(-)	Rivet, 1/2" x 2-3/4" (2 used)
31	A 890 R	(-)	Washer, Thrust (4 used)
32	E 1743 R	(-)	Pin, Dowel (4 used) (Sub. for D186R)

PC-330-(3-60)

Early styled Model BW and BWH front end. *John Deere Archives*

TRACTORS—MODELS "B," "BN," "BNH," "BW," "BWH" (STYLED) 87

"BW" AND "BWH" FRONT END ASSEMBLY—Continued

(Serial No. B60000-B200999)

Key	Part No.	Serial No.	Description
33	AB 1352 R	(-B200999)	Extension, B1210R (Short) ("BWH" only)
	AB 1353 R	(-B200999)	Extension, B1211R (Long) ("BWH" only)
34	C 1494 R	(-B200999)	Stud, 5/8" x 2-7/8" ("BWH" only) (8 used)
35	A 887 R	(-B200999)	Bolt (2 used)
36	A 1101 R	(-B200999)	Bolt, Lock (2 used)
37	B 829 R	(-B200999)	Arm, Steering
38	....	(-B200999)	Bolt, Mach., with Nut, 3/4" x 4-3/4" (2 used)
39	A 880 R	(-B200999)	Pin, Pivot (Front)
40	AA 729 R	(-B200999)	Housing, A1100R ("BW" only)
	AB 1354 R	(-B200999)	Housing, B1207R ("BWH" only)
41	A 876 R	(-B200999)	Bushing, Pivot (Front)
42	....	(-B200999)	Nut, Jam, 5/8" (4 used)
43	A 893 R	(-B200999)	Clamp, Half (Upper) (4 used)
44	11H 49 R	(–)	Pin, Cotter, 1/8" x 2" (4 used)
45	13H 93 R	(–	Bolt, Stove, with Nut, No. 10 x 5/8" (4 used)
46	AC 352 R	(–)	Cover, Drag Link, Dust, Complete (4 used)
	C 1400 R	(–)	Cover, Drag Link, Dust (Outer) (4 used) (Sub. AC352R)
47	C 1401 R	(–)	Cover, Drag Link, Dust (Inner) (4 used) (Sub. AC352R)
48	C 840 R	(–)	Plug, Screw (4 used)
49	C 838 R	(–)	Bearing, Ball Stud (8 used)
50	H 982 R	(-B200999)	End, Tie Rod (4 used) (Sub. for C1109R)
51	C 985 R	(–)	Nut, Jam, 7/8" (4 used) (Sub. for AC1318R)
52	A 892 R	(-B200999)	Rod, Drag Link (4 used) ("BW" only)
	B 1221 R	(-B200999)	Rod, Drag Link (6 used) (Used with Extensions)
	B 1205 R	(-B200999)	Rod, D ag Link (2 used) ("BWH" R.H.)
	B 1206 R	(-B200999)	Rod, Drag Link (2 used) ("BWH" L.H.)
53	3H 715 R	(-B200999)	Bolt, Carriage, 5/8" x 2-3/4"
54	B 1233 R	(-B200999)	Clamp, Half (Bottom) (4 used)

Early styled Model BW and BWH front end (continued). *John Deere Archives*

TRACTORS—MODELS "B," "BN," "BNH," "BW," "BWH" (STYLED) 89

"BW" FRONT END—Continued

(SERIAL No. B201000-)

Key	Part No.	Serial No.	Description
34	F 1743 R	(–)	Pin, Dowel (4 used) (Sub. for D186R)
35	17H 138 A	(–)	Rivet, 1/2" x 2-3/4" (2 used)
36	....	(–)	Screw, Cap, 3/8" x 1-1/4"
37	12H 11 R	(–)	Washer, Lock, 3/8" (8 used)
38	12H 10 R	(–)	Washer, Lock, 5/16" (10 used)
39	....	(–)	Screw, Cap, 5/16" x 1-1/4" (Special) (6 used)
40	AA 1407 R	(–)	Cap, A1555R, Hub (2 used)
41	A 1556 R	(–)	Gasket (2 used) (Packed 10 in a Pkg.)
42	AD 452 R	(–)	Nut Assembly (2 used)
43	....	(–)	Pin, Cotter, 3/16" x 1-1/2" (2 used)
44	JD 7216 R	(–)	Cone with Rollers (2 used)
45	JD 7266 R	(–)	Cup, Outer Bearing (2 used)
46	AF 912 R	(B201000-)	Hub, F843R, with Bearing Cups (2 used)
47	JD 7270 R	(–)	Cup, Inner Bearing (2 used)
48	JD 7224 R	(–)	Cone with Rollers (2 used)
49	D 635 R	(–)	Retainer, Felt (2 used)
50	D 636 R	(–)	Washer, Felt (4 used) (Sub. for AA663R)
51	JD 19 R	(B201000-)	Bolt, Hub (12 used)
52	A 890 R	(–)	Washer, Thrust (4 used)
53	B 2693 R	(B201000-)	Shield, Dust (2 used)
54	AB 3630 R	(B201000-)	Knee, Front Axle, with Bushing and Dust Shield (2 used)
	AB 4006 R*	(B201000-)	Knee, Front Axle, with Bushing and Dust Shield (2 used)
	AB 4046 R	(B201000-)	Knee, Front Axle, with Bushing and Dust Shield (2 used)
55	....	(–)	Bolt, Stove, No. 10 x 5/8", with Nut (2 used)
56	AC 352 R	(–)	Cover, Drag Link, Complete (2 used)
	C 1400 R	(–)	Cover, Outer Dust (2 used) (Sub. AC352R)
57	C 1401 R	(–)	Cover, Inner Dust (2 used) (Sub. AC352R)
58	11H 49 R	(–)	Pin, Cotter, 1/8" x 2" (4 used)
59	C 840 R	(–)	Plug, Screw (4 used)
60	C 838 R	(–)	Bearing, Ball Stud (8 used) (Packed 10 in a Pkg.)
61	H 982 R	(B201000-)	End, Drag Link Rod (2 used)
62	C 985 R	(–)	Nut, Jam (2 used) (Sub. for AC1318R)
63	B 2696 R	(B201000-)	Rod, Drag Link (2 used)
	B 2729 R	(B201000-)	Rod, Drag Link (Used with Knee Extension)
	B 2842 R°	(B201000-)	Rod, Drag Link (2 used)
64	24H 143 R	(B201000-)	Washer (4 used)
65	....	(B201000-)	Nut, 5/16" (4 used)
66	AF 1187 R	(B201000-)	Sleeve, Drag Link (2 used) (Sub. for AB3632R)
67	JD 7760	(–)	Fitting, Grease (2 used)
68	B 2694 R	(B201000-)	Bolt, Lock (2 used)
	B 2694 R	(B201000-)	Bolt, Lock (3 used with Knee Extension)
69	....	(B201000-)	Screw, Cap, 5/16" x 1-1/2" (4 used)
70	AF 1182 R	(B201000-)	Housing, B2690R and F1018R, Front Axle, with Bushing (Sub. for AB3629R)
	AB 4045 R°	(B201000-)	Housing, B2840R, with Pin and Bushing
71	B 2728 R	(B201000-)	Extension, Knee

*Parts for Adjustable Tread Front Axle Type.
°Parts for Tractor with 38" Fixed Tread Front Axle Assembly.

Late styled Model BW front end (continued). *John Deere Archives*

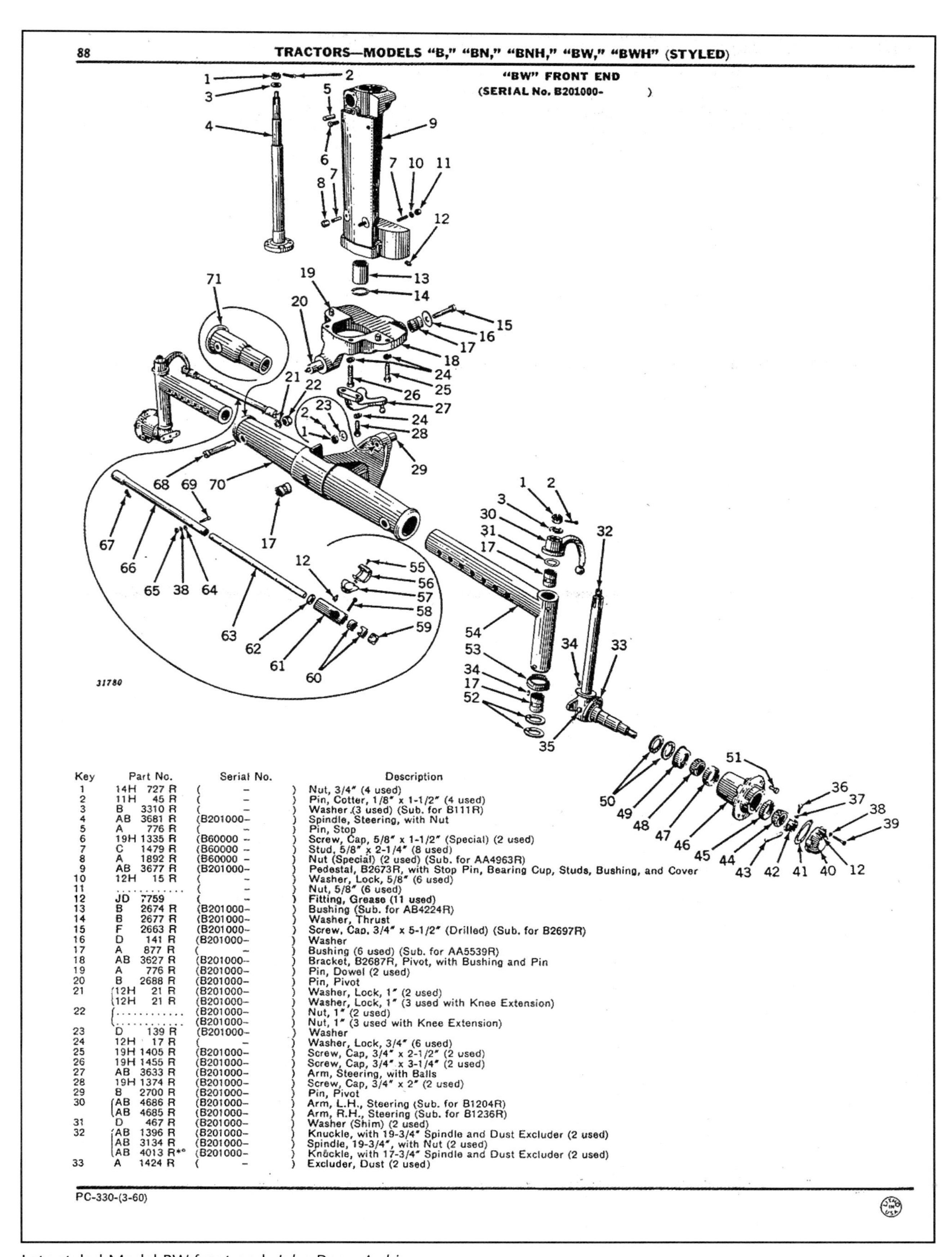

88 TRACTORS—MODELS "B," "BN," "BNH," "BW," "BWH" (STYLED)

"BW" FRONT END
(SERIAL No. B201000-)

31780

Key	Part No.	Serial No.	Description
1	14H 727 R	(–)	Nut, 3/4" (4 used)
2	11H 45 R	(–)	Pin, Cotter, 1/8" x 1-1/2" (4 used)
3	B 3310 R	(–)	Washer (3 used) (Sub. for B111R)
4	AB 3681 R	(B201000–)	Spindle, Steering, with Nut
5	A 776 R	(–)	Pin, Stop
6	19H 1335 R	(B60000 –)	Screw, Cap, 5/8" x 1-1/2" (Special) (2 used)
7	C 1479 R	(B60000 –)	Stud, 5/8" x 2-1/4" (8 used)
8	A 1892 R	(B60000 –)	Nut (Special) (2 used) (Sub. for AA4963R)
9	AB 3677 R	(B201000–)	Pedestal, B2673R, with Stop Pin, Bearing Cup, Studs, Bushing, and Cover
10	12H 15 R	(–)	Washer, Lock, 5/8" (6 used)
11	....	(–)	Nut, 5/8" (6 used)
12	JD 7759	(–)	**Fitting, Grease (11 used)**
13	B 2674 R	(B201000–)	Bushing (Sub. for AB4224R)
14	B 2677 R	(B201000–)	Washer, Thrust
15	F 2663 R	(B201000–)	Screw, Cap, 3/4" x 5-1/2" (Drilled) (Sub. for B2697R)
16	D 141 R	(B201000–)	Washer
17	A 877 R	(–)	Bushing (6 used) (Sub. for AA5539R)
18	AB 3627 R	(B201000–)	Bracket, B2687R, Pivot, with Bushing and Pin
19	A 776 R	(B201000–)	Pin, Dowel (2 used)
20	B 2688 R	(B201000–)	Pin, Pivot
21	12H 21 R	(B201000–)	Washer, Lock, 1" (2 used)
	12H 21 R	(B201000–)	Washer, Lock, 1" (3 used with Knee Extension)
22	....	(B201000–)	Nut, 1" (2 used)
	....	(B201000–)	Nut, 1" (3 used with Knee Extension)
23	D 139 R	(B201000–)	Washer
24	12H 17 R	(–)	Washer, Lock, 3/4" (6 used)
25	19H 1405 R	(B201000–)	Screw, Cap, 3/4" x 2-1/2" (2 used)
26	19H 1455 R	(B201000–)	Screw, Cap, 3/4" x 3-1/4" (2 used)
27	AB 3633 R	(B201000–)	Arm, Steering, with Balls
28	19H 1374 R	(B201000–)	Screw, Cap, 3/4" x 2" (2 used)
29	B 2700 R	(B201000–)	Pin, Pivot
30	AB 4686 R	(B201000–)	Arm, L.H., Steering (Sub. for B1204R)
	AB 4685 R	(B201000–)	Arm, R.H., Steering (Sub. for B1236R)
31	D 467 R	(B201000–)	Washer (Shim) (2 used)
32	AB 1396 R	(B201000–)	Knuckle, with 19-3/4" Spindle and Dust Excluder (2 used)
	AB 3134 R	(B201000–)	Spindle, 19-3/4", with Nut (2 used)
	AB 4013 R*°	(B201000–)	Knuckle, with 17-3/4" Spindle and Dust Excluder (2 used)
33	A 1424 R	(–)	Excluder, Dust (2 used)

PC-330-(3-60)

Late styled Model BW front end. *John Deere Archives*

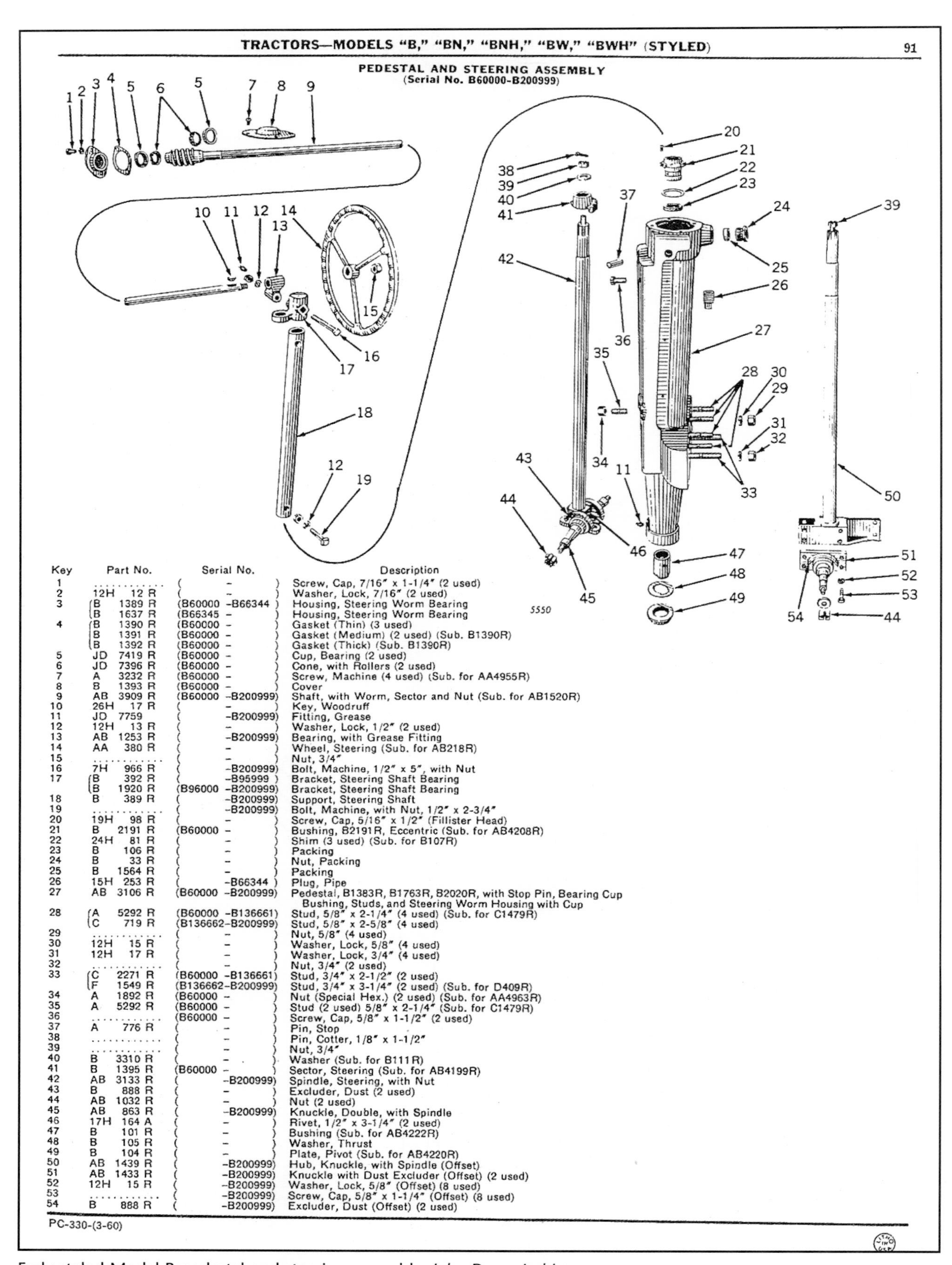

TRACTORS—MODELS "B," "BN," "BNH," "BW," "BWH" (STYLED) 91

PEDESTAL AND STEERING ASSEMBLY
(Serial No. B60000-B200999)

Key	Part No.	Serial No.	Description
1	....	(-)	Screw, Cap, 7/16" x 1-1/4" (2 used)
2	12H 12 R	(-)	Washer, Lock, 7/16" (2 used)
3	B 1389 R	(B60000 -B66344)	Housing, Steering Worm Bearing
	B 1637 R	(B66345 -)	Housing, Steering Worm Bearing
4	B 1390 R	(B60000 -)	Gasket (Thin) (3 used)
	B 1391 R	(B60000 -)	Gasket (Medium) (2 used) (Sub. B1390R)
	B 1392 R	(B60000 -)	Gasket (Thick) (Sub. B1390R)
5	JD 7419 R	(B60000 -)	Cup, Bearing (2 used)
6	JD 7396 R	(B60000 -)	Cone, with Rollers (2 used)
7	A 3232 R	(B60000 -)	Screw, Machine (4 used) (Sub. for AA4955R)
8	B 1393 R	(B60000 -)	Cover
9	AB 3909 R	(B60000 -B200999)	Shaft, with Worm, Sector and Nut (Sub. for AB1520R)
10	26H 17 R	(-)	Key, Woodruff
11	JD 7759	(-B200999)	Fitting, Grease
12	12H 13 R	(-)	Washer, Lock, 1/2" (2 used)
13	AB 1253 R	(-B200999)	Bearing, with Grease Fitting
14	AA 380 R	(-)	Wheel, Steering (Sub. for AB218R)
15	....	(-)	Nut, 3/4"
16	7H 966 R	(-B200999)	Bolt, Machine, 1/2" x 5", with Nut
17	B 392 R	(-B95999)	Bracket, Steering Shaft Bearing
	B 1920 R	(B96000 -B200999)	Bracket, Steering Shaft Bearing
18	B 389 R	(-B200999)	Support, Steering Shaft
19	....	(-B200999)	Bolt, Machine, with Nut, 1/2" x 2-3/4"
20	19H 98 R	(-)	Screw, Cap, 5/16" x 1/2" (Fillister Head)
21	B 2191 R	(B60000 -)	Bushing, B2191R, Eccentric (Sub. for AB4208R)
22	24H 81 R	(-)	Shim (3 used) (Sub. for B107R)
23	B 106 R	(-)	Packing
24	B 33 R	(-)	Nut, Packing
25	B 1564 R	(-)	Packing
26	15H 253 R	(-B66344)	Plug, Pipe
27	AB 3106 R	(B60000 -B200999)	Pedestal, B1383R, B1763R, B2020R, with Stop Pin, Bearing Cup Bushing, Studs, and Steering Worm Housing with Cup
28	A 5292 R	(B60000 -B136661)	Stud, 5/8" x 2-1/4" (4 used) (Sub. for C1479R)
	C 719 R	(B136662-B200999)	Stud, 5/8" x 2-5/8" (4 used)
29	....	(-)	Nut, 5/8" (4 used)
30	12H 15 R	(-)	Washer, Lock, 5/8" (4 used)
31	12H 17 R	(-)	Washer, Lock, 3/4" (4 used)
32	....	(-)	Nut, 3/4" (2 used)
33	C 2271 R	(B60000 -B136661)	Stud, 3/4" x 2-1/2" (2 used)
	F 1549 R	(B136662-B200999)	Stud, 3/4" x 3-1/4" (2 used) (Sub. for D409R)
34	A 1892 R	(B60000 -)	Nut (Special Hex.) (2 used) (Sub. for AA4963R)
35	A 5292 R	(B60000 -)	Stud (2 used) 5/8" x 2-1/4" (Sub. for C1479R)
36	....	(B60000 -)	Screw, Cap, 5/8" x 1-1/2" (2 used)
37	A 776 R	(-)	Pin, Stop
38	....	(-)	Pin, Cotter, 1/8" x 1-1/2"
39	....	(-)	Nut, 3/4"
40	B 3310 R	(-)	Washer (Sub. for B111R)
41	B 1395 R	(B60000 -)	Sector, Steering (Sub. for AB4199R)
42	AB 3133 R	(-B200999)	Spindle, Steering, with Nut
43	B 888 R	(-)	Excluder, Dust (2 used)
44	AB 1032 R	(-)	Nut (2 used)
45	AB 863 R	(-B200999)	Knuckle, Double, with Spindle
46	17H 164 A	(-)	Rivet, 1/2" x 3-1/4" (2 used)
47	B 101 R	(-)	Bushing (Sub. for AB4222R)
48	B 105 R	(-)	Washer, Thrust
49	B 104 R	(-)	Plate, Pivot (Sub. for AB4220R)
50	AB 1439 R	(-B200999)	Hub, Knuckle, with Spindle (Offset)
51	AB 1433 R	(-B200999)	Knuckle with Dust Excluder (Offset) (2 used)
52	12H 15 R	(-B200999)	Washer, Lock, 5/8" (Offset) (8 used)
53	....	(-B200999)	Screw, Cap, 5/8" x 1-1/4" (Offset) (8 used)
54	B 888 R	(-B200999)	Excluder, Dust (Offset) (2 used)

PC-330-(3-60)

Early styled Model B pedestal and steering assembly. *John Deere Archives*

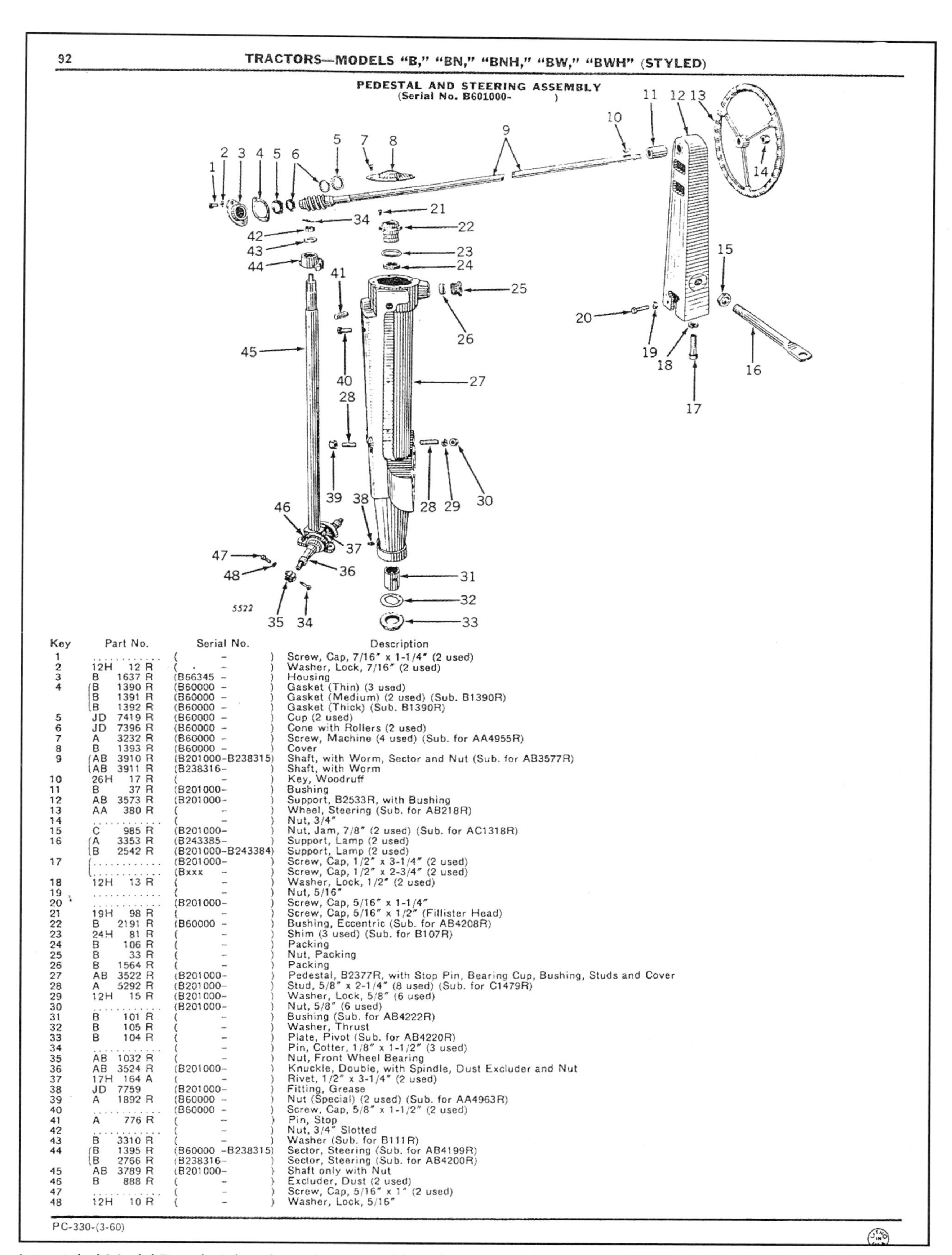

92 TRACTORS—MODELS "B," "BN," "BNH," "BW," "BWH" (STYLED)

PEDESTAL AND STEERING ASSEMBLY
(Serial No. B601000-)

Key	Part No.	Serial No.	Description
1	....	(-)	Screw, Cap, 7/16" x 1-1/4" (2 used)
2	12H 12 R	(-)	Washer, Lock, 7/16" (2 used)
3	B 1637 R	(B66345 -)	Housing
4	B 1390 R	(B60000 -)	Gasket (Thin) (3 used)
	B 1391 R	(B60000 -)	Gasket (Medium) (2 used) (Sub. B1390R)
	B 1392 R	(B60000 -)	Gasket (Thick) (Sub. B1390R)
5	JD 7419 R	(B60000 -)	Cup (2 used)
6	JD 7396 R	(B60000 -)	Cone with Rollers (2 used)
7	A 3232 R	(B60000 -)	Screw, Machine (4 used) (Sub. for AA4955R)
8	B 1393 R	(B60000 -)	Cover
9	AB 3910 R	(B201000-B238315)	Shaft, with Worm, Sector and Nut (Sub. for AB3577R)
	AB 3911 R	(B238316-)	Shaft, with Worm
10	26H 17 R	(-)	Key, Woodruff
11	B 37 R	(B201000-)	Bushing
12	AB 3573 R	(B201000-)	Support, B2533R, with Bushing
13	AA 380 R	(-)	Wheel, Steering (Sub. for AB218R)
14	....	(-)	Nut, 3/4"
15	C 985 R	(B201000-)	Nut, Jam, 7/8" (2 used) (Sub. for AC1318R)
16	A 3353 R	(B243385-)	Support, Lamp (2 used)
	B 2542 R	(B201000-B243384)	Support, Lamp (2 used)
17	....	(B201000-)	Screw, Cap, 1/2" x 3-1/4" (2 used)
	....	(Bxxx -)	Screw, Cap, 1/2" x 2-3/4" (2 used)
18	12H 13 R	(-)	Washer, Lock, 1/2" (2 used)
19	....	(-)	Nut, 5/16"
20	....	(B201000-)	Screw, Cap, 5/16" x 1-1/4"
21	19H 98 R	(-)	Screw, Cap, 5/16" x 1/2" (Fillister Head)
22	B 2191 R	(B60000 -)	Bushing, Eccentric (Sub. for AB4208R)
23	24H 81 R	(-)	Shim (3 used) (Sub. for B107R)
24	B 106 R	(-)	Packing
25	B 33 R	(-)	Nut, Packing
26	B 1564 R	(-)	Packing
27	AB 3522 R	(B201000-)	Pedestal, B2377R, with Stop Pin, Bearing Cup, Bushing, Studs and Cover
28	A 5292 R	(B201000-)	Stud, 5/8" x 2-1/4" (8 used) (Sub. for C1479R)
29	12H 15 R	(B201000-)	Washer, Lock, 5/8" (6 used)
30	....	(B201000-)	Nut, 5/8" (6 used)
31	B 101 R	(-)	Bushing (Sub. for AB4222R)
32	B 105 R	(-)	Washer, Thrust
33	B 104 R	(-)	Plate, Pivot (Sub. for AB4220R)
34	....	(-)	Pin, Cotter, 1/8" x 1-1/2" (3 used)
35	AB 1032 R	(-)	Nut, Front Wheel Bearing
36	AB 3524 R	(B201000-)	Knuckle, Double, with Spindle, Dust Excluder and Nut
37	17H 164 A	(-)	Rivet, 1/2" x 3-1/4" (2 used)
38	JD 7759	(B201000-)	Fitting, Grease
39	A 1892 R	(B60000 -)	Nut (Special) (2 used) (Sub. for AA4963R)
40	....	(B60000 -)	Screw, Cap, 5/8" x 1-1/2" (2 used)
41	A 776 R	(-)	Pin, Stop
42	....	(-)	Nut, 3/4" Slotted
43	B 3310 R	(-)	Washer (Sub. for B111R)
44	B 1395 R	(B60000 -B238315)	Sector, Steering (Sub. for AB4199R)
	B 2766 R	(B238316-)	Sector, Steering (Sub. for AB4200R)
45	AB 3789 R	(B201000-)	Shaft only with Nut
46	B 888 R	(-)	Excluder, Dust (2 used)
47	....	(-)	Screw, Cap, 5/16" x 1" (2 used)
48	12H 10 R	(-)	Washer, Lock, 5/16"

PC-330-(3-60)

Late styled Model B pedestal and steering assembly. *John Deere Archives*

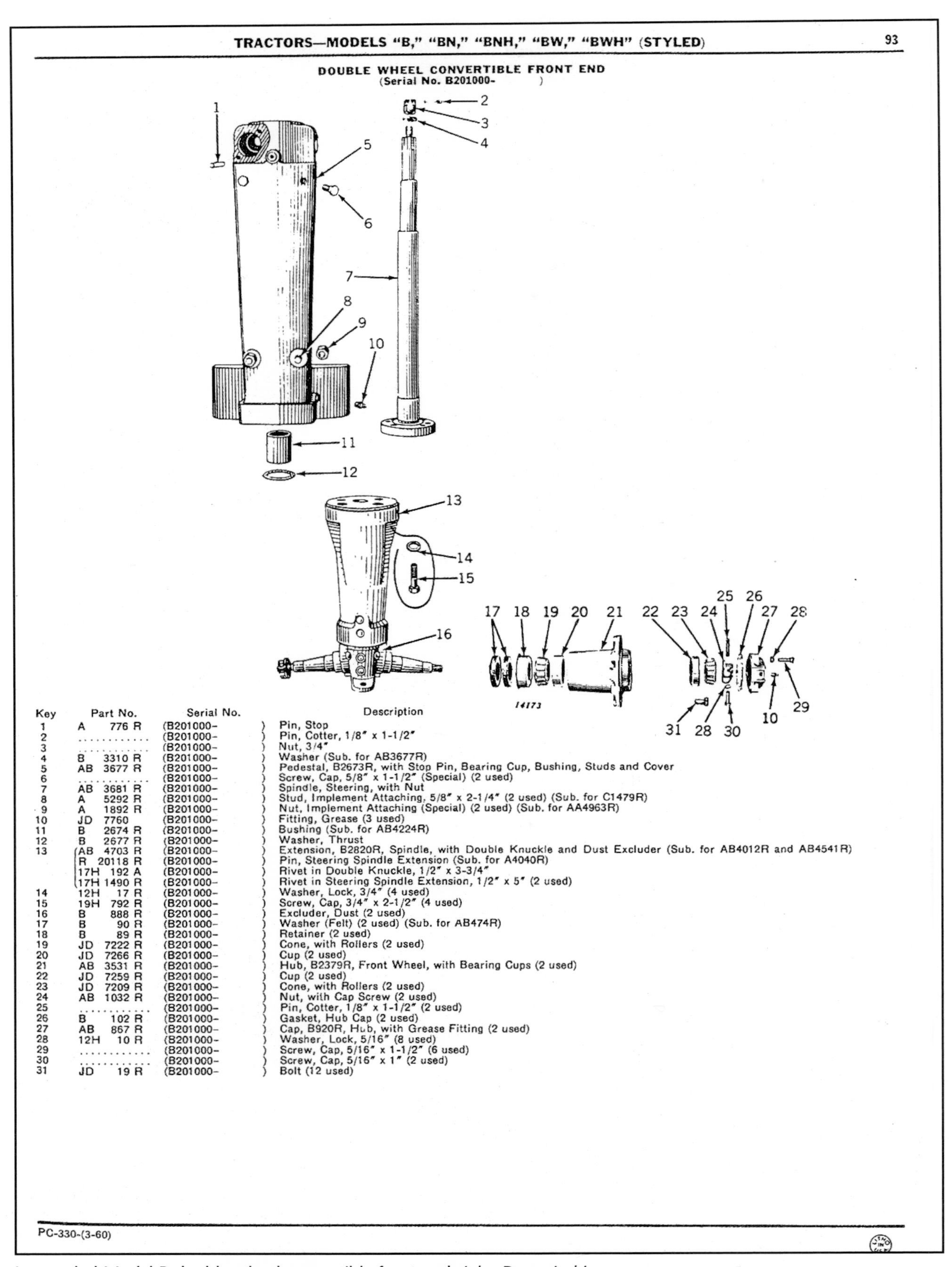

TRACTORS—MODELS "B," "BN," "BNH," "BW," "BWH" (STYLED) 93

DOUBLE WHEEL CONVERTIBLE FRONT END
(Serial No. B201000-)

Key	Part No.	Serial No.	Description
1	A 776 R	(B201000-)	Pin, Stop
2	....	(B201000-)	Pin, Cotter, 1/8" x 1-1/2"
3	....	(B201000-)	Nut, 3/4"
4	B 3310 R	(B201000-)	Washer (Sub. for AB3677R)
5	AB 3677 R	(B201000-)	Pedestal, B2673R, with Stop Pin, Bearing Cup, Bushing, Studs and Cover
6	....	(B201000-)	Screw, Cap, 5/8" x 1-1/2" (Special) (2 used)
7	AB 3681 R	(B201000-)	Spindle, Steering, with Nut
8	A 5292 R	(B201000-)	Stud, Implement Attaching, 5/8" x 2-1/4" (2 used) (Sub. for C1479R)
9	A 1892 R	(B201000-)	Nut, Implement Attaching (Special) (2 used) (Sub. for AA4963R)
10	JD 7760	(B201000-)	Fitting, Grease (3 used)
11	B 2674 R	(B201000-)	Bushing (Sub. for AB4224R)
12	B 2677 R	(B201000-)	Washer, Thrust
13	AB 4703 R	(B201000-)	Extension, B2820R, Spindle, with Double Knuckle and Dust Excluder (Sub. for AB4012R and AB4541R)
	R 20118 R	(B201000-)	Pin, Steering Spindle Extension (Sub. for A4040R)
	17H 192 A	(B201000-)	Rivet in Double Knuckle, 1/2" x 3-3/4"
	17H 1490 R	(B201000-)	Rivet in Steering Spindle Extension, 1/2" x 5" (2 used)
14	12H 17 R	(B201000-)	Washer, Lock, 3/4" (4 used)
15	19H 792 R	(B201000-)	Screw, Cap, 3/4" x 2-1/2" (4 used)
16	B 888 R	(B201000-)	Excluder, Dust (2 used)
17	B 90 R	(B201000-)	Washer (Felt) (2 used) (Sub. for AB474R)
18	B 89 R	(B201000-)	Retainer (2 used)
19	JD 7222 R	(B201000-)	Cone, with Rollers (2 used)
20	JD 7266 R	(B201000-)	Cup (2 used)
21	AB 3531 R	(B201000-)	Hub, B2379R, Front Wheel, with Bearing Cups (2 used)
22	JD 7259 R	(B201000-)	Cup (2 used)
23	JD 7209 R	(B201000-)	Cone, with Rollers (2 used)
24	AB 1032 R	(B201000-)	Nut, with Cap Screw (2 used)
25	....	(B201000-)	Pin, Cotter, 1/8" x 1-1/2" (2 used)
26	B 102 R	(B201000-)	Gasket, Hub Cap (2 used)
27	AB 867 R	(B201000-)	Cap, B920R, Hub, with Grease Fitting (2 used)
28	12H 10 R	(B201000-)	Washer, Lock, 5/16" (8 used)
29	....	(B201000-)	Screw, Cap, 5/16" x 1-1/2" (6 used)
30	....	(B201000-)	Screw, Cap, 5/16" x 1" (2 used)
31	JD 19 R	(B201000-)	Bolt (12 used)

PC-330-(3-60)

Late styled Model B double-wheel convertible front end. *John Deere Archives*

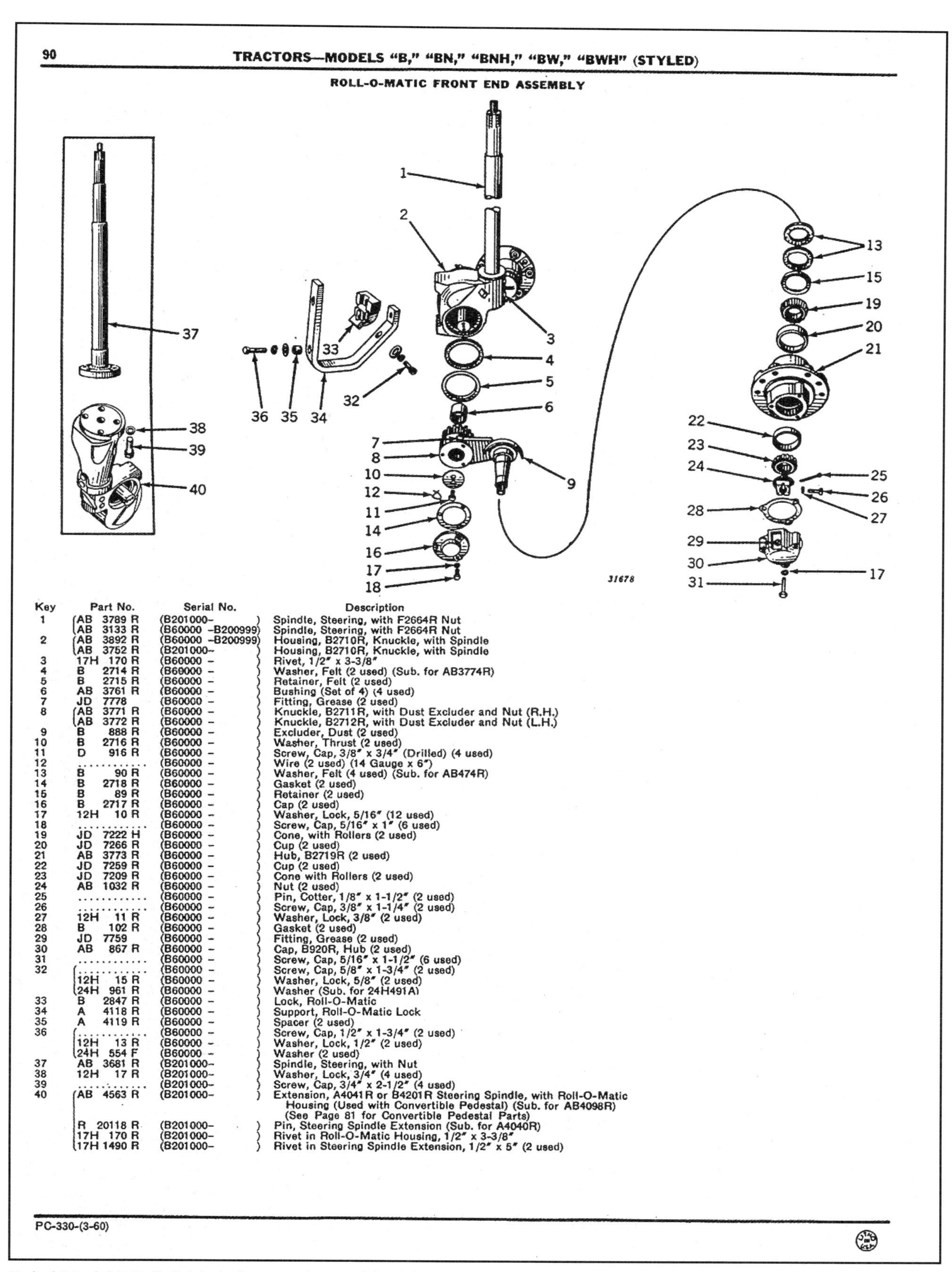

90 TRACTORS—MODELS "B," "BN," "BNH," "BW," "BWH" (STYLED)

ROLL-O-MATIC FRONT END ASSEMBLY

Key	Part No.	Serial No.	Description
1	AB 3789 R	(B201000–)	Spindle, Steering, with F2664R Nut
	AB 3133 R	(B60000 –B200999)	Spindle, Steering, with F2664R Nut
2	AB 3892 R	(B60000 –B200999)	Housing, B2710R, Knuckle, with Spindle
	AB 3752 R	(B201000–)	Housing, B2710R, Knuckle, with Spindle
3	17H 170 R	(B60000 –)	Rivet, 1/2" x 3-3/8"
4	B 2714 R	(B60000 –)	Washer, Felt (2 used) (Sub. for AB3774R)
5	B 2715 R	(B60000 –)	Retainer, Felt (2 used)
6	AB 3761 R	(B60000 –)	Bushing (Set of 4) (4 used)
7	JD 7778	(B60000 –)	Fitting, Grease (2 used)
8	AB 3771 R	(B60000 –)	Knuckle, B2711R, with Dust Excluder and Nut (R.H.)
	AB 3772 R	(B60000 –)	Knuckle, B2712R, with Dust Excluder and Nut (L.H.)
9	B 888 R	(B60000 –)	Excluder, Dust (2 used)
10	B 2716 R	(B60000 –)	Washer, Thrust (2 used)
11	D 916 R	(B60000 –)	Screw, Cap, 3/8" x 3/4" (Drilled) (4 used)
12	....	(B60000 –)	Wire (2 used) (14 Gauge x 6")
13	B 90 R	(B60000 –)	Washer, Felt (4 used) (Sub. for AB474R)
14	B 2718 R	(B60000 –)	Gasket (2 used)
15	B 89 R	(B60000 –)	Retainer (2 used)
16	B 2717 R	(B60000 –)	Cap (2 used)
17	12H 10 R	(B60000 –)	Washer, Lock, 5/16" (12 used)
18	....	(B60000 –)	Screw, Cap, 5/16" x 1" (6 used)
19	JD 7222 H	(B60000 –)	Cone, with Rollers (2 used)
20	JD 7266 R	(B60000 –)	Cup (2 used)
21	AB 3773 R	(B60000 –)	Hub, B2719R (2 used)
22	JD 7259 R	(B60000 –)	Cup (2 used)
23	JD 7209 R	(B60000 –)	Cone with Rollers (2 used)
24	AB 1032 R	(B60000 –)	Nut (2 used)
25	....	(B60000 –)	Pin, Cotter, 1/8" x 1-1/2" (2 used)
26	....	(B60000 –)	Screw, Cap, 3/8" x 1-1/4" (2 used)
27	12H 11 R	(B60000 –)	Washer, Lock, 3/8" (2 used)
28	B 102 R	(B60000 –)	Gasket (2 used)
29	JD 7759	(B60000 –)	Fitting, Grease (2 used)
30	AB 867 R	(B60000 –)	Cap, B920R, Hub (2 used)
31	....	(B60000 –)	Screw, Cap, 5/16" x 1-1/2" (6 used)
32	....	(B60000 –)	Screw, Cap, 5/8" x 1-3/4" (2 used)
	12H 15 R	(B60000 –)	Washer, Lock, 5/8" (2 used)
	24H 961 R	(B60000 –)	Washer (Sub. for 24H491A)
33	B 2847 R	(B60000 –)	Lock, Roll-O-Matic
34	A 4118 R	(B60000 –)	Support, Roll-O-Matic Lock
35	A 4119 R	(B60000 –)	Spacer (2 used)
36	....	(B60000 –)	Screw, Cap, 1/2" x 1-3/4" (2 used)
	12H 13 R	(B60000 –)	Washer, Lock, 1/2" (2 used)
	24H 554 F	(B60000 –)	Washer (2 used)
37	AB 3681 R	(B201000–)	Spindle, Steering, with Nut
38	12H 17 R	(B201000–)	Washer, Lock, 3/4" (4 used)
39	....	(B201000–)	Screw, Cap, 3/4" x 2-1/2" (4 used)
40	AB 4563 R	(B201000–)	Extension, A4041R or B4201R Steering Spindle, with Roll-O-Matic Housing (Used with Convertible Pedestal) (Sub. for AB4098R) (See Page 81 for Convertible Pedestal Parts)
	R 20118 R	(B201000–)	Pin, Steering Spindle Extension (Sub. for A4040R)
	17H 170 R	(B201000–)	Rivet in Roll-O-Matic Housing, 1/2" x 3-3/8"
	17H 1490 R	(B201000–)	Rivet in Steering Spindle Extension, 1/2" x 5" (2 used)

PC-330-(3-60)

Styled Model B Roll-O-Matic front end assembly. *John Deere Archives*

Chapter 5

Wheels and Tires

The tires and wheels on an antique tractor are among the first things to catch the eye. First off, the rear wheels are the largest, most obvious part on the tractor. Secondly, tire wear suggests the condition of the rest of the machine. Finally, the trained eye recognizes whether or not the tread, the rim, and the wheel are correct.

Here's a set of standard (for 1937) steel wheels on a 1937 Model BW. The tractor also has a nice set of round-top fenders.

A classic view of a John Deere Model B equipped with early rubber tires. Note the original tread pattern on the tires; a set of these are difficult to find today, but add a lot to a restoration if they are appropriate for the model. *John Deere Archives*

This is true for steel wheels as well as for rubber-tired tractors. As original steel wheels wore out, exact replacements were not always available, and improvisation often took place.

Today, tires, rims, and wheels present one of the biggest challenges for the restorer, even for the relatively common tractors. To do a first-class restoration job you need the correct rims, wheels, and tires.

According to my count, there are about seventeen types of Model B tractors, including the styled and unstyled high, low, wide, etc. For each type, there are appropriate wheels. In most cases, there are several types of appropriate wheels.

Aftermarket wheels such as French and Hecht or Kay Brunner can add value over Deere wheels, so long as they are appropriate for the year the tractor was built. There was a time that F&H wheels were supplied by Deere.

Accessories like the rim extensions, or scrapers, adds interest and value to steel wheels.

Some purists want to see the tractor on steel if it was originally delivered on steel. To my mind, that is not important, since rubber tires were optional on all Bs.

Rear Tires

Wouldn't it be great if you could find a nice set of the old knobby-tread tires from the mid-thirties? I know of a Ford tractor collector who has a set of tires on his 9N that have the Ford trademark script on them and they still hold air after fifty years. A Model B should have rear tires with the 45º tread rather than the modern 35º tread. Companies such as Gempler's (see appendix) sell tires with 45º lugs. Some collectors are finding 45º tread tires made in Czechoslovakia. I personally feel that modern 35º tires are just fine on a common late styled Model B. I would much rather see that than worn-down old style tires.

Steel Rear Wheels

Most of the early unstyled Model Bs came equipped with a flat-spoke steel rear wheel 48in in diameter and 5 1/4in wide (John Deere part JD1215R, or its replacement JD1265R). Extensions of 5 1/4in were available. Standard tread Bs used an 8in-wide version of the same diameter wheel, part number JD1221R.

Skeleton wheels, JD1266R, were optional equipment. These were 48in in diameter by just under 2in wide. Some of these were made for Deere by French and Hecht and have smooth hubs. There were also some narrow skeleton wheels known as tiptoe wheels, with a rim width of only 1/2in. These carried Deere part number JD1231R and are now very rare. Regular skeleton wheels are appropriate for 1936 or later tractors. Tiptoe wheels, used to minimize soil compaction, were available only for 1937 and 1938 unstyled Bs.

Lugs

A plethora of lugs are appropriate for the John Deere Model B. There were 4in and 5in regular and heavy-duty spade lugs. There were cast lugs for the skeleton wheels, including those for the tiptoe wheels that bolted to the sides. Sand lugs, or two-bolt A lugs, were available in 5in heights. Then there were cone lugs, spud lugs, and button lugs. Button lugs were later used when it was important not to disturb the turf, for tasks like making hay and grooming golf courses. All types were available for both row-crops and standard treads, except for those for the skeleton wheels. Finally, road bands were available to cover these lugs.

Rear Wheels for Rubber

Extant parts breakdowns show only the flat-spoke rear wheels for rubber tires, but these were not available as original equipment. Originally, a round-spoke wheel, part number AB375R, was used. Flat-spoke rims are appropriate for tractors from 1940 to 1947 (early styled).

In late 1936 or early 1937

Note the great set of oval knob rear tires on this John Deere Model B. The photo was taken in 1938, but the ring-type drawbar indicates the tractor is a 1937 (or earlier) model. *John Deere Archives*

Skeleton rear wheels and cast disk front wheels are used on this Model shown planting cotton near Alvarado, Texas, using a John Deere B-37 bedder-planter. The picture was taken in May of 1937. *John Deere Archives*

cast iron disk wheels, with removable rims, became available. In 1938, with styling, the pressed-steel rim was added to the lineup. Both types were used to the end of production. The normal rear tire size was 7.50x36 or 9.00x36 for row-crops, and 11.25x24 for standard treads. The part number AB1316R wheel, for 9.00x40 rubber, was used on early styled BNH and BWH tractors. Remember, there were no late styled BNH or BWH machines, nor were steel wheels used on late styled Model Bs.

Front Wheels and Tires

The AB358R steel wheel was the original 22in-diameter by 3.25in-wide front wheel for dual tricycle General Purpose tractors. You will notice that this has been replaced in the parts breakdown by AB2708R. Either number is acceptable for a quality restoration. Steering bands of 1.5, 2.0 and 2.5in in height were available and are still shown in the breakdown. Front wheel weights were also originally available.

Wide-front Model Bs used a similar wheel (part number AC885R), while standard treads used part number AB642R. All of the above were round-spoke types.

The AB415R cast disk wheel was a popular option on dual narrow front tractors and seemed especially appropriate with the skeleton rears. This wheel is different from other Deere cast disk wheels in that it did not have the demountable hub.

John Deere Model BN tractors were originally equipped with a wide, round-spoke wheel (part number AB427R). This was later replaced by part number AA847R. Both are acceptable and both types can add guide bands and extension rims.

Notice the unusual, for 1941, combination of rubber rear tires with steel in front. Also note that the right rear wheel is at its full extension, and reversed, to keep from running over the windrows. *John Deere Archives*

Rubber

For rubber tires, AB808R round-spoke front wheels were used for all but the BN models up to serial number 29,631. After that, AB1023R pressed-steel front wheels were available. The tire was a 5.00x15 on the B, a 5.25 or 5.50x16 was used on the BR-BO-BI series, and a 5.50x16 was the standard tire for the BW. Model BNH tractors used 6.50x16 or 7.50x16 tires.

For late styled Model Bs (serial number 201,000 and up), steel wheels were not an option. Two types of front wheels were used, those for four- or six-ply tires, and those for eight-ply.

Model BNs, serial numbers 60,000 to 200,999 (early styled), employed a two-piece wheel. Either a 7.50x10 or a 9.00x10 tire could be fitted. For early styled BNH tractors, a spoked wheel was used (part number AB1336R) receiving a 6.50x16 or 7.50x16 tire. Late styled Bs used a single piece disk-type wheel. Part number AB3686R is used with the standard pedestal, and P/N AA847R is used with the convertible pedestal.

A late styled Model B with weighted cast wheels. These wheels, with removable rims, are common on all styled Bs. One-piece pressed-steel wheels were also available. Spoked rear wheels were available for early styled Bs.

Right, strange-looking front wheels for an early unstyled Model B? Yes, these were provided for some 120 Model Bs by International Harvester when the Deere employees who made wheels went on strike.

Note the spoked wheels on this John Deere Model B that is pulling a No. 9 combine through the fields of South Dakota. This photo was taken in August 1939. *John Deere Archives*

Note the rear wheel weights on this John Deere Model BW. The tractor is working with a cultivator-fertilizer in the San Fernando Valley of California in 1938. *John Deere Archives*

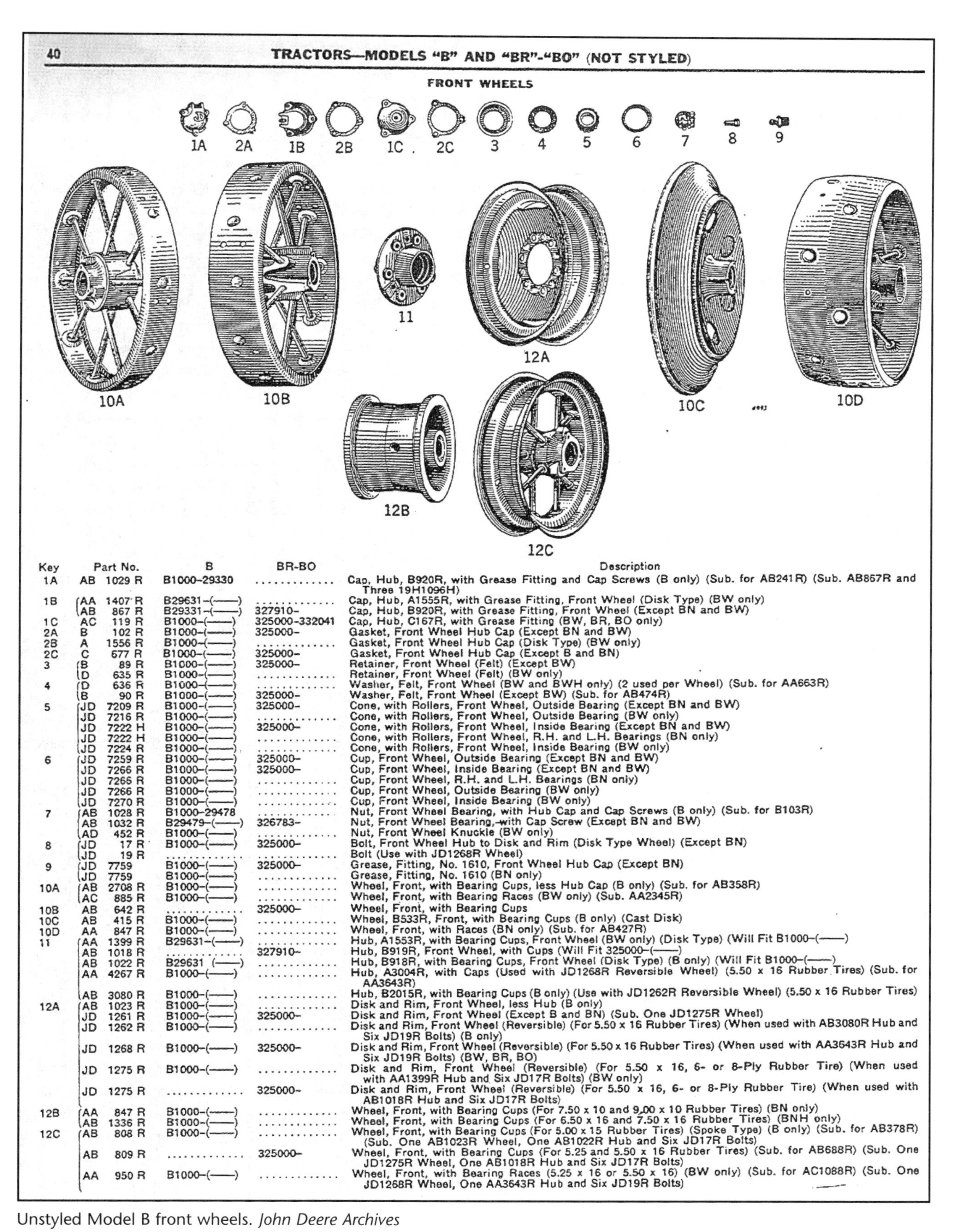

40 TRACTORS—MODELS "B" AND "BR"-"BO" (NOT STYLED)

FRONT WHEELS

Key	Part No.	B	BR-BO	Description
1A	AB 1029 R	B1000-29330	....	Cap, Hub, B920R, with Grease Fitting and Cap Screws (B only) (Sub. for AB241R) (Sub. AB867R and Three 19H1096H)
1B	AA 1407 R	B29631-(——)	....	Cap, Hub, A1555R, with Grease Fitting, Front Wheel (Disk Type) (BW only)
	AB 867 R	B29331-(——)	327910-	Cap, Hub, B920R, with Grease Fitting, Front Wheel (Except BN and BW)
1C	AC 119 R	B1000-(——)	325000-332041	Cap, Hub, C167R, with Grease Fitting (BW, BR, BO only)
2A	B 102 R	B1000-(——)	325000-	Gasket, Front Wheel Hub Cap (Except BN and BW)
2B	A 1556 R	B1000-(——)	....	Gasket, Front Wheel Hub Cap (Disk Type) (BW only)
2C	C 677 R	B1000-(——)	325000-	Gasket, Front Wheel Hub Cap (Except B and BN)
3	B 89 R	B1000-(——)	325000-	Retainer, Front Wheel (Felt) (Except BW)
	D 635 R	B1000-(——)	....	Retainer, Front Wheel (Felt) (BW only)
4	D 636 R	B1000-(——)	....	Washer, Felt, Front Wheel (BW and BWH only) (2 used per Wheel) (Sub. for AA663R)
	B 90 R	B1000-(——)	325000-	Washer, Felt, Front Wheel (Except BW) (Sub. for AB474R)
5	JD 7209 R	B1000-(——)	325000-	Cone, with Rollers, Front Wheel, Outside Bearing (Except BN and BW)
	JD 7216 R	B1000-(——)	....	Cone, with Rollers, Front Wheel, Outside Bearing (BW only)
	JD 7222 H	B1000-(——)	325000-	Cone, with Rollers, Front Wheel, Inside Bearing (Except BN and BW)
	JD 7222 H	B1000-(——)	....	Cone, with Rollers, Front Wheel, R.H. and L.H. Bearings (BN only)
	JD 7224 R	B1000-(——)	....	Cone, with Rollers, Front Wheel, Inside Bearing (BW only)
6	JD 7259 R	B1000-(——)	325000-	Cup, Front Wheel, Outside Bearing (Except BN and BW)
	JD 7266 R	B1000-(——)	325000-	Cup, Front Wheel, Inside Bearing (Except BN and BW)
	JD 7266 R	B1000-(——)	....	Cup, Front Wheel, R.H. and L.H. Bearings (BN only)
	JD 7266 R	B1000-(——)	....	Cup, Front Wheel, Outside Bearing (BW only)
	JD 7270 R	B1000-(——)	....	Cup, Front Wheel, Inside Bearing (BW only)
7	AB 1028 R	B1000-29478	....	Nut, Front Wheel Bearing, with Hub Cap and Cap Screws (B only) (Sub. for B103R)
	AB 1032 R	B29479-(——)	326783-	Nut, Front Wheel Bearing, with Cap Screw (Except BN and BW)
	AD 452 R	B1000-(——)	....	Nut, Front Wheel Knuckle (BW only)
8	JD 17 R	B1000-(——)	325000-	Bolt, Front Wheel Hub to Disk and Rim (Disk Type Wheel) (Except BN)
	JD 19 R	....	....	Bolt (Use with JD1268R Wheel)
9	JD 7759	B1000-(——)	325000-	Grease, Fitting, No. 1610, Front Wheel Hub Cap (Except BN)
	JD 7759	B1000-(——)	....	Grease, Fitting, No. 1610 (BN only)
10A	AB 2708 R	B1000-(——)	....	Wheel, Front, with Bearing Cups, less Hub Cap (B only) (Sub. for AB358R)
	AC 885 R	B1000-(——)	....	Wheel, Front, with Bearing Races (BW only) (Sub. AA2345R)
10B	AB 642 R	....	325000-	Wheel, Front, with Bearing Cups
10C	AB 415 R	B1000-(——)	....	Wheel, B533R, Front, with Bearing Cups (B only) (Cast Disk)
10D	AA 847 R	B1000-(——)	....	Wheel, Front, with Races (BN only) (Sub. for AB427R)
11	AA 1399 R	B29631-(——)	....	Hub, A1553R, with Bearing Cups, Front Wheel (BW only) (Disk Type) (Will Fit B1000-(——)
	AB 1018 R		327910-	Hub, B919R, Front Wheel, with Cups (Will Fit 325000-(——)
	AB 1022 R	B29631 (——)	....	Hub, B918R, with Bearing Cups, Front Wheel (Disk Type) (B only) (Will Fit B1000-(——)
	AA 4267 R	B1000-(——)	....	Hub, A3004R, with Caps (Used with JD1268R Reversible Wheel) (5.50 x 16 Rubber Tires) (Sub. for AA3643R)
	AB 3080 R	B1000-(——)	....	Hub, B2015R, with Bearing Cups (B only) (Use with JD1262R Reversible Wheel) (5.50 x 16 Rubber Tires)
12A	AB 1023 R	B1000-(——)	....	Disk and Rim, Front Wheel, less Hub (B only)
	JD 1261 R	B1000-(——)	325000-	Disk and Rim, Front Wheel (Except B and BN) (Sub. One JD1275R Wheel)
	JD 1262 R	B1000-(——)	....	Disk and Rim, Front Wheel (Reversible) (For 5.50 x 16 Rubber Tires) (When used with AB3080R Hub and Six JD19R Bolts) (B only)
	JD 1268 R	B1000-(——)	325000-	Disk and Rim, Front Wheel (Reversible) (For 5.50 x 16 Rubber Tires) (When used with AA3643R Hub and Six JD19R Bolts) (BW, BR, BO)
	JD 1275 R	B1000-(——)	....	Disk and Rim, Front Wheel (Reversible) (For 5.50 x 16, 6- or 8-Ply Rubber Tire) (When used with AA1399R Hub and Six JD17R Bolts) (BW only)
	JD 1275 R	....	325000-	Disk and Rim, Front Wheel (Reversible) (For 5.50 x 16, 6- or 8-Ply Rubber Tire) (When used with AB1018R Hub and Six JD17R Bolts)
12B	AA 847 R	B1000-(——)	....	Wheel, Front, with Bearing Cups (For 7.50 x 10 and 9.00 x 10 Rubber Tires) (BN only)
	AB 1336 R	B1000-(——)	....	Wheel, Front, with Bearing Cups (For 6.50 x 16 and 7.50 x 16 Rubber Tires) (BNH only)
12C	AB 808 R	B1000-(——)	....	Wheel, Front, with Bearing Cups (For 5.00 x 15 Rubber Tires) (Spoke Type) (B only) (Sub. for AB378R) (Sub. One AB1023R Wheel, One AB1022R Hub and Six JD17R Bolts)
	AB 809 R	....	325000-	Wheel, Front, with Bearing Cups (For 5.25 and 5.50 x 16 Rubber Tires) (Sub. for AB688R) (Sub. One JD1275R Wheel, One AB1018R Hub and Six JD17R Bolts)
	AA 950 R	B1000-(——)	....	Wheel, Front, with Bearing Races (5.25 x 16 or 5.50 x 16) (BW only) (Sub. for AC1088R) (Sub. One JD1268R Wheel, One AA3643R Hub and Six JD19R Bolts)

Unstyled Model B front wheels. *John Deere Archives*

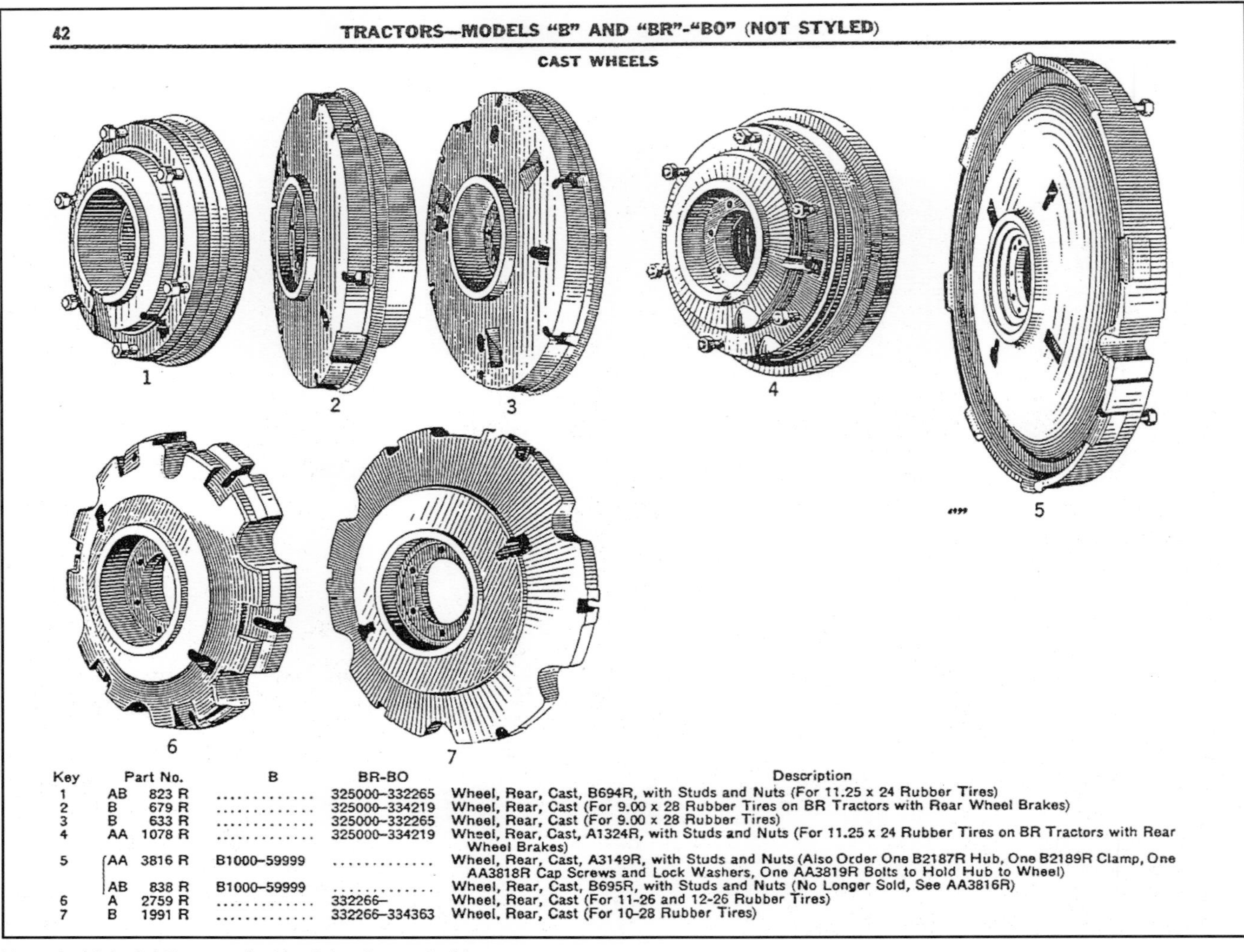

42 TRACTORS—MODELS "B" AND "BR"-"BO" (NOT STYLED)

CAST WHEELS

Key	Part No.	B	BR-BO	Description
1	AB 823 R	....	325000–332265	Wheel, Rear, Cast, B694R, with Studs and Nuts (For 11.25 x 24 Rubber Tires)
2	B 679 R	....	325000–334219	Wheel, Rear, Cast (For 9.00 x 28 Rubber Tires on BR Tractors with Rear Wheel Brakes)
3	B 633 R	....	325000–332265	Wheel, Rear, Cast (For 9.00 x 28 Rubber Tires)
4	AA 1078 R	....	325000–334219	Wheel, Rear, Cast, A1324R, with Studs and Nuts (For 11.25 x 24 Rubber Tires on BR Tractors with Rear Wheel Brakes)
5	AA 3816 R	B1000–59999	....	Wheel, Rear, Cast, A3149R, with Studs and Nuts (Also Order One B2187R Hub, One B2189R Clamp, One AA3818R Cap Screws and Lock Washers, One AA3819R Bolts to Hold Hub to Wheel)
	AB 838 R	B1000–59999	....	Wheel, Rear, Cast, B695R, with Studs and Nuts (No Longer Sold, See AA3816R)
6	A 2759 R	....	332266–	Wheel, Rear, Cast (For 11-26 and 12-26 Rubber Tires)
7	B 1991 R	....	332266–334363	Wheel, Rear, Cast (For 10-28 Rubber Tires)

Unstyled Model B cast wheels. *John Deere Archives*

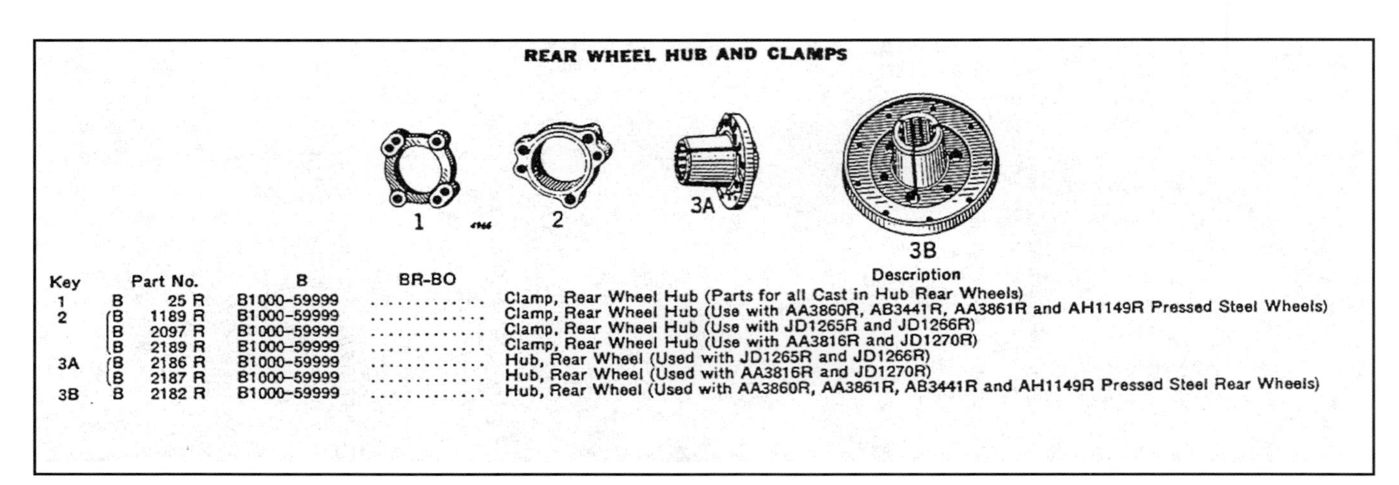

REAR WHEEL HUB AND CLAMPS

Key	Part No.	B	BR-BO	Description
1	B 25 R	B1000–59999	....	Clamp, Rear Wheel Hub (Parts for all Cast in Hub Rear Wheels)
2	B 1189 R	B1000–59999	....	Clamp, Rear Wheel Hub (Use with AA3860R, AB3441R, AA3861R and AH1149R Pressed Steel Wheels)
	B 2097 R	B1000–59999	....	Clamp, Rear Wheel Hub (Use with JD1265R and JD1266R)
	B 2189 R	B1000–59999	....	Clamp, Rear Wheel Hub (Use with AA3816R and JD1270R)
3A	B 2186 R	B1000–59999	....	Hub, Rear Wheel (Used with JD1265R and JD1266R)
	B 2187 R	B1000–59999	....	Hub, Rear Wheel (Used with AA3816R and JD1270R)
3B	B 2182 R	B1000–59999	....	Hub, Rear Wheel (Used with AA3860R, AA3861R, AB3441R and AH1149R Pressed Steel Rear Wheels)

Unstyled Model B rear wheel hub and clamps. *John Deere Archives*

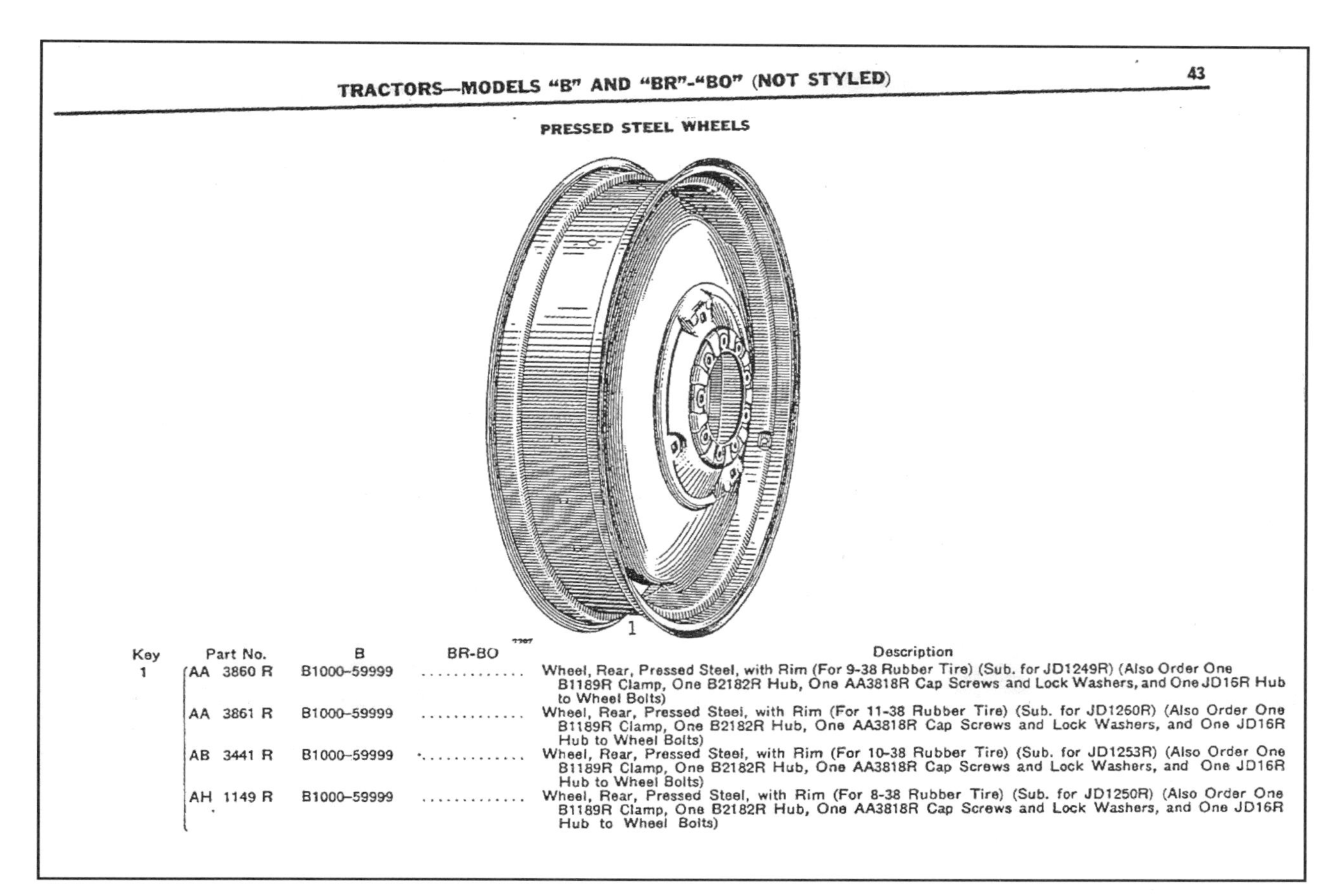

TRACTORS—MODELS "B" AND "BR"-"BO" (NOT STYLED) 43

PRESSED STEEL WHEELS

Key	Part No.	B	BR-BO	Description
1	AA 3860 R	B1000–59999	....	Wheel, Rear, Pressed Steel, with Rim (For 9-38 Rubber Tire) (Sub. for JD1249R) (Also Order One B1189R Clamp, One B2182R Hub, One AA3818R Cap Screws and Lock Washers, and One JD16R Hub to Wheel Bolts)
	AA 3861 R	B1000–59999	....	Wheel, Rear, Pressed Steel, with Rim (For 11-38 Rubber Tire) (Sub. for JD1250R) (Also Order One B1189R Clamp, One B2182R Hub, One AA3818R Cap Screws and Lock Washers, and One JD16R Hub to Wheel Bolts)
	AB 3441 R	B1000–59999	....	Wheel, Rear, Pressed Steel, with Rim (For 10-38 Rubber Tire) (Sub. for JD1253R) (Also Order One B1189R Clamp, One B2182R Hub, One AA3818R Cap Screws and Lock Washers, and One JD16R Hub to Wheel Bolts)
	AH 1149 R	B1000–59999	....	Wheel, Rear, Pressed Steel, with Rim (For 8-38 Rubber Tire) (Sub. for JD1250R) (Also Order One B1189R Clamp, One B2182R Hub, One AA3818R Cap Screws and Lock Washers, and One JD16R Hub to Wheel Bolts)

Unstyled Model B pressed-steel wheel. *John Deere Archives*

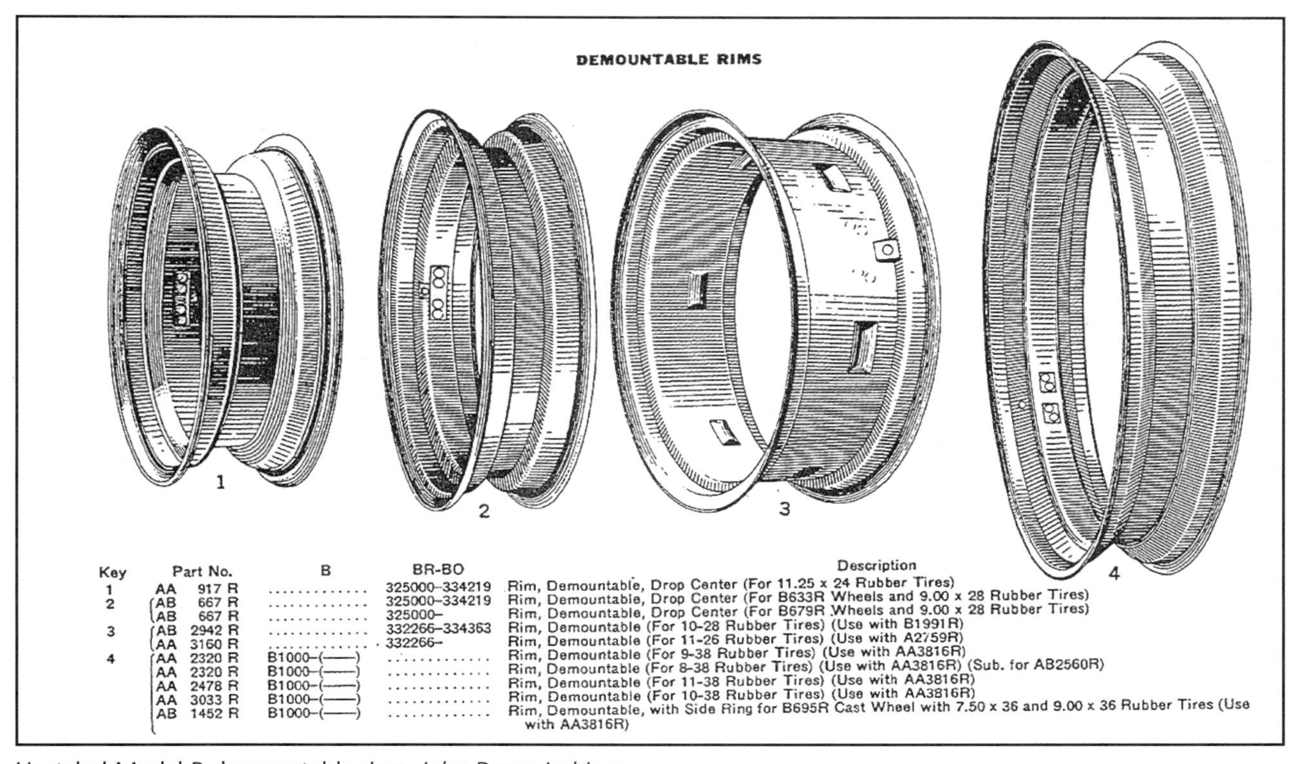

DEMOUNTABLE RIMS

Key	Part No.	B	BR-BO	Description
1	AA 917 R	....	325000–334219	Rim, Demountable, Drop Center (For 11.25 x 24 Rubber Tires)
2	AB 667 R	....	325000–334219	Rim, Demountable, Drop Center (For B633R Wheels and 9.00 x 28 Rubber Tires)
	AB 667 R	....	325000–	Rim, Demountable, Drop Center (For B679R Wheels and 9.00 x 28 Rubber Tires)
3	AB 2942 R	....	332266–334363	Rim, Demountable (For 10-28 Rubber Tires) (Use with B1991R)
	AA 3160 R	....	332266–	Rim, Demountable (For 11-26 Rubber Tires) (Use with A2759R)
4	AA 2320 R	B1000–(——)	....	Rim, Demountable (For 9-38 Rubber Tires) (Use with AA3816R)
	AA 2320 R	B1000–(——)	....	Rim, Demountable (For 8-38 Rubber Tires) (Use with AA3816R) (Sub. for AB2560R)
	AA 2478 R	B1000–(——)	....	Rim, Demountable (For 11-38 Rubber Tires) (Use with AA3816R)
	AA 3033 R	B1000–(——)	....	Rim, Demountable (For 10-38 Rubber Tires) (Use with AA3816R)
	AB 1452 R	B1000–(——)	....	Rim, Demountable, with Side Ring for B695R Cast Wheel with 7.50 x 36 and 9.00 x 36 Rubber Tires (Use with AA3816R)

Unstyled Model B demountable rims. *John Deere Archives*

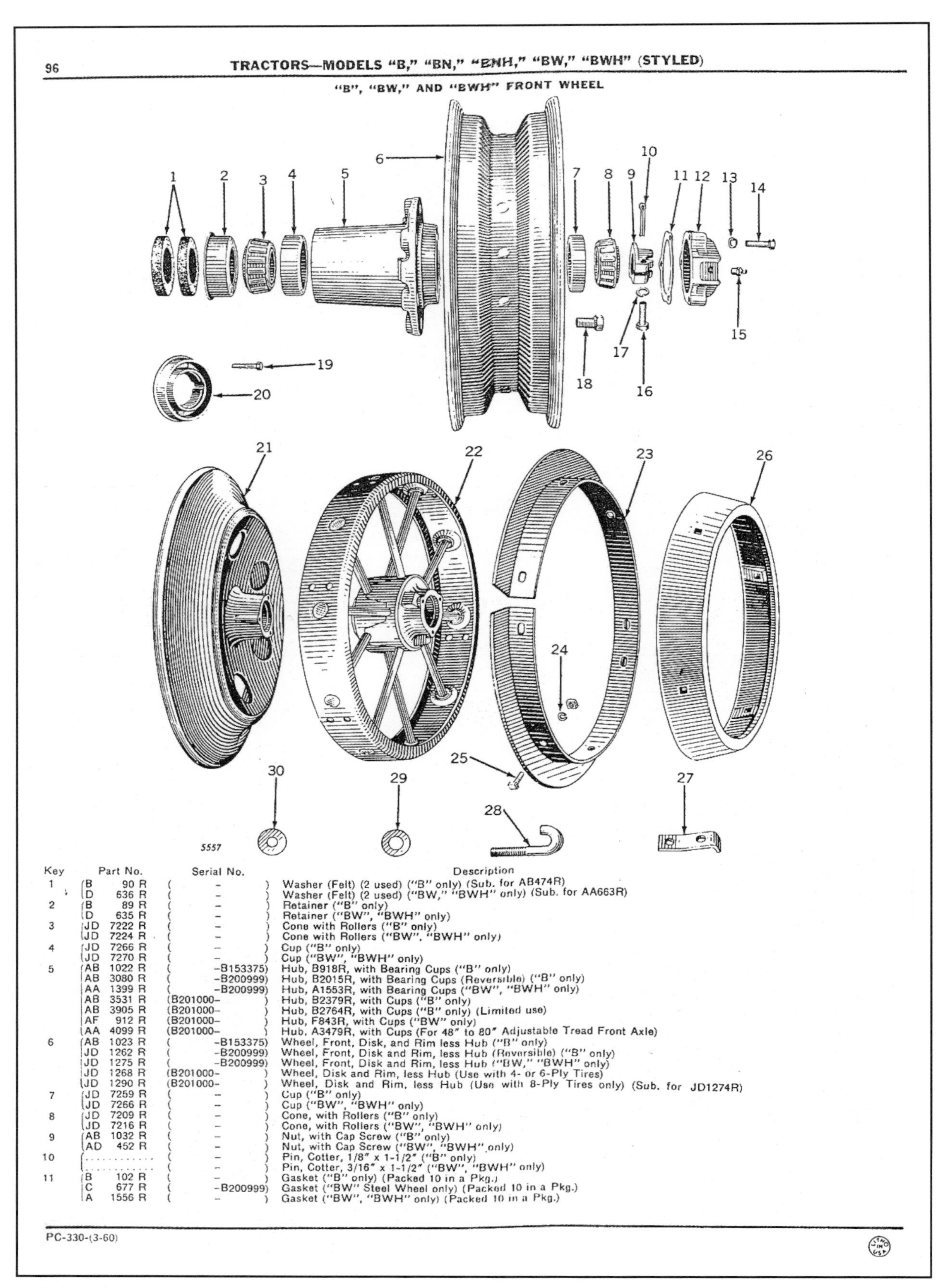

96 TRACTORS—MODELS "B," "BN," "BNH," "BW," "BWH" (STYLED)

"B", "BW," AND "BWH" FRONT WHEEL

Key	Part No.	Serial No.	Description
1	B 90 R	(–)	Washer (Felt) (2 used) ("B" only) (Sub. for AB474R)
	D 636 R	(–)	Washer (Felt) (2 used) ("BW," "BWH" only) (Sub. for AA663R)
2	B 89 R	(–)	Retainer ("B" only)
	D 635 R	(–)	Retainer ("BW", "BWH" only)
3	JD 7222 R	(–)	Cone with Rollers ("B" only)
	JD 7224 R	(–)	Cone with Rollers ("BW". "BWH" only)
4	JD 7266 R	(–)	Cup ("B" only)
	JD 7270 R	(–)	Cup ("BW", "BWH" only)
5	AB 1022 R	(–B153375)	Hub, B918R, with Bearing Cups ("B" only)
	AB 3080 R	(–B200999)	Hub, B2015R, with Bearing Cups (Reversible) ("B" only)
	AA 1399 R	(–B200999)	Hub, A1553R, with Bearing Cups ("BW", "BWH" only)
	AB 3531 R	(B201000–)	Hub, B2379R, with Cups ("B" only)
	AB 3905 R	(B201000–)	Hub, B2764R, with Cups ("B" only) (Limited use)
	AF 912 R	(B201000–)	Hub, F843R, with Cups ("BW" only)
	AA 4099 R	(B201000–)	Hub, A3479R, with Cups (For 48" to 80" Adjustable Tread Front Axle)
6	AB 1023 R	(–B153375)	Wheel, Front, Disk, and Rim less Hub ("B" only)
	JD 1262 R	(–B200999)	Wheel, Front, Disk and Rim, less Hub (Reversible) ("B" only)
	JD 1275 R	(–B200999)	Wheel, Front, Disk and Rim, less Hub ("BW," "BWH" only)
	JD 1268 R	(B201000–)	Wheel, Disk and Rim, less Hub (Use with 4- or 6-Ply Tires)
	JD 1290 R	(B201000–)	Wheel, Disk and Rim, less Hub (Use with 8-Ply Tires only) (Sub. for JD1274R)
7	JD 7259 R	(–)	Cup ("B" only)
	JD 7266 R	(–)	Cup ("BW", "BWH" only)
8	JD 7209 R	(–)	Cone, with Rollers ("B" only)
	JD 7216 R	(–)	Cone, with Rollers ("BW", "BWH" only)
9	AB 1032 R	(–)	Nut, with Cap Screw ("B" only)
	AD 452 R	(–)	Nut, with Cap Screw ("BW", "BWH" only)
10	....	(–)	Pin, Cotter, 1/8" x 1-1/2" ("B" only)
	....	(–)	Pin, Cotter, 3/16" x 1-1/2" ("BW", "BWH" only)
11	B 102 R	(–)	Gasket ("B" only) (Packed 10 in a Pkg.)
	C 677 R	(–B200999)	Gasket ("BW" Steel Wheel only) (Packed 10 in a Pkg.)
	A 1556 R	(–)	Gasket ("BW", "BWH" only) (Packed 10 in a Pkg.)

PC-330-(3-60)

Styled Model B front wheel. *John Deere Archives*

"B", "BW", AND "BWH" FRONT WHEEL—Continued

Key	Part No.	Serial No.	Description
12	AB 867 R	–	Cap, B920R, Hub, with Grease Fitting ("B" only)
	AC 119 R	–B200999	Cap, C167R, Hub, with Grease Fitting ("BW" Steel Wheel only)
	AA 1407 R	–	Cap, A1555R, Hub, with Grease Fitting ("BW," "BWH" only)
13	12H 10 R	–	Washer, Lock, 5/16" (3 used)
14	....	–	Screw, Cap, 5/16" x 1-1/2" (3 used) ("B" only)
	....	–	Screw, Cap, 5/16" x 1-1/4" (3 used) ("BW," "BWH" only)
15	JD 7759	–	Fitting, Grease
16	....	–	Screw, Cap, 5/16" x 1" ("B" only)
	....	–	Screw, Cap, 3/8" x 1-1/4" ("BW," "BWH" only)
17	12H 10 R	–	Washer, Lock, 5/16" ("B" only)
	12H 11 R	–	Washer, Lock, 3/8" ("BW", "BWH" only)
18	JD 17 R	–B153375	Bolt (6 used) ("B" only)
	JD 19 R	B153376–	Bolt (6 used) ("B" Bowl)
	JD 17 R	–B200999	Bolt (6 used) ("BW", "BWH" only)
	JD 19 R	B201000–	Bolt (6 used) ("BW" only)
19	JD 18 R	–B200999	Bolt, Wheel Hub Spacer (6 used per Wheel)
20	AA 2106 R	–B200999	Spacer, Wheel Hub (Two A2275R) (Attachment, List on Separate Order)
21	AB 415 R	–B200999	Wheel, B533R, Cast Disk, with Bearing Cups ("B" only)
22	AB 2708 R	–B200999	Wheel, Front (Steel) with Bearing Cups ("B" only)
	AA 2345 R	–B200999	Wheel, Front (Steel) with Bearing Cups ("BW" only)
23	AB 203 R	–B200999	Band, Front Wheel Guide (Two B10R) 1-1/2" High ("B" only)
	AB 418 R	–B200999	Band, Front Wheel Guide (Two B557R) 2" High ("B" only)
	AB 521 R	–B200999	Band, Front Wheel Guide (Two B605R) 2-1/2" High ("B" only) (Sub. AB418R)
	AC 650 R	–B200999	Band, Front Wheel Guide (Two C1732R) 2-1/2" High ("BW" only)
24	12H 12 R	–B200999	Washer, Lock, 7/16" (8 used)
25	....	–B200999	Bolt, with Nut, 7/16" x 1" (8 used)
26	AB 466 R	–B200999	Rim, Extension (One B575R with Clip and Bolt) ("B" only)
27	C 2309 R	–B200999	Clip, Extension Rim ("B" only)
28	B 559 R	–B200999	Bolt, Hook, Front Wheel Weight (Spoke Type) ("B" only) (3 used)
	D 2184 R	–B200999	Bolt, Hook, Front Wheel Weight (Spoke Type) ("BW" only) (3 used)
29	24H 993 R	–B200999	Washer on Hook Bolt (3 used) ("B" only) (Sub. for 24H490R)
30	D 2186 R	–B200999	Washer on Hook Bolt (3 used) ("BW" only)

Styled Model B front wheel (continued). *John Deere Archives*

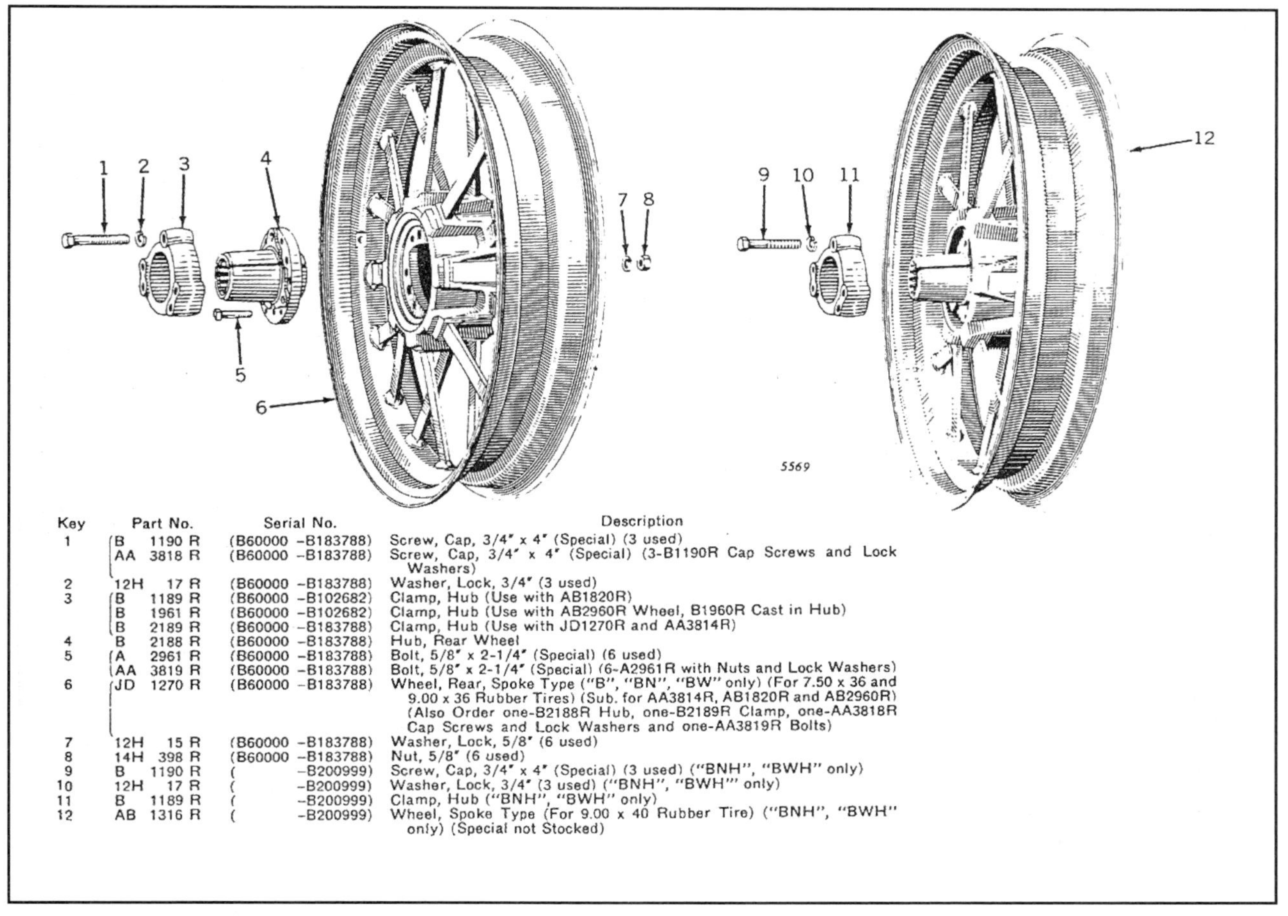

Key	Part No.	Serial No.	Description
1	B 1190 R	(B60000 –B183788)	Screw, Cap, 3/4" x 4" (Special) (3 used)
	AA 3818 R	(B60000 –B183788)	Screw, Cap, 3/4" x 4" (Special) (3-B1190R Cap Screws and Lock Washers)
2	12H 17 R	(B60000 –B183788)	Washer, Lock, 3/4" (3 used)
3	B 1189 R	(B60000 –B102682)	Clamp, Hub (Use with AB1820R)
	B 1961 R	(B60000 –B102682)	Clamp, Hub (Use with AB2960R Wheel, B1960R Cast in Hub)
	B 2189 R	(B60000 –B183788)	Clamp, Hub (Use with JD1270R and AA3814R)
4	B 2188 R	(B60000 –B183788)	Hub, Rear Wheel
5	A 2961 R	(B60000 –B183788)	Bolt, 5/8" x 2-1/4" (Special) (6 used)
	AA 3819 R	(B60000 –B183788)	Bolt, 5/8" x 2-1/4" (Special) (6-A2961R with Nuts and Lock Washers)
6	JD 1270 R	(B60000 –B183788)	Wheel, Rear, Spoke Type ("B", "BN", "BW" only) (For 7.50 x 36 and 9.00 x 36 Rubber Tires) (Sub. for AA3814R, AB1820R and AB2960R) (Also Order one-B2188R Hub, one-B2189R Clamp, one-AA3818R Cap Screws and Lock Washers and one-AA3819R Bolts)
7	12H 15 R	(B60000 –B183788)	Washer, Lock, 5/8" (6 used)
8	14H 398 R	(B60000 –B183788)	Nut, 5/8" (6 used)
9	B 1190 R	(–B200999)	Screw, Cap, 3/4" x 4" (Special) (3 used) ("BNH", "BWH" only)
10	12H 17 R	(–B200999)	Washer, Lock, 3/4" (3 used) ("BNH", "BWH" only)
11	B 1189 R	(–B200999)	Clamp, Hub ("BNH", "BWH" only)
12	AB 1316 R	(–B200999)	Wheel, Spoke Type (For 9.00 x 40 Rubber Tire) ("BNH", "BWH" only) (Special not Stocked)

Styled Model B spoked steel wheels to be used with rubber tires. *John Deere Archives*

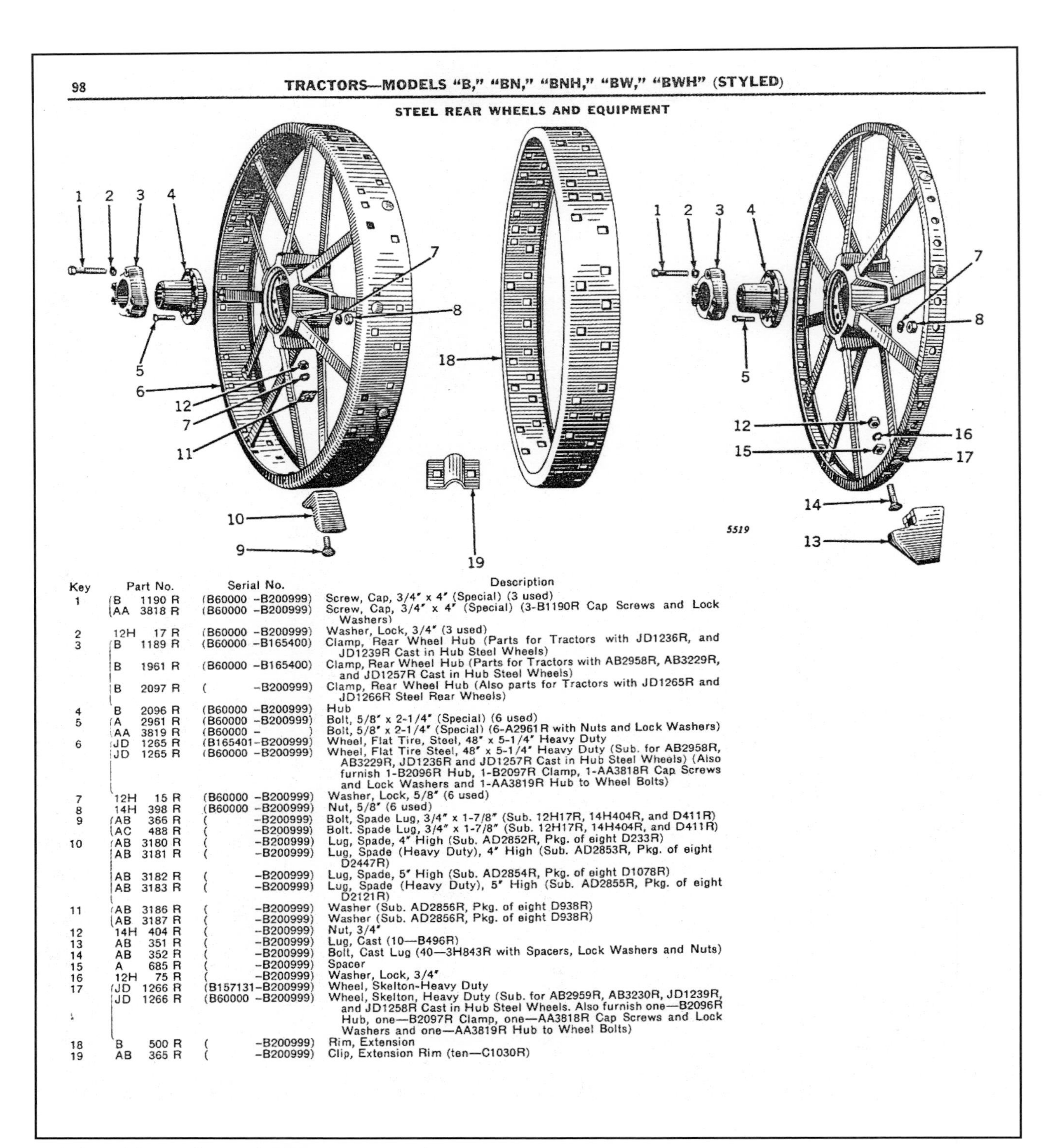

98 TRACTORS—MODELS "B," "BN," "BNH," "BW," "BWH" (STYLED)

STEEL REAR WHEELS AND EQUIPMENT

Key	Part No.	Serial No.	Description
1	B 1190 R	(B60000 -B200999)	Screw, Cap, 3/4" x 4" (Special) (3 used)
	AA 3818 R	(B60000 -B200999)	Screw, Cap, 3/4" x 4" (Special) (3-B1190R Cap Screws and Lock Washers)
2	12H 17 R	(B60000 -B200999)	Washer, Lock, 3/4" (3 used)
3	B 1189 R	(B60000 -B165400)	Clamp, Rear Wheel Hub (Parts for Tractors with JD1236R, and JD1239R Cast in Hub Steel Wheels)
	B 1961 R	(B60000 -B165400)	Clamp, Rear Wheel Hub (Parts for Tractors with AB2958R, AB3229R, and JD1257R Cast in Hub Steel Wheels)
	B 2097 R	(-B200999)	Clamp, Rear Wheel Hub (Also parts for Tractors with JD1265R and JD1266R Steel Rear Wheels)
4	B 2096 R	(B60000 -B200999)	Hub
5	A 2961 R	(B60000 -B200999)	Bolt, 5/8" x 2-1/4" (Special) (6 used)
	AA 3819 R	(B60000 -)	Bolt, 5/8" x 2-1/4" (Special) (6-A2961R with Nuts and Lock Washers)
6	JD 1265 R	(B165401-B200999)	Wheel, Flat Tire, Steel, 48" x 5-1/4" Heavy Duty
	JD 1265 R	(B60000 -B200999)	Wheel, Flat Tire Steel, 48" x 5-1/4" Heavy Duty (Sub. for AB2958R, AB3229R, JD1236R and JD1257R Cast in Hub Steel Wheels) (Also furnish 1-B2096R Hub, 1-B2097R Clamp, 1-AA3818R Cap Screws and Lock Washers and 1-AA3819R Hub to Wheel Bolts)
7	12H 15 R	(B60000 -B200999)	Washer, Lock, 5/8" (6 used)
8	14H 398 R	(B60000 -B200999)	Nut, 5/8" (6 used)
9	AB 366 R	(-B200999)	Bolt, Spade Lug, 3/4" x 1-7/8" (Sub. 12H17R, 14H404R, and D411R)
	AC 488 R	(-B200999)	Bolt. Spade Lug, 3/4" x 1-7/8" (Sub. 12H17R, 14H404R, and D411R)
10	AB 3180 R	(-B200999)	Lug, Spade, 4" High (Sub. AD2852R, Pkg. of eight D233R)
	AB 3181 R	(-B200999)	Lug, Spade (Heavy Duty), 4" High (Sub. AD2853R, Pkg. of eight D2447R)
	AB 3182 R	(-B200999)	Lug, Spade, 5" High (Sub. AD2854R, Pkg. of eight D1078R)
	AB 3183 R	(-B200999)	Lug, Spade (Heavy Duty), 5" High (Sub. AD2855R, Pkg. of eight D2121R)
11	AB 3186 R	(-B200999)	Washer (Sub. AD2856R, Pkg. of eight D938R)
	AB 3187 R	(-B200999)	Washer (Sub. AD2856R, Pkg. of eight D938R)
12	14H 404 R	(-B200999)	Nut, 3/4"
13	AB 351 R	(-B200999)	Lug, Cast (10—B496R)
14	AB 352 R	(-B200999)	Bolt, Cast Lug (40—3H843R with Spacers, Lock Washers and Nuts)
15	A 685 R	(-B200999)	Spacer
16	12H 75 R	(-B200999)	Washer, Lock, 3/4"
17	JD 1266 R	(B157131-B200999)	Wheel, Skelton-Heavy Duty
	JD 1266 R	(B60000 -B200999)	Wheel, Skelton, Heavy Duty (Sub. for AB2959R, AB3230R, JD1239R, and JD1258R Cast in Hub Steel Wheels. Also furnish one—B2096R Hub, one—B2097R Clamp, one—AA3818R Cap Screws and Lock Washers and one—AA3819R Hub to Wheel Bolts)
18	B 500 R	(-B200999)	Rim, Extension
19	AB 365 R	(-B200999)	Clip, Extension Rim (ten—C1030R)

Styled Model B steel rear wheels. *John Deere Archives*

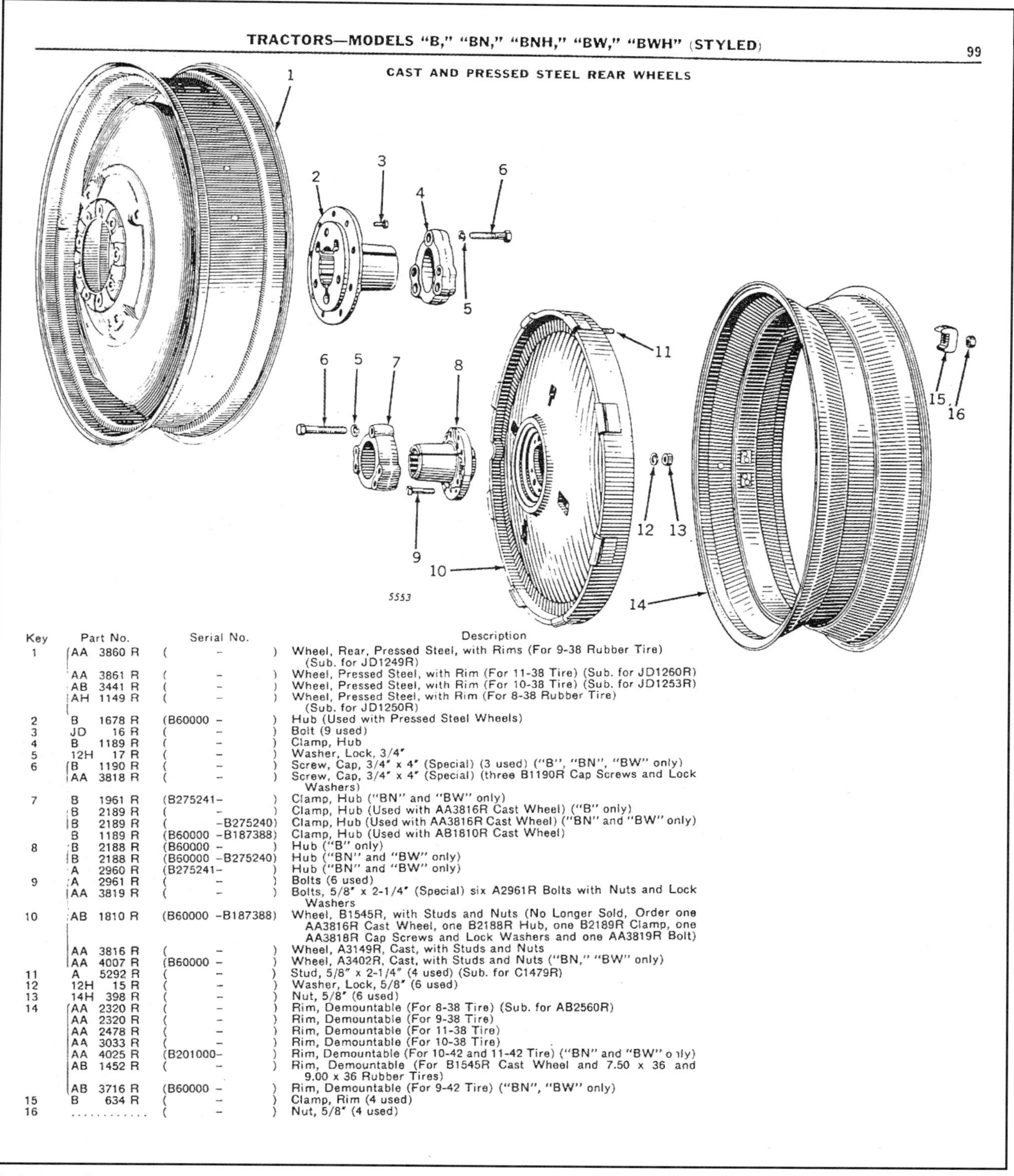

TRACTORS—MODELS "B," "BN," "BNH," "BW," "BWH" (STYLED) 99

CAST AND PRESSED STEEL REAR WHEELS

5553

Key	Part No.	Serial No.	Description
1	AA 3860 R	(–)	Wheel, Rear, Pressed Steel, with Rims (For 9-38 Rubber Tire) (Sub. for JD1249R)
	AA 3861 R	(–)	Wheel, Pressed Steel, with Rim (For 11-38 Tire) (Sub. for JD1260R)
	AB 3441 R	(–)	Wheel, Pressed Steel, with Rim (For 10-38 Tire) (Sub. for JD1253R)
	AH 1149 R	(–)	Wheel, Pressed Steel, with Rim (For 8-38 Rubber Tire) (Sub. for JD1250R)
2	B 1678 R	(B60000 –)	Hub (Used with Pressed Steel Wheels)
3	JD 16 R	(–)	Bolt (9 used)
4	B 1189 R	(–)	Clamp, Hub
5	12H 17 R	(–)	Washer, Lock, 3/4"
6	B 1190 R	(–)	Screw, Cap, 3/4" x 4" (Special) (3 used) ("B", "BN", "BW" only)
	AA 3818 R	(–)	Screw, Cap, 3/4" x 4" (Special) (three B1190R Cap Screws and Lock Washers)
7	B 1961 R	(B275241–)	Clamp, Hub ("BN" and "BW" only)
	B 2189 R	(–)	Clamp, Hub (Used with AA3816R Cast Wheel) ("B" only)
	B 2189 R	(–B275240)	Clamp, Hub (Used with AA3816R Cast Wheel) ("BN" and "BW" only)
	B 1189 R	(B60000 –B187388)	Clamp, Hub (Used with AB1810R Cast Wheel)
8	B 2188 R	(B60000 –)	Hub ("B" only)
	B 2188 R	(B60000 –B275240)	Hub ("BN" and "BW" only)
	A 2960 R	(B275241–)	Hub ("BN" and "BW" only)
9	A 2961 R	(–)	Bolts (6 used)
	AA 3819 R	(–)	Bolts, 5/8" x 2-1/4" (Special) six A2961R Bolts with Nuts and Lock Washers
10	AB 1810 R	(B60000 –B187388)	Wheel, B1545R, with Studs and Nuts (No Longer Sold, Order one AA3816R Cast Wheel, one B2188R Hub, one B2189R Clamp, one AA3818R Cap Screws and Lock Washers and one AA3819R Bolt)
	AA 3816 R	(–)	Wheel, A3149R, Cast, with Studs and Nuts
	AA 4007 R	(B60000 –)	Wheel, A3402R, Cast, with Studs and Nuts ("BN," "BW" only)
11	A 5292 R	(–)	Stud, 5/8" x 2-1/4" (4 used) (Sub. for C1479R)
12	12H 15 R	(–)	Washer, Lock, 5/8" (6 used)
13	14H 398 R	(–)	Nut, 5/8" (6 used)
14	AA 2320 R	(–)	Rim, Demountable (For 8-38 Tire) (Sub. for AB2560R)
	AA 2320 R	(–)	Rim, Demountable (For 9-38 Tire)
	AA 2478 R	(–)	Rim, Demountable (For 11-38 Tire)
	AA 3033 R	(–)	Rim, Demountable (For 10-38 Tire)
	AA 4025 R	(B201000–)	Rim, Demountable (For 10-42 and 11-42 Tire) ("BN" and "BW" only)
	AB 1452 R	(–)	Rim, Demountable (For B1545R Cast Wheel and 7.50 x 36 and 9.00 x 36 Rubber Tires)
	AB 3716 R	(B60000 –)	Rim, Demountable (For 9-42 Tire) ("BN", "BW" only)
15	B 634 R	(–)	Clamp, Rim (4 used)
16	....	(–)	Nut, 5/8" (4 used)

Styled Model B cast- and pressed-steel rear wheels to be used with rubber tires. *John Deere Archives*

Chapter 6

Hydraulics

Hydraulics were one of the most significant improvements to the tractor. Prior to hydraulics, tractors had two uses: prime mover (power supply via the belt pulley or PTO) and traction engine (for pulling loads via the drawbar). Hydraulics added the dimension of lifting and carrying.

This late styled Model B has an aftermarket three-point hitch. A drawbar is installed between the two lower hitch points, while the upper point has the top link held up by a rope. The Powr-Trol hydraulic system raises and lowers the lower points. This hitch greatly adds to the utility of the Model B. For correct restoration, however, the genuine Deere hitch is preferred.

A Model BI with a Parsons Landscoop dumps a load of sand into a 1932 Chevrolet truck. Note the hard rubber front wheels and the rear wheel weights. Note also that the bucket is raised and tipped hydraulically. *John Deere Archives*

The first production tractor with a built-in hydraulic system was the 1930 Allis Chalmers IU with Trackson crawler tracks. It used integral hydraulics to lift its dozer blade. The John Deere Model A was the first production wheel tractor to have built-in hydraulics. Ferguson-Brown, introduced in 1936, incorporated the first hydraulic three-point hitch; it was the forerunner of the Ford-Ferguson 9N. Other manufacturers soon followed, installing various types of hydraulic systems.

Power lifting of implements did not, however, originate with tractor hydraulic systems. As early as 1886, a Peerless steam tractor manufactured by the Geiser Manufacturing Company in Waynesboro, Pennsylvania, could be equipped with a steam lift plow.

The John Deere Model B row-crop was the second production tractor (after the A) to have an integral hydraulic lift system. Actually, the John Deere Model GP tractor had pioneered power implement lifting back in 1928. Its lift, however, was mechanical rather than hydraulic. The WPA (Works Projects Administration, a "New Deal" Great Depression measure) estimated that the power lift saved the farmer 30min per day. Deere estimated it increased the work capacity by ten percent. While none of the standard tread Model Bs had hydraulics, some of the BO Lindeman Crawlers operated their dozer blades with hydraulics. This hydraulic system was made by Lindeman.

John Deere advertising of 1936 touted the hydraulic lift as being a real advance over the mechanical type because it was quick, positive, and provided a cushioned drop. There were fewer parts, and the parts operated in a constant bath of oil.

The original lift was operated by heel-pedals (either left or right, so that the other foot was available for the brake). Sometime in 1936, the size of the pedal pad was increased. In 1947, with the late styled Model B, came Powr-Trol. This was an improved lift system that was operated by a hand lever on the right side of the driver's seat. Powr-Trol had the advantage of being able to operate remote cylinders, as well as the internal rock-shaft cylinder.

Because the power lift was not standard equipment, Deere used a separate serial number

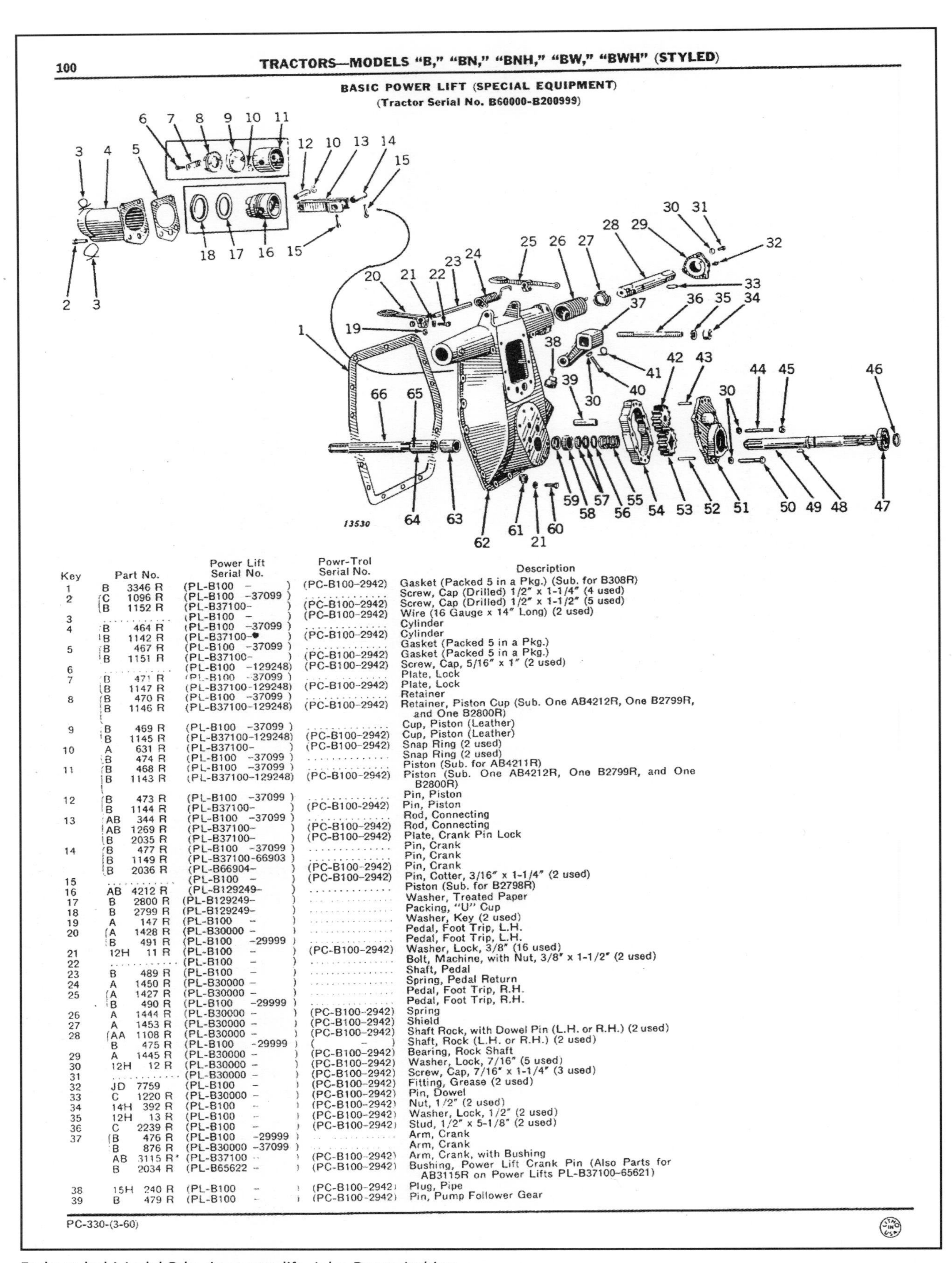

100 TRACTORS—MODELS "B," "BN," "BNH," "BW," "BWH" (STYLED)

BASIC POWER LIFT (SPECIAL EQUIPMENT)

(Tractor Serial No. B60000-B200999)

Key	Part No.	Power Lift Serial No.	Powr-Trol Serial No.	Description
1	B 3346 R	(PL-B100 –)	(PC-B100-2942)	Gasket (Packed 5 in a Pkg.) (Sub. for B308R)
2	C 1096 R	(PL-B100 -37099)	...	Screw, Cap (Drilled) 1/2" x 1-1/4" (4 used)
	B 1152 R	(PL-B37100-)	(PC-B100-2942)	Screw, Cap (Drilled) 1/2" x 1-1/2" (5 used)
3	...	(PL-B100 –)	(PC-B100-2942)	Wire (16 Gauge x 14" Long) (2 used)
4	B 464 R	(PL-B100 -37099)	...	Cylinder
	B 1142 R	(PL-B37100-•)	(PC-B100-2942)	Cylinder
5	B 467 R	(PL-B100 -37099)	...	Gasket (Packed 5 in a Pkg.)
	B 1151 R	(PL-B37100-)	(PC-B100-2942)	Gasket (Packed 5 in a Pkg.)
6	...	(PL-B100 -129248)	(PC-B100-2942)	Screw, Cap, 5/16" x 1" (2 used)
7	B 471 R	(PL-B100 -37099)	...	Plate, Lock
	B 1147 R	(PL-B37100-129248)	(PC-B100-2942)	Plate, Lock
8	B 470 R	(PL-B100 -37099)	...	Retainer
	B 1146 R	(PL-B37100-129248)	(PC-B100-2942)	Retainer, Piston Cup (Sub. One AB4212R, One B2799R, and One B2800R)
9	B 469 R	(PL-B100 -37099)	...	Cup, Piston (Leather)
	B 1145 R	(PL-B37100-129248)	(PC-B100-2942)	Cup, Piston (Leather)
10	A 631 R	(PL-B37100-)	(PC-B100-2942)	Snap Ring (2 used)
	B 474 R	(PL-B100 -37099)	...	Snap Ring (2 used)
11	B 468 R	(PL-B100 -37099)	...	Piston (Sub. for AB4211R)
	B 1143 R	(PL-B37100-129248)	(PC-B100-2942)	Piston (Sub. One AB4212R, One B2799R, and One B2800R)
12	B 473 R	(PL-B100 -37099)	...	Pin, Piston
	B 1144 R	(PL-B37100-)	(PC-B100-2942)	Pin, Piston
13	AB 344 R	(PL-B100 -37099)	...	Rod, Connecting
	AB 1269 R	(PL-B37100-)	(PC-B100-2942)	Rod, Connecting
	B 2035 R	(PL-B37100-)	(PC-B100-2942)	Plate, Crank Pin Lock
14	B 477 R	(PL-B100 -37099)	...	Pin, Crank
	B 1149 R	(PL-B37100-66903)	...	Pin, Crank
	B 2036 R	(PL-B66904-)	(PC-B100-2942)	Pin, Crank
15	...	(PL-B100 –)	(PC-B100-2942)	Pin, Cotter, 3/16" x 1-1/4" (2 used)
16	AB 4212 R	(PL-B129249-)	...	Piston (Sub. for B2798R)
17	B 2800 R	(PL-B129249-)	...	Washer, Treated Paper
18	B 2799 R	(PL-B129249-)	...	Packing, "U" Cup
19	A 147 R	(PL-B100 –)	...	Washer, Key (2 used)
20	A 1428 R	(PL-B30000 –)	...	Pedal, Foot Trip, L.H.
	B 491 R	(PL-B100 -29999)	...	Pedal, Foot Trip, L.H.
21	12H 11 R	(PL-B100 –)	(PC-B100-2942)	Washer, Lock, 3/8" (16 used)
22	...	(PL-B100 –)	...	Bolt, Machine, with Nut, 3/8" x 1-1/2" (2 used)
23	B 489 R	(PL-B100 –)	...	Shaft, Pedal
24	A 1450 R	(PL-B30000 –)	...	Spring, Pedal Return
25	A 1427 R	(PL-B30000 –)	...	Pedal, Foot Trip, R.H.
	B 490 R	(PL-B100 -29999)	...	Pedal, Foot Trip, R.H.
26	A 1444 R	(PL-B30000 –)	(PC-B100-2942)	Spring
27	A 1453 R	(PL-B30000 –)	(PC-B100-2942)	Shield
28	AA 1108 R	(PL-B30000 –)	(PC-B100-2942)	Shaft Rock, with Dowel Pin (L.H. or R.H.) (2 used)
	B 475 R	(PL-B100 -29999)	(–)	Shaft, Rock (L.H. or R.H.) (2 used)
29	A 1445 R	(PL-B30000 –)	(PC-B100-2942)	Bearing, Rock Shaft
30	12H 12 R	(PL-B30000 –)	(PC-B100-2942)	Washer, Lock, 7/16" (5 used)
31	...	(PL-B30000 –)	(PC-B100-2942)	Screw, Cap, 7/16" x 1-1/4" (3 used)
32	JD 7759	(PL-B100 –)	(PC-B100-2942)	Fitting, Grease (2 used)
33	C 1220 R	(PL-B30000 –)	(PC-B100-2942)	Pin, Dowel
34	14H 392 R	(PL-B100 –)	(PC-B100-2942)	Nut, 1/2" (2 used)
35	12H 13 R	(PL-B100 –)	(PC-B100-2942)	Washer, Lock, 1/2" (2 used)
36	C 2239 R	(PL-B100 –)	(PC-B100-2942)	Stud, 1/2" x 5-1/8" (2 used)
37	B 476 R	(PL-B100 -29999)	...	Arm, Crank
	B 876 R	(PL-B30000 -37099)	...	Arm, Crank
	AB 3115 R*	(PL-B37100 –)	(PC-B100-2942)	Arm, Crank, with Bushing
	B 2034 R	(PL-B65622 –)	(PC-B100-2942)	Bushing, Power Lift Crank Pin (Also Parts for AB3115R on Power Lifts PL-B37100-65621)
38	15H 240 R	(PL-B100 –)	(PC-B100-2942)	Plug, Pipe
39	B 479 R	(PL-B100 –)	(PC-B100-2942)	Pin, Pump Follower Gear

PC-330-(3-60)

Early styled Model B basic power lift. *John Deere Archives*

TRACTORS—MODELS "B," "BN," "BNH," "BW," "BWH" (STYLED) 1

BASIC POWER LIFT (SPECIAL EQUIPMENT)—Continued

(Tractor Serial No. B60000-B200999)

Key	Part No.	Power Lift Serial No.	Powr-Trol Serial No.	Description
40	A 634 R	(PL-B100 -130660)	(PC-B100-2942)	Screw, Cap, 7/16" x 2" (Drilled) (2 used)
	A 4168 R	(PL-B130661-)	....	Pin, Crank Arm (2 used)
	....	(PL-B130661-)	....	Pin, Cotter, 1/8" x 5/8" (4 used)
41	....	(PL-B100 -)	(PC-B100-2942)	Wire (16 Gauge x 6" Long)
42	AB 4173 R	(PL-B100 -)	(PC-B100-2942)	Gear, with Bushing Pump Follower (Sub. for AB345R)
	B 494 R	(PL-B100 -)	(PC-B100-2942)	Bushing, Pump Follower Gear
43	A 4879 R	(PL-B100 -)	(PC-B100-2942)	Pin, Dowel (Upper) (Sub. for B153R)
44	B 485 R	(PL-B100 -)	(PC-B100-2942)	Stud, 7/16" x 2-9/16" (4 used)
45	....	(PL-B100 -)	(PC-B100-2942)	Nut, 7/16" (4 used)
46	A 572 R	(PL-B100 -)	(PC-B100-2942)	Snap Ring
47	JD 7664 R	(PL-B100 -)	(PC-B100-2942)	Bearing
48	26H 19 R	(PL-B100 -)	(PC-B100-2942)	Key, Woodruff
49	B 487 R	(PL-B100 -79999)	....	Shaft, Pump, 1-7/64" x 14-5/8"
	B 2071 R	(PL-B80000 -)	(PC-B100-2942)	Shaft, Pump, 1-3/8" x 16-1/2"
50	....	(PL-B100 -)	(PC-B100-2942)	Screw, Cap, 7/16" x 2" (6 used)
51	A 817 R	(PL-B100 -)	(PC-B100-2942)	Cover, Pump Body
52	B 484 R	(PL-B100 -)	(PC-B100-2942)	Pin, Dowel (Lower)
53	B 482 R	(PL-B100 -)	(PC-B100-2942)	Gear, B482R, Drive (Sub. for AB4171R)
54	B 483 R	(PL-B100 -)	(PC-B100-2942)	Body, B483R, Pump (Sub. for AB4239R)
55	A 670 R	(PL-B100 -)	(PC-B100-2942)	Spring
56	24H 272 R	(PL-B100 -)	(PC-B100-2942)	Washer, Oil Seal
57	A 668 R	(PL-B100 -)	(PC-B100-2942)	Packing (2 used)
58	A 667 R	(PL-B100 -)	(PC-B100-2942)	Cup
59	A 621 R	(PL-B100 -)	(PC-B100-2942)	Bearing, Oil Seal
60	....	(PL-B100 -)	(PC-B100-2942)	Screw, Cap, 3/8" x 1" (14 used)
61	15H 237 R	(PL-B30000 -)	(PC-B100-2942)	Plug, Pipe
62	AB 339 R	(PL-B100 -29999)	....	Housing, B463R, with Oil Seal Bearing
	AB 846 R	(PL-B30000 -37099)	....	Housing, B875R, with Pump Shaft Bushing, Oil Seal Bearing, and Pump Follower Gear Pin
	AB 1272 R	(PL-B37100 -)	(PC-B100-2942)	Housing, B1150R, with Pump Shaft Bushing, Oil Seal Bearing, and Pump Follower Gear Pin
63	A 805 R	(PL-B100 -)	(PC-B100-2942)	Bushing
64	A 802 R	(PL-B100 -)	(PC-B100-2942)	Coupling
65	16H 765 A	(PL-B100 -)	(PC-B100-2942)	Rivet, 1/4" x 2"
66	AB 347 R	(PL-B100 -)	(PC-B100-2942)	Shaft with Coupling

*When AB3115R Crank Arm with Bushing is ordered on PL-B100-130660, also furnish two A4168R Pins and four 1/8" x 5/8" Cotter Pins.

Early styled Model B basic power lift (continued). *John Deere Archives*

system for them with the prefix PLB, or PLB after serial number 60,000. With the late styled Model Bs in 1947 (serial number 201,000), the basic lift system was standard, with Powr-Trol optional. Interestingly, this standard lift system was operated with a single centered pedal.

Although there were considerable detail variations in hydraulic lift components over the years, the basic system remained much the same. It was a rather clever unit that bolted over the PTO, and which was essentially self-contained. The PTO provided power for the side-by-side gear pump. The rock-shaft and cylinder were built into the top of the unit, while the valve pack was bolted on the back. Valve pack serial numbers can be found on the tractor build records.

An interesting, but not well known, variation for Model Bs after serial number 60,000 is a live hydraulic pump option. In this configuration, a separate pump is mounted on the distributor/magneto drive pad, with the distributor/magneto mounted to, and driven by, the pump. The PTO-driven pump is then not used. This was not offered as a production option, but was furnished as a kit in 1952.

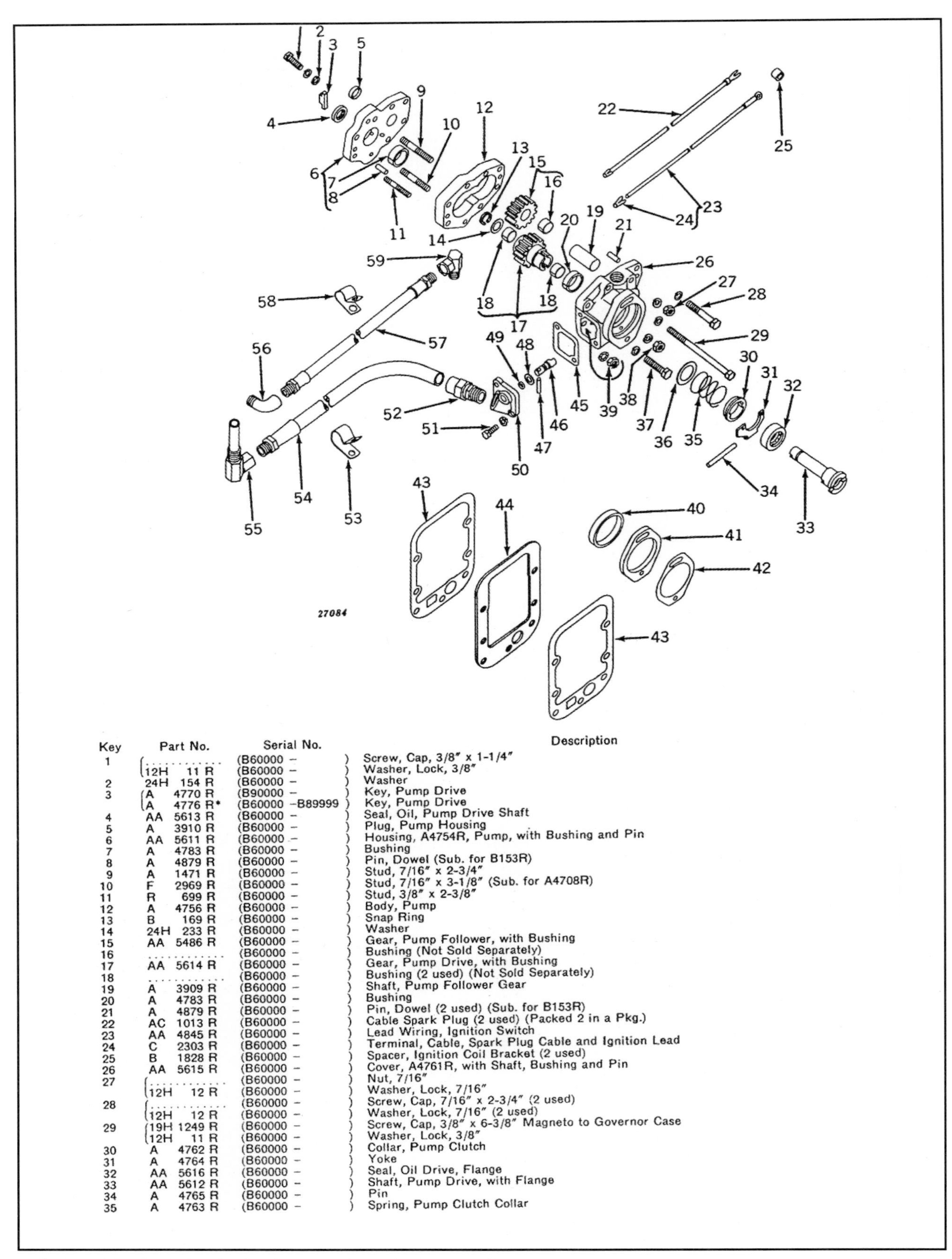

Key	Part No.	Serial No.	Description
1	....	(B60000 –)	Screw, Cap, 3/8" x 1-1/4"
	12H 11 R	(B60000 –)	Washer, Lock, 3/8"
2	24H 154 R	(B60000 –)	Washer
3	A 4770 R	(B90000 –)	Key, Pump Drive
	A 4776 R*	(B60000 –B89999)	Key, Pump Drive
4	AA 5613 R	(B60000 –)	Seal, Oil, Pump Drive Shaft
5	A 3910 R	(B60000 –)	Plug, Pump Housing
6	AA 5611 R	(B60000 –)	Housing, A4754R, Pump, with Bushing and Pin
7	A 4783 R	(B60000 –)	Bushing
8	A 4879 R	(B60000 –)	Pin, Dowel (Sub. for B153R)
9	A 1471 R	(B60000 –)	Stud, 7/16" x 2-3/4"
10	F 2969 R	(B60000 –)	Stud, 7/16" x 3-1/8" (Sub. for A4708R)
11	R 699 R	(B60000 –)	Stud, 3/8" x 2-3/8"
12	A 4756 R	(B60000 –)	Body, Pump
13	B 169 R	(B60000 –)	Snap Ring
14	24H 233 R	(B60000 –)	Washer
15	AA 5486 R	(B60000 –)	Gear, Pump Follower, with Bushing
16	....	(B60000 –)	Bushing (Not Sold Separately)
17	AA 5614 R	(B60000 –)	Gear, Pump Drive, with Bushing
18	....	(B60000 –)	Bushing (2 used) (Not Sold Separately)
19	A 3909 R	(B60000 –)	Shaft, Pump Follower Gear
20	A 4783 R	(B60000 –)	Bushing
21	A 4879 R	(B60000 –)	Pin, Dowel (2 used) (Sub. for B153R)
22	AC 1013 R	(B60000 –)	Cable Spark Plug (2 used) (Packed 2 in a Pkg.)
23	AA 4845 R	(B60000 –)	Lead Wiring, Ignition Switch
24	C 2303 R	(B60000 –)	Terminal, Cable, Spark Plug Cable and Ignition Lead
25	B 1828 R	(B60000 –)	Spacer, Ignition Coil Bracket (2 used)
26	AA 5615 R	(B60000 –)	Cover, A4761R, with Shaft, Bushing and Pin
27	....	(B60000 –)	Nut, 7/16"
	12H 12 R	(B60000 –)	Washer, Lock, 7/16"
28	....	(B60000 –)	Screw, Cap, 7/16" x 2-3/4" (2 used)
	12H 12 R	(B60000 –)	Washer, Lock, 7/16" (2 used)
29	19H 1249 R	(B60000 –)	Screw, Cap, 3/8" x 6-3/8" Magneto to Governor Case
	12H 11 R	(B60000 –)	Washer, Lock, 3/8"
30	A 4762 R	(B60000 –)	Collar, Pump Clutch
31	A 4764 R	(B60000 –)	Yoke
32	AA 5616 R	(B60000 –)	Seal, Oil Drive, Flange
33	AA 5612 R	(B60000 –)	Shaft, Pump Drive, with Flange
34	A 4765 R	(B60000 –)	Pin
35	A 4763 R	(B60000 –)	Spring, Pump Clutch Collar

Styled Model B basic live hydraulic pump kit. *John Deere Archives*

Styled Model B basic live hydraulic pump kit (continued). *John Deere Archives*

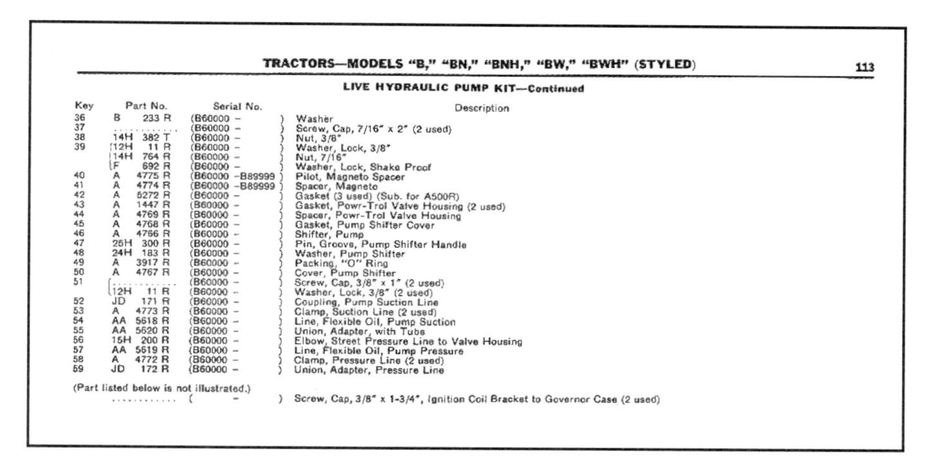

TRACTORS—MODELS "B," "BN," "BNH," "BW," "BWH" (STYLED) 113

LIVE HYDRAULIC PUMP KIT—Continued

Key	Part No.	Serial No.	Description
36	B 233 R	(B60000 –)	Washer
37	....	(B60000 –)	Screw, Cap, 7/16" x 2" (2 used)
38	14H 382 T	(B60000 –)	Nut, 3/8"
39	12H 11 R	(B60000 –)	Washer, Lock, 3/8"
	14H 764 R	(B60000 –)	Nut, 7/16"
	F 692 R	(B60000 –)	Washer, Lock, Shake Proof
40	A 4775 R	(B60000 –B89999)	Pilot, Magneto Spacer
41	A 4774 R	(B60000 –B89999)	Spacer, Magneto
42	A 5272 R	(B60000 –)	Gasket (3 used) (Sub. for A500R)
43	A 1447 R	(B60000 –)	Gasket, Powr-Trol Valve Housing (2 used)
44	A 4769 R	(B60000 –)	Spacer, Powr-Trol Valve Housing
45	A 4768 R	(B60000 –)	Gasket, Pump Shifter Cover
46	A 4766 R	(B60000 –)	Shifter, Pump
47	25H 300 R	(B60000 –)	Pin, Groove, Pump Shifter Handle
48	24H 183 R	(B60000 –)	Washer, Pump Shifter
49	A 3917 R	(B60000 –)	Packing, "O" Ring
50	A 4767 R	(B60000 –)	Cover, Pump Shifter
51	....	(B60000 –)	Screw, Cap, 3/8" x 1" (2 used)
	12H 11 R	(B60000 –)	Washer, Lock, 3/8" (2 used)
52	JD 171 R	(B60000 –)	Coupling, Pump Suction Line
53	A 4773 R	(B60000 –)	Clamp, Suction Line (2 used)
54	AA 5618 R	(B60000 –)	Line, Flexible Oil, Pump Suction
55	AA 5620 R	(B60000 –)	Union, Adapter, with Tube
56	15H 200 R	(B60000 –)	Elbow, Street Pressure Line to Valve Housing
57	AA 5619 R	(B60000 –)	Line, Flexible Oil, Pump Pressure
58	A 4772 R	(B60000 –)	Clamp, Pressure Line (2 used)
59	JD 172 R	(B60000 –)	Union, Adapter, Pressure Line

(Part listed below is not illustrated.)

Key	Part No.	Serial No.	Description
	....	(–)	Screw, Cap, 3/8" x 1-3/4", Ignition Coil Bracket to Governor Case (2 used)

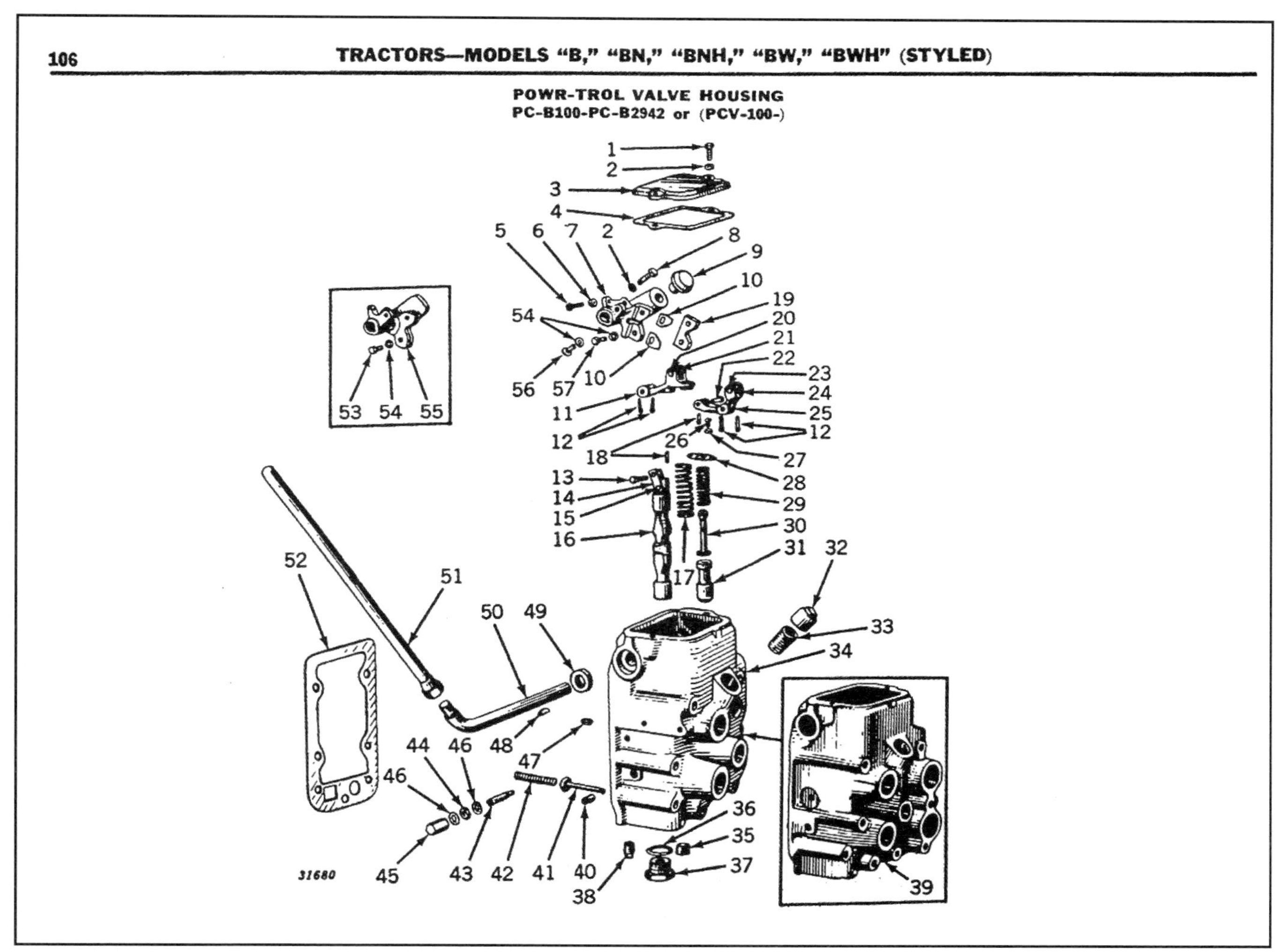

106
TRACTORS—MODELS "B," "BN," "BNH," "BW," "BWH" (STYLED)
POWR-TROL VALVE HOUSING
PC-B100-PC-B2942 or (PCV-100-)
31680

Styled Model B Powr-Trol valve housing. *John Deere Archives*

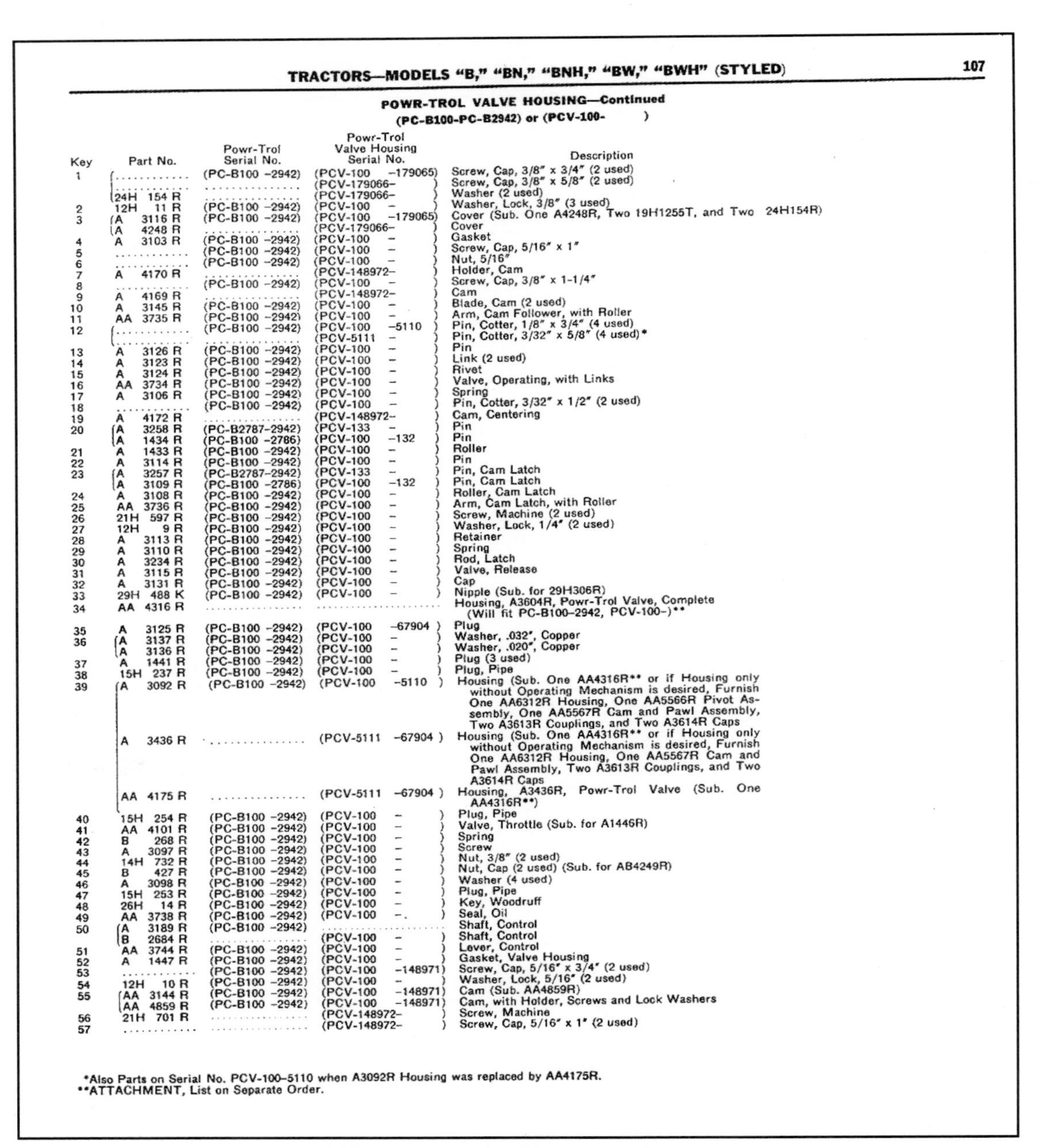

TRACTORS—MODELS "B," "BN," "BNH," "BW," "BWH" (STYLED) 107

POWR-TROL VALVE HOUSING—Continued

(PC-B100-PC-B2942) or (PCV-100-)

Key	Part No.	Powr-Trol Serial No.	Powr-Trol Valve Housing Serial No.	Description
1		(PC-B100 –2942)	(PCV-100 –179065)	Screw, Cap, 3/8" x 3/4" (2 used)
			(PCV-179066–)	Screw, Cap, 3/8" x 5/8" (2 used)
	24H 154 R		(PCV-179066–)	Washer (2 used)
2	12H 11 R	(PC-B100 –2942)	(PCV-100 –)	Washer, Lock, 3/8" (3 used)
3	A 3116 R	(PC-B100 –2942)	(PCV-100 –179065)	Cover (Sub. One A4248R, Two 19H1255T, and Two 24H154R)
	A 4248 R		(PCV-179066–)	Cover
4	A 3103 R	(PC-B100 –2942)	(PCV-100 –)	Gasket
5		(PC-B100 –2942)	(PCV-100 –)	Screw, Cap, 5/16" x 1"
6		(PC-B100 –2942)	(PCV-100 –)	Nut, 5/16"
7	A 4170 R		(PCV-148972–)	Holder, Cam
8		(PC-B100 –2942)	(PCV-100 –)	Screw, Cap, 3/8" x 1-1/4"
9	A 4169 R		(PCV-148972–)	Cam
10	A 3145 R	(PC-B100 –2942)	(PCV-100 –)	Blade, Cam (2 used)
11	AA 3735 R	(PC-B100 –2942)	(PCV-100 –)	Arm, Cam Follower, with Roller
12		(PC-B100 –2942)	(PCV-100 –5110)	Pin, Cotter, 1/8" x 3/4" (4 used)
			(PCV-5111 –)	Pin, Cotter, 3/32" x 5/8" (4 used)*
13	A 3126 R	(PC-B100 –2942)	(PCV-100 –)	Pin
14	A 3123 R	(PC-B100 –2942)	(PCV-100 –)	Link (2 used)
15	A 3124 R	(PC-B100 –2942)	(PCV-100 –)	Rivet
16	AA 3734 R	(PC-B100 –2942)	(PCV-100 –)	Valve, Operating, with Links
17	A 3106 R	(PC-B100 –2942)	(PCV-100 –)	Spring
18		(PC-B100 –2942)	(PCV-100 –)	Pin, Cotter, 3/32" x 1/2" (2 used)
19	A 4172 R		(PCV-148972–)	Cam, Centering
20	A 3258 R	(PC-B2787–2942)	(PCV-133 –)	Pin
	A 1434 R	(PC-B100 –2786)	(PCV-100 –132)	Pin
21	A 1433 R	(PC-B100 –2942)	(PCV-100 –)	Roller
22	A 3114 R	(PC-B100 –2942)	(PCV-100 –)	Pin
23	A 3257 R	(PC-B2787–2942)	(PCV-133 –)	Pin, Cam Latch
	A 3109 R	(PC-B100 –2786)	(PCV-100 –132)	Pin, Cam Latch
24	A 3108 R	(PC-B100 –2942)	(PCV-100 –)	Roller, Cam Latch
25	AA 3736 R	(PC-B100 –2942)	(PCV-100 –)	Arm, Cam Latch, with Roller
26	21H 597 R	(PC-B100 –2942)	(PCV-100 –)	Screw, Machine (2 used)
27	12H 9 R	(PC-B100 –2942)	(PCV-100 –)	Washer, Lock, 1/4" (2 used)
28	A 3113 R	(PC-B100 –2942)	(PCV-100 –)	Retainer
29	A 3110 R	(PC-B100 –2942)	(PCV-100 –)	Spring
30	A 3234 R	(PC-B100 –2942)	(PCV-100 –)	Rod, Latch
31	A 3115 R	(PC-B100 –2942)	(PCV-100 –)	Valve, Release
32	A 3131 R	(PC-B100 –2942)	(PCV-100 –)	Cap
33	29H 488 K	(PC-B100 –2942)	(PCV-100 –)	Nipple (Sub. for 29H306R)
34	AA 4316 R			Housing, A3604R, Powr-Trol Valve, Complete (Will fit PC-B100–2942, PCV-100–)**
35	A 3125 R	(PC-B100 –2942)	(PCV-100 –67904)	Plug
36	A 3137 R	(PC-B100 –2942)	(PCV-100 –)	Washer, .032", Copper
	A 3136 R	(PC-B100 –2942)	(PCV-100 –)	Washer, .020", Copper
37	A 1441 R	(PC-B100 –2942)	(PCV-100 –)	Plug (3 used)
38	15H 237 R	(PC-B100 –2942)	(PCV-100 –)	Plug, Pipe
39	A 3092 R	(PC-B100 –2942)	(PCV-100 –5110)	Housing (Sub. One AA4316R** or if Housing only without Operating Mechanism is desired, Furnish One AA6312R Housing, One AA5566R Pivot Assembly, One AA5567R Cam and Pawl Assembly, Two A3613R Couplings, and Two A3614R Caps
	A 3436 R		(PCV-5111 –67904)	Housing (Sub. One AA4316R** or if Housing only without Operating Mechanism is desired, Furnish One AA6312R Housing, One AA5567R Cam and Pawl Assembly, Two A3613R Couplings, and Two A3614R Caps
	AA 4175 R		(PCV-5111 –67904)	Housing, A3436R, Powr-Trol Valve (Sub. One AA4316R**)
40	15H 254 R	(PC-B100 –2942)	(PCV-100 –)	Plug, Pipe
41	AA 4101 R	(PC-B100 –2942)	(PCV-100 –)	Valve, Throttle (Sub. for A1446R)
42	B 268 R	(PC-B100 –2942)	(PCV-100 –)	Spring
43	A 3097 R	(PC-B100 –2942)	(PCV-100 –)	Screw
44	14H 732 R	(PC-B100 –2942)	(PCV-100 –)	Nut, 3/8" (2 used)
45	B 427 R	(PC-B100 –2942)	(PCV-100 –)	Nut, Cap (2 used) (Sub. for AB4249R)
46	A 3098 R	(PC-B100 –2942)	(PCV-100 –)	Washer (4 used)
47	15H 253 R	(PC-B100 –2942)	(PCV-100 –)	Plug, Pipe
48	26H 14 R	(PC-B100 –2942)	(PCV-100 –)	Key, Woodruff
49	AA 3738 R	(PC-B100 –2942)	(PCV-100 –)	Seal, Oil
50	A 3189 R	(PC-B100 –2942)		Shaft, Control
	B 2684 R		(PCV-100 –)	Shaft, Control
51	AA 3744 R	(PC-B100 –2942)	(PCV-100 –)	Lever, Control
52	A 1447 R	(PC-B100 –2942)	(PCV-100 –)	Gasket, Valve Housing
53		(PC-B100 –2942)	(PCV-100 –148971)	Screw, Cap, 5/16" x 3/4" (2 used)
54	12H 10 R	(PC-B100 –2942)	(PCV-100 –)	Washer, Lock, 5/16" (2 used)
55	AA 3144 R	(PC-B100 –2942)	(PCV-100 –148971)	Cam (Sub. AA4859R)
	AA 4859 R	(PC-B100 –2942)	(PCV-100 –148971)	Cam, with Holder, Screws and Lock Washers
56	21H 701 R		(PCV-148972–)	Screw, Machine
57			(PCV-148972–)	Screw, Cap, 5/16" x 1" (2 used)

*Also Parts on Serial No. PCV-100–5110 when A3092R Housing was replaced by AA4175R.
**ATTACHMENT, List on Separate Order.

Styled Model B Powr-Trol valve housing (continued). *John Deere Archives*

TRACTORS—MODELS "B," "BN," "BNH," "BW," "BWH" (STYLED) 103

BASIC POWER LIFT (STANDARD EQUIPMENT)—Continued

(SERIAL No. B201000-)

Key	Part No.	Serial No	Description
44	JD 7190 R	(B201000–)	Bearing
45	F 215 R	(B201000–)	Snap Ring (5 used)
46	26H 19 R	(B201000–)	Key, Woodruff
47		(B201000–)	Screw, Cap, 7/16" x 2-1/4" (6 used)
48	A 819 R	(B201000–)	Pin, Dowel
49	B 2616 R	(B201000–)	Gear, Pump Drive (Sub. for AB4172R)
50	A 2435 R	(B201000–)	Spring
51	24H 316 R	(B201000–)	Washer, Oil Seal (Steel) (Sub. for A2434R)
52	A 2436 R	(B201000–)	Packing (2 used)
53	A 2432 R	(B201000–)	Cup, Oil Seal
54	A 2480 R	(B201000–)	Bearing, Oil Seal
55	15H 237 R	(B201000–)	Plug, Pipe
56		(B201000–)	Screw, Cap, 3/8" x 1" (11 used)
57	12H 11 R	(B201000–)	Washer, Lock, 3/8" (11 used)
58	A 2428 R	(B201000–)	Coupling (2 used) (Sub. for A3401R)
59	B 2625 R	(B201000–)	Shaft, Drive
60	B 2626 R	(B201000–)	Bushing

*When AB3115R Crank Arm with Bushing on B201000-B273841 is ordered, also furnish two A4168R Pins and four 1/8" x 5/8" Cotter Pins.

Styled Model B power lift (continued). *John Deere Archives*

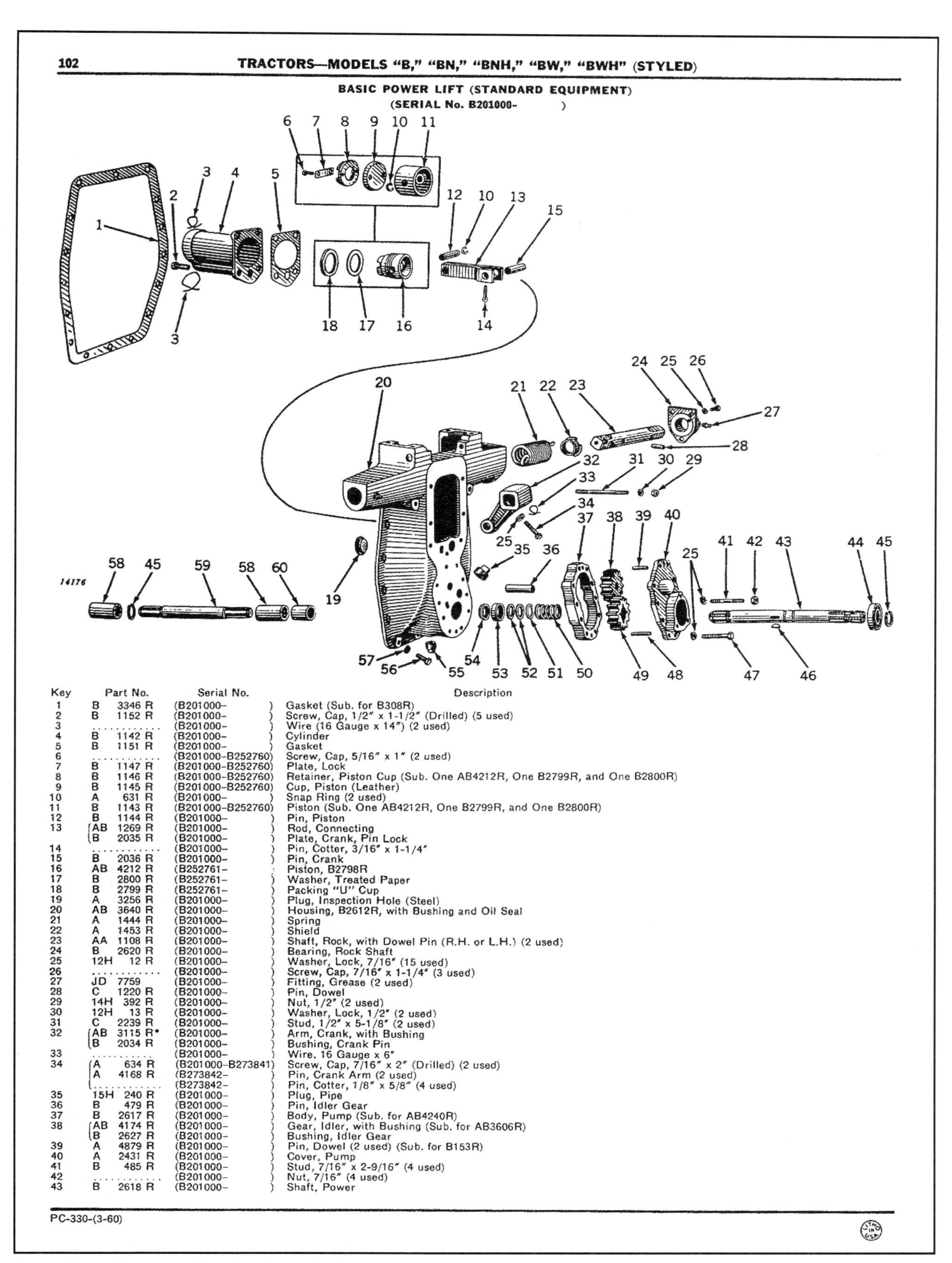

102 TRACTORS—MODELS "B," "BN," "BNH," "BW," "BWH" (STYLED)

BASIC POWER LIFT (STANDARD EQUIPMENT)

(SERIAL No. B201000-)

Key	Part No.	Serial No.	Description
1	B 3346 R	(B201000-)	Gasket (Sub. for B308R)
2	B 1152 R	(B201000-)	Screw, Cap, 1/2" x 1-1/2" (Drilled) (5 used)
3	....	(B201000-)	Wire (16 Gauge x 14") (2 used)
4	B 1142 R	(B201000-)	Cylinder
5	B 1151 R	(B201000-)	Gasket
6	....	(B201000-B252760)	Screw, Cap, 5/16" x 1" (2 used)
7	B 1147 R	(B201000-B252760)	Plate, Lock
8	B 1146 R	(B201000-B252760)	Retainer, Piston Cup (Sub. One AB4212R, One B2799R, and One B2800R)
9	B 1145 R	(B201000-B252760)	Cup, Piston (Leather)
10	A 631 R	(B201000-)	Snap Ring (2 used)
11	B 1143 R	(B201000-B252760)	Piston (Sub. One AB4212R, One B2799R, and One B2800R)
12	B 1144 R	(B201000-)	Pin, Piston
13	AB 1269 R	(B201000-)	Rod, Connecting
	B 2035 R	(B201000-)	Plate, Crank, Pin Lock
14	....	(B201000-)	Pin, Cotter, 3/16" x 1-1/4"
15	B 2036 R	(B201000-)	Pin, Crank
16	AB 4212 R	(B252761-)	Piston, B2798R
17	B 2800 R	(B252761-)	Washer, Treated Paper
18	B 2799 R	(B252761-)	Packing "U" Cup
19	A 3256 R	(B201000-)	Plug, Inspection Hole (Steel)
20	AB 3640 R	(B201000-)	Housing, B2612R, with Bushing and Oil Seal
21	A 1444 R	(B201000-)	Spring
22	A 1453 R	(B201000-)	Shield
23	AA 1108 R	(B201000-)	Shaft, Rock, with Dowel Pin (R.H. or L.H.) (2 used)
24	B 2620 R	(B201000-)	Bearing, Rock Shaft
25	12H 12 R	(B201000-)	Washer, Lock, 7/16" (15 used)
26	....	(B201000-)	Screw, Cap, 7/16" x 1-1/4" (3 used)
27	JD 7759	(B201000-)	Fitting, Grease (2 used)
28	C 1220 R	(B201000-)	Pin, Dowel
29	14H 392 R	(B201000-)	Nut, 1/2" (2 used)
30	12H 13 R	(B201000-)	Washer, Lock, 1/2" (2 used)
31	C 2239 R	(B201000-)	Stud, 1/2" x 5-1/8" (2 used)
32	AB 3115 R*	(B201000-)	Arm, Crank, with Bushing
	B 2034 R	(B201000-)	Bushing, Crank Pin
33	....	(B201000-)	Wire, 16 Gauge x 6"
34	A 634 R	(B201000-B273841)	Screw, Cap, 7/16" x 2" (Drilled) (2 used)
	A 4168 R	(B273842-)	Pin, Crank Arm (2 used)
	....	(B273842-)	Pin, Cotter, 1/8" x 5/8" (4 used)
35	15H 240 R	(B201000-)	Plug, Pipe
36	B 479 R	(B201000-)	Pin, Idler Gear
37	B 2617 R	(B201000-)	Body, Pump (Sub. for AB4240R)
38	AB 4174 R	(B201000-)	Gear, Idler, with Bushing (Sub. for AB3606R)
	B 2627 R	(B201000-)	Bushing, Idler Gear
39	A 4879 R	(B201000-)	Pin, Dowel (2 used) (Sub. for B153R)
40	A 2431 R	(B201000-)	Cover, Pump
41	B 485 R	(B201000-)	Stud, 7/16" x 2-9/16" (4 used)
42	....	(B201000-)	Nut, 7/16" (4 used)
43	B 2618 R	(B201000-)	Shaft, Power

PC-330-(3-60)

Styled Model B power lift. *John Deere Archives*

Chapter 7

Electrical System

Surprisingly, tractor lights were not common until the model year 1939. Caterpillar and Cletrac offered lights as early as 1928, but these were exceptions. Some Massey-Harris pictures from 1930 show lights as well, but it was the 1935 Oliver 70 that established the optional tractor electrical system, with both lights and the self-starter.

This rare example of an unstyled Model B with a headlight is a 1936 John Deere Model BW with a B&B cultivator operating near Phoenix, Arizona. Note the early style Firestone rear treads. *John Deere Archives*

Lighting

Lighting outfits were available from John Deere as early as the late 1920s for both the D and GP tractors. Model A and B tractors were offered with K-W electric lighting outfits from the start of production. Electric starting and lighting were offered as optional equipment beginning in September 1939 for the 1939 model tractors.

For model years 1939 and 1940, 7in lights were provided with the option. After that, from 1941 and on, 5in lights were used.

Hood end caps with three instrument holes were used when equipped with an electrical system. An ammeter was installed, in addition to the oil pressure and temperature gauges. Slant-dash hood end caps were used in 1939 and 1940. After that, vertical end caps were used.

Delco-Remy six-volt generators were used throughout production, although there were several different part numbers used (see parts breakdown figure). Voltage regulators, rather than cutouts, were used after serial number 201,000. Delco-Remy starters were also used.

Fabric-covered wires are appropriate for prewar and wartime tractors.

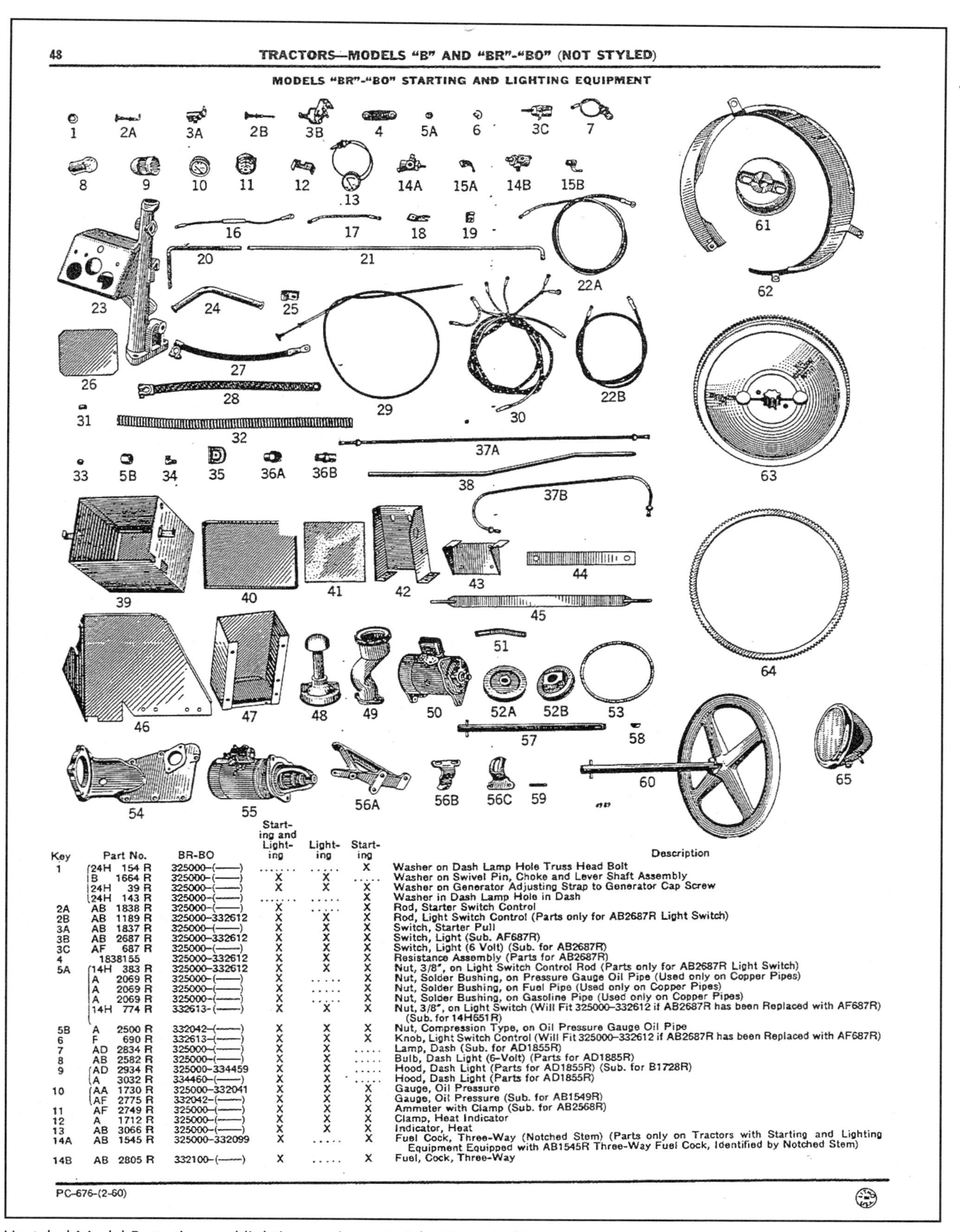

48 TRACTORS—MODELS "B" AND "BR"-"BO" (NOT STYLED)

MODELS "BR"-"BO" STARTING AND LIGHTING EQUIPMENT

Key	Part No.	BR-BO	Starting and Lighting	Lighting	Starting	Description
1	24H 154 R	325000-(——)	....	.....	X	Washer on Dash Lamp Hole Truss Head Bolt
	B 1664 R	325000-(——)	X	X	.....	Washer on Swivel Pin, Choke and Lever Shaft Assembly
	24H 39 R	325000-(——)	X	X	X	Washer on Generator Adjusting Strap to Generator Cap Screw
	24H 143 R	325000-(——)	....	.....	X	Washer in Dash Lamp Hole in Dash
2A	AB 1838 R	325000-(——)	X	.....	X	Rod, Starter Switch Control
2B	AB 1189 R	325000-332612	X	X	X	Rod, Light Switch Control (Parts only for AB2687R Light Switch)
3A	AB 1837 R	325000-(——)	X	X	X	Switch, Starter Pull
3B	AB 2687 R	325000-332612	X	X	X	Switch, Light (Sub. AF687R)
3C	AF 687 R	325000-(——)	X	X	X	Switch, Light (6 Volt) (Sub. for AB2687R)
4	1838155	325000-332612	X	X	X	Resistance Assembly (Parts for AB2687R)
5A	14H 383 R	325000-332612	X	X	X	Nut, 3/8", on Light Switch Control Rod (Parts only for AB2687R Light Switch)
	A 2069 R	325000-(——)	X	.....	X	Nut, Solder Bushing, on Pressure Gauge Oil Pipe (Used only on Copper Pipes)
	A 2069 R	325000-(——)	X	.....	X	Nut, Solder Bushing, on Fuel Pipe (Used only on Copper Pipes)
	A 2069 R	325000-(——)	X	.....	X	Nut, Solder Bushing, on Gasoline Pipe (Used only on Copper Pipes)
	14H 774 R	332613-(——)	X	X	X	Nut, 3/8", on Light Switch (Will Fit 325000-332612 if AB2687R has been Replaced with AF687R) (Sub. for 14H651R)
5B	A 2500 R	332042-(——)	X	X	X	Nut, Compression Type, on Oil Pressure Gauge Oil Pipe
6	F 690 R	332613-(——)	X	X	X	Knob, Light Switch Control (Will Fit 325000-332612 if AB2687R has been Replaced with AF687R)
7	AD 2834 R	325000-(——)	X	X	.....	Lamp, Dash (Sub. for AD1855R)
8	AB 2582 R	325000-(——)	X	X	.....	Bulb, Dash Light (6-Volt) (Parts for AD1885R)
9	AD 2934 R	325000-334459	X	X	.....	Hood, Dash Light (Parts for AD1855R) (Sub. for B1728R)
	A 3032 R	334460-(——)	X	X	.....	Hood, Dash Light (Parts for AD1855R)
10	AA 1730 R	325000-332041	X	X	X	Gauge, Oil Pressure
	AF 2775 R	332042-(——)	X	X	X	Gauge, Oil Pressure (Sub. for AB1549R)
11	AF 2749 R	325000-(——)	X	X	X	Ammeter with Clamp (Sub. for AB2568R)
12	A 1712 R	325000-(——)	X	X	X	Clamp, Heat Indicator
13	AB 3066 R	325000-(——)	X	X	X	Indicator, Heat
14A	AB 1545 R	325000-332099	X	.....	X	Fuel Cock, Three-Way (Notched Stem) (Parts only on Tractors with Starting and Lighting Equipment Equipped with AB1545R Three-Way Fuel Cock, Identified by Notched Stem)
14B	AB 2805 R	332100-(——)	X	.....	X	Fuel, Cock, Three-Way

PC-676-(2-60)

Unstyled Model B starting and lighting equipment. *John Deere Archives*

MODELS "BR"-"BO" STARTING AND LIGHTING EQUIPMENT—Continued

Key		Part No.	BR-BO	Starting and Lighting	Lighting	Starting	Description
15A	B	1535 R	325000–332099	X	.....	X	Indexing, Stop, Three-Way Fuel Cock (Parts only on Tractors with Starting and Lighting Equipment Equipped with AB1545R Three-Way Fuel Cock Identified by Notched Stem)
15B	B	1901 R	332100–(——)	X	.....	X	Indexing Stop, Three-Way Fuel (Parts only on Tractors with Starting and Lighting Equipment Equipped with AB2805R Three-Way Fuel Cock Identified by Round Stem)
16	AF	701 R	332613–(——)	X	X	X	Fuse, Lead Ammeter to Light Switch (Will Fit 325000–332612 if AB2687 has been Replaced with AF687R)
17	AA	4845 R	325000–(——)	X	.....	X	Wire, Ammeter to Starting Switch (Sub. for AB1840R)
18	B	1592 R	325000–(——)	X	.....	X	Support, Choke Tube
19	A	2610 R	325000–(——)	X	X	X	Clip, Wiring Harness to Tractor (Sub. for A1225R)
	A	2610 R	325000–(——)	X	X	X	Clip, Rear Lamp Wire to Tractor (Sub. for A1225R)
	A	2610 R	325000–(——)	X	.....	X	Clip, Choke Tube to Tank Support (Sub. for A1225R)
20	B	1655 R	325000–(——)	X	X	X	Shaft, Speed Control
21	B	1651 R	325000–332099	X	.....	X	Rod, Fuel Control (Parts only on Tractors with Starting and Lighting Equipment Equipped with AB1545R Three-Way Fuel Cock, Identified by Notched Stem)
	B	1903 R	325000–(——)	X	.....	X	Rod, Fuel Control (Parts only on Tractors with Starting and Lighting Equipment Equipped with AB2805R Three-Way Fuel Cock Identified by Round Stem)
22A	AB	1964 R	325000–(——)	X	.....	X	Wire, Starter Switch to Magnetic Switch
	AB	1965 R	325000–(——)	X	.....	X	Wire, Ammeter to Magnetic Switch
	AB	1978 R	325000–(——)	....	X	.....	Wire, Ammeter to Battery
22B	AB	1963 R	325000–(——)	X	X	.....	Wire, Rear Lamp
23	B	1642 R	325000–(——)	X	X	X	Support, Dash and Steering Shaft
24	B	1647 R	325000–(——)	X	X	X	Conduit, Wiring Harness
25	B	1588 R	325000–(——)	X	X	X	Clip, Conduit
26	B	1645 R	325000–(——)	X	X	X	Cover, Dash
27	AB	1968 R	325000–(——)	X	.....	X	Cable, Magnetic Switch to Battery
28	AB	1197 R	325000–(——)	X	X	X	Cable, Battery Ground
29	AB	4227 R	325000–(——)	X	.....	X	Rod and Tube, Choke (Sub. for AB1961R)
30	AB	1962 R	325000–(——)	X	X	.....	Harness, Wiring
	AB	1979 R	325000–(——)	....	.....	X	Harness, Generator Wiring
31	E	2150 R	325000–(——)	X	.....	X	Gland, Solder Bushing, on Fuel Pipe (Used only on Copper Pipes)
	E	2150 R	325000–(——)	X	.....	X	Gland, Solder Bushing, on Gasoline Pipe (Used only on Copper Pipes)
	E	2150 R	325000–(——)	X	X	X	Gland, Solder Bushing, on Pressure Gauge Pipe (Used only on Copper Pipes)
32	B	1644 R	325000–(——)	X	X	X	Conduit, Starting and Lighting Control
33	A	2499 R	332042-(——)	X	X	X	Sleeve on Oil Pressure Gauge Oil Pipe
34	D	417 R	325000–332041	X	X	X	Elbow, Pressure Gauge Oil Pipe to Governor Case
35	B	1654 R	325000–(——)	X	.....	X	Bracket, Fuel Control
36A	A	2564 R	332042–(——)	X	X	X	Connector, Compression Type, Oil Pressure Gauge to Oil Pressure Gauge Oil Pipe
36B	A	2502 R	332042–(——)	X	X	X	Connector, Governor Case to Oil Pressure Gauge Oil Pipe
37A	AB	1960 R	325000–332041	X	X	X	Pipe, Oil Pressure Gauge
37B	AB	1970 R	325000–(——)	X	.....	X	Pipe, Fuel
	AB	1971 R	325000–(——)	X	.....	X	Pipe, Gasoline
38	B	1646 R	325000–(——)	X	X	X	Pipe, Ventilator
39	AB	1194 R	325000–(——)	X	X	X	Box, Battery
40	B	1029 R	325000–(——)	X	X	X	Lid, Battery Box
41	B	1589 R	325000–(——)	X	X	X	Pad, Battery
42	B	999 R	325000–(——)	X	X	X	Support, Battery Box
43	B	1025 R	325000–(——)	X	X	X	Brace, Battery Box
44	B	998 R	325000–(——)	X	X	X	Plate, Battery Clamp Cross
45	AB	1196 R	325000–(——)	X	X	X	Clamp, Battery, with Bolts
46	AB	1973 R	325000–(——)	X	.....	X	Front, Orchard Fender, L.H.
47	AA	1911 R	325000–(——)	X	X	X	Box, Tool
48	AB	1969 R	325000–(——)	X	.....	X	Cover, B55R, Breather, with Stack
49	B	1649 R	325000–(——)	X	.....	X	Body, Breather
50	A	1204 R	325000–(——)	X	X	X	Generator (Delco-Remy No. 1101356 or No. 1101385) (Sub. AP19305H)
51	B	1033 R	325000–(——)	X	X	X	Strap, Generator Adjusting
52A	B	1030 R	325000–(——)	X	X	X	Pulley, Generator
52B	AA	1930 R	325000–(——)	X	X	X	Pulley, D2911R, Generator Drive
53	A	1230 R	325000-(——)	X	X	X	Belt, Generator
54	AB	2598 R	325000–(——)	X	.....	X	Cover, B1595R, Crankcase
55	AB	1845 R	325000–(——)	X	.....	X	Motor, Starting, with Magnetic Switch (Delco-Remy No. 110724) (Sub. AB4092R)
56A	B	1031 R	325000–(——)	X	X	X	Bracket, Generator
56B	B	1028 R	325000–(——)	X	X	.....	Bracket, Head Lamp
56C	D	2914 R	325000–(——)	X	X	.....	Bracket, Lamp, Rear
57	AB	2571 R	325000–(——)	X	.....	X	Shaft, Cranking (Use with Steering Wheel)
58	26H	17 R	325000–(——)	X	.....	X	Key, Woodruff, in Cranking Shaft
59	B	1662 R	325000–(——)	X	.....	X	Pin, Cranking Shaft
60	AB	1956 R	325000–332058	X	.....	X	Wheel, Cranking, with Shaft and Pin
61	B	1608 R	325000–(——)	X	.....	X	Ratchet, Flywheel Crank
62	AB	1856 R	325000–(——)	X	.....	X	Guard, Flywheel, with Supports
63	AB	2686 R	325000–(——)	X	.....	X	Flywheel, B1606R, with Crank Ratchet
64	B	1607 R	325000–(——)	X	.....	X	Gear, Flywheel Starter
65	AB	3144 R	325000–(——)	X	X	.....	Lamp, R.H. (7" Dia.)
	AB	3145 R	325000–(——)	X	X	.....	Lamp, L.H. (7" Dia.)
	AD	2450 R	325000–(——)	X	X	.....	Lamp, Rear (7" Dia.)
(Parts listed below are not illustrated.)							
	A	2791 R	332042–(——)	X	X	X	Pipe, Oil, Oil Pressure Gauge
	B	997 R	325000–(——)	X	X	X	Bolt, Battery Clamp
	A	3082 R	325000–(——)	X	.....	X	Cover, Starting Motor Terminal

Unstyled Model B starting and lighting equipment (continued). *John Deere Archives*

This rather unusual 1939 photo shows a Model B plowing at night with a hood-mounted headlight. It does appear that the tractor does have a generator, but the wiring and light seem to be temporary. *John Deere Archives*

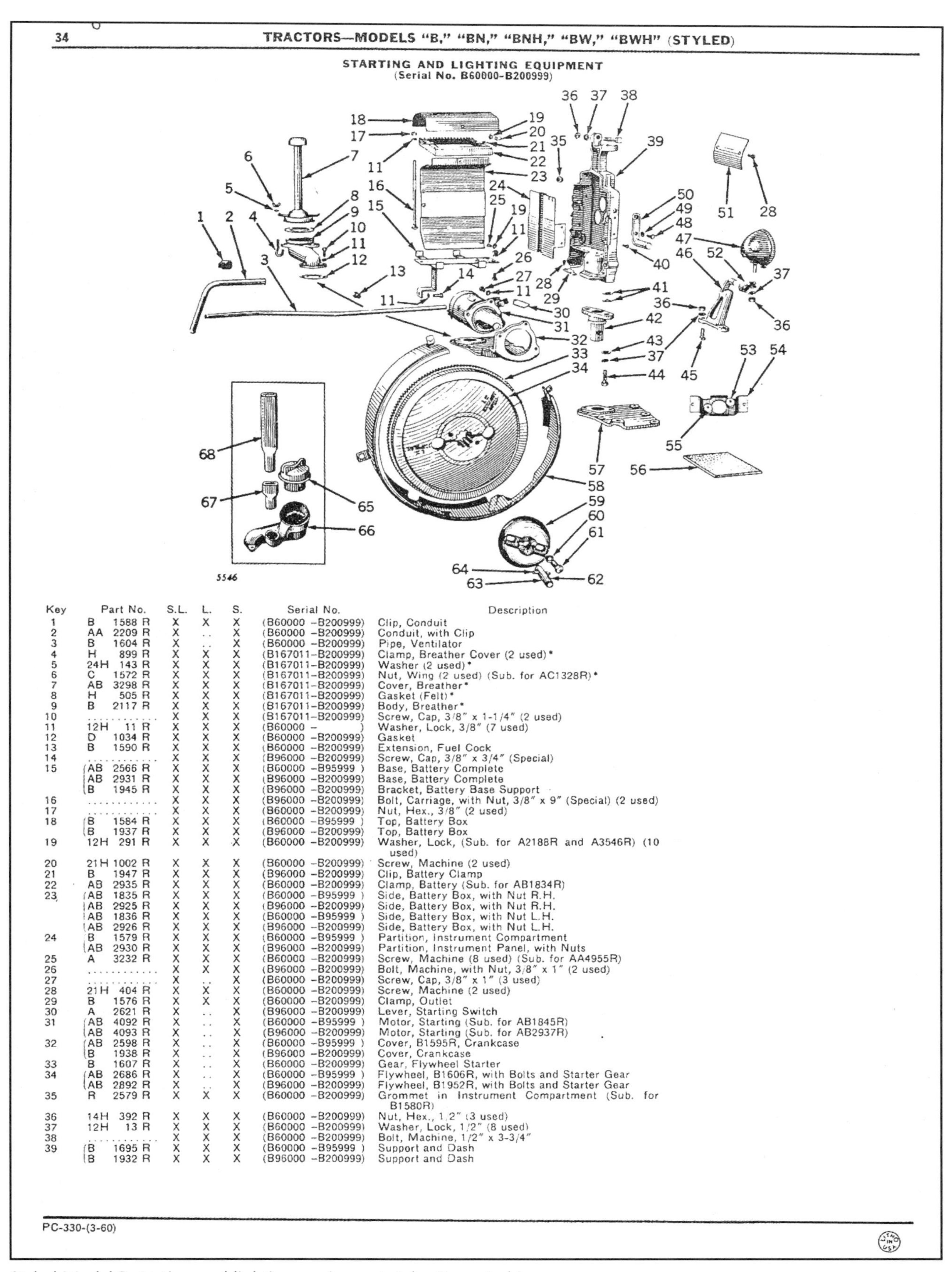

STARTING AND LIGHTING EQUIPMENT

(Serial No. B60000-B200999)

Key	Part No.	S.L.	L.	S.	Serial No.	Description
1	B 1588 R	X	X	X	(B60000 -B200999)	Clip, Conduit
2	AA 2209 R	X	..	X	(B60000 -B200999)	Conduit, with Clip
3	B 1604 R	X	..	X	(B60000 -B200999)	Pipe, Ventilator
4	H 899 R	X	X	X	(B167011-B200999)	Clamp, Breather Cover (2 used)*
5	24H 143 R	X	X	X	(B167011-B200999)	Washer (2 used)*
6	C 1572 R	X	X	X	(B167011-B200999)	Nut, Wing (2 used) (Sub. for AC1328R)*
7	AB 3298 R	X	X	X	(B167011-B200999)	Cover, Breather*
8	H 505 R	X	X	X	(B167011-B200999)	Gasket (Felt)*
9	B 2117 R	X	X	X	(B167011-B200999)	Body, Breather*
10	....	X	X	X	(B167011-B200999)	Screw, Cap, 3/8" x 1-1/4" (2 used)
11	12H 11 R	X	X	X	(B60000 –)	Washer, Lock, 3/8" (7 used)
12	D 1034 R	X	X	X	(B60000 -B200999)	Gasket
13	B 1590 R	X	X	X	(B60000 -B200999)	Extension, Fuel Cock
14	....	X	X	X	(B96000 -B200999)	Screw, Cap, 3/8" x 3/4" (Special)
15	AB 2566 R	X	X	X	(B60000 -B95999)	Base, Battery Complete
	AB 2931 R	X	X	X	(B96000 -B200999)	Base, Battery Complete
	B 1945 R	X	X	X	(B96000 -B200999)	Bracket, Battery Base Support
16	....	X	X	X	(B96000 -B200999)	Bolt, Carriage, with Nut, 3/8" x 9" (Special) (2 used)
17	....	X	X	X	(B60000 -B200999)	Nut, Hex., 3/8" (2 used)
18	B 1584 R	X	X	X	(B60000 -B95999)	Top, Battery Box
	B 1937 R	X	X	X	(B96000 -B200999)	Top, Battery Box
19	12H 291 R	X	X	X	(B60000 -B200999)	Washer, Lock, (Sub. for A2188R and A3546R) (10 used)
20	21H 1002 R	X	X	X	(B60000 -B200999)	Screw, Machine (2 used)
21	B 1947 R	X	X	X	(B96000 -B200999)	Clip, Battery Clamp
22	AB 2935 R	X	X	X	(B60000 -B200999)	Clamp, Battery (Sub. for AB1834R)
23	AB 1835 R	X	X	X	(B60000 -B95999)	Side, Battery Box, with Nut R.H.
	AB 2925 R	X	X	X	(B96000 -B200999)	Side, Battery Box, with Nut R.H.
	AB 1836 R	X	X	X	(B60000 -B95999)	Side, Battery Box, with Nut L.H.
	AB 2926 R	X	X	X	(B96000 -B200999)	Side, Battery Box, with Nut L.H.
24	B 1579 R	X	X	X	(B60000 -B95999)	Partition, Instrument Compartment
	AB 2930 R	X	X	X	(B96000 -B200999)	Partition, Instrument Panel, with Nuts
25	A 3232 R	X	X	X	(B60000 -B200999)	Screw, Machine (8 used) (Sub. for AA4955R)
26	....	X	X	X	(B96000 -B200999)	Bolt, Machine, with Nut, 3/8" x 1" (2 used)
27	....	X	..	X	(B60000 -B200999)	Screw, Cap, 3/8" x 1" (3 used)
28	21H 404 R	X	X	X	(B60000 -B200999)	Screw, Machine (2 used)
29	B 1576 R	X	X	X	(B60000 -B200999)	Clamp, Outlet
30	A 2621 R	X	..	X	(B96000 -B200999)	Lever, Starting Switch
31	AB 4092 R	X	..	X	(B60000 -B95999)	Motor, Starting (Sub. for AB1845R)
	AB 4093 R	X	..	X	(B96000 -B200999)	Motor, Starting (Sub. for AB2937R)
32	AB 2598 R	X	..	X	(B60000 -B95999)	Cover, B1595R, Crankcase
	B 1938 R	X	..	X	(B96000 -B200999)	Cover, Crankcase
33	B 1607 R	X	..	X	(B60000 -B200999)	Gear, Flywheel Starter
34	AB 2686 R	X	..	X	(B60000 -B95999)	Flywheel, B1606R, with Bolts and Starter Gear
	AB 2892 R	X	..	X	(B96000 -B200999)	Flywheel, B1952R, with Bolts and Starter Gear
35	R 2579 R	X	X	X	(B60000 -B200999)	Grommet in Instrument Compartment (Sub. for B1580R)
36	14H 392 R	X	X	X	(B60000 -B200999)	Nut, Hex., 1/2" (3 used)
37	12H 13 R	X	X	X	(B60000 -B200999)	Washer, Lock, 1/2" (8 used)
38	....	X	X	X	(B60000 -B200999)	Bolt, Machine, 1/2" x 3-3/4"
39	B 1695 R	X	X	X	(B60000 -B95999)	Support and Dash
	B 1932 R	X	X	X	(B96000 -B200999)	Support and Dash

PC-330-(3-60)

Styled Model B starting and lighting equipment. *John Deere Archives*

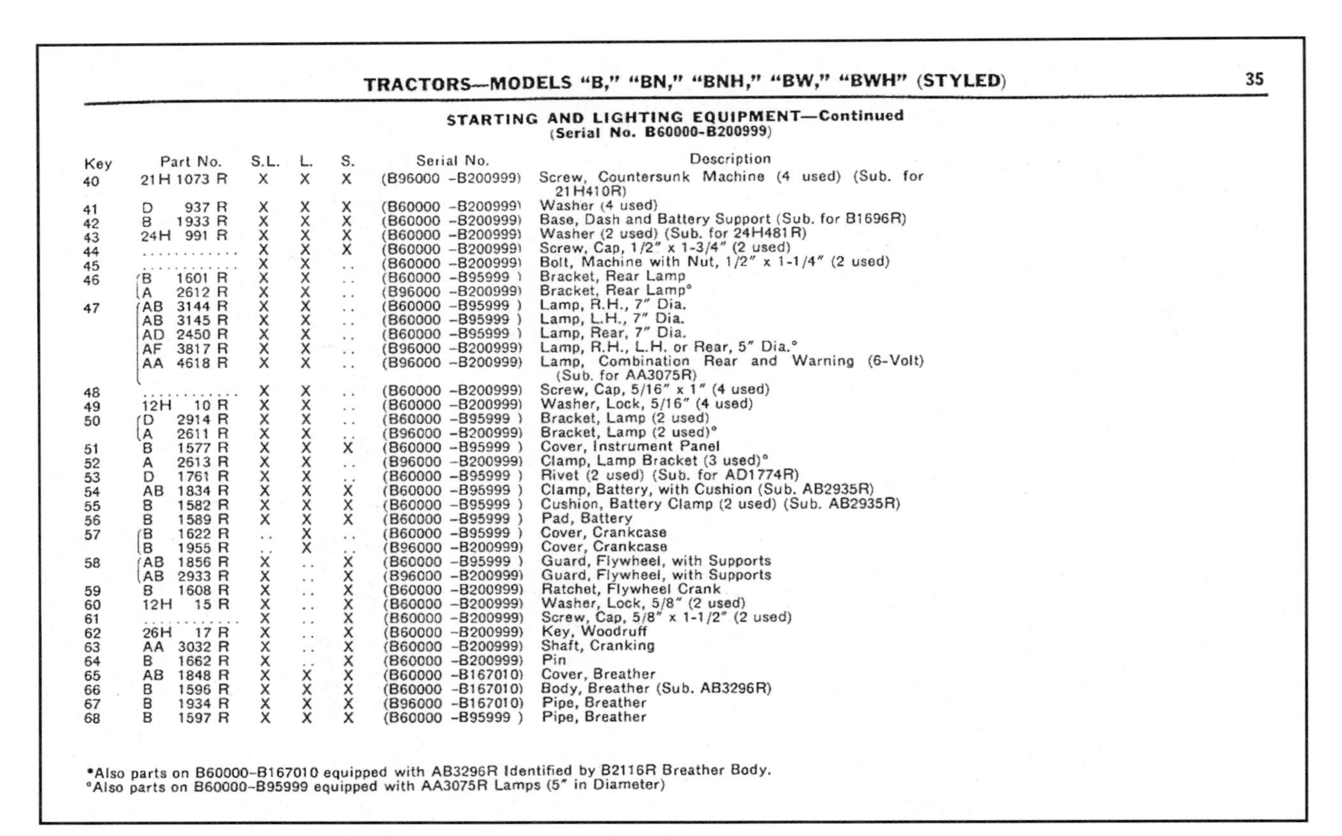

STARTING AND LIGHTING EQUIPMENT—Continued
(Serial No. B60000-B200999)

Key	Part No.	S.L.	L.	S.	Serial No.	Description
40	21H 1073 R	X	X	X	(B96000 -B200999)	Screw, Countersunk Machine (4 used) (Sub. for 21H410R)
41	D 937 R	X	X	X	(B60000 -B200999)	Washer (4 used)
42	B 1933 R	X	X	X	(B60000 -B200999)	Base, Dash and Battery Support (Sub. for B1696R)
43	24H 991 R	X	X	X	(B60000 -B200999)	Washer (2 used) (Sub. for 24H481R)
44	....	X	X	X	(B60000 -B200999)	Screw, Cap, 1/2" x 1-3/4" (2 used)
45	....	X	X	..	(B60000 -B200999)	Bolt, Machine with Nut, 1/2" x 1-1/4" (2 used)
46	B 1601 R	X	X	..	(B60000 -B95999)	Bracket, Rear Lamp
	A 2612 R	X	X	..	(B96000 -B200999)	Bracket, Rear Lamp°
47	AB 3144 R	X	X	..	(B60000 -B95999)	Lamp, R.H., 7" Dia.
	AB 3145 R	X	X	..	(B60000 -B95999)	Lamp, L.H., 7" Dia.
	AD 2450 R	X	X	..	(B60000 -B95999)	Lamp, Rear, 7" Dia.
	AF 3817 R	X	X	..	(B96000 -B200999)	Lamp, R.H., L.H. or Rear, 5" Dia.°
	AA 4618 R	X	X	..	(B96000 -B200999)	Lamp, Combination Rear and Warning (6-Volt) (Sub. for AA3075R)
48	....	X	X	..	(B60000 -B200999)	Screw, Cap, 5/16" x 1" (4 used)
49	12H 10 R	X	X	..	(B60000 -B200999)	Washer, Lock, 5/16" (4 used)
50	D 2914 R	X	X	..	(B60000 -B95999)	Bracket, Lamp (2 used)
	A 2611 R	X	X	..	(B96000 -B200999)	Bracket, Lamp (2 used)°
51	B 1577 R	X	X	X	(B60000 -B95999)	Cover, Instrument Panel
52	A 2613 R	X	X	..	(B96000 -B200999)	Clamp, Lamp Bracket (3 used)°
53	D 1761 R	X	X	..	(B60000 -B95999)	Rivet (2 used) (Sub. for AD1774R)
54	AB 1834 R	X	X	X	(B60000 -B95999)	Clamp, Battery, with Cushion (Sub. AB2935R)
55	B 1582 R	X	X	X	(B60000 -B95999)	Cushion, Battery Clamp (2 used) (Sub. AB2935R)
56	B 1589 R	X	X	X	(B60000 -B95999)	Pad, Battery
57	B 1622 R	..	X	..	(B60000 -B95999)	Cover, Crankcase
	B 1955 R	..	X	..	(B96000 -B200999)	Cover, Crankcase
58	AB 1856 R	X	..	X	(B60000 -B95999)	Guard, Flywheel, with Supports
	AB 2933 R	X	..	X	(B96000 -B200999)	Guard, Flywheel, with Supports
59	B 1608 R	X	..	X	(B60000 -B200999)	Ratchet, Flywheel Crank
60	12H 15 R	X	..	X	(B60000 -B200999)	Washer, Lock, 5/8" (2 used)
61	....	X	..	X	(B60000 -B200999)	Screw, Cap, 5/8" x 1-1/2" (2 used)
62	26H 17 R	X	..	X	(B60000 -B200999)	Key, Woodruff
63	AA 3032 R	X	..	X	(B60000 -B200999)	Shaft, Cranking
64	B 1662 R	X	..	X	(B60000 -B200999)	Pin
65	AB 1848 R	X	X	X	(B60000 -B167010)	Cover, Breather
66	B 1596 R	X	X	X	(B60000 -B167010)	Body, Breather (Sub. AB3296R)
67	B 1934 R	X	X	X	(B96000 -B167010)	Pipe, Breather
68	B 1597 R	X	X	X	(B60000 -B95999)	Pipe, Breather

•Also parts on B60000-B167010 equipped with AB3296R Identified by B2116R Breather Body.
°Also parts on B60000-B95999 equipped with AA3075R Lamps (5" in Diameter)

Styled Model B starting and lighting equipment (continued). *John Deere Archives*

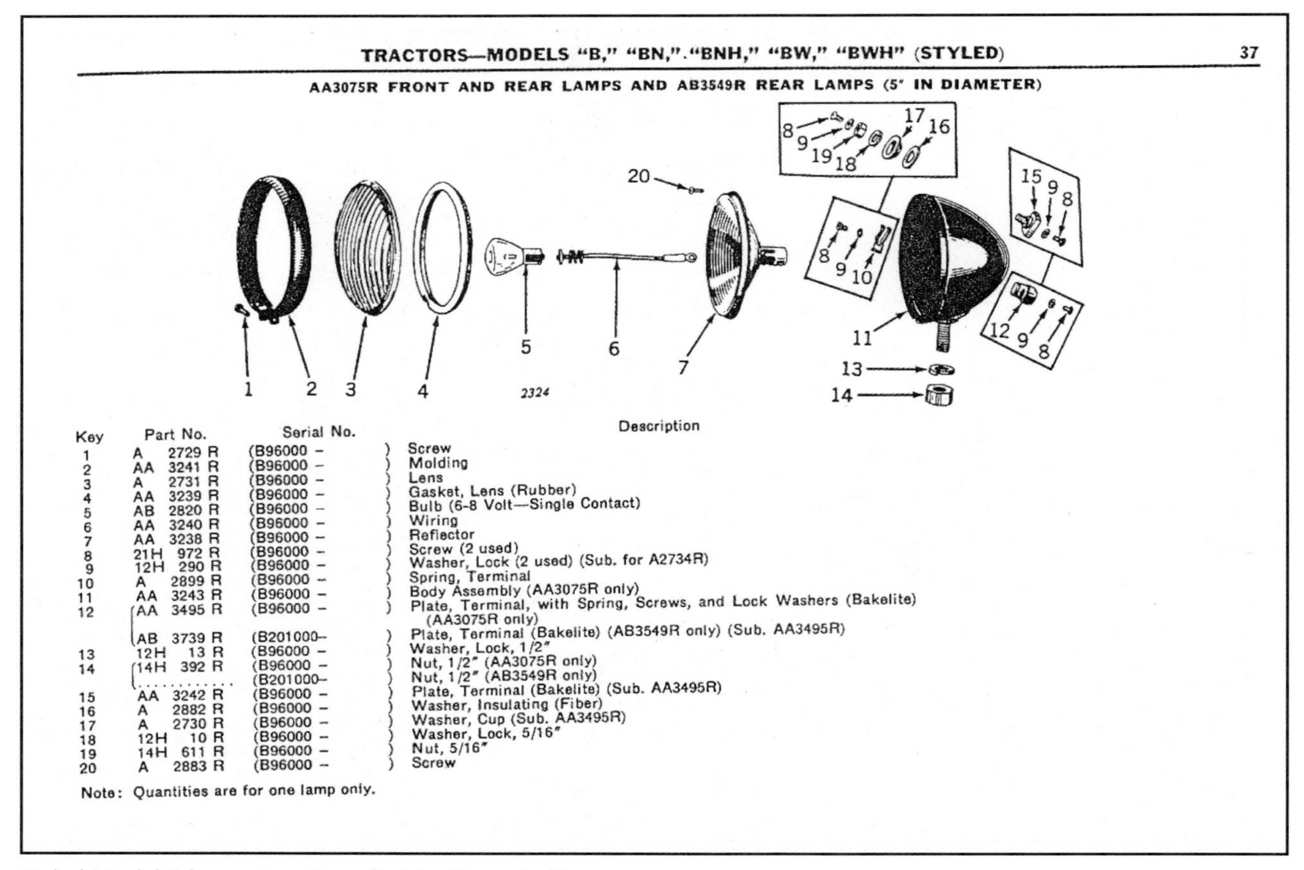

AA3075R FRONT AND REAR LAMPS AND AB3549R REAR LAMPS (5" IN DIAMETER)

Key	Part No.	Serial No.	Description
1	A 2729 R	(B96000 -)	Screw
2	AA 3241 R	(B96000 -)	Molding
3	A 2731 R	(B96000 -)	Lens
4	AA 3239 R	(B96000 -)	Gasket, Lens (Rubber)
5	AB 2820 R	(B96000 -)	Bulb (6-8 Volt—Single Contact)
6	AA 3240 R	(B96000 -)	Wiring
7	AA 3238 R	(B96000 -)	Reflector
8	21H 972 R	(B96000 -)	Screw (2 used)
9	12H 290 R	(B96000 -)	Washer, Lock (2 used) (Sub. for A2734R)
10	A 2899 R	(B96000 -)	Spring, Terminal
11	AA 3243 R	(B96000 -)	Body Assembly (AA3075R only)
12	AA 3495 R	(B96000 -)	Plate, Terminal, with Spring, Screws, and Lock Washers (Bakelite) (AA3075R only)
	AB 3739 R	(B201000-)	Plate, Terminal (Bakelite) (AB3549R only) (Sub. AA3495R)
13	12H 13 R	(B96000 -)	Washer, Lock, 1/2"
14	14H 392 R	(B96000 -)	Nut, 1/2" (AA3075R only)
	....	(B201000-)	Nut, 1/2" (AB3549R only)
15	AA 3242 R	(B96000 -)	Plate, Terminal (Bakelite) (Sub. AA3495R)
16	A 2882 R	(B96000 -)	Washer, Insulating (Fiber)
17	A 2730 R	(B96000 -)	Washer, Cup (Sub. AA3495R)
18	12H 10 R	(B96000 -)	Washer, Lock, 5/16"
19	14H 611 R	(B96000 -)	Nut, 5/16"
20	A 2883 R	(B96000 -)	Screw

Note: Quantities are for one lamp only.

Styled Model B lamps (continued). *John Deere Archives*

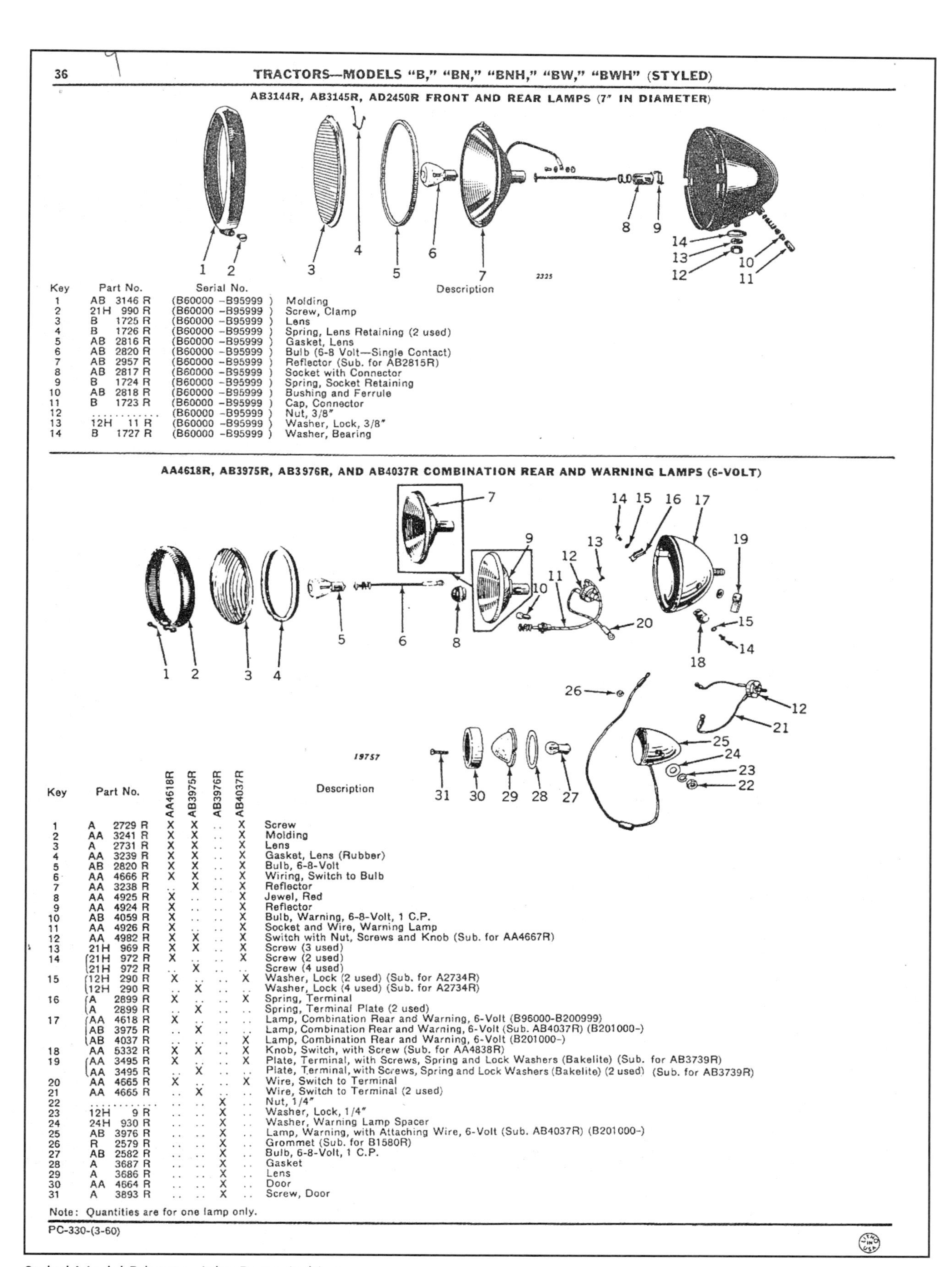

36 TRACTORS—MODELS "B," "BN," "BNH," "BW," "BWH" (STYLED)

AB3144R, AB3145R, AD2450R FRONT AND REAR LAMPS (7" IN DIAMETER)

Key	Part No.	Serial No.	Description
1	AB 3146 R	(B60000 –B95999)	Molding
2	21H 990 R	(B60000 –B95999)	Screw, Clamp
3	B 1725 R	(B60000 –B95999)	Lens
4	B 1726 R	(B60000 –B95999)	Spring, Lens Retaining (2 used)
5	AB 2816 R	(B60000 –B95999)	Gasket, Lens
6	AB 2820 R	(B60000 –B95999)	Bulb (6-8 Volt—Single Contact)
7	AB 2957 R	(B60000 –B95999)	Reflector (Sub. for AB2815R)
8	AB 2817 R	(B60000 –B95999)	Socket with Connector
9	B 1724 R	(B60000 –B95999)	Spring, Socket Retaining
10	AB 2818 R	(B60000 –B95999)	Bushing and Ferrule
11	B 1723 R	(B60000 –B95999)	Cap, Connector
12	....	(B60000 –B95999)	Nut, 3/8"
13	12H 11 R	(B60000 –B95999)	Washer, Lock, 3/8"
14	B 1727 R	(B60000 –B95999)	Washer, Bearing

AA4618R, AB3975R, AB3976R, AND AB4037R COMBINATION REAR AND WARNING LAMPS (6-VOLT)

Key	Part No.	AA4618R	AB3975R	AB3976R	AB4037R	Description
1	A 2729 R	X	X	..	X	Screw
2	AA 3241 R	X	X	..	X	Molding
3	A 2731 R	X	X	..	X	Lens
4	AA 3239 R	X	X	..	X	Gasket, Lens (Rubber)
5	AB 2820 R	X	X	..	X	Bulb, 6-8-Volt
6	AA 4666 R	X	X	..	X	Wiring, Switch to Bulb
7	AA 3238 R	..	X	..	X	Reflector
8	AA 4925 R	X	..	..	X	Jewel, Red
9	AA 4924 R	X	..	..	X	Reflector
10	AB 4059 R	X	..	..	X	Bulb, Warning, 6-8-Volt, 1 C.P.
11	AA 4926 R	X	..	..	X	Socket and Wire, Warning Lamp
12	AA 4982 R	X	X	..	X	Switch with Nut, Screws and Knob (Sub. for AA4667R)
13	21H 969 R	X	X	..	X	Screw (3 used)
14	21H 972 R	X	..	..	X	Screw (2 used)
	21H 972 R	..	X	..	..	Screw (4 used)
15	12H 290 R	X	..	..	X	Washer, Lock (2 used) (Sub. for A2734R)
	12H 290 R	..	X	..	..	Washer, Lock (4 used) (Sub. for A2734R)
16	A 2899 R	X	..	..	X	Spring, Terminal
	A 2899 R	..	X	..	..	Spring, Terminal Plate (2 used)
17	AA 4618 R	X	..	..	..	Lamp, Combination Rear and Warning, 6-Volt (B96000-B200999)
	AB 3975 R	..	X	..	..	Lamp, Combination Rear and Warning, 6-Volt (Sub. AB4037R) (B201000-)
	AB 4037 R	..	..	..	X	Lamp, Combination Rear and Warning, 6-Volt (B201000-)
18	AA 5332 R	X	X	..	X	Knob, Switch, with Screw (Sub. for AA4838R)
19	AA 3495 R	X	..	..	X	Plate, Terminal, with Screws, Spring and Lock Washers (Bakelite) (Sub. for AB3739R)
	AA 3495 R	..	X	..	..	Plate, Terminal, with Screws, Spring and Lock Washers (Bakelite) (2 used) (Sub. for AB3739R)
20	AA 4665 R	X	..	..	X	Wire, Switch to Terminal
21	AA 4665 R	..	X	..	..	Wire, Switch to Terminal (2 used)
22	....	..	..	X	..	Nut, 1/4"
23	12H 9 R	..	..	X	..	Washer, Lock, 1/4"
24	24H 930 R	..	..	X	..	Washer, Warning Lamp Spacer
25	AB 3976 R	..	..	X	..	Lamp, Warning, with Attaching Wire, 6-Volt (Sub. AB4037R) (B201000-)
26	R 2579 R	..	..	X	..	Grommet (Sub. for B1580R)
27	AB 2582 R	..	..	X	..	Bulb, 6-8-Volt, 1 C.P.
28	A 3687 R	..	..	X	..	Gasket
29	A 3686 R	..	..	X	..	Lens
30	AA 4664 R	..	..	X	..	Door
31	A 3893 R	..	..	X	..	Screw, Door

Note: Quantities are for one lamp only.

PC-330-(3-60)

Styled Model B lamps. *John Deere Archives*

STARTING AND LIGHTING EQUIPMENT

(SERIAL No. B60000-B200999)

GREEN ON YELLOW
POSITIVE (+) GROUND
BLACK
BLACK ON YELLOW
CONNECT TO RELAY TERMINAL MARKED "BAT"
BATTERY TO AMMETER
GREEN ON YELLOW
CONNECT TO GENERATOR TERMINAL MARKED "F"
BLACK ON YELLOW
CONNECT TO STARTING MOTOR
5547

Key	Part No.	Serial No.	Description
1	AB 3144 R	(B60000 –B95999)	Lamp, R.H., 7" Diameter
	AB 3145 R	(B60000 –B95999)	Lamp, L.H., 7" Diameter
	AD 2450 R	(B60000 –B95999)	Lamp, Rear, 7" Diameter
	AF 3817 R	(B96000 –B200999)	Lamp, R.H., L.H. or Rear, 5" Diameter (3 used) (Sub. for AA3075R)°
	AA 4618 R	(B96000 –B200999)	Lamp, Combination Rear and Warning (6 Volt)°
2	AB 1833 R	(B60000 –B200999)	Cable, Ground
3	AB 4241 R	(B60000 –B95999)	Lamp, Dash (Sub. for AB1829R)
	AD 2834 R	(B96000 –B200999)	Lamp, Dash (Sub. for AD1855R)
	AB 2582 R	(B60000 –B200999)	Bulb, Dash Light
4	21H 404 R	(B60000 –B95999)	Screw, Machine
5	B 1574 R	(B60000 –B95999)	Bracket, Dash Lamp
6	AD 2834 R	(B96000 –B174675)	Hood, Dash Lamp (Sub. for B1728R)
	A 3032 R	(B174676–B200999)	Hood, Dash Lamp
7	AB 2687 R	(B60000 –B133724)	Switch, Light (Sub. AF687R)
	AF 687 R	(B133725–B200999)	Switch, Light (Sub. for AB2687R)
8	F 692 R	(B133725–)	Washer, Lock•
9	14H 651 R	(B133725–)	Nut, Jam, 3/8"•
10	F 690 R	(B133725–)	Knob, Switch•
11	AB 1189 R	(B60000 –B133724)	Rod, Switch Control (Parts only for Light Switch AB2687R)
12	AF 701 R	(B133725–B200999)	Lead, Fuse•
13	1838155	(B60000 –B133724)	Resistance Unit (Parts for AB2687R only)
14	....	(B60000 –B200999)	Nut, 1/4" (2 used)
15	12H 9 R	(B20000 –B200999)	Washer, Lock, 1/4" (2 used)
16	21H 597 R	(B60000 –B200999)	Screw, Machine (2 used)
17	B 2007 R	(B60000 –B200999)	Clip, Starting Motor Cable
18	AA 4442 R	(B60000 –B95999)	Wire, Battery to Ammeter (Sub. for AB1830R and AD2639R)
	AA 4442 R	(B96000– B200999)	Wire, Starting Motor to Ammeter (Sub. for AB1830R and AD2639R)
19	AA 4422 R	(B60000 –B200999)	Cable, Starting Motor (Sub. for AB1842R)
20	AF 2749 R	(B60000 –)	Ammeter, with Clamp (Sub. for AB2568R)
21	A 2610 R	(B60000 –B200999)	Clip, Cable (3 used) (Sub. for A1225R)
22	AB 1860 R	(B60000 –B200999)	Clamp, Negative Terminal
23	AA 4442 R	(B60000 –B200999)	Wire, Battery to Ammeter (Lighting only) (Sub. for AB1830R and AD2639R)
24	AB 1831 R	(B60000 –B95999)	Harness, Wiring
	AA 3077 R	(B96000 –B200999)	Harness, Wiring°
	AB 1913 R	(B60000 –B95999)	Harness, Wiring, Generator (Starting only)
25	AA 4845 R	(B60000 –B95999)	Wire, Ammeter to Switch (Sub. for AB1840R)
26	14H 383 R	(B60000 –B133724)	Nut, Jam, 3/8"
27	AB 1838 R	(B60000 –B95999)	Rod, Starter Switch Control
28	AB 1837 R	(B60000 –B95999)	Switch, Starter
29	AA 4845 R	(B60000 –B95999)	Wire, Starter Switch to Magnetic Switch (Part only on Tractors with Dash Light) (Sub. for AA2076R)

°Part on B60000–B95999 equipped with AA3075R Lamp.
•Will Fit B60000–B133724 if AB2687R has been replaced with AF687R.

Styled Model B starting and lighting equipment. *John Deere Archives*

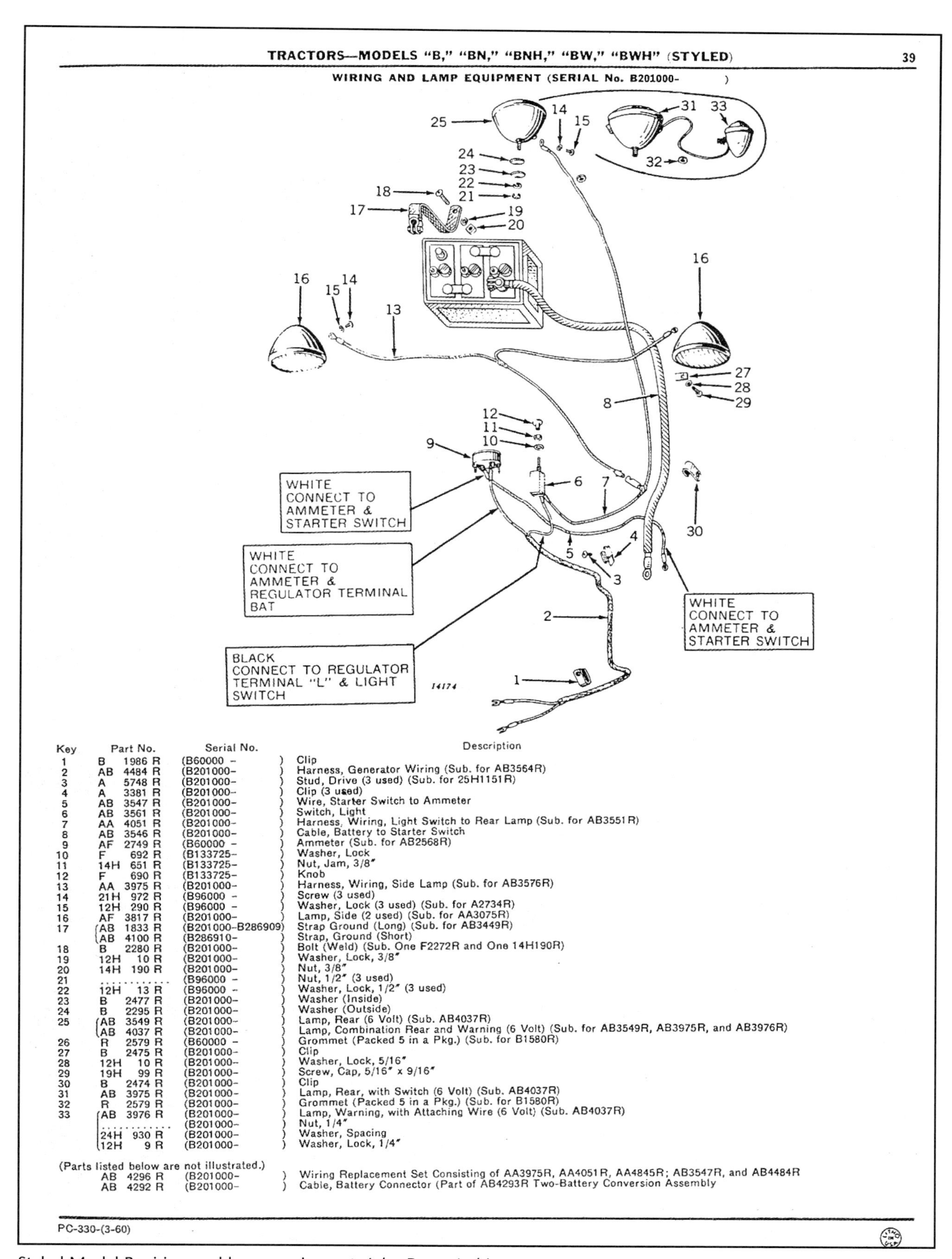

TRACTORS—MODELS "B," "BN," "BNH," "BW," "BWH" (STYLED) **39**

WIRING AND LAMP EQUIPMENT (SERIAL No. B201000-)

Key	Part No.	Serial No.	Description
1	B 1986 R	(B60000 -)	Clip
2	AB 4484 R	(B201000-)	Harness, Generator Wiring (Sub. for AB3564R)
3	A 5748 R	(B201000-)	Stud, Drive (3 used) (Sub. for 25H1151R)
4	A 3381 R	(B201000-)	Clip (3 used)
5	AB 3547 R	(B201000-)	Wire, Starter Switch to Ammeter
6	AB 3561 R	(B201000-)	Switch, Light
7	AA 4051 R	(B201000-)	Harness, Wiring, Light Switch to Rear Lamp (Sub. for AB3551R)
8	AB 3546 R	(B201000-)	Cable, Battery to Starter Switch
9	AF 2749 R	(B60000 -)	Ammeter (Sub. for AB2568R)
10	F 692 R	(B133725-)	Washer, Lock
11	14H 651 R	(B133725-)	Nut, Jam, 3/8"
12	F 690 R	(B133725-)	Knob
13	AA 3975 R	(B201000-)	Harness, Wiring, Side Lamp (Sub. for AB3576R)
14	21H 972 R	(B96000 -)	Screw (3 used)
15	12H 290 R	(B96000 -)	Washer, Lock (3 used) (Sub. for A2734R)
16	AF 3817 R	(B201000-)	Lamp, Side (2 used) (Sub. for AA3075R)
17	AB 1833 R	(B201000-B286909)	Strap Ground (Long) (Sub. for AB3449R)
	AB 4100 R	(B286910-)	Strap, Ground (Short)
18	B 2280 R	(B201000-)	Bolt (Weld) (Sub. One F2272R and One 14H190R)
19	12H 10 R	(B201000-)	Washer, Lock, 3/8"
20	14H 190 R	(B201000-)	Nut, 3/8"
21	....	(B96000 -)	Nut, 1/2" (3 used)
22	12H 13 R	(B96000 -)	Washer, Lock, 1/2" (3 used)
23	B 2477 R	(B201000-)	Washer (Inside)
24	B 2295 R	(B201000-)	Washer (Outside)
25	AB 3549 R	(B201000-)	Lamp, Rear (6 Volt) (Sub. AB4037R)
	AB 4037 R	(B201000-)	Lamp, Combination Rear and Warning (6 Volt) (Sub. for AB3549R, AB3975R, and AB3976R)
26	R 2579 R	(B60000 -)	Grommet (Packed 5 in a Pkg.) (Sub. for B1580R)
27	B 2475 R	(B201000-)	Clip
28	12H 10 R	(B201000-)	Washer, Lock, 5/16"
29	19H 99 R	(B201000-)	Screw, Cap, 5/16" x 9/16"
30	B 2474 R	(B201000-)	Clip
31	AB 3975 R	(B201000-)	Lamp, Rear, with Switch (6 Volt) (Sub. AB4037R)
32	R 2579 R	(B201000-)	Grommet (Packed 5 in a Pkg.) (Sub. for B1580R)
33	AB 3976 R	(B201000-)	Lamp, Warning, with Attaching Wire (6 Volt) (Sub. AB4037R)
	....	(B201000-)	Nut, 1/4"
	24H 930 R	(B201000-)	Washer, Spacing
	12H 9 R	(B201000-)	Washer, Lock, 1/4"

(Parts listed below are not illustrated.)

Part No.	Serial No.	Description
AB 4296 R	(B201000-)	Wiring Replacement Set Consisting of AA3975R, AA4051R, AA4845R; AB3547R, and AB4484R
AB 4292 R	(B201000-)	Cable, Battery Connector (Part of AB4293R Two-Battery Conversion Assembly

PC-330-(3-60)

Styled Model B wiring and lamp equipment. *John Deere Archives*

Chapter 8

Chassis

Frame

The structure commonly called the frame is identified as the "front end support" in the illustrated parts figures. This is an important part of a John Deere tractor, since the transverse engine is not used to carry any of the front end loads as is the case with many other brands with inline engines.

This engine and frame arrangement began back in about 1917 with the Waterloo Boy outfit, the pioneer tractor company Deere bought in 1918. Waterloo Boy engineers were working on a replacement for the Waterloo Boy Model N tractor, which was to be less like a steamer with an internal combustion engine and more like what was becoming the conventional tractor layout.

The big players in the tractor field at that time were International Harvester, Case, Allis-Chalmers, and Ford. A prominent feature of many of these manufacturer's designs was the all-enclosed frameless structure. This had been originated by Wallis—which became part of Case—but had been taken to its ultimate on the Fordson. The Fordson had its front end attached directly to the front of the engine, with the engine providing the structure. Waterloo Boy had copied the Wallis approach, which used a tub-shaped frame to cover the bottom of its engine and to provide an attach point for the front wheels. This Waterloo Boy tractor, the predecessor to the John Deere Model D, was called "the bathtub tractor." After Deere took over from Waterloo Boy, the basic design was continued and refined and introduced as the Model D in 1923. Deere tractors, with two-cylinder transverse engines, have all used modifications of this approach.

There were eight basic frames used on Model B tractors. One frame, part number B813R, was used for all standard tread models. For row-crop tractors, the first frame was used only through serial number 3,042. These were the Bs with the four-bolt front pedestal. This frame's part number is AB244R.

Next, there was the short-frame Model B, through serial number 42,199. This frame was part number AB437R. Next came the long-frame unstyled Bs, which used part number AB1163R frame through serial number 59,999.

Early styled Model Bs used the AB1509R welded frame from serial numbers 60,000 to 136,661. During the war years of 1942 through 1944, the frame was switched to a cast iron type, part number B2013R. After serial number 167,000, Model Bs again used the AB1509R welded frame to serial number 200,999.

For late styled Bs, two different pressed-steel frames were used. From serial number 201,000 to serial number 275,393 (1950), frame part number AB3537R was originally installed. After that, a beefed-up frame—which looks the same—was substituted. The new frame was part number AB4247R. Many pre-1950 Model Bs had their original frames replaced by the later type, which is preferred for restoration purposes.

Left, a right-side view of the pressed-steel frame of the late styled Model B. The exhaust manifold is severely corroded.

Drawbar

The classic ring-type drawbar end is appropriate for tractors up through the year model 1937 for both row-crops and standard treads. After that, straight-ended drawbars were used through the end of the unstyled tractors. These used a simple roller affair to provide the swing feature.

Styled tractors began with a complex swinging straight drawbar. This was used through serial number 186,133 (1946). Then a much-simplified assembly was adopted and used to the end of production. This latter type did not use a roller for the swing function. It was not straight like its predecessor, but had a reversible kick-up end, for adjusting the height of the pull.

A right-side detail showing the angle iron frame of an early styled B.

Platform

Only three types of small sheet-metal platforms were used for the entire series of row-crop tractors: one for unstyled, one for early styled, and one for late styled. Standard tread Model Bs were another matter. The parts breakdown figure shows no fewer than thirteen different part numbers. The reasons for all the variations are no longer known. Likely, some differences were for BOs, BIs, and BRs. And, likely the Lindeman used a different platform (if it was supplied by Deere).

Left, another detail photo of the right side of an early styled Model B, showing the angle iron frame and tool box.

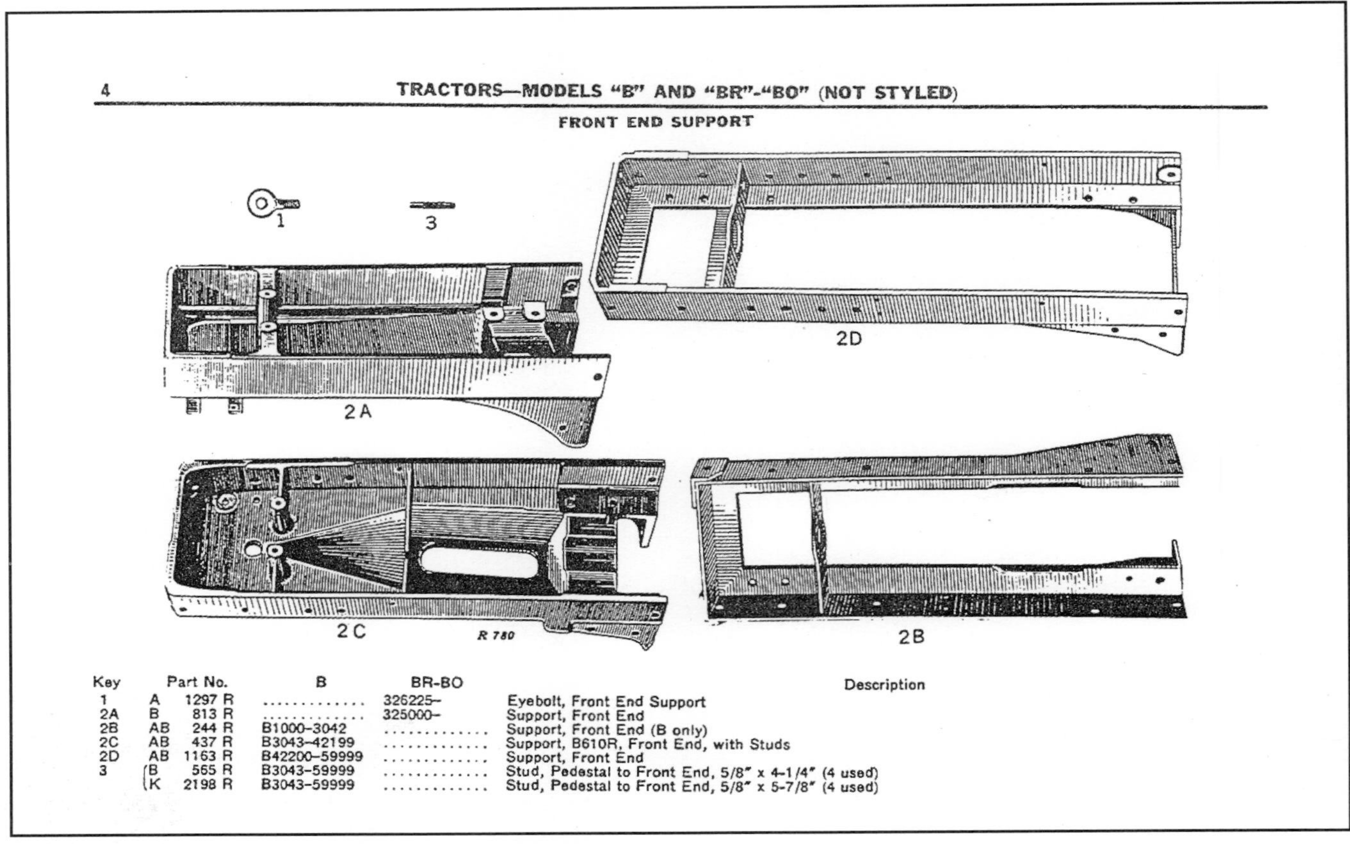

4 TRACTORS—MODELS "B" AND "BR"-"BO" (NOT STYLED)

FRONT END SUPPORT

Key	Part No.	B	BR-BO	Description
1	A 1297 R	....	326225–	Eyebolt, Front End Support
2A	B 813 R	....	325000–	Support, Front End
2B	AB 244 R	B1000–3042	....	Support, Front End (B only)
2C	AB 437 R	B3043–42199	....	Support, B610R, Front End, with Studs
2D	AB 1163 R	B42200–59999	....	Support, Front End
3	B 565 R	B3043–59999	....	Stud, Pedestal to Front End, 5/8" x 4-1/4" (4 used)
	K 2198 R	B3043–59999	....	Stud, Pedestal to Front End, 5/8" x 5-7/8" (4 used)

Unstyled Model B front end support. *John Deere Archives*

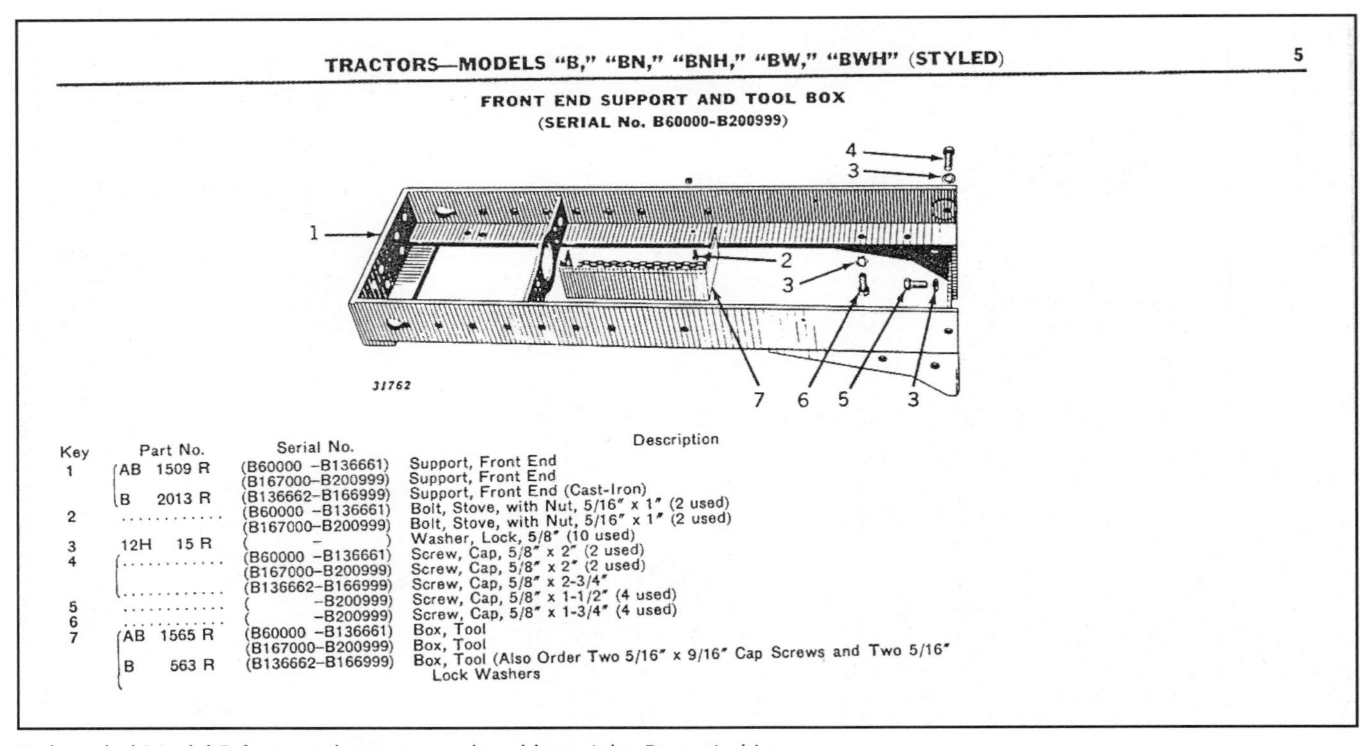

TRACTORS—MODELS "B," "BN," "BNH," "BW," "BWH" (STYLED) 5

FRONT END SUPPORT AND TOOL BOX

(SERIAL No. B60000–B200999)

Key	Part No.	Serial No.	Description
1	AB 1509 R	(B60000 –B136661)	Support, Front End
		(B167000–B200999)	Support, Front End
	B 2013 R	(B136662–B166999)	Support, Front End (Cast-Iron)
2	....	(B60000 –B136661)	Bolt, Stove, with Nut, 5/16" x 1" (2 used)
		(B167000–B200999)	Bolt, Stove, with Nut, 5/16" x 1" (2 used)
3	12H 15 R	(–)	Washer, Lock, 5/8" (10 used)
4	....	(B60000 –B136661)	Screw, Cap, 5/8" x 2" (2 used)
		(B167000–B200999)	Screw, Cap, 5/8" x 2" (2 used)
	....	(B136662–B166999)	Screw, Cap, 5/8" x 2-3/4"
5	....	(–B200999)	Screw, Cap, 5/8" x 1-1/2" (4 used)
6	....	(–B200999)	Screw, Cap, 5/8" x 1-3/4" (4 used)
7	AB 1565 R	(B60000 –B136661)	Box, Tool
		(B167000–B200999)	Box, Tool
	B 563 R	(B136662–B166999)	Box, Tool (Also Order Two 5/16" x 9/16" Cap Screws and Two 5/16" Lock Washers

Early styled Model B front end support and tool box. *John Deere Archives*

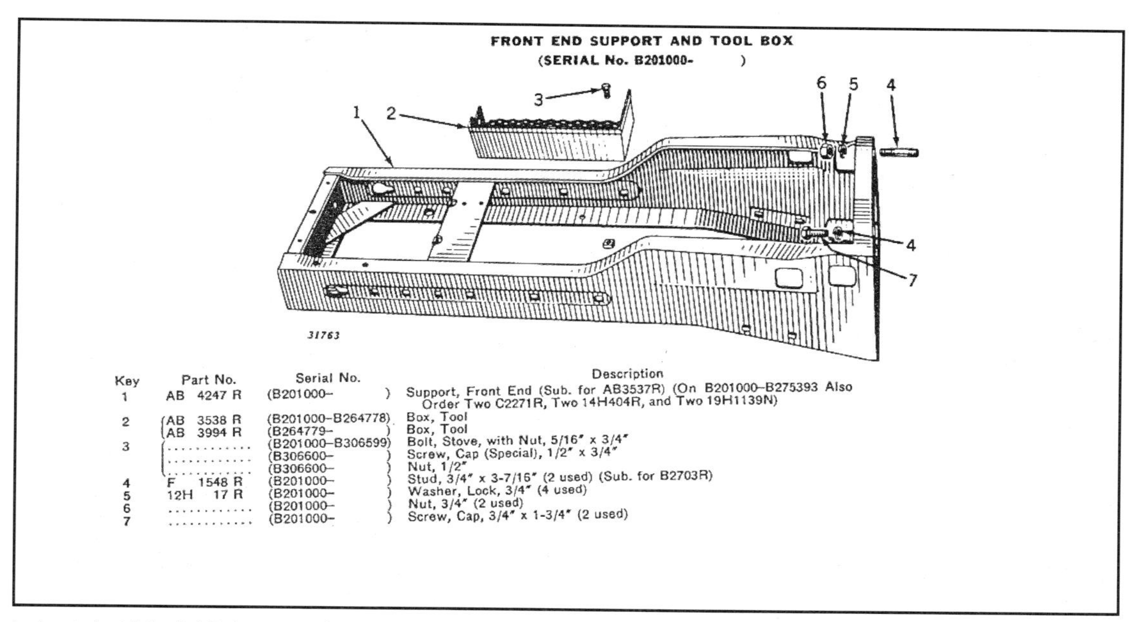
FRONT END SUPPORT AND TOOL BOX
(SERIAL No. B201000-   )

31763

Key	Part No.	Serial No.	Description
1	AB 4247 R	(B201000-)	Support, Front End (Sub. for AB3537R) (On B201000–B275393 Also Order Two C2271R, Two 14H404R, and Two 19H1139N)
2	AB 3538 R	(B201000–B264778)	Box, Tool
	AB 3994 R	(B264779-)	Box, Tool
3	....	(B201000–B306599)	Bolt, Stove, with Nut, 5/16" x 3/4"
	....	(B306600-)	Screw, Cap (Special), 1/2" x 3/4"
	....	(B306600-)	Nut, 1/2"
4	F 1548 R	(B201000-)	Stud, 3/4" x 3-7/16" (2 used) (Sub. for B2703R)
5	12H 17 R	(B201000-)	Washer, Lock, 3/4" (4 used)
6	....	(B201000-)	Nut, 3/4" (2 used)
7	....	(B201000-)	Screw, Cap, 3/4" x 1-3/4" (2 used)

Late styled Model B front end support and tool box. *John Deere Archives*

Note the curved drawbar on this late styled Model B. Also note that this type does not have a roller to support the swing function.

Left, the classic ring-type drawbar end is appropriate for tractors up through the year model 1937 for both row-crops and standard treads. After that, straight-ended drawbars were used through the end of the unstyled tractors.

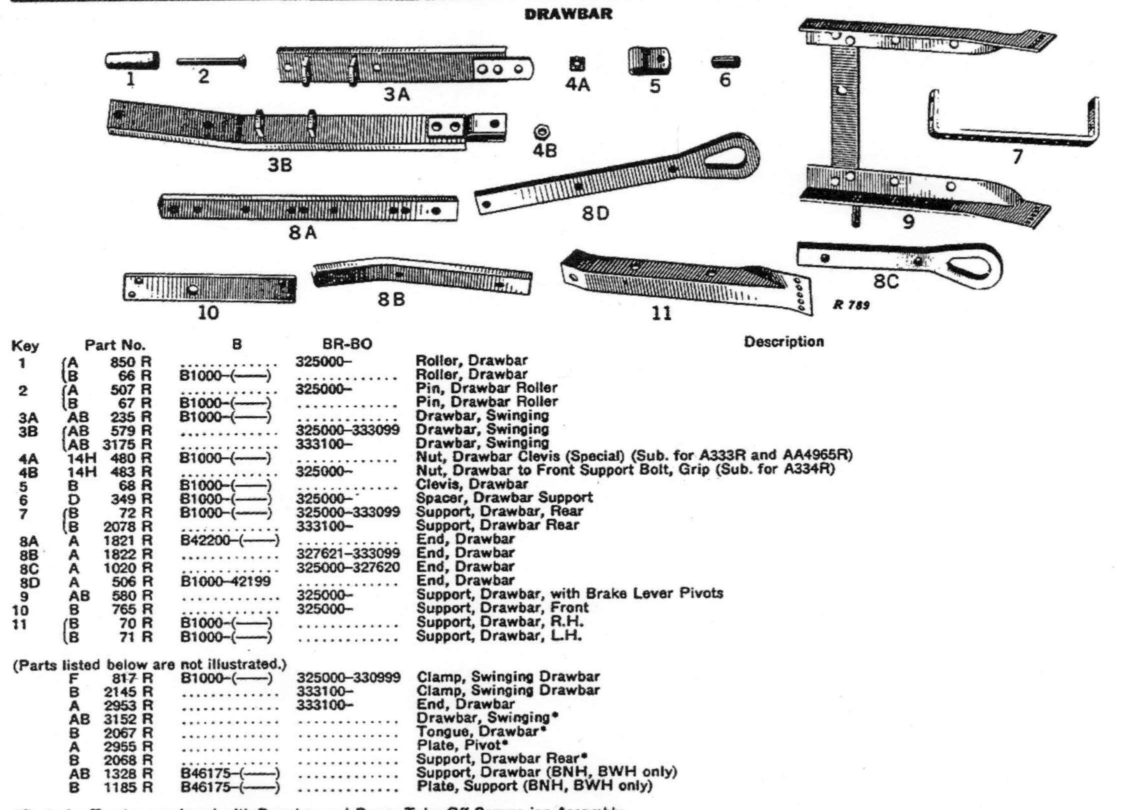

TRACTORS—MODELS "B" AND "BR"-"BO" (NOT STYLED) 31

DRAWBAR

Key	Part No.	B	BR-BO	Description
1	(A 850 R	....	325000–	Roller, Drawbar
	(B 66 R	B1000–(——)	....	Roller, Drawbar
2	(A 507 R	....	325000–	Pin, Drawbar Roller
	(B 67 R	B1000–(——)	....	Pin, Drawbar Roller
3A	AB 235 R	B1000–(——)	....	Drawbar, Swinging
3B	(AB 579 R	....	325000–333099	Drawbar, Swinging
	(AB 3175 R	....	333100–	Drawbar, Swinging
4A	14H 480 R	B1000–(——)	....	Nut, Drawbar Clevis (Special) (Sub. for A333R and AA4965R)
4B	14H 483 R	....	325000–	Nut, Drawbar to Front Support Bolt, Grip (Sub. for A334R)
5	B 68 R	B1000–(——)	....	Clevis, Drawbar
6	D 349 R	B1000–(——)	325000–	Spacer, Drawbar Support
7	(B 72 R	B1000–(——)	325000–333099	Support, Drawbar, Rear
	(B 2078 R	....	333100–	Support, Drawbar Rear
8A	A 1821 R	B42200–(——)	....	End, Drawbar
8B	A 1822 R	....	327621–333099	End, Drawbar
8C	A 1020 R	....	325000–327620	End, Drawbar
8D	A 506 R	B1000–42199	....	End, Drawbar
9	AB 580 R	....	325000–	Support, Drawbar, with Brake Lever Pivots
10	B 765 R	....	325000–	Support, Drawbar, Front
11	(B 70 R	B1000–(——)	....	Support, Drawbar, R.H.
	(B 71 R	B1000–(——)	....	Support, Drawbar, L.H.
(Parts listed below are not illustrated.)				
	F 817 R	B1000–(——)	325000–330999	Clamp, Swinging Drawbar
	B 2145 R	....	333100–	Clamp, Swinging Drawbar
	A 2953 R	....	333100–	End, Drawbar
	AB 3152 R	....	....	Drawbar, Swinging*
	B 2067 R	....	....	Tongue, Drawbar*
	A 2955 R	....	....	Plate, Pivot*
	B 2068 R	....	....	Support, Drawbar Rear*
	AB 1328 R	B46175–(——)	....	Support, Drawbar (BNH, BWH only)
	B 1185 R	B46175–(——)	....	Plate, Support (BNH, BWH only)

*Parts for Tractors equipped with Drawbar and Power Take-Off Conversion Assembly.

(Serial No. B186134-)

Part No.	Serial No.	Description
B 3262 R	(B186134–)	Drawbar, Swinging (Sub. for B2450R)
12H 13 R	(–)	Washer, Lock, 1/2" (2 used)
(AB 3507 R	(B186134–B200999)	Support, Drawbar ("B," "BN," "BW" only)
AB 3507 R	(B201000–)	Support, Drawbar ("B" only)
AB 3618 R	(B186134–B200999)	Support, Drawbar ("BNH," "BWH" only)
(AB 3618 R	(B201000–)	Support, Drawbar ("BN," "BW" only)
AA 5365 R	(B186134–)	Pivot, Drawbar (Sub. for B2198R)
12H 15 R	(–)	Washer, Lock, 5/8" (4 used)
(A 5292 R	(B186134–B200999)	Stud, 5/8" x 2-1/4" (4 used) ("B," "BN," "BW" only) (Sub. for A284R)
(A 5292 R	(B201000–)	Stud, 5/8" x 2-1/4" (4 used) ("B" only) (Sub. for A284R)
(19H 1335 R	(B186134–B200999)	Screw, Cap, 5/8" x 1-1/2" (2 used) ("BNH," BWH" only)
(19H 1335 R	(B201000–)	Screw, Cap, 5/8" x 1-1/2" (2 used) ("BN," "BW" only)
(............	(B186134–B200999)	Nut, 5/8" (4 used) ("B," "BN," "BW" only)
(............	(B201000–)	Nut, 5/8" (4 used) ("B" only)
(19H 1373 R	(B186134–B200999)	Screw, Cap, 5/8" x 2" ("BNH," "BWH" only)
(19H 1373 R	(B201000–)	Screw, Cap, 5/8" x 2" ("BN," "BW" only)
....	(B186134–)	Bolt, Machine, with Nut, 1/2" x 2-3/4" (2 used)

Unstyled Model B drawbar. *John Deere Archives*

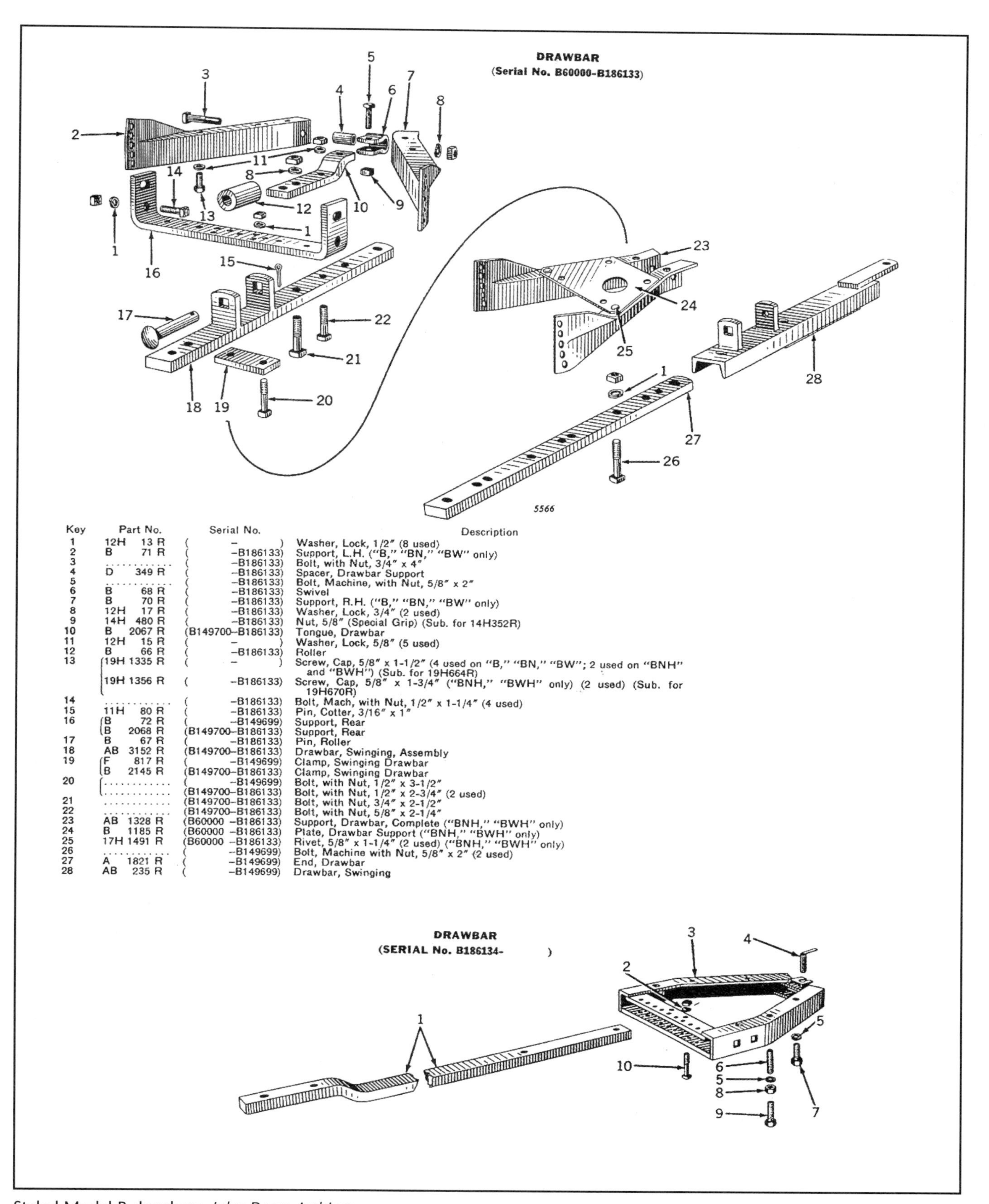

DRAWBAR
(Serial No. B60000–B186133)

Key	Part No.	Serial No.	Description
1	12H 13 R	(–)	Washer, Lock, 1/2″ (8 used)
2	B 71 R	(–B186133)	Support, L.H. ("B," "BN," "BW" only)
3	....	(–B186133)	Bolt, with Nut, 3/4″ x 4″
4	D 349 R	(–B186133)	Spacer, Drawbar Support
5	....	(–B186133)	Bolt, Machine, with Nut, 5/8″ x 2″
6	B 68 R	(–B186133)	Swivel
7	B 70 R	(–B186133)	Support, R.H. ("B," "BN," "BW" only)
8	12H 17 R	(–B186133)	Washer, Lock, 3/4″ (2 used)
9	14H 480 R	(–B186133)	Nut, 5/8″ (Special Grip) (Sub. for 14H352R)
10	B 2067 R	(B149700–B186133)	Tongue, Drawbar
11	12H 15 R	(–)	Washer, Lock, 5/8″ (5 used)
12	B 66 R	(–B186133)	Roller
13	19H 1335 R	(–)	Screw, Cap, 5/8″ x 1-1/2″ (4 used on "B," "BN," "BW"; 2 used on "BNH" and "BWH") (Sub. for 19H664R)
	19H 1356 R	(–B186133)	Screw, Cap, 5/8″ x 1-3/4″ ("BNH," "BWH" only) (2 used) (Sub. for 19H670R)
14	....	(–B186133)	Bolt, Mach, with Nut, 1/2″ x 1-1/4″ (4 used)
15	11H 80 R	(–B186133)	Pin, Cotter, 3/16″ x 1″
16	B 72 R	(–B149699)	Support, Rear
	B 2068 R	(B149700–B186133)	Support, Rear
17	B 67 R	(–B186133)	Pin, Roller
18	AB 3152 R	(B149700–B186133)	Drawbar, Swinging, Assembly
19	F 817 R	(–B149699)	Clamp, Swinging Drawbar
	B 2145 R	(B149700–B186133)	Clamp, Swinging Drawbar
20	....	(–B149699)	Bolt, with Nut, 1/2″ x 3-1/2″
	....	(B149700–B186133)	Bolt, with Nut, 1/2″ x 2-3/4″ (2 used)
21	....	(B149700–B186133)	Bolt, with Nut, 3/4″ x 2-1/2″
22	....	(B149700–B186133)	Bolt, with Nut, 5/8″ x 2-1/4″
23	AB 1328 R	(B60000 –B186133)	Support, Drawbar, Complete ("BNH," "BWH" only)
24	B 1185 R	(B60000 –B186133)	Plate, Drawbar Support ("BNH," "BWH" only)
25	17H 1491 R	(B60000 –B186133)	Rivet, 5/8″ x 1-1/4″ (2 used) ("BNH," "BWH" only)
26	....	(–B149699)	Bolt, Machine with Nut, 5/8″ x 2″ (2 used)
27	A 1821 R	(–B149699)	End, Drawbar
28	AB 235 R	(–B149699)	Drawbar, Swinging

DRAWBAR
(SERIAL No. B186134–)

Styled Model B drawbars. *John Deere Archives*

A detail of the platform of an early styled B. Note the seat spring.

TRACTORS—MODELS "B" AND "BR"-"BO" (NOT STYLED) 33

PLATFORM—Continued

Key	Part No.	B	BR-BO	Description
1A	B 819 R	....	325000–327159	Platform
	B 895 R	....	327160–331076	Platform
	B 901 R	....	325000–331076	Platform (Parts for BR Tractors equipped with Rear Wheel Brakes)
1B	B 1697 R	....	331077–	Platform
2	AB 299 R	B1000–(——)	....	Platform with Brake Latch Supports
3	AB 330 R	B1000–(——)	....	Support, Brake Latch, with Pivot
4A	B 821 R	....	325000–326008	Support, Platform, L.H.
	B 862 R	....	326009–327159	Support, Platform, L.H.
4B	B 820 R	....	325000–326008	Support, Platform, R.H.
	B 861 R	....	326009–327159	Support, Platform, R.H.
4C	B 897 R	....	325000–331076	Support, Platform, L.H. (Parts for BR Tractors Equipped with Rear Wheel Brakes)
	B 897 R	....	327160–331076	Support, Platform, L.H.
	B 1701 R	....	331077–	Support, Platform, L.H.
4D	B 896 R	....	325000–331076	Support, Platform, R.H. (Parts for BR Tractors Equipped with Rear Wheel Brakes)
	B 896 R	....	327160–331076	Support, Platform, R.H.
	B 1700 R	....	331077–	Support, Platform, R.H.
5A	AB 552 R	....	325000–326008	Platform with Support and Cross Angle
	AB 740 R	....	326009–327159	Platform with Support and Cross Angle
	AB 985 R	....	327160–331076	Platform with Support and Cross Angles (Sub. AB2611R)
5B	AB 991 R	....	325000–331076	Platform with Support and Cross Angles (Sub. AB2612R) (Parts for BR Tractors Equipped with Rear Wheel Brakes)
	AB 2611 R	....	331077–333099	Platform with Supports (Sub. for AB985R)
	AB 2612 R	....	331077–333099	Platform with Supports (Sub. for AB991R)
6	B 822 R	....	325000–326008	Cross Angle, Platform, 53-5/8" Long
	B 860 R	....	326009–327159	Cross Angle, Platform, 52-1/4" Long
	B 898 R	....	325000–331076	Cross Angle, Fender (Parts for BR Tractors Equipped with Rear Wheel Brakes)
	B 898 R	....	327160–331076	Cross Angle, Fender
7A	B 1709 R	....	331077–	Plate, Reinforcing, R.H.
7B	B 1710 R	....	331077–	Plate, Reinforcing, L.H.
8	B 1705 R	....	331077–333099	Support, Pivot Plate
9A	B 1702 R	....	331077–	Angle, R.H.
9B	B 1703 R	....	331077–	Angle, L.H.
10	A 2542 R	....	331077–332099	Plate, Pivot, Universal Shield
11	B 1706 R	....	331077–	Reinforcement, Platform
(Parts listed below are not illustrated.)				
	A 2955 R	....	333100–	Plate, Pivot, Universal Shield
	AB 3177 R	....	333100–	Platform with Supports
	AB 3213 R	....	333100–	Platform with Supports (Parts for BR Tractors Equipped with Rear Wheel Brakes)
	B 1698 R	....	331077–	Platform (Parts for BR Tractors Equipped with Rear Wheel Brakes)
	B 2080 R	....	333100–	Support, Pivot Plate
	AB 3177 R	....	....	Platform with Supports
	AB 3213 R	....	....	Platform with Supports (Used on Tractors with Rear Wheel Brakes)

*Parts for tractors equipped with Drawbar and Power Take-Off Conversion Assembly.)

Unstyled Model B platform (continued). *John Deere Archives*

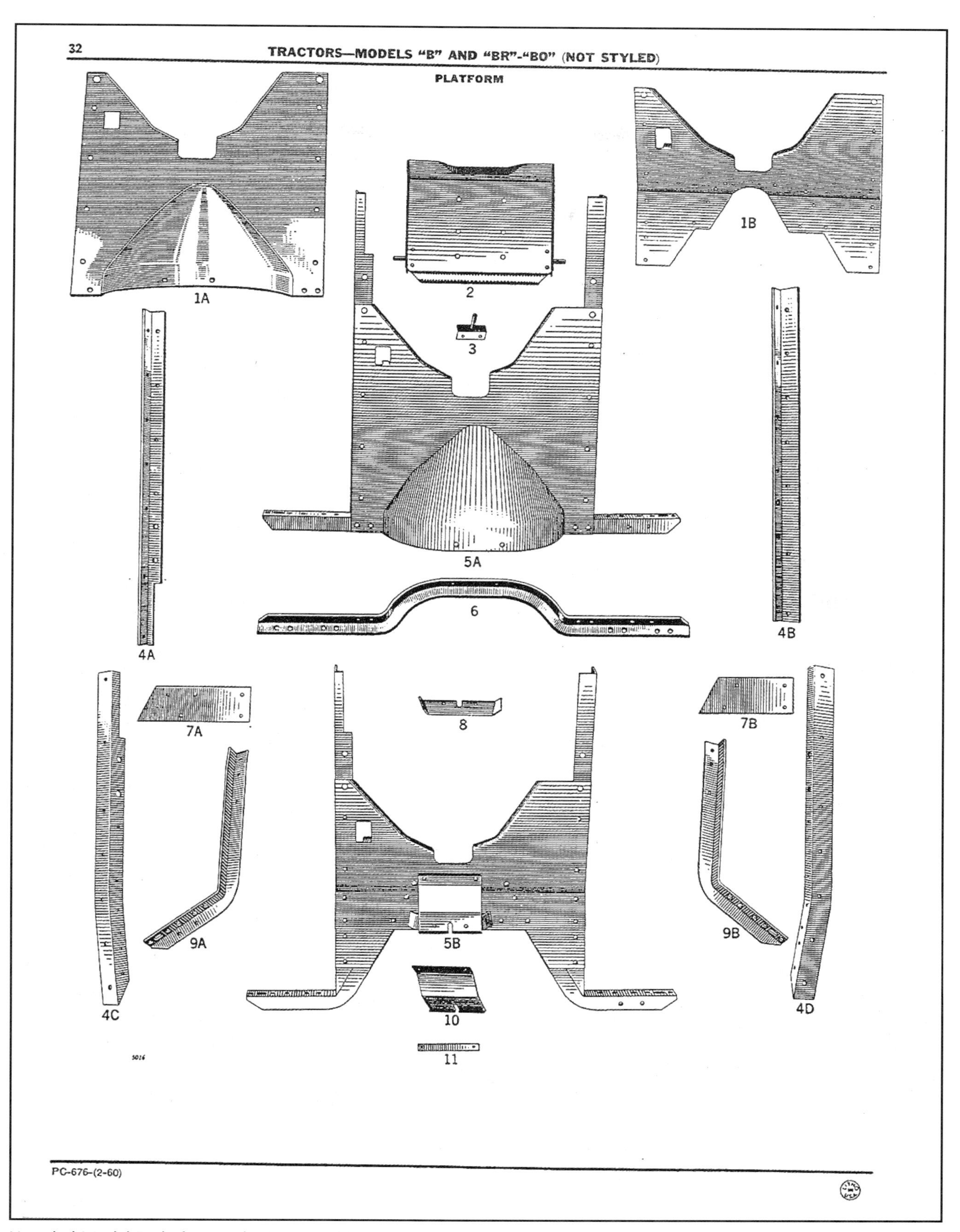

Unstyled Model B platform. *John Deere Archives*

Chapter 9

Cosmetics

According to Webster's Dictionary, the word "cosmetic" comes from the Greek *kosmetikos*, and the French *kosmein*, meaning to arrange, adorn, and beautify externally, and to correct defects. Therefore, we use the term here as the title of the chapter pertaining to sheet metal, paint, trim, and other appearance items.

No matter how much time and money you put into making the details on your Model B correct, clean, straight bodywork and fresh paint are essential for a quality restoration. Patrick Flanigan's nicely finished 1948 Model B is a fine example.

Paint and Body

It is surprising how nice a freshly painted (but roughly finished) John Deere looks from a distance even if the hood, grille, fenders, and other parts are less than perfect. Perhaps this is good enough for a work tractor, but for restoration, the cosmetics are no place to skimp!

First of all, every bit of old paint must be removed and every nick and dent must be fixed. For styled Model Bs, the hood has likely had the exhaust pipe hole enlarged for easy muffler replacement; this must be repaired. In many cases, a replacement hood is cheaper than having quality bodywork done. Check with Geyer Hoods in Oxford, Iowa (see appendix).

Fenders are also available from aftermarket vendors.

Hood

Row-crop tractors from serial number 1,000 to 1,509 had filler ports for the gasoline and kerosene tanks located in the center of the hood. In order to make it easier to pour in fuel, subsequent models had the filler ports offset to the left. The length of the frame was increased at serial number 42,200, so the hood is longer after that number. The longer hood, part number AB1263R, has a guide for the shutter control rod that was not used on the short hood.

For standard tread Model Bs, note that orchard hoods could be ordered for BR tractors, so you may find a mix of parts that are correct. Contact the John Deere Archives (see chapter one) for build record data.

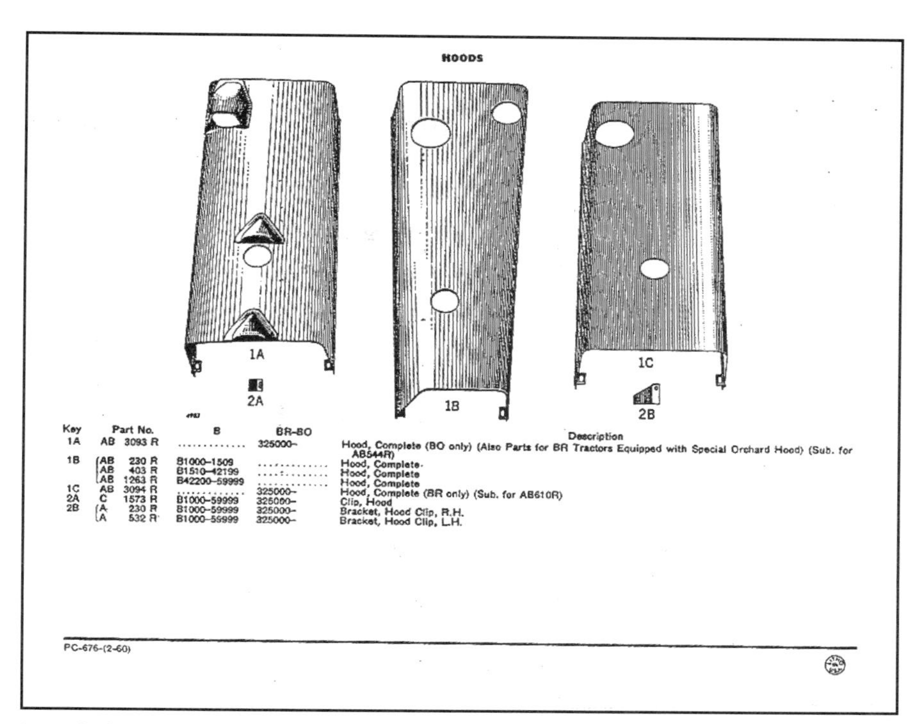

HOODS

Key	Part No.	B	BR-BO	Description
1A	AB 3093 R	....	325000–	Hood, Complete (BO only) (Also Parts for BR Tractors Equipped with Special Orchard Hood) (Sub. for AB544R)
1B	AB 230 R	B1000–1509	....	Hood, Complete
	AB 403 R	B1510–42199	....	Hood, Complete
	AB 1263 R	B42200–59999	....	Hood, Complete
1C	AB 3094 R	....	325000–	Hood, Complete (BR only) (Sub. for AB610R)
2A	C 1573 R	B1000–59999	325000–	Clip, Hood
2B	A 230 R	B1000–59999	325000–	Bracket, Hood Clip, R.H.
	A 532 R	B1000–59999	325000–	Bracket, Hood Clip, L.H.

PC-676-(2-60)

Unstyled Model B hoods. *John Deere Archives*

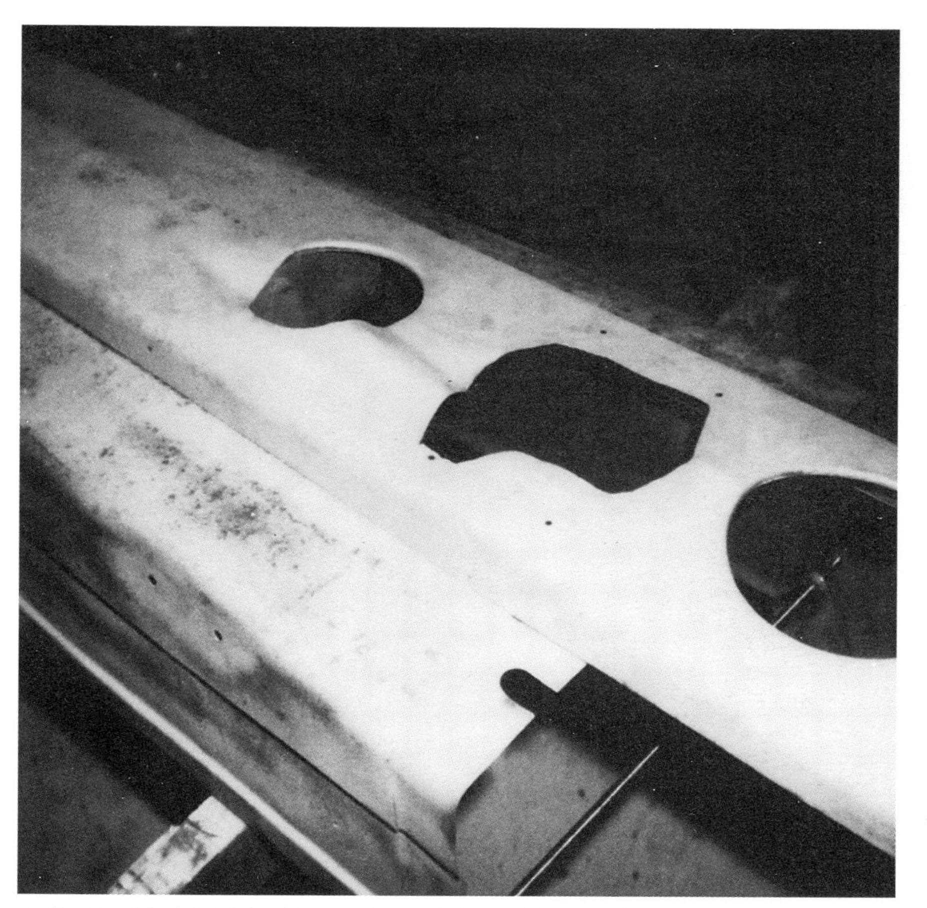

Unlike the Model A John Deere, the styled Model B muffler bolts were under the hood. Almost invariably, rather than remove the hood to get at these bolts, a cold chisel and hacksaw were used to enlarge the hood hole. Such a damaged hood is unacceptable for restoration and must be patched.

This top view of an early unstyled Model B shows the taper to the hood that allowed great visibility for cultivating. Also note the ring-type drawbar.

Here is the same hood shown previously, after being patched. The patch was cut from the hood of a scrapped John Deere Model 60 and welded into place. After hours of sanding, sealing, and priming, the finished result is a correctly restored hood, ready for paint.

Another look at the restored hood, painted and mounted on a 1948 Model B.

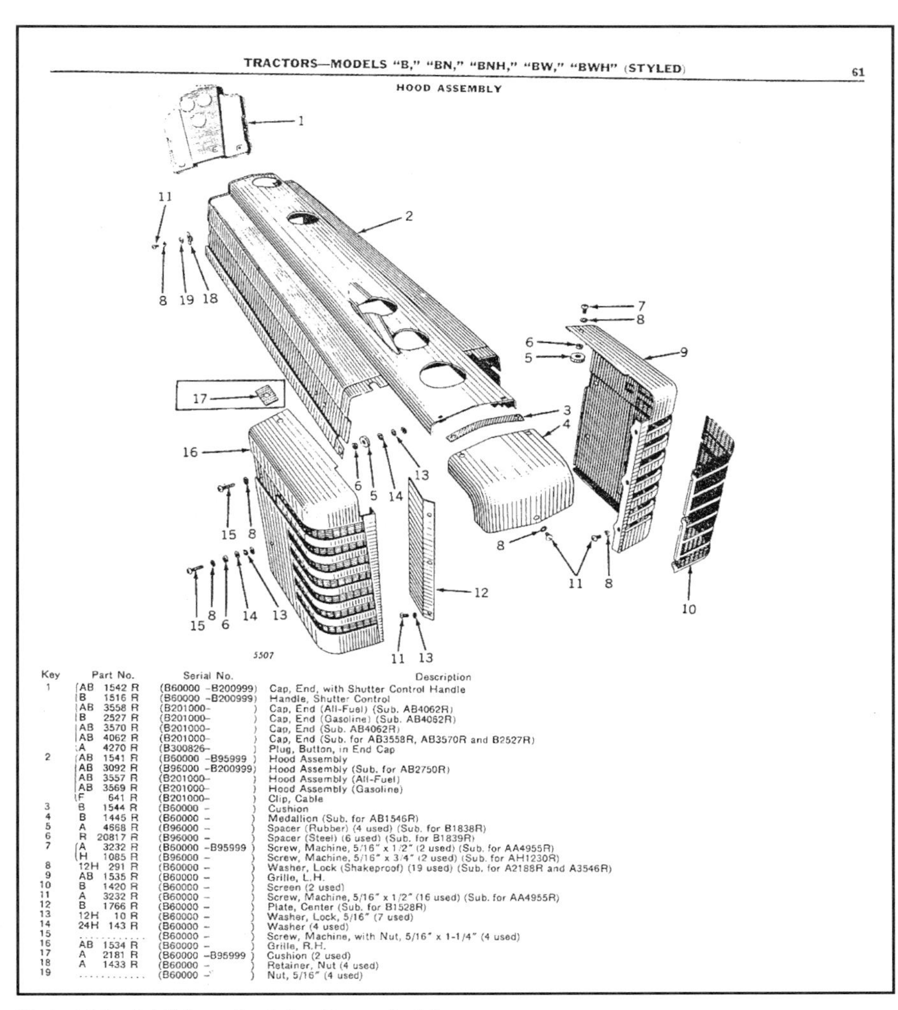

TRACTORS—MODELS "B," "BN," "BNH," "BW," "BWH" (STYLED) 61

HOOD ASSEMBLY

5507

Key	Part No.	Serial No.	Description
1	AB 1542 R	(B60000 -B200999)	Cap, End, with Shutter Control Handle
	B 1516 R	(B60000 -B200999)	Handle, Shutter Control
	AB 3558 R	(B201000-)	Cap, End (All-Fuel) (Sub. AB4062R)
	B 2527 R	(B201000-)	Cap, End (Gasoline) (Sub. AB4062R)
	AB 3570 R	(B201000-)	Cap, End (Sub. AB4062R)
	AB 4062 R	(B201000-)	Cap, End (Sub. for AB3558R, AB3570R and B2527R)
	A 4270 R	(B300826-)	Plug, Button, in End Cap
2	AB 1541 R	(B60000 -B95999)	Hood Assembly
	AB 3092 R	(B96000 -B200999)	Hood Assembly (Sub. for AB2750R)
	AB 3557 R	(B201000-)	Hood Assembly (All-Fuel)
	AB 3569 R	(B201000-)	Hood Assembly (Gasoline)
	F 641 R	(B201000-)	Clip, Cable
3	B 1544 R	(B60000 -)	Cushion
4	B 1445 R	(B60000 -)	Medallion (Sub. for AB1546R)
5	A 4668 R	(B96000 -)	Spacer (Rubber) (4 used) (Sub. for B1838R)
6	R 20817 R	(B96000 -)	Spacer (Steel) (6 used) (Sub. for B1839R)
7	A 3232 R	(B60000 -B95999)	Screw, Machine, 5/16" x 1/2" (2 used) (Sub. for AA4955R)
	H 1085 R	(B96000 -)	Screw, Machine, 5/16" x 3/4" (2 used) (Sub. for AH1230R)
8	12H 291 R	(B60000 -)	Washer, Lock (Shakeproof) (19 used) (Sub. for A2188R and A3546R)
9	AB 1535 R	(B60000 -)	Grille, L.H.
10	B 1420 R	(B60000 -)	Screen (2 used)
11	A 3232 R	(B60000 -)	Screw, Machine, 5/16" x 1/2" (16 used) (Sub. for AA4955R)
12	B 1766 R	(B60000 -)	Plate, Center (Sub. for B1528R)
13	12H 10 R	(B60000 -)	Washer, Lock, 5/16" (7 used)
14	24H 143 R	(B60000 -)	Washer (4 used)
15	....	(B60000 -)	Screw, Machine, with Nut, 5/16" x 1-1/4" (4 used)
16	AB 1534 R	(B60000 -)	Grille, R.H.
17	A 2181 R	(B60000 -B95999)	Cushion (2 used)
18	A 1433 R	(B60000 -)	Retainer, Nut (4 used)
19	....	(B60000 -)	Nut, 5/16" (4 used)

Styled Model B hoods. *John Deere Archives*

Fenders

There are a surprising number of fender variations. For unstyled row-crops, round-top fenders (AA467R right and AA468R left) were available from the beginning, but not common.

After 1937, Model Bs used the more modern-looking round-top fender (AA1582R right and AA1583R left). Note that these fenders can be used on earlier tractors, unless a hand-lift cultivator is going to be fitted. These same later fenders are appropriate on early styled and late styled Model Bs up to serial number 260,983 (mid-1950); later models used a clam shell fender.

For BR tractors, note that different fenders and braces are used when individual wheel brakes are fitted.

Clam shell fenders on a late styled Model B. Also, note the newer forty-five-degree angle tread tires, which are correct.

Round-top fenders grace an early styled Model B.

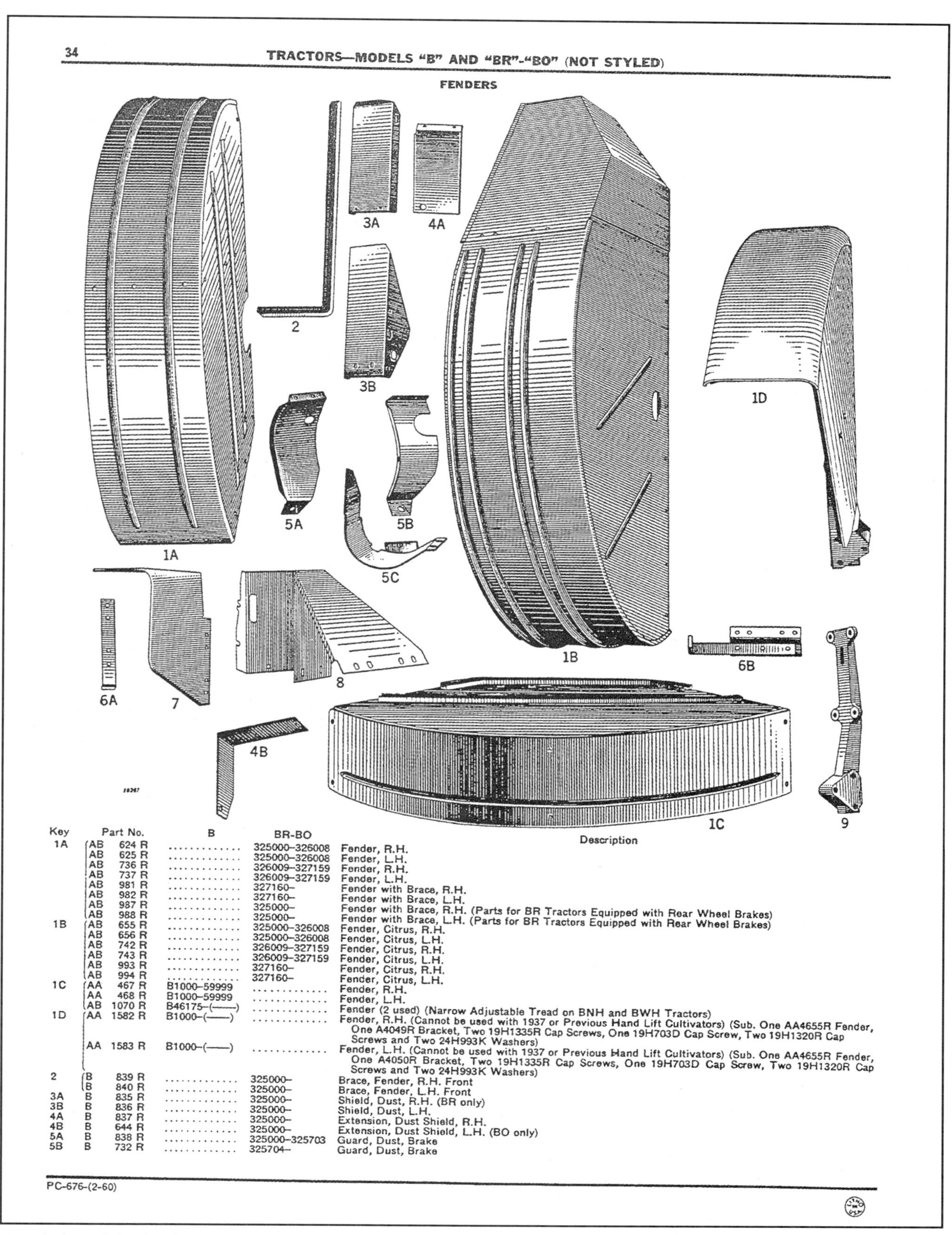

34 TRACTORS—MODELS "B" AND "BR"-"BO" (NOT STYLED)

FENDERS

Key	Part No.	B	BR-BO	Description
1A	AB 624 R	....	325000–326008	Fender, R.H.
	AB 625 R	....	325000–326008	Fender, L.H.
	AB 736 R	....	326009–327159	Fender, R.H.
	AB 737 R	....	326009–327159	Fender, L.H.
	AB 981 R	....	327160–	Fender with Brace, R.H.
	AB 982 R	....	327160–	Fender with Brace, L.H.
	AB 987 R	....	325000–	Fender with Brace, R.H. (Parts for BR Tractors Equipped with Rear Wheel Brakes)
	AB 988 R	....	325000–	Fender with Brace, L.H. (Parts for BR Tractors Equipped with Rear Wheel Brakes)
1B	AB 655 R	....	325000–326008	Fender, Citrus, R.H.
	AB 656 R	....	325000–326008	Fender, Citrus, L.H.
	AB 742 R	....	326009–327159	Fender, Citrus, R.H.
	AB 743 R	....	326009–327159	Fender, Citrus, L.H.
	AB 993 R	....	327160–	Fender, Citrus, R.H.
	AB 994 R	....	327160–	Fender, Citrus, L.H.
1C	AA 467 R	B1000–59999	....	Fender, R.H.
	AA 468 R	B1000–59999	....	Fender, L.H.
	AB 1070 R	B46175–(——)	....	Fender (2 used) (Narrow Adjustable Tread on BNH and BWH Tractors)
1D	AA 1582 R	B1000–(——)	....	Fender, R.H. (Cannot be used with 1937 or Previous Hand Lift Cultivators) (Sub. One AA4655R Fender, One A4049R Bracket, Two 19H1335R Cap Screws, One 19H703D Cap Screw, Two 19H1320R Cap Screws and Two 24H993K Washers)
	AA 1583 R	B1000–(——)	....	Fender, L.H. (Cannot be used with 1937 or Previous Hand Lift Cultivators) (Sub. One AA4655R Fender, One A4050R Bracket, Two 19H1335R Cap Screws, One 19H703D Cap Screw, Two 19H1320R Cap Screws and Two 24H993K Washers)
2	B 839 R	....	325000–	Brace, Fender, R.H. Front
	B 840 R	....	325000–	Brace, Fender, L.H. Front
3A	B 835 R	....	325000–	Shield, Dust, R.H. (BR only)
3B	B 836 R	....	325000–	Shield, Dust, L.H.
4A	B 837 R	....	325000–	Extension, Dust Shield, R.H.
4B	B 644 R	....	325000–	Extension, Dust Shield, L.H. (BO only)
5A	B 838 R	....	325000–325703	Guard, Dust, Brake
5B	B 732 R	....	325704–	Guard, Dust, Brake

PC-676-(2-60)

Unstyled Model B fenders. *John Deere Archives*

TRACTORS—MODELS "B" AND "BR"-"BO" (NOT STYLED) 35

FENDERS—Continued

Key	Part No.	B	BR-BO	Description
5C	AB 788 R	....	325000–	Guard, Dust, Brake (Parts for BR Tractors Equipped with Rear Wheel Brakes)
6A	B 630 R	....	325000–	Support, Cirtus Fender, L.H., Front
6B	AB 659 R	....	325000–	Support, Cirtus Fender, R H., Front
7	AB 836 R	....	325795–	Fender, Front, L.H. (BO only)
8	AB 628 R	....	325000–	Guard, Pulley
9	A 792 R	B1000–59999	....	Bracket, Fender, R.H. and L.H.
	B 960 R	B46175–(——)	....	Bracket, Fender, R.H. and L.H. (Narrow Adjustable Tread on BNH and BWH Tractors)
(Parts listed below are not illustrated.)				
	B 906 R	....	327160–	Support, Side, Citrus Fender, R.H.
	B 907 R	....	327160–	Support, Side, Citrus Fender, L.H.

Unstyled Model B fenders (continued). *John Deere Archives*

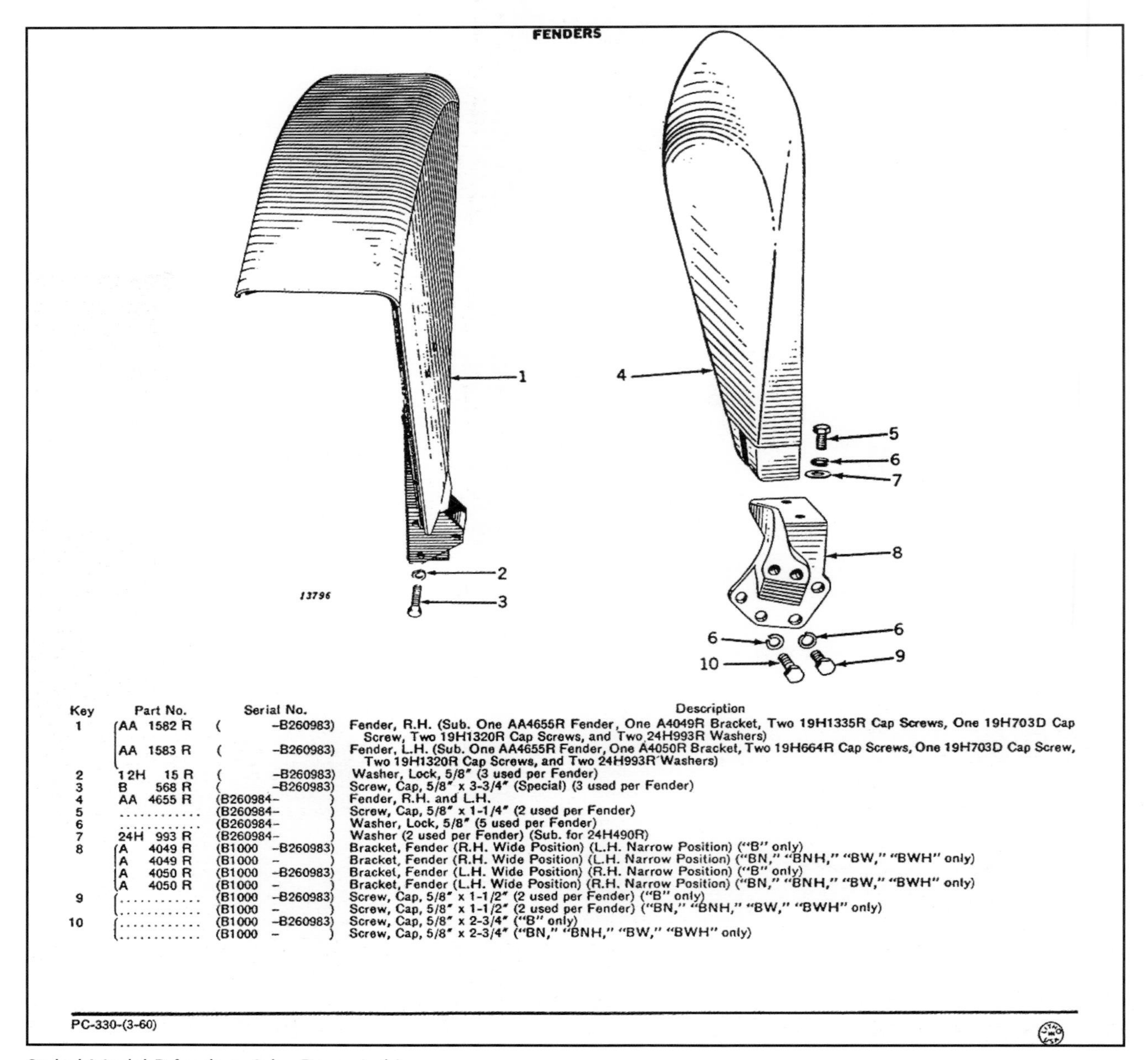

Key	Part No.	Serial No.	Description
1	AA 1582 R	(–B260983)	Fender, R.H. (Sub. One AA4655R Fender, One A4049R Bracket, Two 19H1335R Cap Screws, One 19H703D Cap Screw, Two 19H1320R Cap Screws, and Two 24H993R Washers)
	AA 1583 R	(–B260983)	Fender, L.H. (Sub. One AA4655R Fender, One A4050R Bracket, Two 19H664R Cap Screws, One 19H703D Cap Screw, Two 19H1320R Cap Screws, and Two 24H993R Washers)
2	12H 15 R	(–B260983)	Washer, Lock, 5/8" (3 used per Fender)
3	B 568 R	(–B260983)	Screw, Cap, 5/8" x 3-3/4" (Special) (3 used per Fender)
4	AA 4655 R	(B260984–)	Fender, R.H. and L.H.
5	....	(B260984–)	Screw, Cap, 5/8" x 1-1/4" (2 used per Fender)
6	....	(B260984–)	Washer, Lock, 5/8" (5 used per Fender)
7	24H 993 R	(B260984–)	Washer (2 used per Fender) (Sub. for 24H490R)
8	A 4049 R	(B1000 –B260983)	Bracket, Fender (R.H. Wide Position) (L.H. Narrow Position) ("B" only)
	A 4049 R	(B1000 –)	Bracket, Fender (R.H. Wide Position) (L.H. Narrow Position) ("BN," "BNH," "BW," "BWH" only)
	A 4050 R	(B1000 –B260983)	Bracket, Fender (L.H. Wide Position) (R.H. Narrow Position) ("B" only)
	A 4050 R	(B1000 –)	Bracket, Fender (L.H. Wide Position) (R.H. Narrow Position) ("BN," "BNH," "BW," "BWH" only)
9	....	(B1000 –B260983)	Screw, Cap, 5/8" x 1-1/2" (2 used per Fender) ("B" only)
	....	(B1000 –)	Screw, Cap, 5/8" x 1-1/2" (2 used per Fender) ("BN," "BNH," "BW," "BWH" only)
10	....	(B1000 –B260983)	Screw, Cap, 5/8" x 2-3/4" ("B" only)
	....	(B1000 –)	Screw, Cap, 5/8" x 2-3/4" ("BN," "BNH," "BW," "BWH" only)

PC-330-(3-60)

Styled Model B fenders. *John Deere Archives*

New John Deere gauges have been fitted to this Model B. The correct, original gauges have white faces and the words "John Deere" on the face. These gauges were not available for some time due to copyright restrictions, but the copyright was lifted and Antique Gauges in Laurel, Delaware, now has correct gauges available. While the black-faced gauges shown above are not correct for restoration purposes, they do the job just fine. Note that the ammeter is showing a charge and the oil pressure gauge reads plenty of pressure, disproving the old advertising slogan that you can't take a clear picture of a running John Deere.

This slant-dash is correct for Model Bs equipped with electrical systems. The picture was taken in September of 1939. *John Deere Archives*

Gauges

All original Model B instruments had white faces. Instruments currently supplied by Deere have black faces, which will not do for a correct restoration. Contact Antique Gauges, Inc., Laurel, Delaware (see appendix), for replacements, or you can try touching up the old instrument if it still works. You can get the bezel rechromed, if that was original. Remember, tractors prior to serial number 12,743 were not originally equipped with a temperature gauge. At one time, trademark restrictions prohibited anyone other than John Deere from putting the words "John Deere" on the face of the instrument. Those trademark restrictions were lifted, however, and replacement white-face gauges with "John Deere" on them are available from Antique Gauges.

The correct gauges are shown in this two-gauge panel for an early styled Model B. Note the white faces and "John Deere" type.

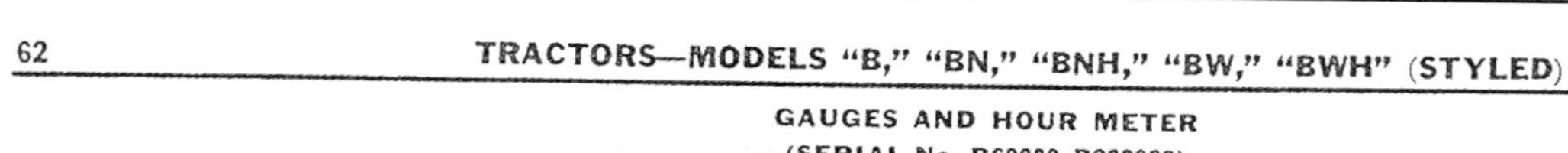

62 **TRACTORS—MODELS "B," "BN," "BNH," "BW," "BWH" (STYLED)**

GAUGES AND HOUR METER
(SERIAL No. B60000-B200999)

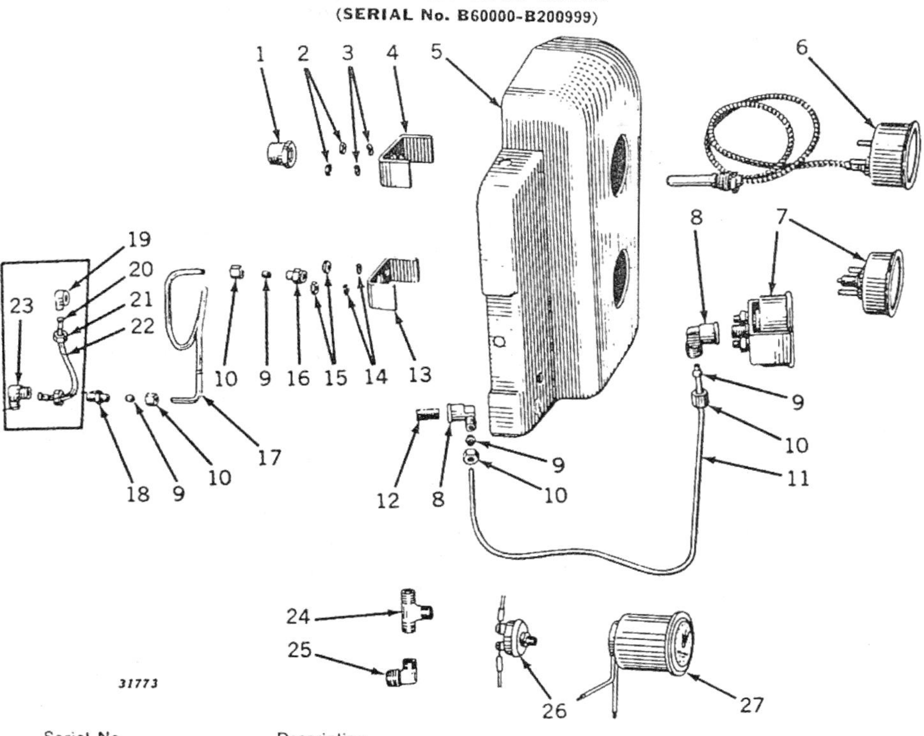

Key	Part No.	Serial No.	Description
1	A 1248 R	(–)	Bushing, Heat Indicator Tube
2	....	(B60000 –)	Nut (2 used)
3	....	(B60000 –)	Washer, Lock (2 used)
4	A 1712 R	(B60000 –)	Clamp
5	AB 1542 R	(B60000 –B200999)	Cap, End
6	AA 883 R	((–B148499)	Heat Indicator with Nuts and Lock Washers
		(B167000–)	Heat Indicator with Nuts and Lock Washers
	AA 3538 R	(B148500–B166999)	Heat, Indicator with Nuts and Lock Washers
	AA 1342 R	(B60000 –B148499) (B167000–B200999)	Heat Indicator with Nuts and Lock Washers (Used on Tractors with Electric Starting Equipment) (Sub. AA6295R)
	AA 3534 R	(B148500–B166999)	Heat Indicator with Nuts and Lock Washers (Used on Tractors with Electric Starting Equipment) (Sub. AA6295R)
7	AF 2775 R	(B60000 –)	Gauge, Oil Pressure (Sub. for AB1549R)
	AA 1730 R	(B60000 –B95999)	Gauge, Oil Pressure (Used on Tractors with Electric Starting Equipment)
8	A 2501 R	(B96000 –B200999)	Elbow (2 used) (Used on Tractors with Electric Starting Equipment)
9	A 2499 R	(B144538–)	Sleeve (2 used) (Also used on Tractors (B96000–) equipped with Electric Starting)
10	A 2500 R	(B144538–)	Nut, Compression (2 used) (Also used on Tractors (B96000–) equipped with Electric Starting)
11	AB 1832 R	(B60000 –B95999)	Pipe, Oil Pressure Gauge (Used on Tractors with Electric Starting Equipment)
	B 1941 R	(B96000 –B200999)	Pipe, Oil Pressure Gauge (Used on Tractors with Electric Starting Equipment)
12	29H 483 R	(B96000 –B200999)	Nipple (Used on Tractors with Electric Starting Equipment)
13	....	(B60000 –)	Clamp
14	....	(B60000 –)	Washer, Lock (2 used)
15	....	(B60000 –)	Nut (2 used)
16	A 2564 R	(B144538–)	Connector
17	B 2011 R	(B144538–B200999)	Pipe, Oil Pressure Gauge
18	A 2502 R	(B144538–)	Connector
19	B 1479 R	(B60000 –B144537)	Elbow
20	E 2150 R	(B60000 –B80496)	Gland, Solder Bushing (2 used) (Used only on Copper Pipes)
	B 1675 R	(B80497 –B144537)	Gland, Solder Bushing (2 used) (Used only on Copper Pipes)
21	A 2069 R	(B60000 –B144537)	Nut (2 used)
22	AB 1634 R	(B60000 –B144537)	Pipe, Oil Pressure Gauge, and Elbow
23	A 258 R	(–B80496)	Connector (Sub. for D392R)
	D 417 R	(B80497 –B144537)	Elbow (Also parts to Tractor (B60000–B80496) equipped with Governor Case Oil Indicator Gauge Oil Pipe 1/4" in Diameter)
24	15H 541 R	(B60000 –)	Tee, Pipe (Used with Hour Meter Pressure Switch)
25	D 3159 R	(B60000 –)	Elbow (Used with Hour Meter Pressure Switch)
26	AA 5337 R	(B60000 –)	Switch, Hour Meter Pressure, with Elbow and Tee (ATTACHMENT, List on Separate Order)
	AR 720 R	(B60000 –)	Switch, Hour Meter
27	AB 4282 R	(B60000 –)	Meter, Hour, 6 Volt (ATTACHMENT, List on Separate Order) (For Service send to John W Hobbs Corporation, Springfield, Illinois)

Early styled Model B gauges. *John Deere Archives*

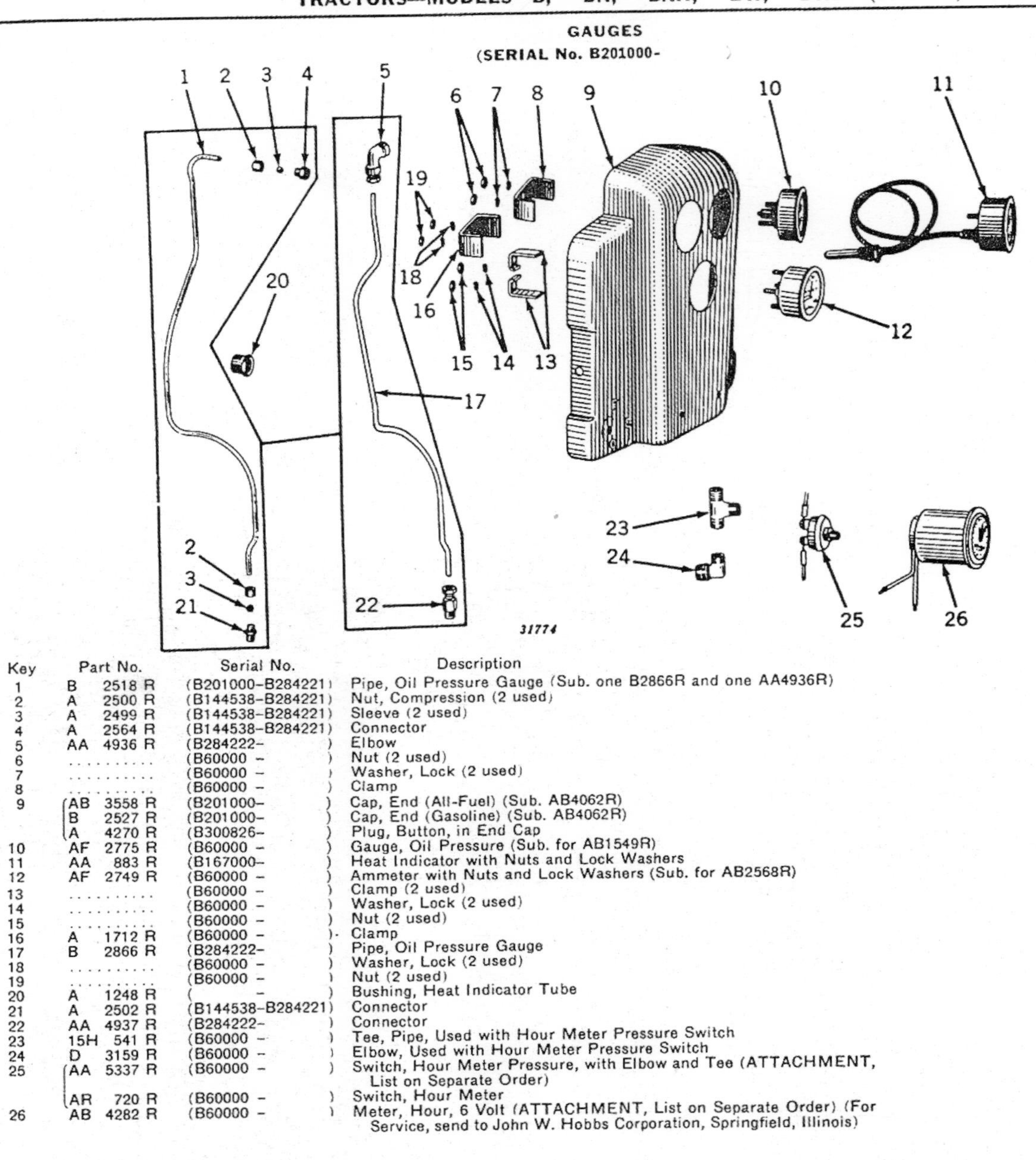

TRACTORS—MODELS "B," "BN," "BNH," "BW," "BWH" (STYLED) 63

GAUGES

(SERIAL No. B201000-)

Key	Part No.	Serial No.	Description
1	B 2518 R	(B201000–B284221)	Pipe, Oil Pressure Gauge (Sub. one B2866R and one AA4936R)
2	A 2500 R	(B144538–B284221)	Nut, Compression (2 used)
3	A 2499 R	(B144538–B284221)	Sleeve (2 used)
4	A 2564 R	(B144538–B284221)	Connector
5	AA 4936 R	(B284222–)	Elbow
6	....	(B60000 –)	Nut (2 used)
7	....	(B60000 –)	Washer, Lock (2 used)
8	....	(B60000 –)	Clamp
9	AB 3558 R	(B201000–)	Cap, End (All-Fuel) (Sub. AB4062R)
	B 2527 R	(B201000–)	Cap, End (Gasoline) (Sub. AB4062R)
	A 4270 R	(B300826–)	Plug, Button, in End Cap
10	AF 2775 R	(B60000 –)	Gauge, Oil Pressure (Sub. for AB1549R)
11	AA 883 R	(B167000–)	Heat Indicator with Nuts and Lock Washers
12	AF 2749 R	(B60000 –)	Ammeter with Nuts and Lock Washers (Sub. for AB2568R)
13	....	(B60000 –)	Clamp (2 used)
14	....	(B60000 –)	Washer, Lock (2 used)
15	....	(B60000 –)	Nut (2 used)
16	A 1712 R	(B60000 –)	Clamp
17	B 2866 R	(B284222–)	Pipe, Oil Pressure Gauge
18	....	(B60000 –)	Washer, Lock (2 used)
19	....	(B60000 –)	Nut (2 used)
20	A 1248 R	(–)	Bushing, Heat Indicator Tube
21	A 2502 R	(B144538–B284221)	Connector
22	AA 4937 R	(B284222–)	Connector
23	15H 541 R	(B60000 –)	Tee, Pipe, Used with Hour Meter Pressure Switch
24	D 3159 R	(B60000 –)	Elbow, Used with Hour Meter Pressure Switch
25	AA 5337 R	(B60000 –)	Switch, Hour Meter Pressure, with Elbow and Tee (ATTACHMENT, List on Separate Order)
	AR 720 R	(B60000 –)	Switch, Hour Meter
26	AB 4282 R	(B60000 –)	Meter, Hour, 6 Volt (ATTACHMENT, List on Separate Order) (For Service, send to John W. Hobbs Corporation, Springfield, Illinois)

Late styled Model B gauges. *John Deere Archives*

Note the leaping deer between "General" and "Purpose" on this very early John Deere B running a No. 5 corn sheller. This photo was taken in January 1937 in Jasper, Montana. Also note the model designator on the rear of the gasoline tank. *John Deere Archives*

Decals

Originally, insignias, trademarks, logos, and the like were applied by the process of silk screening. In 1941, this process was supplanted by decalcomania, or decals. Now, the latest method of applying such is by laser-cut pressure-sensitive logotype. Most restoration authorities prefer this later type (available from Travis Jorde, see appendix), regardless of what was originally used. Experienced restorers avoid decal sets supplied by John Deere. Deere decals have been generalized to fit a variety of tractors and most are not exactly right for any one model. Also, some say Deere decals fade or crack when exposed to the sun for extended periods.

The earliest John Deere Model Bs, up to about serial number 6,000 (May 1935), had a leaping deer silk-screened between "John" and "Deere." With the leaping deer, the model designation was applied to the rear of the fuel tank. The "G" in General Purpose was also more script-like than the later block letter.

The "B" in the black circle logo is not correct on this rare early styled Model BNH. Early styled Model Bs should have the model designation, "Model BNH" in this case, on the seat strut. The rear brake cover indicates that this model is a pre-1941 model.

Model Bs after serial number 6,000 had the model designation moved to the seat support (readable from the pulley side). Also, the rear of the fuel tank bore the leaping deer and the words "John Deere - Moline, Ill."

Styled tractors omitted the "General Purpose" script from the logo on the side of the hood. The "John Deere" decal on the side of the hood was centered on styled Model Bs until 1950, when the decal was moved forward, just behind the circular model designation logo (see photos). The model designation was on the seat support until the late styled tractors appeared. Late styled tractors have the model designation in a circular decal on the front sides of the hood.

One of the simplest ways to get the correct decals and placement for your Model B is to order them through Travis Jorde in Rochester, Minnesota (see appendix for address). If you supply your tractor's model and serial number with your order, Travis will send you the correct decals and instructions for placement.

Paint

John Deere's famous Deere Implement Green is available from DuPont as code 262 in Dulux, Imron, and Centari. The yellow is code 263 in Dulux and Centari. For John Deere Model BI machines, use DuPont Construction Yellow code 43007 in Dulux. The John Deere company also has restoration-quality paint.

This beautiful Model BW restoration is marred by the wrong hood decal. Either the straight-topped "G" in General Purpose is wrong, or the leaping deer between "John" and "Deere" is wrong. The leaping deer and curved "G" were discontinued in mid-1935. After that, the deer was on the rear of the gasoline tank and the flat-topped "G" was used.

The leaping deer between "John" and "Deere" is not correct for the BR, nor are the letters "BR" on the hood. Correct decal type and placement have been a challenge for John Deere restorers.

This archival photo shows the correct decal placement for early styled Model Bs. The "John Deere" decal is centered on the hood, and the model designation (not quite visible) is on the seat strut. This photo was taken in 1939. *John Deere Archives*

This photo shows the correct placement of the model designation on early styled Model Bs. Also note the pan-type seat, which is correct for early styled Bs.

The tractor in this archival photo has the correct decals for late styled Model B tractors. The "B" logo in a black circle was added to late styled Model B tractors, while the "John Deere" type should be centered on styled Model Bs built before 1950. The type was moved forward on styled Model Bs built in 1950 or later. *John Deere Archives*

This archival photo shows a late styled Model B with the correct logos for 1950 and later Model Bs. The "John Deere" type on the hood is positioned towards the front rather than centered. *John Deere Archives*

This restorer likely got his decals from Deere & Company, and got more than he needed for this late styled Model B. The "Custom Powr-Trol" decal, on the side of the battery box, would be appropriate for a Model 520. Note the "Be Careful" logo, which is correct.

Here's an example of the padded seat used on late styled Model Bs. This 1951 photo was taken near Dubuque, Iowa. *John Deere Archives*

Seat

The same steel stamped seat pan was used on all Model Bs, except the BI, until the late styled tractors of 1947. The BI used a bench—or armchair—seat. Unfortunately, the BI seat is not shown on the figures. Late styled tractors have an upholstered bench seat on top of the battery box.

Serial Number Plates

It is nice to polish brass serial number plates to a soft, gold-like glow. Aluminum plates can be painted black and then sanded lightly with fine-grit paper to make the letters stand out. Under no circumstances should you alter the number plate. In most cases it is illegal to do so. If you want to change the transmission case on your Model B and install your old serial plate on the new case, most experts agree that is okay. It is also possible to get a duplicate plate. Contact your Deere & Company dealer.

Replacement aluminum "warning" plates can be obtained from Brandon Pfeiffer Tractor Plates, Mount Vernon, Indiana (see appendix).

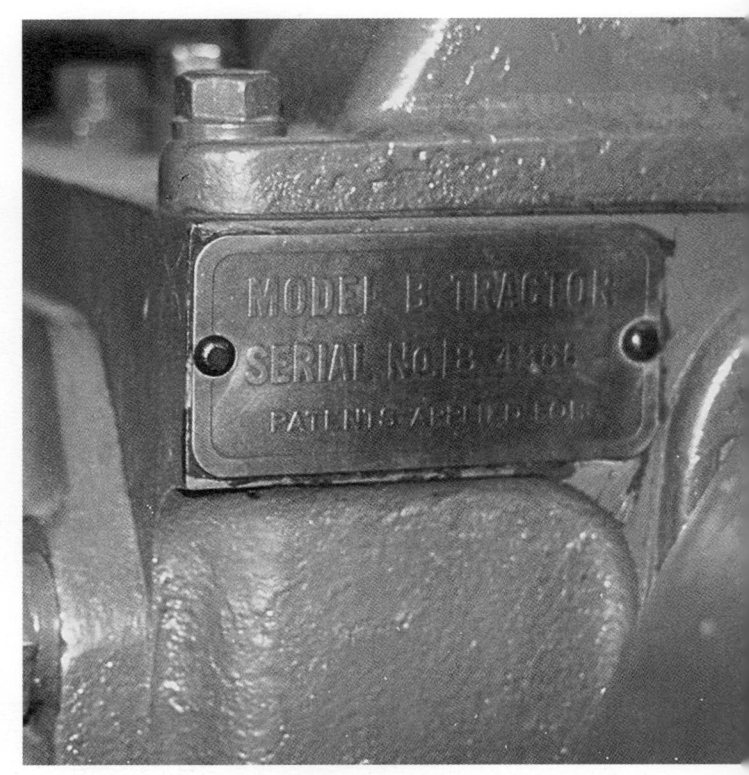

The serial number plate is above the flywheel on unstyled John Deere Model B tractors.

Note the pan-type seat on this Model B. The pan-type seat is correct for early styled Model Bs. The seats were notoriously uncomfortable and, according to author Randy Leffingwell, the seat was shaped to fit Pete, who was simply the guy in the factory with the biggest behind. *John Deere Archives*

Late styled Model Bs use this type of seat with a back support.

The unpadded armchair seat used on the Model BI Industrial tractor. This one belongs to Bruce Johnson of Lily Lake, Illinois.

A 1936 Model BI mows the shoulder of a country road. This gives a good view of the armchair seat unique to the Model BI. *John Deere Archives*

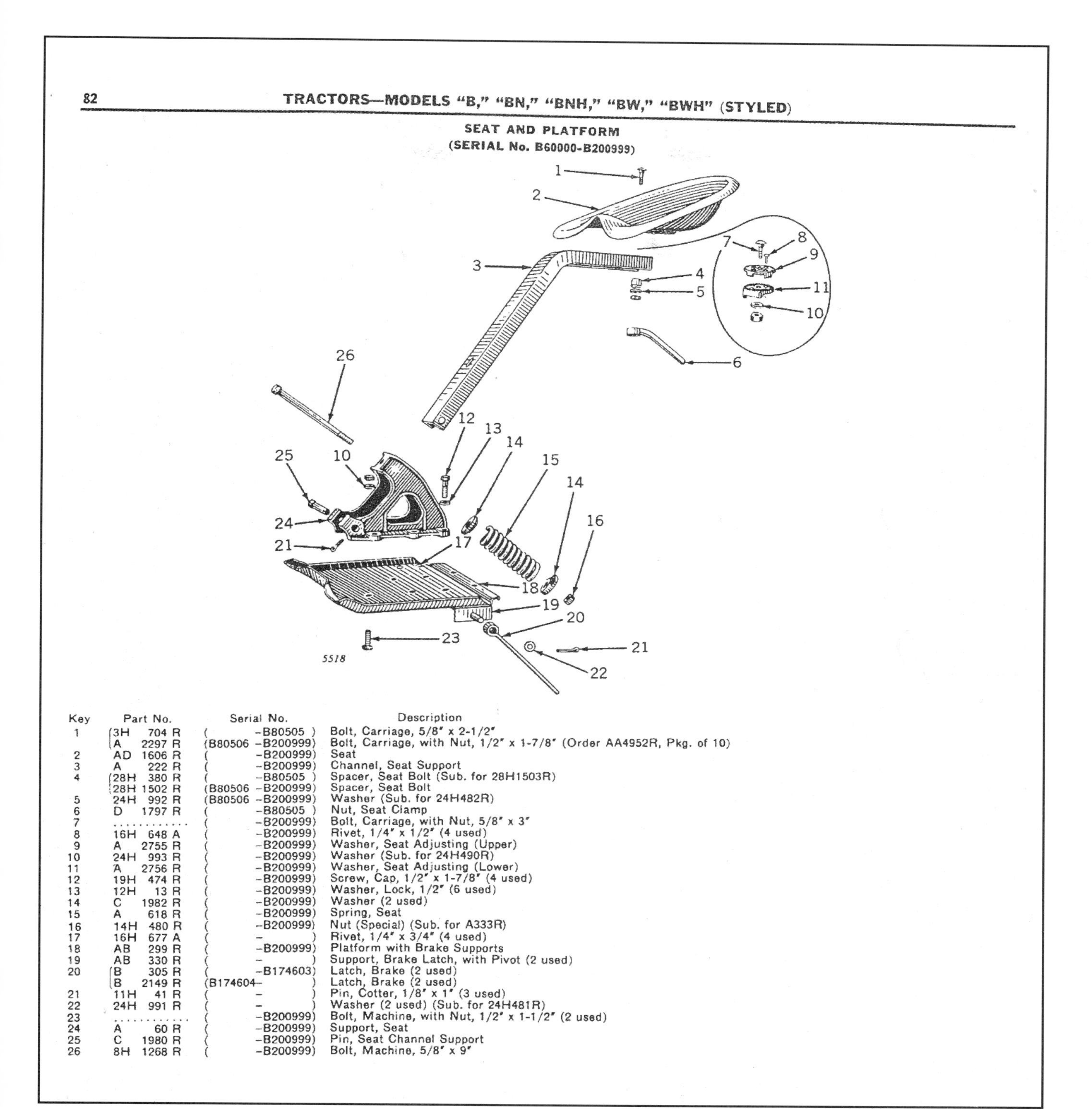

82 TRACTORS—MODELS "B," "BN," "BNH," "BW," "BWH" (STYLED)

SEAT AND PLATFORM
(SERIAL No. B60000-B200999)

Key	Part No.	Serial No.	Description
1	3H 704 R	(-B80505)	Bolt, Carriage, 5/8" x 2-1/2"
	A 2297 R	(B80506 -B200999)	Bolt, Carriage, with Nut, 1/2" x 1-7/8" (Order AA4952R, Pkg. of 10)
2	AD 1606 R	(-B200999)	Seat
3	A 222 R	(-B200999)	Channel, Seat Support
4	28H 380 R	(-B80505)	Spacer, Seat Bolt (Sub. for 28H1503R)
	28H 1502 R	(B80506 -B200999)	Spacer, Seat Bolt
5	24H 992 R	(B80506 -B200999)	Washer (Sub. for 24H482R)
6	D 1797 R	(-B80505)	Nut, Seat Clamp
7	....	(-B200999)	Bolt, Carriage, with Nut, 5/8" x 3"
8	16H 648 A	(-B200999)	Rivet, 1/4" x 1/2" (4 used)
9	A 2755 R	(-B200999)	Washer, Seat Adjusting (Upper)
10	24H 993 R	(-B200999)	Washer (Sub. for 24H490R)
11	A 2756 R	(-B200999)	Washer, Seat Adjusting (Lower)
12	19H 474 R	(-B200999)	Screw, Cap, 1/2" x 1-7/8" (4 used)
13	12H 13 R	(-B200999)	Washer, Lock, 1/2" (6 used)
14	C 1982 R	(-B200999)	Washer (2 used)
15	A 618 R	(-B200999)	Spring, Seat
16	14H 480 R	(-B200999)	Nut (Special) (Sub. for A333R)
17	16H 677 A	(–)	Rivet, 1/4" x 3/4" (4 used)
18	AB 299 R	(-B200999)	Platform with Brake Supports
19	AB 330 R	(–)	Support, Brake Latch, with Pivot (2 used)
20	B 305 R	(-B174603)	Latch, Brake (2 used)
	B 2149 R	(B174604–)	Latch, Brake (2 used)
21	11H 41 R	(–)	Pin, Cotter, 1/8" x 1" (3 used)
22	24H 991 R	(–)	Washer (2 used) (Sub. for 24H481R)
23	....	(-B200999)	Bolt, Machine, with Nut, 1/2" x 1-1/2" (2 used)
24	A 60 R	(-B200999)	Support, Seat
25	C 1980 R	(-B200999)	Pin, Seat Channel Support
26	8H 1268 R	(-B200999)	Bolt, Machine, 5/8" x 9"

Pan-style seat and bracketry used on early styled Model Bs. *John Deere Archives*

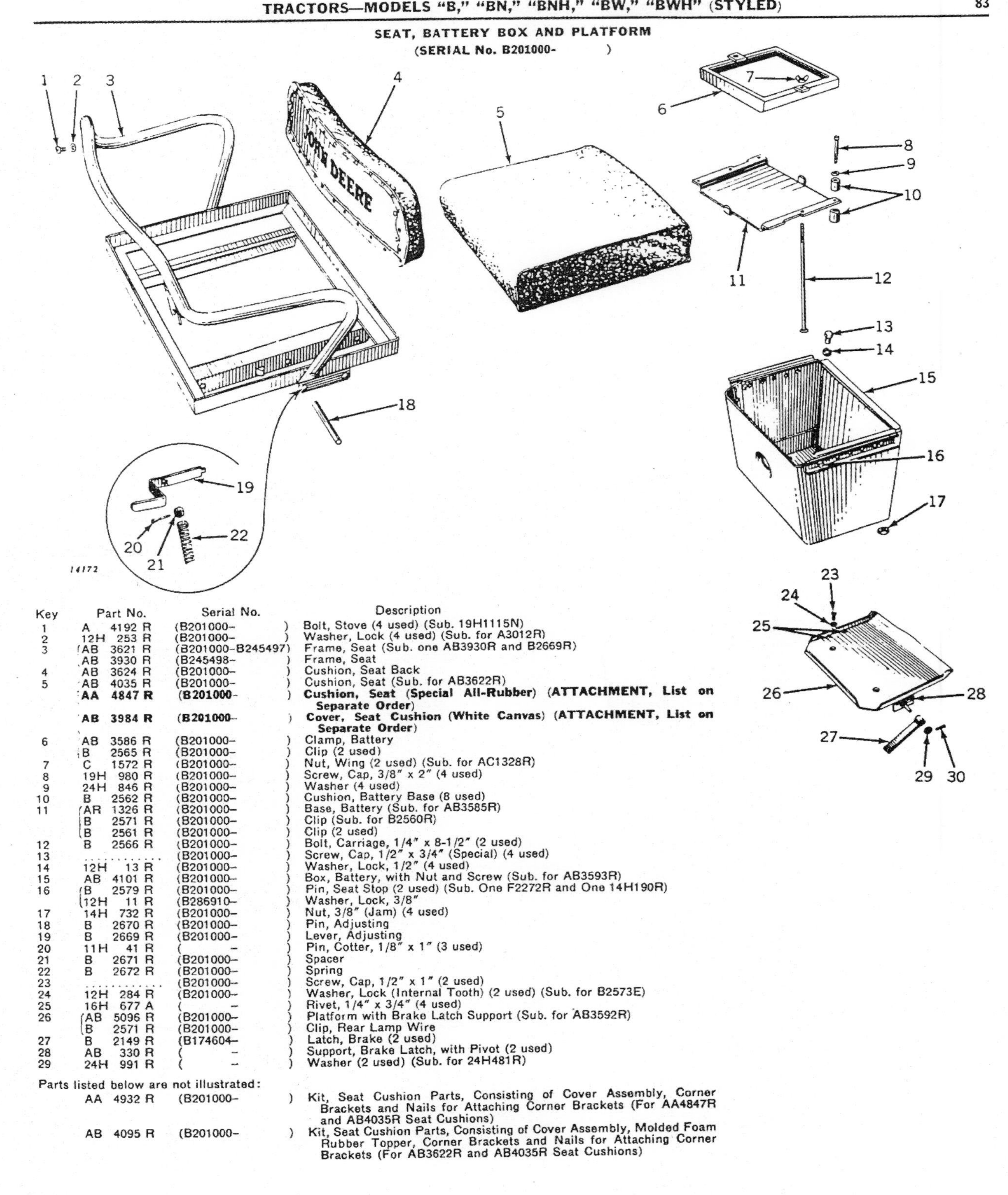

TRACTORS—MODELS "B," "BN," "BNH," "BW," "BWH" (STYLED) 83

SEAT, BATTERY BOX AND PLATFORM

(SERIAL No. B201000-)

Key	Part No.	Serial No.	Description
1	A 4192 R	(B201000-)	Bolt, Stove (4 used) (Sub. 19H1115N)
2	12H 253 R	(B201000-)	Washer, Lock (4 used) (Sub. for A3012R)
3	AB 3621 R	(B201000-B245497)	Frame, Seat (Sub. one AB3930R and B2669R)
	AB 3930 R	(B245498-)	Frame, Seat
4	AB 3624 R	(B201000-)	Cushion, Seat Back
5	AB 4035 R	(B201000-)	Cushion, Seat (Sub. for AB3622R)
	AA 4847 R	**(B201000-)**	**Cushion, Seat (Special All-Rubber) (ATTACHMENT, List on Separate Order)**
	AB 3984 R	**(B201000-)**	**Cover, Seat Cushion (White Canvas) (ATTACHMENT, List on Separate Order)**
6	AB 3586 R	(B201000-)	Clamp, Battery
	B 2565 R	(B201000-)	Clip (2 used)
7	C 1572 R	(B201000-)	Nut, Wing (2 used) (Sub. for AC1328R)
8	19H 980 R	(B201000-)	Screw, Cap, 3/8" x 2" (4 used)
9	24H 846 R	(B201000-)	Washer (4 used)
10	B 2562 R	(B201000-)	Cushion, Battery Base (8 used)
11	AR 1326 R	(B201000-)	Base, Battery (Sub. for AB3585R)
	B 2571 R	(B201000-)	Clip (Sub. for B2560R)
	B 2561 R	(B201000-)	Clip (2 used)
12	B 2566 R	(B201000-)	Bolt, Carriage, 1/4" x 8-1/2" (2 used)
13	....	(B201000-)	Screw, Cap, 1/2" x 3/4" (Special) (4 used)
14	12H 13 R	(B201000-)	Washer, Lock, 1/2" (4 used)
15	AB 4101 R	(B201000-)	Box, Battery, with Nut and Screw (Sub. for AB3593R)
16	B 2579 R	(B201000-)	Pin, Seat Stop (2 used) (Sub. One F2272R and One 14H190R)
	12H 11 R	(B286910-)	Washer, Lock, 3/8"
17	14H 732 R	(B201000-)	Nut, 3/8" (Jam) (4 used)
18	B 2670 R	(B201000-)	Pin, Adjusting
19	B 2669 R	(B201000-)	Lever, Adjusting
20	11H 41 R	(-)	Pin, Cotter, 1/8" x 1" (3 used)
21	B 2671 R	(B201000-)	Spacer
22	B 2672 R	(B201000-)	Spring
23	....	(B201000-)	Screw, Cap, 1/2" x 1" (2 used)
24	12H 284 R	(B201000-)	Washer, Lock (Internal Tooth) (2 used) (Sub. for B2573E)
25	16H 677 A	(-)	Rivet, 1/4" x 3/4" (4 used)
26	AB 5096 R	(B201000-)	Platform with Brake Latch Support (Sub. for AB3592R)
	B 2571 R	(B201000-)	Clip, Rear Lamp Wire
27	B 2149 R	(B174604-)	Latch, Brake (2 used)
28	AB 330 R	(-)	Support, Brake Latch, with Pivot (2 used)
29	24H 991 R	(-)	Washer (2 used) (Sub. for 24H481R)

Parts listed below are not illustrated:

Part No.	Serial No.	Description
AA 4932 R	(B201000-)	Kit, Seat Cushion Parts, Consisting of Cover Assembly, Corner Brackets and Nails for Attaching Corner Brackets (For AA4847R and AB4035R Seat Cushions)
AB 4095 R	(B201000-)	Kit, Seat Cushion Parts, Consisting of Cover Assembly, Molded Foam Rubber Topper, Corner Brackets and Nails for Attaching Corner Brackets (For AB3622R and AB4035R Seat Cushions)

Padded seat, battery box, and platform used on late styled Model Bs. *John Deere Archives*

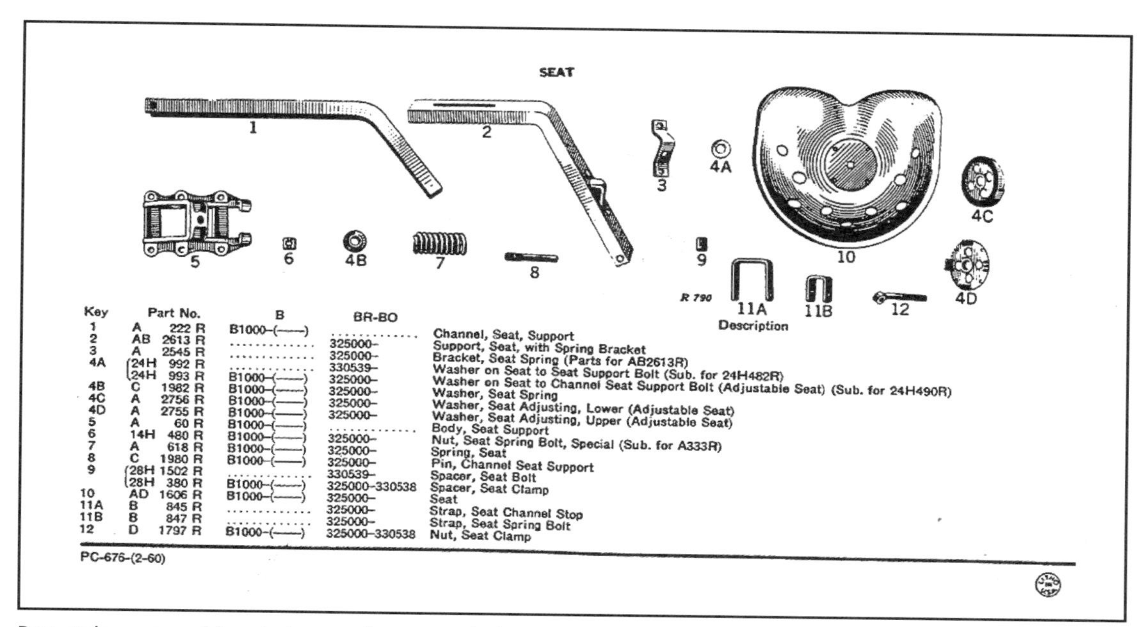

SEAT

1 2 3 4A 4B 4C 4D 5 6 7 8 9 10 11A 11B 12

R 790

Key	Part No.	B	BR-BO	Description
1	A 222 R	B1000-(——)	....	Channel, Seat, Support
2	AB 2613 R	....	325000-	Support, Seat, with Spring Bracket
3	A 2545 R	....	325000-	Bracket, Seat Spring (Parts for AB2613R)
4A	24H 992 R	....	330539-	Washer on Seat to Seat Support Bolt (Sub. for 24H482R)
	24H 993 R	B1000-(——)	325000-	Washer on Seat to Channel Seat Support Bolt (Adjustable Seat) (Sub. for 24H490R)
4B	C 1982 R	B1000-(——)	325000-	Washer, Seat Spring
4C	A 2756 R	B1000-(——)	325000-	Washer, Seat Adjusting, Lower (Adjustable Seat)
4D	A 2755 R	B1000-(——)	325000-	Washer, Seat Adjusting, Upper (Adjustable Seat)
5	A 60 R	B1000-(——)	....	Body, Seat Support
6	14H 480 R	B1000-(——)	325000-	Nut, Seat Spring Bolt, Special (Sub. for A333R)
7	A 618 R	B1000-(——)	325000-	Spring, Seat
8	C 1980 R	B1000-(——)	325000-	Pin, Channel Seat Support
9	28H 1502 R	....	330539-	Spacer, Seat Bolt
	28H 380 R	B1000-(——)	325000-330538	Spacer, Seat Clamp
10	AD 1606 R	B1000-(——)	325000-	Seat
11A	B 845 R	....	325000-	Strap, Seat Channel Stop
11B	B 847 R	....	325000-	Strap, Seat Spring Bolt
12	D 1797 R	B1000-(——)	325000-330538	Nut, Seat Clamp

PC-676-(2-60)

Pan-style seat and bracketry used on unstyled Model Bs. *John Deere Archives*

The owner of this Model B probably should have found a better grille and screen before painting.

Grille

For a quality restoration, extreme care must be taken with the grille and grille screen on styled Model Bs. It is quite unrealistic to expect these to have soldiered for fifty-plus years without some damage. In most cases, the grille can be straightened by good body and fender techniques. If the grille screen has been distorted and torn, it may be carefully shaped back to original and spot soldered. If it is too badly damaged, perhaps a better one can be found, or at least a better piece can be cut from another and soldered in.

Note that the original styled Bs had twisted wire grille screens through most of the 1939 model year. After that the stamped mesh screen was used.

For unstyled tractors, radiator curtains were used through mid-1937 (serial number 34,951). After that shutters were used. A functioning curtain, or shutters, are important for a proper restoration. For kerosene tractors, they are also important for proper operation.

Appendix

Recommended Reading

Books

Broehl, Wayne G. Jr. *John Deere's Company.* Doubleday and Company, 1984.

Gray, R.B. *The Agricultural Tractor 1855–1950.* ASAE, 1954.

Huber, Donald S., and Hughes, Ralph C. *How Johnny Popper Replaced The Horse.* Deere & Company publication, 1988.

Leffingwell, Randy. *John Deere Farm Tractors.* Motorbooks International, 1993.

Macmillan, Don, and Jones, Russell. *John Deere Tractors And Equipment.* ASAE, 1988, two volumes.

Pripps, Robert N. *Illustrated John Deere Two-Cylinder Tractor Buyer's Guide.* Motorbooks International, 1992.

Rasmussen, Henry. *John Deere Tractors, Big Green Machines in Review.* Motorbooks International, 1987.

Robert C. Williams., *Fordson, Farmall, and Poppin' Johnny.* University of Illinois Press, 1987.

John Deere Tractors 1918-1976, reprinted by ASAE by permission of Deere & Company, 1987.

(Most of the above books are available from Motorbooks International Publishers and Wholesalers Inc., 729 Prospect Avenue, Osceola, WI 54020. Call 800-826-6600 to order books.)

Clubs and Magazines

Clubs and publications are the single-best source for the collector or restorer. The articles, reader letters, and so on are helpful and informative, and the advertisements and classified ads are almost priceless. New suppliers are cropping up everyday, and it's quite possible that a company or individual has surfaced with just the rare reproduction or NOS part that you have been searching for. New suppliers have undoubtedly surfaced since the time of this book's publication, and they can probably be found in one of the enthusiast magazines.

Two-Cylinder
P.O. Box 219
Grundy Center, IA 50638-219
Bimonthly magazine published for John Deere two-cylinder enthusiasts.

Green Magazine
RR 1, P.O. Box 7
Bee, NE 68314
Monthly publication for John Deere enthusiasts.

Swap Meet
RR 1, Box 7
Bee, NE 68314
(402) 643-6269
(402) 643-3912
Monthly advertising-only publication

Tractor Digest
P.O. Box 31
Eldora, IA 50627-0031
(800) 831-5176
Quarterly publication featuring John Deere tractors.

The Review
P.O. Box 322
Grundy Center, IA 50638
(800) 831-5176
Semi-monthly publication for John Deere enthusiasts.

Successful Farming
1716 Locust St
Des Moines, IA 50309-3023
Monthly farming publication; includes *Ageless Iron,* which is devoted to tractor collectors (all brands).

Restoration Specialists and Parts Suppliers

Antique Gauges, Inc.
Joyce Carmine
RR 2, Box 225A
Laurel, DE 19956
(302) 875-5255
White-faced gauges.

Antique Tractor Company
P.O. Box 247
Leaf River, IL 61047
(815) 738-2251
FAX (815) 738-2257
NOS and used parts, restoration service.

Beyer's Two-Cylinder Restoration
Carl Beyer
Lanark, IL
(815) 493-6593
Complete restoration services.

Raymond Beutel
4487 Sunset Drive
Lockport, NY 14094
(716) 433-4657
Reproduction manifolds for BR and BO.

Branson Enterprises
7722 Elm Avenue
Rockford, IL 61115
(815) 633-4262
Carburetor and magneto repair.

Doug Burry
18028 Monroeville
Monroeville, IN 46773
Carburetor rebuilding.

Tom Detwiler Sales and Service
S3266 Highway 13 South
Spencer, WI 54479
(715) 659-4252
Parts.

Gempler's
P.O. Box 270-A1
Mount Horeb, WI 53572
(800) 382-8473
Reproduction tires and liners.

Gerry's Motor Clinic
324 E. Washington
Freeport, IL
Starter, generator, magneto repair; complete restoration service.

Hinrichs Repair
Morrison, IL
(815) 772-4513
New oversize piston and ring sets.

John Deere Distribution and Service Center
Department SP
P.O. Box 136
Moline, IL 61266-1086
(800) 522-7448
Operators manuals, parts books, and service manuals for John Deere tractors and equipment.

K. Johnson
6530 Maple Grove Road
Cloquet, MN 55720
(218) 729-7143
New and used parts.

Travis Jorde
935 9th Avenue NE
Rochester, MN 55906
(507) 288-5483
Decals; if you supply your tractor's serial number with your order, Travis will send you the correct decals and instruction for placement.

K & K Antique Tractors
RR 3 Box 384X
Shelbyville, IN 46176
(317) 398-9883
Reproduction mufflers, air stacks, and decals; restoration services.

Jack Kreeger
7529 Beford Ave
Omaha, NE 68134
John Deere LI and L manuals.

Charles Krekow
270 50th Street
Marcus, IA 51035
(712) 376-2663
Reproduction radiator guards and curtains; tool boxes.

Al Larkin
407 West Pickwick Drive
Syracuse, IN 46567
(219) 457-4071
Reproduction fenders.

Magneeders
Jack Chandler
RR 5, Box 505
Carthage, MO 64836
(417) 385-7863
Magneto repair and parts; new Wico magnetos.

M.E. Miller Tire Company
17386 State Highway 2
Wauseon, OH 43567
Restoration.

Minn-Kota Repair
RR 1, Box 99
Milbank, SD 57252
Steering wheel restoration, radiator filler necks.

Brandon Pfieffer Tractor Plates
7810 Upper Mt. Vernon Road
Mt. Vernon, IN 47620
Parts, reproduction warning plates.

Polacek Implement
Hwy. 13 South
Phillips, WI 54555
Restoration.

Dennis Polk Equipment
72435 SR 15
New Paris, IN 46553
(219) 831-3555
(219) 831-5717
New, used, and reproduction parts.

Rosewood Machine and Tool
Box 17
Rosewood, OH 43070
Reproduction cast parts.

Leland Schwandt
RR 2, Box 141
Wilmot, SD 57279-9101

Stephen Equipment Company
7460 East Highway 86
Franktown, CO 80116
(303) 688-3151
NOS and reproduction parts.

Tim Serien
1320 Highway 92
Keota, IA 52248
(319) 698-4042
Reproduction radiator shutters.

Treadwell Carburetor Company
HC 87 Box 24
Treadwell, NY 13846
(607) 829-8321
Carburetor repair, NOS carburetors.

Wengers, Incorporated
251 S. Race Street
Meyerstown, PA 17067
Parts.

Wilson Farms
20552 Old Mansfield Road
Frederickstown, OH 43019
Grilles and fenders.

Index